Deep Blue

Springer

New York
Berlin
Heidelberg
Hong Kong
London
Milan
Paris
Tokyo

Monty Newborn

Deep Blue

An Artificial Intelligence Milestone

Foreword by Charles E. Lieserson

With 94 Figures

 Springer

Monty Newborn
School of Computer Science
McGill University
Montreal, Quebec H3A 2A7
Canada
newborn@cs.mcgill.ca

Library of Congress Cataloging-in-Publication Data
Newborn, Monroe.
    Deep Blue : an artificial intelligence milestone / Monty Newborn.
        p. cm.
    Includes bibliographical references and index.
    ISBN 0-387-95461-9 (alk. paper)
        1. Computer Chess.   2. Deep Blue (Computer)   I. Title.
    GV1449.3 .N47 2002
    794.1'72—dc21   2002070741

ISBN 0-387-95461-9   Printed on acid-free paper.

Printed in the United States of America.

9 8 7 6 5 4 3 2 1   SPIN 10869464

Typesetting: Pages created by the author.

www.springer-ny.com

Springer-Verlag   New York Berlin Heidelberg
A member of BertelsmannSpringer Science+Business Media GmbH

Foreword

As a competitor of the Deep Blue team, I had mixed emotions as I watched their chess-playing machine defeat World Chess Champion Garry Kasparov during their 1997 Rematch. On the one hand, it meant that our MIT program, *Socrates, would not be the first program to defeat a human World Chess Champion. On the other hand, I felt great admiration for the monumental engineering accomplishment that Deep Blue's victory represented, and proud for the small part that my own team had played in advancing computer-chess research. After over 50 years of concerted effort to produce a chess-playing machine capable of beating the best human, Deep Blue finally attained the goal that so many computer scientists had sought.

In this entertaining and informative book, Monty Newborn chronicles the story of Deep Blue, from its origins as Chiptest at Carnegie Mellon University to its winning the Rematch as a top IBM research project. You do not have to be a chess player or a computer scientist to enjoy this marvelous tale of man and machine. Monty paints the characters of this drama in vivid colors, from the technical geniuses CB Hsu, Murray Campbell, and Thomas Anantharaman to the visionary manager CJ Tan. As only an insider can, Monty recreates the excitement of the event, including the IBM marketing hype and the marvelous compendium of editorial cartoons.

When my Supercomputing Technologies research group at the MIT Laboratory for Computer Science produced its first chess-playing program, Deep Thought was already a legend. My group's goal was to explore how modern parallel-processing technology could be leveraged for nonnumerical problems. Computer chess was a perfect vehicle, representing a dynamic and unstructured computation atypical of the static and regular structure of traditional numerical computations. For us, computer chess began as a bit of a lark to gain some P. R. for our work on parallel computation. While the Deep Blue team aimed its sights on Garry Kasparov, we were focused on them, since Deep Thought represented the pinnacle of computer chess at that time.

My research group's first program, StarTech, was written by Bradley Kuszmaul. Running on a 512-processor Connection Machine CM5 at the University of Illinois, StarTech won 3rd prize in the 1993 ACM International

Computer Chess Championship, not bad for a first outing. At that tournament we met Don Dailey and Larry Kaufman, whose Socrates program won the tournament running on a personal computer. We joined forces to produce the *Socrates parallel program. Don Dailey wrote most of the chess code, and Chris Joerg wrote most of the parallel-processing code in the new "multithreaded" language Cilk which my research group was developing. In our first outing with *Socrates, we finally faced Deep Thought II at the 1994 ACM International Computer Chess Championship. Playing White to Deep Thought's Black, *Socrates succumbed to a brilliant Sicilian Defense in what some commentators at the time called the best chess game ever played between computers.

*Socrates faced Deep Thought II for the second time in the 1995 ICCA World Computer Chess Championship in Hong Kong. This time, running on an 1824-node Intel Paragon at Sandia National Laboratories. Our opening book was much improved but it didn't matter. Playing Black to Deep Thought II's White, *Socrates lost in 51 moves. Fortunately, this loss to Deep Thought II was our only loss in the five rounds of play, which tied us with the program Fritz4 for 1st prize, which actually beat Deep Thought II in the tournament. Watching via the Internet from my home in Massachusetts, my elation at our 1st-place tie turned to disappointment as *Socrates lost to Fritz4 in the playoff, giving Fritz4 the crown of World Computer Chess Champion. Our disappointment could not compare to that of the Deep Blue team, however. Poor Deep Thought II lost its bid to regain the World Championship and had to settle for 3rd prize, an inauspicious omen for its upcoming rematch with Garry Kasparov. How quickly things can change in the world of computer chess!

Now, five years later, I cannot look back at the events leading up to the Rematch without nostalgia for the excitement which Monty so accurately portrays in this book. At the same time, I must wonder, was Deep Blue's defeat of Garry Kasparov good or bad for computer chess? Finding sponsors for computer-chess tournaments, always challenging, has become near impossible. My own computer-chess team at MIT has been disbanded. Yet, despite widespread sentiment to the contrary, research on computer chess is far from finished, even though a computer has beat a World Champion. Should we blame Deep Blue for the current loss of interest in a rich area of research?

I believe that we must view computer-chess research in its historical context. Computer chess taught the world much, from efficient algorithms for heuristic search to languages for programming parallel processors. Moreover, research in other areas of computer game playing, such as Go, continues to intrigue researchers. If we can look towards an analogy, Charles Lindbergh's solo across the Atlantic in 1927 not only captured the imagination of the 1927 public, it heralded numerous other aviation feats, including the 1969 Apollo landing on the moon. So, too, Deep Blue's defeat of Garry Kasparov does not signal the end of a line of research; rather, it portends many future accomplishments in the engineering of artificially intelligent systems. In this respect, Monty's book offers a bold tribute to a historic milestone which future researchers will doubtless look back on for inspiration.

Charles E. Lieserson
Massachusetts Institute of Technology
Cambridge, Massachusetts
May 2002

Preface

In 1989 IBM took on a scientific project that would eventually hold the world spellbound. Three Carnegie Mellon University Ph.D. graduates, Feng-Hsiung Hsu, Murray Campbell, and Thomas Anantharaman, were recruited to continue the work they had begun as students. The objective: to create a chess-playing computer that would outplay the best human on planet Earth.

Eight years later, two of the original three, Hsu and Campbell, together now with a large team of other IBM researchers, made it into the annals of history. Their creation, Deep Blue, defeated World Champion Garry Kasparov in a six-game match in New York in early May of 1997. IBM celebrated, the chess grandmasters of the world went into a state of shock, and the average person on the street wondered what it was all about.

For the Deep Blue team and for IBM, the match was a monumental triumph, ranking as one of the great technological achievements of the 20th century. It can be compared with Orville Wright's first flight in 1906 and with NASA's moon landing in 1969. In addition, for IBM, the match was possibly the single greatest public relations event in the company's century-long history. The match was also the subject of the most successful Internet broadcast to that time. Over the next several years, sales of IBM supercomputers mushroomed.

The following pages tell the story of this historic showdown between Deep Blue and Kasparov, exploring the years of work leading up to and surrounding their final battles. It is a story of how a super-talented team of scientists and engineers designed their dream. It is about how one of America's mightiest corporations nurtured the team, even though important voices inside were concerned with each setback. It is a story filled with drama and surprises, disappointments, and incredible successes. Deep Blue's success raises many questions about our future relationship with this new exciting tool, the digital computer, now a half-century old, and destined to be our companion for centuries to come.

My own involvement in the world of computers and chess dates back many years. Chess, of course, came first, since there were no computers when, as a child, I was taught to play chess by my parents. My main opponent was my brother, with whom I played countless games.

My interest continued through university studies and included participation on The Ohio State University chess team in the 1960s. I participated in a number of tournaments during those years, including one in Michigan that featured Bobby Fischer and that I will never forget. On the eve of the final round of the competition, I watched Fischer, who was then in his early 20s, gamble on one speed chess game after another with a Chicago chess master. Fischer was winning even though spotting his opponent various pieces. I retired around 11:00 p.m. only to find the two still battling one another the following morning. The final round started, if I recall correctly, at 10:00 a.m. Fischer, who was paired with Arthur Bisguier, one of the top several players in the United States, fell into a deep sleep at the board when the game began. With his clock ticking and the audience silently watching, Fischer slept soundly for some time, possibly as long as an hour! When he awoke, he quickly polished off Bisguier. It was an amazing performance.

My interest in computers began in the early 1960s after I graduated from Rensselaer Polytechnic Institute in Troy, New York. I went to work at Douglas Aircraft in Los Angeles and was involved in maintaining a large computer that used vacuum tubes for carrying out logical operations and magnetic cores for storing information. During my subsequent graduate studies at The Ohio State University, I became increasingly interested in logic circuits and at a more abstract level, automata theory. Upon completing my Ph.D. studies, I joined Columbia University's Department of Electrical Engineering, and my interest in automata theory continued.

In 1970 the Association for Computing (then called the Association for Computing Machinery) approached Kenneth King, who was director of Columbia's Computer Center, and me with a request to organize a "Special Events Program" at the Association's annual conference at the New York Hilton Hotel. It was the perfect opportunity to combine my interest in computers and chess: to organize the first major competition between computers that played chess. It was the beginning of a long experiment. A program from Northwestern University called Chess 3.0 won the tournament. The success of the first event led to annual competitions at ACM conferences until 1997 when Deep Blue defeated Garry Kasparov. Working together with Ben Mittman, who was director of Northwestern University's Computer Center, and with British International Master David Levy, I was involved in the organization of one tournament after another.

In 1977 the International Computer Chess Association was formed. Mittman served as the first president. I replaced him three years later, and Levy replaced me three years after that. We organized world championships every three years and world microcomputer championships even more often. I founded the ACM Computer Chess Committee several years later with the support of the ACM's then-president Tony Ralston. I served as head of that committee from its inception through the two Deep Blue versus Kasparov matches.

In 1972 Columbia University student George Arnold and I developed a chess program of our own called Ostrich. Ostrich competed in major competitions around the world until the late 1980s. In 1974 it narrowly missed tying for first place at the First World Computer Chess Championship. It went into the final round of that event with a 2–1 score and was paired with the Soviet program Kaissa. It foxed Kaissa out of material in the middlegame and subsequently found itself in a position where it could force checkmate on its opponent. The mate, however, was one move too deep for the program to see. It played incorrectly and eventually lost the game, leaving Kaissa as the first world computer chess champion. Ostrich managed a draw with Belle during the 1980s. In 1986 Ostrich defeated a barely debugged version of the future Deep Blue in its tournament debut!

From its very first competition, I have followed the progress of what eventually became Deep Blue. I feel fortunate to have had the opportunity to observe both the Deep Blue team and Kasparov from up close as they prepared for and participated in their 1996 and 1997 matches. In my capacity as chairman of the ACM Computer Chess Committee, I served as the organizer of the first match in 1996 in Philadelphia, named the ACM Chess Challenge. In 1997 IBM served as its own organizer, inviting the ACM Computer Chess Committee to participate as the officiating body. That match was named the IBM Kasparov Versus Deep Blue Rematch, or the Rematch, for short. I served as head of the four-person team of officials along with Ken Thompson, Mike Valvo, and Carol Jarecki.

I have developed friendships with members of the Deep Blue team over the years and have followed their progress with great admiration. I have followed Kasparov's ascent to the top of the chess world with equal admiration, beginning with his days at the Moscow chess school of former World Champion Mikhail Botvinnik. When Kasparov was a mere teenager, Botvinnik met with us in the computer chess community and predicted his talented student would be world champion some day. Botvinnik, after retiring from competitive chess and while coaching the elite of the young Soviet chess players, developed his own chess program in the 1960s and 1970s, but it never competed with the other programs.

A detailed record of the chess achievements of IBM's program is presented in my 1997 book, *Kasparov versus Deep Blue: Computer Chess Comes of Age*. The first half of the book covers the history of computer chess prior to the creation of Hsu, Campbell, and Anantharaman's first program Chiptest in 1986; the second half takes the reader through the many matches played by Chiptest and its successors, ending with Deep Blue's match in the

1996 ACM Chess Challenge. Kasparov's encounters with Fritz and Chess Genius in 1994 and 1995 are also covered.

The Rematch spawned several other books on Deep Blue and Kasparov, written from the perspective of strong chess players. These include Bruce Pandolfini's *Kasparov and Deep Blue: The Historic Chess Match Between Man and Machine* (Simon & Schuster), Daniel King's *Kasparov v Deep Blue* (Batsford, London), Michael Khodarkovsky's *A New Era: How Kasparov Changed the World of Chess* (Ballantine Books, New York), and David Goodman and Raymond Keene's *Man Versus Machine: Kasparov Versus Deep Blue* (H3 Publications, Cambridge, MA.). Khodarkovsky was part of Kasparov's inner circle, and his account represents the world champion's perspective.

My intent with this book is to record the story of a great scientific achievement. I am telling the story from my perspective as a computer scientist and lifelong chess enthusiast, and as someone with years of involvement in the field both as participant and as organizer. The book is not meant to be another chess book, though it is hard to avoid chess altogether. The final game of the 1997 Rematch appears in detail in Chapter 13, and there is considerable discussion of the moves of the other five games in the previous three chapters. For historical completeness, I have provided a comprehensive record of every significant game played by IBM's program in the appendices.

The chess-playing system — the IBM RS/6000 SP2, the third-generation VLSI chess chip and accelerator board, and the extensive chess software, collectively called Deep Blue — played its first official game of chess in Philadelphia in 1996. Chess programs that had been developed by members of the Deep Blue team and that eventually led to the creation of Deep Blue were given different names over the years. The first was Chiptest, then Deep Thought and its successive versions, later Deep Thought II. The name Deep Blue was conceived in 1992. In 1993 Nordic Deep Blue competed under the name of Deep Blue, although it was actually a version of Deep Thought II. The single-processor version of Deep Blue called Deep Blue Prototype appeared in 1995, and the next year, the complete Deep Blue finally appeared. Following the Rematch, Deep Blue Prototype was renamed Deep Blue Junior.

Chung-Jen Tan, who headed the Deep Blue team, and Gabby Silberman, currently director of the IBM Center for Advanced Studies and formerly with Tan's group in Yorktown Heights, provided valuable assistance in gethering material and obtaining access to members of the Deep Blue team and others at IBM who played a role. Without their help, I couldn't have assembled the pieces. My university granted me a sabbatical leave for the 1998–99 academic year, during which I began the research and writing of this colorful story. Several years have passed since the historic rematch and even more years since the story of Deep Blue first began. Given its great significance to the scientific world and the chess world and its implications for all of us, recording it for posterity is important.

I would like to express my appreciation to the many who helped create this book, beginning with a special thanks to CJ Tan and Gabby Silberman. I also want to thank the members of the Deep Blue team — Murray Campbell, Feng-hsiung Hsu, Joe Hoane, Jerry Brody, and Joel Benjamin. Let me also express my thanks to others at IBM who played a role in the success of Deep Blue — George Paul, Randy Moulic, Robert Morris, Zeev Barzilai, Barbara Moore, Marcy Holle, and Matt Thoennes. And finally, I would like give special thanks to members of my team of Rematch officials — Ken Thompson, Mike Valvo, and Carol Jarecki.

I would like to thank Charles Leiserson for contributing the Foreword to this book. Leiserson, a professor of computer science at MIT, was in charge of the effort that developed *Socrates (Star Socrates), Deep Blue's main competition in the months leading up to the IBM program's encounters with Garry Kasparov. Charles has had a distinguished research career and is one of the leading experts in the area of computer architecture and algorithms.

Susan Rose provided invaluable editorial assistance with the manuscript, curing it of some of my writing shortcomings. I extend her many thanks for her thorough job.

The photos of Alan Turing, Norbert Weiner, and John von Neumann were provided by the Turing Institute, the MIT Museum, and the IEEE History Center, respectively. I want to thank them for allowing me to include these historical photos in this book. I also want to thank the Lawrence Livermore National Laboratory for the picture of ASCI White, Novag Inc., for the photo of Novag Chess Robot, and IBM for the photos of its Yorktown Heights Thomas J. Watson Research Center, the Hawthorn Annex, and the Beijing Research Center. Carol Moore and Thomas Anantharaman were kind enough to send me photos of themselves, and I want to thank them for this.

The world of cartoonists is a special one, filled with very special people. A number of them gave me permission to reprint their work in this book, and I want to thank them here. This includes Jim Borgman (*Cincinnati Enquirer*, reprinted with permission of King Features Syndicate), Mike Thompson (*Detroit Free Press* with permission of Copley News Service), Mike Luckovich (*Atlanta Journal-Constitution*, with permission of Creators Syndicate), Brian Duffy (*Des Moines Register*), John Deering (*Arkansas Democrat-Gazette*), Bill DeOre (*Dallas Morning News*), Steve Breem (*San Diego Union Tribune* with permission of Copley News Service), Jeff Stahler (*Cin-

cinnati Post with permission of United Feature Syndicate), Richard Crowson (*Wichita Eagle*), John Sherffius (*St. Louis Post Dispatch*), Dwane Powell (*Raleigh News & Observer* with permission of Creators Syndicate), Richard Guindon (*Detroit Free Press*), Etta Hulme (*Fort Worth Star Telegram*), Don Addis (*St. Petersburg Times*), Kirk Walters (*Toledo Blade*), Doug Marlette (*Newsday* and Tribune Media Services), and Mike Graston (*Windsor Star*). These talented individuals will leave a smile on your face when you turn the final page of this book!

Monty Newborn
McGill University
Montreal, Canada
May 2002

Contents

1 Intellectual Equals

We live in a period of remarkable scientific progress. We live longer, healthier, and more interesting lives than did our ancestors. We have created powerful telescopes and microscopes that probe the limits of our universe. We have learned how to use electricity, harness the atom, and transmit great quantities of information at the speed of light. We have built minature robots that navigate inside our bodies. We have cloned sheep and transplanted organs. Nevertheless, we have barely pushed back the frontiers of our understanding of the most fundamental questions about the universe around us. Answers remain hidden, possibly beyond our comprehension for years to come.

Our mind, our very essence, is one of these mysteries. Just how does it function? How does it store ideas and memories? How does it reason? How does it differ from the minds of other earthly creatures? And if we have company in this vast universe, what are their minds like?

In previous centuries, we were reluctant to give up beliefs regarding our position in the universe. We once thought our world was at the very center of the heavens, a motionless body around which the sun and other celestial bodies revolved in giant concentric circles. In the 16th century, there was great resistance to the new heliocentric system proposed by Nicolaus Copernicus and later supported by Galileo Galilei. At that time, it was hard to imagine the Earth moved. At a practical level, why wouldn't buildings topple? At a philosophical level, why would we, the most important creature in the universe, be placed anywhere but at the very center? We now find ourselves living on a small planet circling an undistinguished star moving through space in a universe of unknown size, inconceivable origin, and a future completely beyond the wildest of imaginations.

Not only did we once believe that we were at the center of the universe, we also saw ourselves as unique creatures; we were unquestionably the most intelligent form of life. Of course, a mere — in astronomical terms — 10,000 years, or 400 generations, ago, we ourselves were quite primitive: no books or libraries to say the least. And bathrooms? Is it fair to say that creatures who do not have bathrooms are an intelligent form of life? The animals that shared our planet were considered inferior creatures, there to serve us, our slave labor. If they were unable or unwilling to do that, they became our dinner. Charles Darwin's revelation that we were all cousins was initially resisted. Even if true, it was argued that no one else possessed our intellectual prowess. Our use of language, our ability to reason, and our awareness of ourselves were put forward as arguments for our uniqueness. But in recent years, even on these issues, there is strong evidence that suggests we are not as unique as imagined. A series of thought-provoking articles in a 1998 issue of *Scientific American* addressed these controversial issues.

When I was a child not so long ago, it was generally believed that animals could not be taught languages with words representing abstract concepts. But one gabby parrot named Alex recently seems to have done just that. Irene Pepperberg, a professor in the Biology Department at the University of Arizona, who feeds and cares for her squawky feathered friend, says he understands the concepts "same" and "different," knows his numbers and colors, and can identify, request, and describe more than a hundred objects. In her *Scientific American* article, she ends by saying, "With each new utterance, Alex and his feathered friends strengthen the evidence that parrots are capable of performing complex cognitive tasks. Their skills reflect the innate abilities of parrots and suggest that we should remain open to discovering advanced forms of intelligence in other animals" [2].

In the same *Scientific American* issue, James L. Gould and Carol Grant Gould begin by saying,

> The ability to think and plan is taken by many of us to be the hallmark of the human mind. Reason, which makes thinking possible, is often said to be uniquely human and thus sets us apart from the beasts. In the past two decades, however, this comfortable assumption of intellectual superiority has come under increasingly skeptical scrutiny.

The authors go on to say that "a mounting body of evidence suggests that a number of species can infer concepts, formulate plans and employ simple logic in solving problems" [3]. They then remind the reader that in 1914 German psychologist Wolfgang Kohler showed that a chimpanzee could use insight rather than trial and error in problem solving. They say,

> When Kohler first hung a batch of bananas out of reach, the chimpanzee being observed made a few useless leaps, then went off to a corner and "sulked." But in time he looked back at the bananas, then around the large outdoor enclosure at the various objects he had to play with, back to the bananas, back to one specific toy (a box), then ran directly to the box, dragged it under the fruit, climbed on top, leaped up and grabbed the prize.

Showing how unresolved the issue of animal intelligence is, in another pair of *Scientific American* articles, Gordon Gallop and Daniel Povinelli assume diametrically opposing positions on the question of whether or not animals can empathize — do they have any idea of "self-concept?" [4,5] Gallop studied whether animals could recognize themselves in a mirror, concluding that chimpanzees and orangutans learn that the reflections are images of themselves. He contends that "not only are some animals aware of themselves but that such an awareness enables these animals to infer the mental states of others." Gallop's conclusions are disputed by Povinelli, who concludes his article by stating that "only one primate lineage — the human one — evolved the unique cognitive specialization that enables us to represent explicitly our own psychological states and those of others," and that "other species, including chimpanzees, may simply be incapable of reasoning about mental states — no matter how much we insist on believing that they do."

The issue of animal intelligence on Earth is philosophically dwarfed by the question of whether intelligent life exists, or existed once upon a time, on other worlds. Given the size and age of the universe and the capabilities of our tools to study it, our awareness of distant worlds and ancient events is extremely limited. And yet, even from our narrow window, we have made a start. We seem to have found life-supporting water on the moon and, possibly, primitive forms of life in Martian rocks. But Guillermo Lemarchand's *Scientific American* article points out that it is not necessarily the case that "the emergence of life will lead to the emergence of intelligence, which gives rise to interstellar communications technology" [6].

Along with these considerations, we now have the computer, lifeless, incapable of any action unless told. These calculating machines are certainly good at adding and multiplying, tasks that are clearly mechanical. But, from their very inception, we have asked whether they could be programmmed with our intellgence. Could they be programmed to compete with the best human minds on really difficult problems, ones that seemed to required our intellectual uniqueness? Was there some problem that would serve this purpose — an experimental testing ground — and who would serve as the best human minds? Of the myriad of problems, scientists zeroed in on the game of chess and the grandmasters that played it. Over time, the goal evolved: to design a chess program that would defeat the human world champion. On the way to designing such a program, it was hoped that we would learn more about the human mind. I have been excited to be a part of this effort, as a programmer, organizer, and writer.

Chess is an elegant mental task. The best players are described as creative, artistic, sometimes methodical, aggressive or defensive. They combine brilliant, gifted minds with many years of intensive training. They begin to play at an early age when their minds are flexible and can absorb ideas and concepts more easily than when they are older. They spend a quarter of their waking hours studying the game. They virtually eat and sleep chess.

The game of chess turns out to be ideally suited for the study of intelligence, playing a similar role to the drosophila, the fruit fly, in the field of genetics. It is a game that pits one mind against another. There is no luck as in backgammon, no guessing of hidden information as in blackjack, only a single opponent in contrast to the game of bridge, which involves a partner and two opponents as well as both luck and guessing. All the cards are on the table, so to speak.

Chess is one of few intellectual games where a fairly accurate performance measure exists. All strong chess players in the world have ratings. Just as auto engines are measured in horsepower, computers in mips, and battleships in firepower, the best chess players are all given a numerical rating based on their relative playing strength. The stronger you play, the higher your

My cat, Floyd, was terrific at the keyboard.
He loved to perform the Random Paws Blues (in his coat and tails!).

rating. Garry Kasparov tops the human world with a rating of approximately 2820, the only player ever to exceed 2800. Fewer than 10 players in the world are currently rated over 2700. The approximately 200 players rated over 2600 are typically grandmasters. Masters, ranked over approximately 2200, constitute the next category, with several thousand players in this group. The best masters often hold the title of International Master for perfoming at a sufficiently high level in international competition. International masters are typically rated over 2300. Someone with a good head and a year of experience would likely be rated at approximately 1400. Universities in the United States usually have several players rated over 2000. Statistically, two players are rated 200 points apart if the stronger player wins three out of four points against the weaker one in a four-game match.

What are the implications if and when a computer defeated the world champion? Would it suggest that computers some day will become our intellectual equals in other domains? Will they eventually compose music that draws crowds to Carnegie Hall? Will they, as robots, replace us in the labor market, leaving vast numbers of workers unemployed? Worse yet, will they enslave us, maybe even reproduce themselves, and eventually outnumber us? In theory, we know they can reproduce. Or, perhaps too good to be true, will they usher in a new era in which they serve as our obedient drones, freeing us for a life of leisure? Once fire, the wheel, and the steam engine presented similar concerns. Each has provided countless benefits to mankind, although each has caused great grief as well.

With these controversial thoughts in mind, the pioneers of computer chess gave birth to this challenging project at the end of World War II. Alan Turing, with the University of Manchester in England, and Claude Shannon, with MIT, outlined the basic programming approach in the late 1940s and early 1950s [7,8]. Turing and Shannon rank among the most distinguished pioneers in the field of computers.

Turing is credited with formulating some of the most important concepts related to the theory of computing. The Turing machine, an abstract automaton that performs calculations on a tape of infinite length, was named after the British genius and is studied by every student in the field of computer science. Turing was also instrumental in cracking the secret German Enigma codes during World War II.

Shannon is considered the father of information theory and logical design. In the field of information theory, he showed that the amount of information that could be propagated along a communication channel was related to the channel's bandwidth. In the field of logical design, he showed how to implement the rules of logic with analogous electronic circuits.

In his classic paper entitled "Machine intelligence," Turing said that his interest in chess was motivated by his fascination with whether "it is possible for machines to show intelligent behavior. It is usually assumed without argument that it is not possible." He went on to say that there was

> an unwillingness to admit the possibility that mankind can have any rivals in intellectual power. This occurs as much amongst intellectual people as amongst others; they have more to lose. Those who admit the possibility all agree that its realization would be very disagreeable. The same situation arises in connection with the possibility of our being superseded by some other animal species. This is almost as disagreeable and its theoretical possibility is indisputable.

He concluded his paper by saying,

> The extent to which we regard something as behaving in an intelligent manner is determined as much by our own state of mind and training as

Alan Turing.

by the properties of the object under consideration. If we are able to explain and predict its behavior or if there seems to be little underlying plan, we have little temptation to imagine intelligence. With the same object therefore it is possible that one man would consider it as intelligent and another would not; the second man would have found out the rules of its behavior.

These words drew a response from his colleagues that "Turing was going to infest the countryside with a robot which will live on twigs and scrap iron!" [9]

On whether a chess-playing machine thinks, Shannon said,

The answer depends entirely on how we define thinking. Since there is no general agreement as to the precise connotation of this word, the question has no definite answer. From a behavioristic point of view, the machine acts as though it were thinking. It has always been considered that skillful chess play requires the reasoning faculty. If we regard thinking as a property of external actions rather than internal methods the machine is surely thinking.

Shannon and Turing's interest in chess was paralleled by world-reknowned professors Norbert Weiner and John von Neumann of MIT and

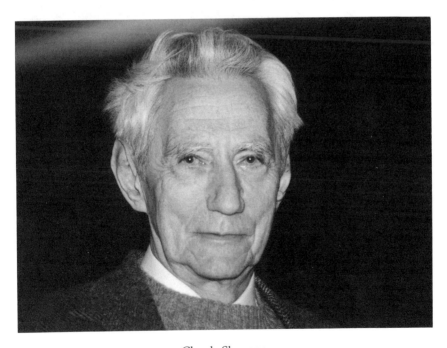

Claude Shannon.

Princeton University, respectively. Weiner's name is synonymous with the field of cybernetics. In 1948 Weiner conjectured that it was possible to construct a machine that "would not only play legal chess, but a chess not so manifestly bad as to be ridiculous . . . . It would probably win over a stupid or careless chess player, and would almost certainly lose to a careful player of any considerable degree of proficiency" [10]. He concluded by saying that it could "attain a pretty fair level of accomplishment." von Neumann is given credit for establishing the very foundations of stored programming. He, along with Oscar Morganstern, also established the validity of the minimax algorithm, the fundamental algorithm of game theory and at the heart of every chess program [11]. Nobody at that time was arguing that the Turing/Shannon approach couldn't yield a program that some day would defeat the human world champion; the possibility was not yet even a subject of speculation.

These exceptional scientists were followed by others who were not only as exceptional but who actually participated in the construction of real, working programs. Carnegie Mellon University's Herbert Simon, Nobel Laureate for his contributions to the field of economics, developed the first "selective-search" program in the late 1950s while working with Alan

Norbert Weiner.

Newell and John Shaw [12]. MIT's John McCarthy, who some consider the father of artificial intelligence and who created the programming language LISP, put together a capable program in the 1960s. Developed with MIT undergraduate Alan Kotok, the program played a postal chess match against a Soviet program in the mid-1960s in the first major computer-chess event [13]. A decade later, Bell Laboratories' Ken Thompson, creator of the UNIX operating system, while working with Joe Condon, gave birth to Belle, the first master-level chess program [14].

Few problems in science have attracted the attention of a more distinguished group of individuals. Of course, great problems attract great minds. Few problems, though, have touched a more sensitive nerve: our intelligence.

The first working programs played very poorly, leading some to believe it was necessary to understand how humans approached the problem so that computers could be programmed to do the same. Some believed there was some aspect of the thought process that defied being programmed — perhaps intuition — which eventually would limit how strongly computers could play. But gradually, computers improved from

John von Neumann.

beginners in the 1960s to experts in the 1970s to masters in the 1980s and then, finally, to grandmasters in the 1990s. With each improvement emerged a contingency of doubters who contended the improvement had run its course. Mostly, wishful thinking!

For computer scientists, the challenge had become how to design a program to search effectively and efficiently through countless sequences of chess moves while trying to decide on the best move. In the typical chess position, there are approximately 30 moves. To each of these 30, there are approximately 30 replies, leading to about 900 different positions after one move by each side. Rounding this number to an even 1000 to make the coming calculation simpler, we find that looking ahead two moves by each side, or a four-level search, leads to about 1000 times 1000, or about 1,000,000 positions. This can be visualized abstractly as a tree with the root corresponding to the given position and with branches corresponding to the possible moves from the given position leading to 30 other positions.

Herbert Simon.

Branches from these 30 first-level positions lead to successor positions that are at the second level, and so on.

To play chess at the level of a world champion, a computer would have to find the best line of play, the principal continuation as it is usually called, to a depth of approximately 12 levels. When looking this deeply, the search examines an incredible 1,000,000,000,000,000,000 positions. Moreover, a computer would have to search many of these positions deeper yet in order to resolve complicated tactical variations. These numbers make the task look virtually impossible. However, by using the alpha-beta algorithm, generally credited to John McCarthy in the United States and Alex Brudno in the former USSR, and by saving information in large memory tables, a chess program can safely ignore most of these positions. Nevertheless, the remaining number of positions is still a monstrous number.

The process of search can be characterized as one that requires intelligence. It is carried out by all living creatures when trying to solve the daily problems they face, and thus to some degree, all living creatures exhibit some intelligence. Plants send out roots in search of nourishment from the soil, while moving their leaves and branches in search of energy from the sun. Animals search the forests and deserts and seas for food and mates and places to live. They spend their days in pursuit of the necessities of life with

John McCarthy.

instincts and other poorly understood thought processes mysteriously guiding them toward warmer places, lighter places, hills that may have caves, and scents that may lead to meals or mates.

Curious humans spend time in search of life's basics, too, but they also have time to search for things more esoteric: good stocks to buy, the Titanic, the Loch Ness Monster, even UFOs. Newspaper readers are given a weekly chance to test their own search strategies at solving chess-mating problems. Millions get up Saturday mornings and attempt to solve their weekly mind-teasing mate-in-two over breakfast coffee, usually giving up after a few minutes' struggle.

Chemists employ programs that search through billions of different molecular structures looking for a rare handful that might satisfy some special set of constraints. Universities depend on large search programs to schedule courses so that students have a minimum number of conflicts. Telephone companies and airlines use search programs to find the cheapest way to route messages and flights from one city to another. The design of computer circuits, in particular VLSI (very large scale integrated) circuits, depends on search programs that route connections from one component to another to minimize various factors including cable length and wire crossings. Programs designed to understand human speech and recognize visual scenes carry out searches trying to match the sounds and images they encounter with those stored in computer memories. Mathematicians call upon automated theorem-proving programs to search for proofs of theorems from a wide spectrum of problems. Programs that perform these tasks are similar to chess programs, and the lessons learned in trying to develop chess programs carry over to them.

It was thus in 1989 that IBM hired a team of talented researchers who had just completed their Ph.D. studies at Carnegie Mellon University to travel the final leg of the trip — to design a chess program that would defeat the human world champion, then Garry Kasparov. When the team joined IBM, it brought along its program, Deep Thought, which was playing at the weak grandmaster level. Further improvement seemed inevitable by using bigger and faster computers and by improving search methods that cleverly encoded and processed sophisticated chess knowledge. The program would have to outdo Kasparov's elegantly flexible but error-prone and definitely fatigable mind with its own inflexible but errorfree indefatigable approach. It would have to defeat a human mind with three decades of learning tucked away into billions of biological neurons.

IBM's role with this great challenge in the final decade of the 20th century can be compared with NASA's challenge of landing a man on the moon in the decade of the 1960s. By 1989 computers were beginning to peck away at the grandmasters, but there was considerable disagreement on how much more improvement was necessary to catch the best of all. This could be compared with the state of space travel and NASA's flights that circled the globe at the beginning of the 1960s. Earlier concerns over the effect of long periods of weightlessness on the human body had been resolved as had concerns over whether a spacecraft could safely reenter the Earth's atmosphere. However, there remained great doubt whether it was possible to make the giant step from circling the Earth to going to the moon and back. Just as with efforts to send a man to the moon, thousands of scientists had contributed to the design of chess programs from the time of Turing and Shannon. And just as NASA's 1969 achievement ushered in a new era of space research, a victory over Kasparov would mark a monumental step forward with our new tool, suggesting further great things to come. The day when a computer defeated the human world chess champion would become a milestone in the history of science.

References

[1] Phillip Yam, "Intelligence considered," *Scientific American*, Exploring Intelligence, pp. 6–11, February 1998.

[2] Irene Pepperberg, "Talking with Alex," *Scientific American*, Exploring Intelligence, pp. 60–65, February 1998.

[3] James L. Gould and Carol Grant Gould, "Reasoning in animals," *Scientific American*, Exploring Intelligence, pp. 52–59, February 1998.

[4] Gordon Gallop, Jr., "Can Animals Empathize? Yes," *Scientific American*, Exploring Intelligence, pp. 66, 68–71, February 1998.

[5] Daniel J. Povinelli, "Can animals emphasize? Maybe not," *Scientific American*, Exploring Intelligence, pp. 67, 72–75, February 1998.

[6] Guillermo A. Lamarchand, "Is there intelligent life out there?" *Scientific American*, Exploring Intelligence, pp. 96–104, February 1998.

[7] Claude Shannon, "Programming a computer for playing chess," *Philosophical Magazine*, 41(7), pp. 256–275, 1950.

[8] Alan Turing, "Digital computers applied to games," in *Faster Than Thought*, B. V. Bowden (ed.), Pitman, London, pp. 286–310, 1953.

[9] Alan Turing, "Intelligent machinery," *Machine Intelligence 5*, University of Edinburgh Press, 1970.

[10] Norbert Wiener, *Cybernetics*, Wiley, New York, 1948.

[11] John von Neumann and Oscar Morganstern, *Theory of Games and Economic Bahavoir*, Princeton University Press, Princeton, NJ, 1944.

[12] Alan Newell, John Shaw, and Herb Simon, "Chess-playing programs and the problem of complexity," *IBM J. of Research and Development*, 2, pp. 320–335, 1958.

[13] Alan Kotok, *A chess playing program for the IBM 7090*, B.S. Thesis, MIT, Cambridge, MA, 1962.

[14] Joe Condon and Ken Thompson, "Belle," in *Chess Skill in Man and Machine*, 2nd ed., Peter Frey, ed., Springer-Verlag, New York, pp. 201–210, 1983.

The Deep Blue team: In the front row are Joel Benjamin and Chung-Jen Tan; in the back row are Murray Campbell, Jerry Brody, Feng-hsiung Hsu, and Joe Hoane

2 Testing the Water

"It appears to have imagination, because it can look ahead and see moves that nobody would have thought of."
Murray Campbell, 1989 [1]

Our story begins on October 23, 1989. It was on that date that an IBM chess program called Deep Thought met World Champion Garry Kasparov for the first of three historic contests. Recent additions to IBM, two of the program's creators, Feng-hsiung Hsu and Murray Campbell, humbly sat across the board from the world champion and his intimidating gaze, managing their protégé. The two-game exhibition match was a hastily arranged coming-out party for the former Carnegie Mellon University graduate students. Thomas Anantharaman, the third member of the group, not yet with IBM, was stationed at Carnegie Mellon, watching over the computing system on which the chess program was running.

Deep Thought was the brainchild and life-long dream of Feng-hsiung Hsu, an exceptional individual and true genius. He was known to his friends as CB, short for "Crazy Bird," a nickname given to him prior to his arrival at Carnegie Mellon. During the mid 1980s, the semiconductor industry had established an ambitious program with American universities to fabricate VLSI circuit chips designed by students. A circuit design whiz

Feng-hsiung(CB) Hsu.

with a degree in electrical engineering from the Taiwan National University, Hsu submitted his design for a high-speed chess move-generator chip in March of 1986. The chip, modeled after one constructed a decade earlier at Bell Laboratories by Ken Thompson and Joe Condon [4,5], was ready in June.

Shortly thereafter, Hsu was joined by Campbell and Anantharaman, and they assembled their first chess-playing system called Chiptest. Andreas Nowatzyk, Mike Browne, and Peter Jansen, also students at Carnegie Mellon, joined the trio during this period. Nowatzyk assisted in optimizing the evaluation function; Browne and Jansen contributed in minor ways, the former with the opening book and the latter with the search heuristics. Hsu's VLSI chess chip, the heart of the system, was designed using 3-micron CMOS technology — that is, using wires three millionths of a meter across — and placed on a circuit board, or more simply, a board, that then was attached to the bus of a SUN 4 computer [6].

Chiptest was followed a year later by a new system containing an improved board and now housing two VLSI chess chips. This system, renamed Deep Thought 0.01 (0.01 for its one board), was soon followed by Deep Thought 0.02, essentially the same system but now containing two boards and four VLSI chess chips. Following Deep Thought 0.02, subsequent variations of the system, no matter how many boards and VLSI chips they incorporated, were simply called Deep Thought.

By the time Deep Thought played Garry Kasparov in this first of their three historic man-machine showdowns, the system contained three dual-processor VLSI chess boards attached to three SUN 4 computers, essentially

Murray Campbell.

Deep Thought 0.03. Each computer was searching an incredible — for that time — 720,000 chess positions per second. The overall system was searching in excess of 2,000,000 chess positions per second. Hsu had plans to eventually assemble a Deep Thought 1.00, a system with 100 computers, with each computer housing a board containing two of his VLSI chess chips. He intended to have that system play a major match some day with Kasparov to see who was the world's best player.

Peter Brown, who, before joining IBM's Thomas J. Watson Research Center, had roomed with Campbell during his student days at Carnegie Mellon, was instrumental in bringing the talented threesome to IBM. After discussing the possibility with Campbell, he then approached Abe Peled, vice president of Systems and Software at IBM Research. The Thomas J. Watson Research Center is one of eight centers and laboratories around the world that constitute IBM Research.

Always on the lookout to bring top computer science talent to IBM, Peled saw the project's potential as exciting science, a "Grand Challenge Problem" in IBM's vernacular, and sent Randy Moulic, one of his project managers, to Carnegie Mellon to check out the group. Moulic was impressed and subsequently invited all three back to IBM for formal interviews. Offers followed, and Moulic soon found himself in charge of a new supertalented research team as first Campbell, then Hsu, and finally Anantharaman accepted the offers and joined IBM.

The project fell into the broad area of parallel computation, an area of special interest to Peled, and one that he felt was very important for the future. It was nurtured under the direction of Zeev Barzilai, who reported directly to Peled and to whom Moulic reported. Until he left the Thomas J. Watson Research Center in 1994 for an assignment with IBM's Tel Aviv's offices, Barzilai was in charge of a group of more than 130 researchers. He

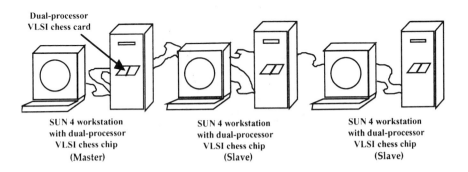

Schematic of Deep Thought 0.03.

had sufficient flexibility in his budget to cater to the chess project's ever-increasing needs. His keen interest in how well the chess program was progressing would often prompt him to travel to the competitions for firsthand observations.

The team was initially assigned to the Hawthorn Annex of the Thomas J. Watson Research Center. The Annex is located about 10 miles southwest of the main IBM facility in Yorktown Heights. The team remained at the Annex until the end of 1993 when they were moved to Yorktown Heights.

When Hsu joined IBM in October of 1989, he brought along Deep Thought and his dream of creating the ultimate chess program. Campbell had arrived a month earlier and Anantharaman would arrive several months later. Shortly after arriving, Hsu began to revise his original plans. Rather than creating Deep Thought 1.00, a system with 200 VLSI chess chips, he would put together a system containing 1000 chess chips — five times as many as his original plan. He reasoned that whatever were the chances of Deep Thought 1.00 defeating Kasparov, the chances of a system with 1000 VLSI chess chips were that much greater.

IBM, on the other hand, had recruited the team with somewhat different expectations. While aware that it had hired three very talented researchers to design the ultimate chess machine, IBM foresaw that some day in the future, if they were still at IBM, these bright guys would be involved in research on very different problems. It would be great if the chess project succeeded, and they would be strongly supported in their efforts, but some day in the future they would likely still be working at IBM but no longer

Thomas Anantharaman.

involved with the chess project. Succeed or fail, their experience on this project would prove useful. Their success thus far indicated they might also succeed on other important problems.

During this period, the company was doing quite well — or perhaps the financial crisis of the early 1990s hadn't yet become apparent — and new speculative directions were being encouraged. One was the creation of the GF-11 [7], a new supercomputer. Randy Moulic, working under Zeev Barzilai, was in charge of the construction of this one-of-a-kind system. The GF-11 was intended to solve various important particle physics problems, including the computation of the mass of a neutron to validate the theory of quantum chromodynamics. Computations that would take hundreds of years on contemporary conventional hardware would take a fraction of the time — perhaps a year or so — on the GF-11. This 576-processor special-purpose supercomputer was designed to perform 11 gigaflops (11 billion floating-point operations per second — hence the name GF-11). In computer jargon, it was a single-instruction, multiple-data machine, meaning that all processors executed the same program, generally stepping together from one instruction to the next. Each computer had its own memory; information was transferred rapidly from one computer to another over a high-speed switching circuit.

The GF-11 went into operation in 1990 with 530 processors, but it was too specialized to be of any use as a chess-playing machine. There was, however, another IBM Research project that would eventually assume special importance to the chess project. Unlike the GF-11, this project, called the RP3 Project ("Research Parallel Processing Prototype"), involved the design of a 64-processor shared-memory system that was intended to function as a general-purpose supercomputer. The project, which began in the early 1980s as a collaborative effort with computer scientists at New York University [8], set the stage for further research projects in parallel processing, including, in particular, the design of the Vulcan prototype [9]. It was the Vulcan that led, in turn, to the SP-series supercomputers, the eventual home for the IBM chess program.

Randy Moulic, along with Chung-Jen (CJ) Tan and Steve Harvey, led the RP3 developmental effort. George Paul later took over supervision of experimental software projects that researchers were designing to run on the system. Tan would eventually be in charge of the Deep Blue team and call upon Paul for assistance.

The Vulcan prototype was designed about the same time that the Carnegie Mellon recruits joined IBM. Unlike the RP3, which used a large shared memory, the Vulcan had no shared memory, but rather transmitted information between computers on an advanced message-passing network. Although the 16-processor Vulcan prototype was never built, based on the optimism shown by those involved in the design, a management decision was made to build the SP1 modeled after it. The first SP1 was delivered in 1992; the first SP2, delivered a year later [10], was the computer used by Deep Blue when it played Kasparov. Subsequent versions of the SP-series computers were simply called SP computers.

The chess project was yet another project under Barzilai, and in turn under Moulic, involving the design of a special-purpose computer. Moulic viewed the project as an experiment, in his words, of "putting search into hardware." While this special-purpose computer was under construction, the chess team continued to improve the chess software and to test improved versions of Deep Thought in competition. The two-game exhibition match with Garry Kasparov in 1989 was the first test.

Prior to their arrival at IBM and their first encounter with Kasparov, Hsu, Campbell, and Anantharaman had established Deep Thought's dominance over the other leading chess-playing computers in May 1989 at the 6th World Computer Chess Championship in Edmonton, Alberta. Deep Thought smashed the field there, finishing with a perfect 5–0 score [11,12]. In November 1988, it also shared first place with Grandmaster Tony Miles, who would play Kasparov for the World Championship several years later, in the Software Toolbox Chess Championship in Long Beach, California, finishing with an incredible 6.5 – 1.5 score [13–15]. During that tournament, it defeated Danish Grandmaster Bent Larsen, once ranked among the several top players in the world. Thus, by the time of the two-game exhibition match with Kasparov in 1989, Deep Thought was recognized as the world's strongest chess-playing computer and, figuratively speaking, as a young budding electronic grandmaster. Such credentials, however, were far short of making the computer a serious opponent for Kasparov.

The 1989 Deep Thought encounter with Kasparov took place at the New York Academy of Art on Lafayette Street on the northern fringe of Greenwich Village. Shelby Lyman organized the event. Lyman, a chess promoter and a syndicated columnist for numerous newspapers, including *The New York Post*, had made his name as the PBS commentator for the 1972 Bobby Fischer versus Boris Spassky World Championship match. Lyman's special talent, along with being a master-level chess player, was his ability to share the stage with his guests during the match. AGS Computers Inc., a unit of the NYNEX Corporation, put up a $10,000 appearance fee for Kasparov. Games were played in a room filled to the brim with the academy's sculptures and paintings. In a commentary room one flight up, Lyman and Grandmaster Edmar Mednis hosted an animated analysis of the play.

The match drew an audience of approximately 100 journalists and 400 chess enthusiasts, including, in particular, Mike Valvo, Jonathan Schaeffer, Hans Berliner, and me. Lyman had personally invited the four of us; he gave us front-row seats to ensure that a few computer supporters would be visible to the media filming the event! We were in the minority.

Mike Valvo, one of the top blindfold chess players in the world and an international master, was well known for serving as tournament director at major computer championships. He had earned the admiration of the chess programmers for appreciating their mission. Beginning in late 1988 and ending in early 1989, he played and defeated Deep Thought 0.02 in a two-game match (played like the old postal games), winning both games.

Jonathan Schaeffer, a professor of computer science at the University of Alberta, was known for his own work on chess-playing programs. He had developed Phoenix, one of the better programs. An expert-level chess player, Schaeffer had hoped to be the one to develop the world's best chess program, but his passion to be the best at whatever he did eventually led him to checkers when he found Phoenix was not quite able to reach the top of the class of chess-playing programs. In the mid-1990s, he used his experience developing Phoenix to develop Chinook, an unbeatable checker program. In 1995 Chinook defeated the human world checker champion.

Hans Berliner was one of the pioneers in the field of computer chess. He was Murray Campbell's thesis advisor at Carnegie Mellon, where the two worked together on the chess program Hitech. Hitech was playing at the

Feng-hsiung Hsu at the chess board among the Academy of Art statues.

level of a strong master at the time. Berliner, a senior researcher at Carnegie Mellon, had stood at the focus of research in computer chess at the Pittsburgh university. When CB Hsu began his studies there, he briefly worked with Berliner. However, the two found themselves at odds on the design of chess circuitry, and Hsu went on to study under the supervision of H. T. Kung, a VLSI technology pioneer. Berliner had won the world correspondence chess championship in the 1960s, when games were played over a several-month period at a rate of a move every several days. It took a special mind to toil over one chess game for so long — and be the best in the world!

An hour prior to the start of the match with Kasparov, the audience was treated to an interview with the participants. Eager journalists peppered Kasparov with one question after another. The two new IBM researchers, blatantly ignored, sat quietly on the stage, from time to time typing on their computer terminal, while Kasparov answered questions in his usual articulate way.

Grandmaster Robert Byrne, *The New York Times* chess columnist, came to watch and to report on Deep Thought. He was among the small minority of spectators not primarily fixated on Kasparov. He had followed Deep Thought's progress for several years, and the field of computer chess for many more. With all the appearance of an Ivy League professor, Byrne, the

Garry Kasparov in conversation with Robert Byrne
before playing Deep Thought.

senior chess columnist in the United States, understood that some day computers would play the game better than any human. Perhaps he wanted his column to serve as a historical record of the progress toward that eventuality. Byrne, himself, drew a two-game exhibition match with Deep Thought hosted by Carnegie Mellon only two months prior to this Deep Thought versus Garry Kasparov battle [16,17]. At one time, Byrne was ranked among the top several chess players in the United States, and even here, in his middle 60s, he remained a tough competitor.

Kasparov told the excited attendees that he had studied Deep Thought's record extensively, playing through as many as 50 of its games—essentially every game on record — on the day before the match. He came well prepared. German computer chess promoter Frederic Friedel had obtained some of Deep Thought's games from Campbell and passed them on to the world champion. Friedel, who over time had become increasingly involved with Kasparov and his chess activities, served the world champion as computer consultant and as a link to the Deep Thought team.

Kasparov felt Deep Thought could take one or two points from him in a 10-game match, and he ventured that a rating of 2480–2500 was appropriate for the computer. Some day a computer might defeat him, but he thought there was still some time before that would happen. "I don't know how we can exist knowing that there exists something mentally stronger than us," he said. The spirit in the room was very pro-Kasparov, to say the least, not that it was anticomputer or anti-Deep Thought, but Kasparov was an extremely popular champion in the chess-playing world, and the audience consisted primarily of chess enthusiasts.

When this two-game match took place, Kasparov had been world champion for about four years. Born in Baku, the capital of Azerbaijan, on April 13, 1963, Kasparov was the son of a Jewish father and an Armenian mother. His father died when he was only seven, and he and his mother moved in with her parents. In January 1976, at the age of 12, Kasparov won the USSR Junior Championship. In 1980, at the age of 17, he was recognized as a grandmaster [18]. His mother, Klara Kasparova, was an engineer by profession until 1981, when she assumed the responsibility of managing her son's mushrooming chess career.

Kasparov's career raced ahead over the next few years. He qualified for the world championship candidates competition, then walked over, in succession, the other candidate finalists — Alexander Beliavsky, Viktor Korchnoi, and Vasily Smyslov — to earn the right to play Karpov for the world championship in 1984. Outclassed by Karpov early in the match and on the brink of losing, Kasparov gradually improved. He eventually appeared on the verge of finding a way to win the match when FIDE (International Chess Federation) authorities stepped in and, astonishingly, canceled the affair. After 48 games, Karpov had 5 wins, Kasparov had 3, and 40 games were drawn. Karpov had effectively taught the 21–year-old Kasparov how to be world champion. The following year, Kasparov showed that he had learned his lessons well when he ended Karpov's 10-year reign in a replay of the canceled match.

The two games between Deep Thought and Kasparov were very one-sided. In the first game which lasted 52 moves, the computer gradually weakened its position and was lost, according to Kasparov, after the 20th move. Kasparov said, "After such a loss, no human would come back for more." But, of course, Deep Thought did, oblivious of its opponent's stature. On the sixth move of the second game, Deep Thought played incorrectly. From that point on its creators waited anxiously for the end of the two-game contest which painfully dragged on for another 31 moves. The audience gave Kasparov a rousing hand when he finished, after which he entertained them with his observations of the match [19,20].

Among grandmasters, the general feeling was one of relief; the day of reckoning remained in the distant future. The news media echoed the same feeling on the following day. *The New York Times* heralded "Kasparov

University of Alberta Professor Jonathan Schaeffer,
developer of Phoenix and Chinook.

beats chess computer (for now) [21]." *The New York Post* and *Newsday* followed suit with "Red chess king quick fries Deep Thought's chips" [22], and "Back to the drawing board. Chess computer's no match for animated Kasparov" [23].

Generally lost in the clamor to praise Kasparov, however, was the fact that an elusive programming bug had plagued the play of Deep Thought. Ridding a chess program of all bugs is something that has most likely never been done. Now, there are many types of bugs, some serious, some mysterious, some both serious and mysterious. This bug fell into the third and nastiest category! The bug, both serious and mysterious, surfaced without detection in both games. Before the match, Deep Thought had been running on a single processor; for this match, and for the first time, Deep Thought was running on three processors acting together when selecting moves. Not present in the single-processor version, the bug lurked in the software of the new and barely tested three-processor version. Detected when it resurfaced several weeks later in a game between Deep Thought and Jonathan Schaeffer's Phoenix in the 20th ACM North American Computer Chess Championship in Reno, the bug was sufficient to cause the computer to lose to Kasparov here in New York [24]. The bug caused Deep Thought to avoid castling unless essentially forced to do so, resulting in its king being unnecessarily exposed to merciless attacks by Kasparov in both games.

Deep Thought also played the first game against Kasparov too rapidly. The programmers hadn't had time to test the computer's play when using the time limits established for the match — each side was allotted 90 minutes to play all its or his moves — and the computer's setting was too conservative. Between games, Hsu corrected the problem, instructing Deep Thought to analyze each move somewhat longer, but the modification had little consequence on the outcome of the second game, given the damage caused by the castling bug.

The bright spot of Deep Thought's play was its ability to defend itself in difficult positions. Computers have earned a reputation for slithering out of what sometimes seems to be certain death when behind, finding incredibly clever ways to stave off defeat. Kasparov thought he had the first game locked up after the 20th move — and most grandmasters would have acquiesced to the world champion soon thereafter — but the computer lasted another 32 moves before finally capitulating.

The Deep Thought team had feared having such problems, since it had only recently joined IBM, and its new three-processor system had hardly been tested. The team would have preferred to play Kasparov several months or even a year or so later, but it didn't want to pass up a concrete opportunity for the uncertainty of playing him at some future date. This marked the team's first match under the IBM banner and its first setback. While the team was accustomed to and prepared for such misfortune, one can only imagine that the management at IBM Research would have preferred reading front-page national newspaper reports of victory to stories about fried chips!

Jerry Present, representing IBM Research's public relations office, attended the match. He was in charge of the PR surrounding Deep Thought until he left in 1995 and was replaced by Marcy Holle. In these early years, IBM Research management watched the project from a distance, concerned that it might never succeed, and not wanting to overpromote a project with such an uncertain future. In the world of research, a conservative approach to claims of great progress and success seems to have been IBM's policy.

One week after losing to Kasparov, Deep Thought put in a second disappointing performance in the Harvard Cup using its three SUN 4 system [25]. Harvard students Chris Chabris and Dan Edelman, the latter a chess master, organized the one-day event on the Harvard University campus. This was the first of several such yearly affairs that the two organized pitting the top the computers against East Coast grandmasters. The event matched four computers, Hitech, Mephisto Portorose, Chiptest, and Deep Thought against four grandmasters, Lev Alburt, Maxim Dlugy,

Carnegie Mellon researcher and creator of Hitech, Hans Berliner.

Boris Gulko, and Michael Rohde, all ranked among the top 20 players in the United States. Chiptest, an earlier version of Deep Thought, was dusted off by the Deep Thought team at the request of the organizers who needed a fourth computer to equalize the number of participating species. Each computer played all four grandmasters. Games were played at a speed of all moves in 30 minutes per side; a game would last at most one hour.

Deep Thought managed to defeat Dlugy but lost to the other three grandmasters. Chiptest lost all four games, although it had a strong position against Alburt when time ran out. Once again, the castling bug mysteriously appeared and possibly cost Deep Thought points. In its only victory, Deep Thought was instructed to castle by its opening book. In its three losses, the bug clearly was a factor. It castled late in two games — on the 16th move against Gulko and on the 12th move against Rohde — and skipped castling altogether in its game against Alburt.

In mid-November 1989, Deep Thought's third contest under the IBM banner was in Reno, Nevada, at the 20th ACM North American Computer Chess Championship [23,26–28]. The program used the same three SUN 4 system. For the record and for comparison with future computing systems used by the IBM chess programs, the SUNs were rated at 8 mips (8 million

Garry Kasparov all aglow after easily disposing of
Deep Thought in New York.

instructions per second) with 32 megabytes (32 million 8-bit words) of memory. The performance again was less than impressive. After winning the first four rounds, Deep Thought was upset in the final fifth round by Richard Lang's Mephisto, resulting in a first-place tie with archrival Hans Berliner's Hitech.

In its first-round victory over Jonathan Schaeffer's Phoenix, the castling bug surfaced again and almost cost Deep Thought another game. During a postgame analysis, the problem was finally grasped, though corrected only after Deep Thought's third-round game with Hitech when there was time for debugging. The victory over Phoenix did illustrate the great strength of Deep Thought's massive search, being able to outplay a capable opponent from an inferior complex middlegame position. The second round was no contest for Deep Thought, who romped over University of London Professor Don Beal's BP in 23 moves.

In the third round, Deep Thought played Hitech. Hans Berliner, who had been in New York to watch as Deep Thought lost to Garry Kasparov, returned to Carnegie Mellon and spent long hours booking lines related to the two games, hoping to use them in this event against Deep Thought. Hitech played White. Berliner watched the first six moves of the game replicate those of the second Garry Kasparov–Deep Thought game. A murmur of excitement went through the audience when it became apparent that Hitech was in the process of leading Deep Thought down a path to a quick slaughter. However, Deep Thought's sixth move avoided the disastrous 6 ... c6 that had led to its downfall in New York.

When I asked, Murray Campbell denied having modified the book to avoid this move, but said that this game was played more slowly than those against Kasparov and the added time led to a different move, fortunately for Deep Thought. Berliner, of course, was hoping that Deep Thought's book had not yet been corrected. In that, he was right. But Deep Thought went off in another direction anyway. Never mind. Berliner had prepared Hitech for alternatives as well, and his program continued to play the first 13 moves of the game from book. Upon leaving book on the 14th move, Hitech had consumed a total of about one minute of time, building up an overwhelming position, while Deep Thought had consumed an hour, giving Hitech a 2–1 time advantage for the coming moves. The position was quite complex. Grandmaster Larry Evans, in his analysis of the game, said that Hitech had "quickly achieved the kind of crushing bind that grandmasters see only in their dreams." But once again, the massive searches carried out by Deep Thought quickly turned the tables on its foe, forcing Hitech to resign on the 29th move. Reflecting on his frustration with the outcome, Berliner observed at the end, "It's hard to win a won game against a program that looks ahead six moves for both sides."

In the fourth round, Deep Thought easily defeated Rebel, confirming that the bug had been fixed when it castled on the eighth move. In the final round against Mephisto, the two sides stood even after 49 moves but, in a rare occurrence, Deep Thought was foxed out of a pawn over the next few moves, leading to its downfall. It finished in a disappointing tie for first place with Hitech.

Thus, after three events played under the IBM banner over a three-month period, the program had yet to deliver an impressive performance. Bugs had made the match with Kasparov uninteresting. The same bugs had led to a poor showing in the Harvard Cup. And from a distance, a tie for first place at the 20th ACM championship was marred by a final-round loss to a program running on a small computer. But these problems, while greatly affecting the level of play, were somewhat superficial and easy to correct. New versions of Deep Thought would be free from these problems, although other problems would step forward to take their place! Progress was clearly being made. However, the complicated three SUN 4 system was temporarily set aside for the former single-processor system.

In December 1989 and after these three lackluster performances, Deep Thought finally displayed the great progress that had been made by chess-

Mephisto, having just played 43 ... Kc7, about to defeat Deep Thought at the 20th ACM North American Computer Chess Championship in Reno.

playing programs during the decade by blitzing British International Master David Levy in a six-game match in London [29]. Levy, who was rated around 2300, had gained fame in 1968 when he wagered four leading computer scientists the sum of $10,000 that no computer would defeat him in a match during the following decade. For an impoverished graduate student, that was a whopping amount of money at the time. He was either pretty sure of victory or an awfully big gambler. When the bet was made, the best computers were playing at the class C level; the year before, Richard Greenblatt's Mac Hack had competed in a tournament with humans in Massachusetts and was credited with playing at around the 1500 level. During the decade following the wager, chess programs made rapid progress, reaching the level of expert by 1976.

When the challenge for the wager took place in 1978, the best programs were not yet equal to the British international master. Levy played David Slate and Larry Atkin's Northwestern University-based world champion program Chess 4.7 in a six-game challenge match at the Canadian National Exhibition in Toronto. To his surprise, Levy drew the first game, shocking himself into more serious play for the next two games. Up 2.5 – 0.5 going into the fourth game, Levy decided he could afford to experiment. He would try to defeat his opponent in a tactical game, and teach it a thing or

International Master David Levy was no match for
Deep Thought in December 1989.

two. He failed! Chess 4.7 set him on his ear. After that, Levy returned to the conservative do-nothing style of his victorious first game, winning the final two games — and his $10,000 wager.

Following the Toronto skirmish, *Omni Magazine* offered an open-ended prize of $5,000 to the first computer to defeat Levy. In 1984 Levy easily put down a challenge from Cray Blitz, developed by Robert Hyatt, with help from Burt Gower and Harry Nelson. In 1989 he finally succumbed to Deep Thought. The British international master was a 3–1 favorite with the London bookmakers even though he predicted his own demise. Levy knew best. He was no match for Deep Thought, getting blown off the table in 36 moves, 42 moves, 22 moves, and 34 moves in the 4 games, a most brutal beating! After the match, Levy was quite humble, praising Deep Thought and stating that he had no excuse for his loss, although his lack of serious competition for over a decade hadn't helped. He said that his understanding of how computers played closed the gulf "between us by as much as 100 or 150 rating points, but the gulf was too wide to start with." Deep Thought had passed a major milestone on the road to the world champion.

Thus, after a several-month residence at IBM, Deep Thought had reaffirmed that it was playing at the grandmaster level, that a British international master was easy pickings, and that Kasparov was clearly superior. Kasparov had given Deep Thought credit for a rating of approximately 2480–2500 before their two-game match, compared to his own 2800

Former World Chess Champion Mikhail Botvinnik with
Kaissa programmer Misha Donskoy.

rating at the time. Deep Thought's performance against Levy suggested a 200-point edge over the 2300-rated British international master. Taken together, a rating of 2500 seemed quite appropriate. Its performance at the 20th ACM North American Computer Chess Championship reconfirmed that it was still the best of it own species, though not by enough to totally write off its electronic competitors.

The challenge facing the Deep Thought team was becoming well defined as the 1990s approached: to catch Kasparov, Deep Thought would

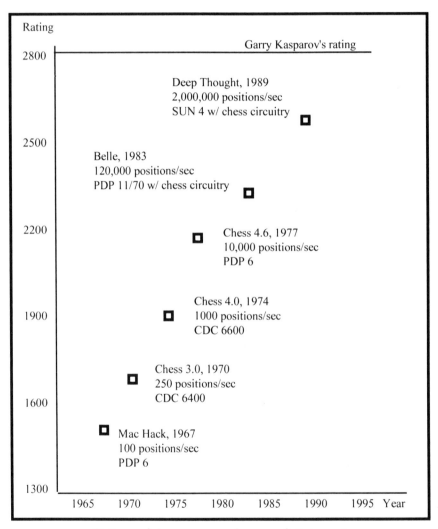

Ratings of chess programs by year of attainment.

have to improve by somewhere in the neighborhood of 300 rating points. Let us look backwards from 1990 to see the continual progress up to that time, and try to draw some conclusions about how many years it might take Deep Thought to improve by the necessary 300 points. Chess programs reached rating levels of 2200 in the early 1980s, improving approximately 300 points by 1990. (See the plot on the preceding page.) In 1983 Ken Thompson's Belle was awarded the title of US Master in recognition of attaining the 2200 level of play, although even in the late 1970s, Slate and Atkin's Chess 4.9 had been playing at near that level. Six years or so prior to that, around 1974–1975, earlier versions of Slate and Atkin's program were playing 300 points weaker, at the 1900 level. Thus, if one assumes that chess programs would continue to improve at the same rate as in the past, about another six to eight years of hard work, coupled with the usual advances in hardware, were necessary to improve Deep Thought by the 300 points needed to challenge the world champion.

There were, however, many who believed that progress would not continue as in the past, and that defeating the world champion was still many years away. A survey of the very individuals who were designing chess programs was carried out in 1989 by David Levy, and the average

Former Northwestern University graduate student David Slate, programmer of Chess 3.0 – Chess 4.6.

prediction was the year 2005 [30]. CB Hsu predicted 1994, and Murray Campbell predicted 1995. A similar survey of the leading chess players, had it been carried out, would have found the average to be even further off. Thus, in 1990 there remained a spectrum of opinions about how many years would pass before the world champion would lose to a computer.

Although Deep Thought had established a clear lead over competing chess programs, these, too, were moving forward at impressive rates. If the Deep Thought team's ultimate goal was to defeat Kasparov, to remain ahead of the silicon competition in the meanwhile was a second and almost equally important goal. The Deep Thought team was not the only one with its sights on the world champion.

Robert Hyatt's Cray Blitz [31–33] and Hans Berliner's Hitech [34] were a notch weaker than Deep Thought, and both Hyatt and Berliner were talented individuals. Neither's program could be ruled out in the race to challenge the world champion. Berliner would have given his left arm to be the first; he had invested the better part of his adult life aiming for this opportunity. Hyatt, a professor at the University of Alabama at Birmingham, would have danced on rooftops for the rest of his life! He had spent a quarter of a century trying to put his various chess programs at the head of the pack. His chess program, Crafty, continues to be one of the rare pieces of outstanding free software available over the Internet.

Robert Hyatt, University of Alabama professor and
programmer of Cray Blitz.

*Socrates [ed: read Star Socrates], developed at MIT under the supervision of computer science Professor Charles Leiserson, emerged as Deep Blue's main electronic rival in the months leading up to the Kasparov matches. *Socrates was an amalgamation of Heuristic Software's Socrates with MIT's software that parallelized the search for a chess move. It was developed by a large group at MIT including Robert Blumofe, Eric Brewer, Michael Halberr, Christopher Joerg, Bradley Kuszmaul, Yuli Zhou, and Leiserson. Heuristic Software's Don Dailey and Larry Kaufman had previously developed the single-processor chess program called Socrates. *Socrates ran on large multiprocessing systems, including a 512-processor Connection Machine CM–5 when it participated in the ACM's 1994 Cape May tournament. The *Socrates team would have waltzed on the Charles River had its protégé wound up at the head of the pack.

Even the commercial PC-based programs, Wchess, Fritz, Mephisto, and Chess Genius, were having major successes. And hidden from view were the efforts of Ken Thompson, who had the potential to create a hardware phenomenon that would usurp the entire field. Mankind's race to land a man on the moon was a prestigious East–West contest, pitting the capitalist system against communism. This race, 30 years later, was squarely among corporate and academic giants like Bell Laboratories, Carnegie Mellon, MIT, Intel, and IBM.

The pattern in the computer-chess world of rapid ascent to the top of the pack, followed by surprising sudden descent, had been very consistent over the years. With one quirky exception, no world champion chess program had been able to successfully defend its title at the next world championship. The race to be number one had been fierce, with no time to look over one's shoulder at the charging competition. Good ideas from one program appeared shortly after in others, refined to work even better. The Deep Thought team thus faced a formidable task just staying ahead of the other computers.

Kaissa, developed by Misha Donskoy and a team of other distinguished scientists at the Institute for Control Science in Moscow, was the first chess program to follow this pattern. In 1974 Kaissa won the 1st World Computer Chess Championship in Stockholm, Sweden, with a perfect 4–0 score. The favorite entering the competition was David Slate and Larry Atkin's Chess 4.0, initially called Chess 3.0, subsequently renamed Chess 3.5, Chess 3.6, Chess 4.0, Chess 4.6, and eventually Chess 4.9 when it retired. Not having been paired during the competition, Kaissa and Chess 4.0 squared off in a friendly one-game match after the final round, playing to a draw where Kaissa had a rook and knight on the board while Chess 4.0 had only a rook. In 1974 Kaissa was clearly the best.

In 1977 at the 2nd World Computer Chess Championship held in Toronto, Kaissa was just another program, finishing an unimpressive third.

The winner was a greatly improved Chess 4.6, an updated version of Chess 4.0, playing on a CDC Cyber 176, one of the big supercomputers of that time. Chess 4.6 dominated that championship, finishing with a perfect 4–0 score. Again, since Kaissa and Chess 4.6 weren't paired in the main competition, their programmers set up a second friendly one-game match where Chess 4.6 confirmed its superiority, routinely disposing of Kaissa in a 45-move game. Kaissa, the best in 1974, was never again a threat to the leading programs. A small but important digression: following the championship, the International Computer Chess Association was formed, and since then, it has organized all world championships.

Three years later in 1980 in Linz, Austria, at the 3rd World Computer Chess Championship, Ken Thompson moved his protégé Belle to the head of the field. Slate and Atkin's program could do no better than finish in the middle of the field. Belle seemed to be the best by far, destined to reign forever. Belle's success rested on newly designed special-purpose chess circuitry, allowing it to search as many as 120,000 chess positions per second, far more than any other chess-playing computer to that time. It had the most extensive opening book yet seen in a chess program, containing as many as 500,000 different positions, and databases for a number of three- and four-piece endgames.

In 1983 at a small ceremony in the middle of the third round of the 4th World Computer Chess Championship in New York, Belle was awarded

IBM Thomas J. Watson Research Center, Hawthorn Annex.

the title of U.S. Master by the United States Chess Federation. It was as though a curse was placed on the program at that point, for it wound up losng that game after winning its first two. A second loss in the final round marked the unexpected end to Belle's domination. The new champion was Robert Hyatt's Cray Blitz, running on a powerful Cray XMP/48. Unlike previous world champions, Cray Blitz led the pack by the smallest of margins, with competitors Belle and Hitech playing just a shade weaker.

Most surprisingly, in 1986 Cray Blitz became the first and only program ever to retain the title of world champion when it won the 5th World Computer Chess Championship in Cologne, Germany. Though four programs finished with four points out of a possible five — Hitech, Bebe, Phoenix, and Cray Blitz — Cray Blitz was awarded first place and the championship on the basis of tie-breaking points, much to the chagrin of the other three. Seeded first in the tournament as reigning world champion, Cray Blitz played a slightly tougher group of opponents, giving it an advantage when tie-breaking points were taken into account to decide the winner.

Three years later in 1989 at the 6th World Computer Chess Championship in Edmonton, Canada, Cray Blitz was dethroned by Deep Thought. Cray Blitz and Hitech finished tied for third. Belle didn't even participate. Deep Thought dominated the championship, winning all five games.

In summary, Deep Thought now had the task of improving by some 300 rating points while remaining ahead of its silicon opponents on its journey to meeting World Champion Garry Kasparov — a most daunting task.

References

[1] Feng-hsiung Hsu, *Large scale parallelization of alpha-beta search: An algorithmic and architectural study with computer chess*, PhD. Thesis, Department of Computer Science, Carnegie Mellon University, 1990.

[2] Murray Campbell, *Chunking as an abstract mechanism*, PhD. thesis, Department of Computer Science, Carnegie Mellon University, 1988.

[3] Thomas S. Anantharaman, *A statistical study of selective min-max search in computer chess*, PhD. thesis, Department of Computer Science, Carnegie Mellon University, 1990.

[4] Joe H. Condon and Ken Thompson, "Belle chess hardware," in *Advances in Computer Chess*, 3, M. R. B. Clarke, ed., Oxford, Pergamon Press, pp. 45–54, 1982.

[5] Joe H. Condon and Ken Thompson, "Belle," in *Chess Skill in Man and Machine*, 2nd ed., P. Frey, ed., Springer-Verlag, New York, pp. 201–210, 1983.

[6] Feng-hsiung Hsu, "A two-million moves/s CMOS single chip chess move generator," *IEEE Journal of Solid-State Circuits*, 22(5), pp. 841–846, 1987.

[7] J. Beetem, M. Denneau, and D. Weingarten, "The GF11 parallel computer," in J. J. Dongarra, ed., *Experimental Parallel Computing Architectures*, North-Holland, Amsterdam, 1987.

[8] Gregory F. Pfister, "An introduction to the RP3," in J. J. Dongarra, ed., *Experimental Parallel Computing Architectures*, North-Holland, Amsterdam, 1987.

[9] C. B. Stunkel, D. G. Shea, B. Abali, M. M. Denneau, P. H. Hochchild, D. J. Joseph, B. J. Nathanson, M. Tsao, and P. R. Varker, "Architecture and implementation of Vulcan," Proceedings of the 8th International Parallel Processing Symposium (Cancun, Mexico), pp. 268–274, April 1994.

[10] T. Agerwala, J. L. Martin, J. H. Mirza, D. C. Sadler, D. M. Dias, and M. Snir, "SP2 system architecture," *IBM Systems Journal*, 34(2), 1995.

[11] Garth E. Courtois, Jr., "The Sixth World Computer-Chess Championship," *ICCA Journal*, 12(2), pp. 84–99, June 1989.

[12] Ray Keene, "Deep thoughts from Edmonton," *ICCA Journal*, 12(2), pp. 84–99, June 1989.

[13] Feng-hsiung Hsu, "The Software Toolworks Open Championship," *ICCA Journal*, 11(3), pp. 199–200, December 1988.

[14] J. Hanken, "Deep Thought has miles to go before it sleeps," *Chess Life*, pp. 22–28, March 1989.

[15] David Levy, "Computer beats grandmaster," *ICCA Journal*, 11(3), pp. 168–170, December 1988.

[16] The DT Team, "Deep Thought versus Byrne," *ICCA Journal*, 12(3), p. 191, September 1989.

[17] Robert Byrne, *The New York Times*, September 26, 1989.

[18] Garry Kasparov (with Donald Trelford), *Unlimited Challenge*, Grove Weidenfeld, New York, 1987. [An autobiography of Kasparov's life up to 1987, revised in 1990; originally published in Great Britain as *Child of Change* in 1987.]

[19] M. Mitchell Waldrop, "Humanity 2, computers 0," *Science*, 246, November 3, 1989, pp. 572–573.

[20] The Editors, "Champ meets champ," *ICCA Journal*, 11(4), p. 230, December 1989.

[21] Harold C. Schonberg, "Kasparov beats chess computer (for now)" *The New York Times*, p. A1, October 23, 1989.

[22] Andrea Privitere, "Red chess king quick fries Deep Thought's chips," *New York Post*, p. 3, October 23, 1989.

[23] Douglas Haberman and George E. Jordan, "Back to the drawing board. Chess computer's no match for animated Kasparov," *New York Newsday*, p. 3, October 23, 1989.

[24] Monty Newborn and Danny Kopec, "The Twentieth Annual ACM North American Computer Chess Championship," *Communications of the ACM*, 33(7), pp. 94–103, July 1990.

[25] Chris Chabris, "The Harvard Cup Man-Versus-Machine Chess Challenge," *ICCA Journal*, 16(1), pp. 57–61, March 1993.

[26] David Levy, "The ACM 20th North American Computer-Chess Championship," *ICCA Journal*, 12(4), pp. 238–243, December 1989.

[27] Larry Evans, "The key game," *ICCA Journal*, 12(4), pp. 244–245, December 1989.

[28] Ben Mittman, "Deep preparations," *ICCA Journal*, 12(4), pp. 246–247, December 1989.

[29] David Levy, "The end of an era," *ICCA Journal*, 13(1), pp. 34–35, March 1990.

[30] David Levy and Monty Newborn, *How Computers Play Chess*, Computer Science Press, New York, 1991.

[31] R. M. Hyatt, B. E. Gower, and H. L. Nelson, "Cray Blitz," *Advances in Computer Chess 4*, D. Beal, ed., Pergamon Press, Oxford, pp. 8–18, 1985.

[32] Robert M. Hyatt, *A high performance parallel algorithm to search depth-first game trees*, PhD. Thesis, Department of Computer Science, University of Alabama, Birmingham, 1988.

[33] R. M. Hyatt, B. W. Suter, and H. L. Nelson, "A parallel alpha-beta tree searching algorithm," *Parallel Computing*, 10(3), pp. 299–308, 1989.

[34] Hans J. Berliner and C. Ebeling, "The SUPREM architecture: a new intelligent paradigm," *Artificial Intelligence*, 28, pp. 3–8, 1986.

[35] Bradley C. Kuszmaul, "The STARTECH massively parallel chess program," *ICCA Journal*, 18(1), pp. 3–19, March 1995.

Summary of Matches during the Period
October 1989 – December 31, 1989

Date: October 23, 1989
Location: New York Academy of the Arts
Event: Exhibition Match with World Champion Garry Kasparov
Time Control: All/90 minutes
Results: Kasparov 2, Deep Thought 0

Versus	Color	Result
Garry Kasparov	White	Deep Thought Lost
Garry Kasparov	Black	Deep Thought Lost

Date: October 29, 1989
Location: Harvard University
Event: The First Harvard Cup
Time Control: All/ 30 minutes
Results: Deep Thought 1, Opponents 3

Versus	Color	Result
Boris Gulko	Black	Deep Thought Lost
Maxim Dlugy	White	Deep Thought Won
Lev Alburt	White	Deep Thought Lost
Michael Rohde	Black	Deep Thought Lost

Date: November 12-15, 1989
Location: Reno, Nevada
Event: ACM's 20th North American Computer Chess Championship
Time Control: 40/2, 20/1 thereafter
Results: Deep Thought 4, Opponents 1

Versus	Color	Result
Sun Phoenix	Black	Deep Thought Won
BP	White	Deep Thought Won
Hitech	Black	Deep Thought Won
Rebel	White	Deep Thought Won
Mephisto	Black	Deep Thought Lost

Date: December 1989
Location: London, England
Event: David Levy Versus Deep Thought Challenge Match
Time Control: 40/2, 20/1 thereafter
Results: Deep Thought 4, David Levy 0

Versus	Color	Result
David Levy	White	Deep Thought Won
David Levy	Black	Deep Thought Won
David Levy	White	Deep Thought Won
David Levy	Black	Deep Thought Won

3 Gaining Experience

"Not the mother of all machines,"
observed Frederic Friedel [7].

S hortly after joining IBM Research, CB Hsu set out to design his dream machine, a computer that would defeat the world chess champion. Efforts to create this new machine would occupy the next several years. During this time, the team would achieve significant success playing with Deep Thought and its successor Deep Thought II.

Hsu planned to design a special-purpose 1000-processor system with 20 VLSI chess chips on each of 50 boards packed into two six-foot high cabinets [1]. The chess chips would be much faster than those developed at Carnegie Mellon. The system would search three billion chess positions per second, more than one thousand times as many as the version that had just battled Garry Kasparov. The big question was how much better this massive system would perform. Using a large army of computers effectively had proven very difficult.

Jerry Brody.

In early 1990 Jerry Brody was added to the team and given the responsibility of transforming Hsu's high-level design plans into real functioning electronic cabinets. In 1959 Brody had received an applied science degree from the RCA Institute in New York. Having joined IBM in 1978, his work with supercomputers dates back to the RP3 project in the middle 1980s. Brody's easygoing personality meshed well with other more complex personalities on the team.

Until the new system was ready, efforts would continue to improve Deep Thought's software, evaluation function, book, and search heuristics, and to test the new versions in competition. Meanwhile, an IBM computer would replace the SUN 4 system at Carnegie Mellon. The software, written mostly in C, and the new circuit boards on which the improved VLSI chess chips would reside would be modified to be compatible with the RS/6000, short for RISC (Reduced Instruction Set Computer) System/6000, IBM's main workstation product.

On February 2, 1990, Deep Thought played a single game against the world's second-ranked player Anatoly Karpov [2]. Karpov had replaced Bobby Fischer as World Champion in 1975 and reigned until toppled by Kasparov in 1985. When he played Deep Thought, his rating was over 2700. At that point, he and Kasparov had battled many times, with Kasparov holding a slim one-game advantage.

Karpov was born on May 23, 1951, in the Soviet city of Zlatoust located near the Ural Mountains. His personality, contrasting sharply with Kasparov's, lacked the visible intensity that permeated Kasparov's demeanor, but reflected a quiet confidence. While Kasparov was likely to be found discussing world politics when his mind wasn't occupied with chess, Karpov was more likely to be found discussing some other board game. Both realized the importance of physical exercise as part of their training; both shared an interest in tennis.

Dan Edelman put together this one-game match between Deep Thought and Karpov on the Harvard University campus. Edelman had organized the Harvard Cup in which Deep Thought participated several months earlier. Karpov was tired from traveling and was given the white pieces to counterbalance his fatigued state, since historical evidence suggests that White has a significant 55% to 45% edge over Black. Each player received an hour on the clock; essentially, the game was played at approximately three times the speed of world championship games.

The Deep Thought team preferred to play two games, but it was unable to get Karpov's agreement. It was also unhappy when Karpov asked to play with the white pieces as a condition of his participation. However, because its main objective was to acquire experience — the more games, the better — and either color would do.

After a long, hard-fought battle, and after putting up great resistance while passing over several opportunities to force a draw, Deep Thought finally succumbed to Karpov on move 65. This was clearly the best one-game performance by a computer to date. Only several months earlier, Deep Thought had put in an unimpressive showing against the world's top-ranked player. Here, against the world's second-ranked player, the computer played like an equal, although one game was hardly conclusive.

Several weeks later, Deep Thought drew both games of a two-game match with the tough German Grandmaster Helmut Pfleger via the telephone [3]. The first game ended with Deep Thought having a one-pawn advantage but no way to make further progress. Deep Thought gave up a small advantage late in the game when it traded one of its two bishops for a knight and pawn, leading six moves later to a draw. When the game ended, several pawns and bishops of opposite color remained on the board. Deep Thought needed additional information on how to handle such situations. It needed to know that bishops of opposite color with one or two pawns on the board usually result in drawn games. In the second game, both sides had a rook and pawn on the board when a draw was agreed upon. Frederic Friedel was instrumental in the arrangements, continuing his close involvement with the Deep Thought team and with the leading players.

Joe Hoane.

In the autumn of 1990 Thomas Anantharaman left IBM to join a Wall Street investment firm interested in his exceptional programming talent. Perhaps the company felt his experience designing chess programs might turn out to be useful in designing software to forecast the direction of stock price movements on the NYSE. He has since moved to the academic world, and he is now with the University of Wisconsin. Randy Moulic quickly replaced Anantharaman with Joe Hoane, concerned that the budget slot might disappear if not filled quickly, as financial problems were beginning to surface at IBM.

Joe Hoane, who had been working on the RP3 and then on the Vulcan prototype, had developed an interest in the chess project. IBM researchers frequently interact with others in different groups and move from one project to another as their interests shift. Hoane, whose office was in close proximity to those of Hsu and Campbell, often discussed Deep Thought with them. The two felt that Hoane could assist them, and they encouraged Randy Moulic to take him on board. Hoane restored to the team the programming talent that left with Anantharaman. Hoane had graduated from the University of Illinois in 1984 and would received a Master of Science degree from Columbia University in 1994. When he joined IBM's Fishkill Division upon graduation, his first assignment involved developing a custom wiring program for multilayer ceramic integrated circuits.

Later in November of 1990 at the 21st ACM North American Computer Chess Championship held in New York while Deep Thought was undergoing major modifications and was not in a state to compete, an earlier version named Deep Thought/88 — the Deep Thought program from 1988 — participated [4,5]. It could do no better than tie for first place. The championship demonstrated how quickly the computer competition was progressing. In 1988 Deep Thought was the outright winner of that year's ACM championship with a score of 3.5/4; two years later, it was fortunate to share first place with Mephisto, a program running on a small computer. Moreover, had Hitech not lost its final round game due to some bad fortune, Deep Thought's arch rival would have won the tournament outright.

In May of 1991, and after a year without competing — excluding the ACM championship in 1990 at which an old version of the program was entered — Deep Thought appeared in the strongest tournament yet that included a computer [6]. At CeBIT, a giant computer exhibition in Hanover, Germany, Deep Thought joined the company of seven grandmasters.

Hsu's giant machine with 1000 VLSI chess chips was still far from ready. With a new batch of the first-generation chess chips fabricated but not yet installed, once more the well-worn version of Deep Thought went off to battle. The system was connected from the Hawthorn facility via telephone lines to the playing hall in Germany, where Campbell and Hsu took turns at the board.

Deep Thought finished with a disappointing 2.5 out of 7 points. Two losses were a direct consequence of errors in Deep Thought's new opening book, prepared in cooperation with Grandmaster Maxim Dlugy, although the errors really were not introduced directly by Dlugy. He had created parts of the book by copying lines from the *Encyclopedia of Chess Openings*. One line, however, contained an incorrect move and another an erroneous evaluation of the position at the end of a line. Deep Thought managed to stumble across these errors; one wonders how many others were present. If the computer had won at least one of the two games affected by these errors, it would have finished with a respectable score. Dlugy's new opening book was short-lived: pouring lines from an encyclopedia was a dangerous procedure. For the near-term, with other priorities needing attention, a better opening book would have to wait.

While in Germany, Campbell and Hsu crossed paths with Garry Kasparov, who had been invited to Hanover by the conference organizers to give a simultaneous exhibition and to meet the press. Frederic Friedel, who was involved in organizing the competition, thought it would be a perfect occasion to give the world champion an interesting examination that is at the soul of artificial intelligence! Friedel would give Kasparov the games from each of the first five rounds of the tournament, one round at a time, and Kasparov was to pick out Deep Thought from the seven other contestants. He was allotted 30 minutes to examine the 20 games. According to Friedel, Kasparov correctly picked Deep Thought's games against Hans-Ulrich Grunberg and Wolfgang Unzicker, but failed to recognize its games against Klaus Bischoff, Eric Lobron, and Uwe Bonsch. Friedel admitted that in Round 3 Kasparov had narrowed the choices to Deep Thought and Raj Tischbierek. Although he finally incorrectly picked Tischbierek, for this waffling, Friedel gave him half credit and awarded him an overall score of 50% on the examination. While Kasparov was not particularly familiar with the German grandmasters, having only played Matthias Wahls when he was much younger, he was very familiar with Deep Thought. The examination showed the difficulty of distinguishing the top computer from top human chess players. If Kasparov can guess correctly only 50% of the time, then the differences must be small and subtle.

On August 28, 1991 and several months after the Hanover tournament, Deep Thought played to a win and a loss in a two-game match with Australia's number two ranked player, Grandmaster Darryl Johansen [7,8]. The match took place in Sydney, Australia, at the 12th International Joint Conference on Artificial Intelligence, a biannual conference that attracts the top researchers in the field of artificial intelligence. This time Randy Moulic was at the game table, connected halfway around the world to IBM's Hawthorn Annex. Each side had one hour to complete all moves.

The first game against Johansen was a tactical battle in which Deep Thought took advantage of a weak sixth move by its opponent and gradually built up an advantage, forcing a resignation on move 44. The second game saw Deep Thought outplayed positionally, with all of the computer's pieces effectively out of play at the end while its opponent was in total control. This was possibly the worst loss on record for the IBM chess machine. The question after the game was how to modify the evaluation function to avoid similar disasters in the future.

In November of 1991 a new version of Deep Thought, called Deep Thought II, finally appeared at the 22nd ACM International Computer Chess Championship in Albuquerque [9,10]. (The name of the annual ACM competitions had been changed for this event to reflect the international composition of the field.) Finishing with a perfect 5–0 score, the new system dominated the event. IBM's RS/6000 workstation was now connected to 12 improved chess boards with the usual two VLSI chess chips apiece. The new boards, though using the same VLSI chess chip, contained improved hardware for evaluating positions. The workstation was rated at 44 mips and contained 192 megabytes of memory — about five times as fast as the

Grandmaster Darryl Johansen.

SUN 4 computer that Deep Thought had been using, and it contained about six times as much memory. A large table that could store information on two million chess positions was used. Deep Thought II was searching 5,000,000 positions per second, almost a factor of 10 more than its predecessor. In comparison, Cray Blitz, the next most powerful system, was running on an eight-processor Cray YMP that was examining a relatively meager 500,000 positions per second.

Deep Thought II outplayed Zarkov and Mchess in the first two rounds and then met archrival Hitech in the third round. Campbell's extended opening book was used for the first time in this championship, and it assisted Deep Thought II in this important game. Hitech played a French Defense for which Deep Thought II was not extensively booked. Berliner worked hard on his opening book to include lines where Deep Thought would be weak. When Deep Thought II's opening book was no longer able to provide moves, the extended opening book took over and provided adequate replies. Deep Thought II eventually wore down Hitech in a well-played endgame. In the final two games of the tournament against Cray Blitz and Chess Machine, Deep Thought II again gradually wore down its opponents, winning two long endgames.

Campbell had implemented Deep Thought II's novel extended opening book just prior to this event. This book contained positions found in several hundred thousand high-caliber games played by grandmasters. For each position, there was information about the moves the grandmasters selected, including how often each of the moves had been selected, the results, and who had played them. This information was boiled down to a single number for each move indicating its apparent quality.

During a game, if a position at the root of the search tree was not found in the o-pening book, Deep Thought II then looked for it in its extended opening book. If it found the position there, the moves in that position were

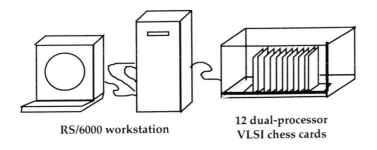

RS/6000 workstation   **12 dual-processor VLSI chess cards**

Schematic of Deep Thought II.

assigned scores from the extended book plus the value found by the search of the game tree. If the score assigned to some move from the extended book was sufficiently high, that move was selected and the usual search was skipped. The extended book turned out to be very effective and was an important factor in the second and sixth games of the 1997 Rematch.

The period 1990–1991, while having its ups and down, thus ended on a positive note for the IBM chess effort. Deep Thought II had solidified its position at the top of the world of chess-playing computers. In tournament-length games against grandmasters during this period, the chess program had compiled one win (Bonsch 2535), three draws (Pfleger twice 2520, Bischoff 2495), and four losses (Lobron 2545, Unzicker 2480, Wahls 2560, Tischbierek 2500). However, Hsu's system with 1000 VLSI chess chips was still nowhere in sight. Two cabinets, one an identical copy of the other, had been assembled by Jerry Brody in anticipation of the eventual electronic circuit boards. Power supplies were put in their places. Fans were mounted in readiness to cool the boards. While waiting for the boards to appear, Brody had gone as far as building dummy boards loaded with heat-dissipating resistors to simulate the worst-case heating scenario that the eventual system might generate. An IBM Power PC was scheduled to serve as the computer for the system.

But progress in science doesn't march in straight lines: Hsu's large system with 1000 VLSI chess chips would never be built. The chip, yes, eventually, but it would be housed in a different home. A detour would soon be made.

Meanwhile, Garry Kasparov continued his reign as world champion, successfully defending his title against Anatoly Karpov in 1990. He defeated his archrival in a 24-game match by a score of 12.5 – 11.5, winning 4 games, losing 3, and drawing 17. Computers were just off his radar screen.

References

[1] Feng-hsiung Hsu, Thomas Anantharaman, Murray Campbell and Andreas Nowatzyk, "A Grandmaster chess machine," *Scientific American*, 263(4), pp. 44–50, October 1990.

[2] Mike Valvo, "Moral victory: Karpov versus Deep Thought at Harvard," *ICCA Journal*, 12(1), pp. 37–40, March 1990.

[3] Frederic Friedel, "Pfleger versus Deep Thought," *ICCA Journal*, 13(1), p. 40, March 1990.

[4] Monty Newborn and Danny Kopec, "The 21st ACM North American Computer Chess Championship," *Communications of the ACM*, 34(11), pp. 85–92, November 1991.

[5] Robert Levinson, "The ACM 21st North American Computer-Chess Championship," *ICCA Journal*, 12(4), pp. 208–214, December 1990.

[6] Frederic Friedel, "Not the mother of all machines," *ICCA Journal*, 14(2), pp. 101–107, June 1991.

[7] Robert Levinson, "Man and machine, theory and practice square off in Sydney," *ICCA Journal*, 14(3), pp. 150–152, September 1991.

[8] ICCA Editorial Board, "Johansen vs. Deep Thought II: A correction," *ICCA Journal*, 14(4), p. 233, December 1991.

[9] Danny Kopec, Monty Newborn, and Mike Valvo, "The 22nd ACM International Computer Chess Championship," *Communications of the ACM*, 35(11), pp. 100–110, November 1992.

[10] Don Beal, "Report on the 22nd ACM International Computer Chess Championship," *ICCA Journal*, 14(4), pp. 214–222, December 1991.

Summary of Matches During the Period
January 1, 1990 – December 31, 1991

Date: February 2, 1990
Location: Harvard University, Boston, Massachusetts
Event: Exhibition Match with Former World Champion Anatoly Karpov
Time Control: All/1
Results: Karpov 1 – Deep Thought 0

Versus	Color	Result
Anatoly Karpov	Black	Deep Thought Lost

Dates: February 1990
Location: Germany
Event: Exhibition Match with Grandmaster Helmut Pfleger
Time Control: 40/2, 20/1 thereafter
Results: Deep Thought 1 – Pfleger 1

Versus	Color	Result
Helmut Pfleger	Black	Draw
Helmut Pfleger	White	Draw

Dates: November 11–14, 1990
Location: New York
Event: 21st ACM North American Computer Chess Championship
Time Control: All/2
Results: Deep Thought/88 won 4 of 5 points and tied for first place with
         Mephisto; performance rating: 2586

Versus	Color	Result
Bebe	White	Deep Thought/88 Won
Belle	Black	Deep Thought/88 Won
Mephisto	White	Deep Thought/88 Won
Hitech	Black	Deep Thought/88 Lost
Zarkov	White	Deep Thought/88 Won

Dates: May, 1991
Location: Hanover, Germany
Event: Hanover Grandmaster Event
Time Control: 40/2, 20/1 thereafter
Results: Deep Thought II won 2.5 of 7 points

Versus	Color	Result
Hans-Ulrich Grunberg	Black	Deep Thought II Won
Klaus Bischoff	White	Draw
Eric Lobron	Black	Deep Thought II Lost
Uwe Bonsch	White	Deep Thought II Won
Wolfgang Unzicker	Black	Deep Thought II Lost
Matthias Wahls	White	Deep Thought II Lost
Raj Tischbierek	Black	Deep Thought II Lost

Date: August 28, 1991
Location: Sydney, Australia
Event: IJCAI Match
Time Control: All/1
Results: Deep Thought II 1 – Darryl Johansen 1

Versus	Color	Result
Darryl Johansen	White	Deep Thought II Won
Darryl Johansen	Black	Deep Thought II Lost

Dates: November 17–20, 1991
Location: Albuquerque, New Mexico
Event: 22nd ACM International Computer Chess Championship
Time Control: 40/2, 20/1 thereafter
Results: Deep Thought II won 5 of 5 points and won the event

Versus	Color	Result
Zarkov	White	Deep Thought II Won
Mchess	Black	Deep Thought II Won
Hitech	White	Deep Thought II Won
Cray Blitz	Black	Deep Thought II Won
Chess Machine	White	Deep Thought II Won

4 Surviving Deep Cuts

"I need some practice and then I will kill it!" Judit Polgar, 1993.

In the spring of 1992, Chung-Jen (CJ) Tan took over the chess project during what had become a difficult period for IBM, possibly the most difficult in the company's modern history. When Tan took over, the value of a share of IBM stock was $60, falling, and with no end in sight. From a high of $175.87 in 1987, the value of a share of IBM's stock fell to a low of $40.63 in 1993; the company's value decreased by a devastating 77% over this six-year period. The company was going through massive reorganization exercises. Then-CEO John Akers was considering a radical proposal of selling off various divisions, including IBM Research. Every research project was being reevaluated, and chess was low on the list of priorities — according to Tan, down near the bottom of the list. Akers' drastic plans were dropped when Lou Gerstner took over in 1993 as CEO; the chess project had survived!

Chung-Jen (CJ) Tan.

Tan took over the chess project at the request of Zeev Barzilai when Randy Moulic moved from IBM Research to another position within the company. Tan added Moulic's assignment, including the chess project, to his ongoing parallel processing research, and from that time on was in charge of the exciting effort to catch Garry Kasparov.

Tan had completed his doctoral studies in electrical engineering at Columbia University in 1969. His research was in the area of logical design —specifically, how to design computer circuits that worked reliably at high speeds. His advisor was Steve Unger, a prominent name in the field of computer circuit design. There Tan and I became colleagues and good friends in 1968 when I was a young first-year professor and he was in his final year of studies. Tan was born in Chongqing, China, and moved to Taiwan with his parents in 1949. After high school, he went on to the University of Seattle for his BS. degree and then the University of California at Berkeley for his MS. degree.

During the days at Columbia, Tan's and my research interests were similar. Beyond his work with Unger, he and I with three other graduate students — Ed Hsieh, Hsieh Hao, and Tom Arnold — published several joint papers on the subject of computer circuit design. It was an exciting and productive period, with lots of blackboard scribbling and discussions over coffee in the students' lounge. Our research led to interesting results. We showed that, in theory, any big computer could be designed by interconnecting many identical small computers. Each small computer could be very, very small — in fact, as small as a computer could be. Moreover, the small computers could be arranged in a rectangular array.

After receiving their doctorates, Ed Hsieh and Hsieh Hao joined IBM and went on to spend almost three decades there. Tom Arnold had been on a work-study program with Bell Laboratories while a doctoral student and chose to remain with the telephone company after graduation. Arnold's younger brother George, an undergraduate in electrical engineering at Columbia and the valedictorian of his class, developed a chess program with me several years later. This was Ostrich, so named because of its tendency to put its head in the sand, so to speak, when in trouble. Ostrich participated in major computer chess events, including five world championships, from the early 1970s through most of the 1980s.

After joining IBM upon graduation, Tan worked initially on automating the design of logic circuits. He later became involved in computer system design, and ultimately in the design of parallel computers, including the RP3 and the RS/6000 SP series. He has had a distinguished career at IBM; his work on computer circuits was recognized in 1989 when he received an IBM Outstanding Technical Achievement Award. In 1994 he received an IBM Research Division Award for his contribution to the design and development of the SP2. For his work on the Deep Blue, he received an IBM Research Outstanding Contribution Award in 1996 and a Special IBM Corporate Award the next year. In 1999 he became a Fellow of the Association for Computing (ACM).

Tan's extensive technical background and managerial experience were the perfect qualifications to supervise the complex chess project. The project had deadlines to meet, budgets to hold, circuits to build and interconnect, programs to write, expert information to encode, and extensive testing to carry out. There were hundreds of design decisions, choices and compromises that had to be made. And the case for the project had to be taken to IBM's upper management levels from time to time and justified. Tan had to explain delays and bugs, while showing progress. The project always advanced more slowly than expectations.

Tan was responsible for supervising CB Hsu, one of the unique talents in the world. Hsu is without question a true genius, a brilliant mind, full of ideas, energy, enthusiasm, with a love and a deep passion for his work. To put his passion in perspective, Murray Campbell likes to tell the story of how his wife, Gina, helped Hsu when he joined IBM. It seems that Hsu was too busy with his work to find time to buy himself a bed. He slept on the floor for a whole month until Gina came to his rescue. She had to buy him a bed for his apartment. Unlike Campbell and Joe Hoane, Hsu was a bachelor — his work got every ounce of his energy.

In 1991 Hsu received the ACM's Grace Murray Hopper Award, which included a $5000 prize, in recognition for being the most "outstanding young professional of the year." Although totally indispensable to the project, he was a challenge to supervise. The design of his VLSI chess chip and board was a neverending story. He always had something more to change or add. His goal was perfection, and he always felt he could achieve it with several more months of work. His mind raced ahead of his words, making explanations of his work difficult to follow. Tan had to give Hsu's creative mind the freedom necessary to design his special-purpose VLSI chess chip and board, intended to outdo Garry Kasparov, but he also had to put pressure on the circuit wizard to force him to complete his complex ideas. A functioning circuit was clearly better than a perfect circuit that never materialized.

Balancing Hsu's outwardly, visible enthusiasm was the quiet, soft-spoken way of Murray Campbell. Campbell, no less talented, exuded an air of calmness. He brought chess expertise to the project, having played at the Master level when he was younger. Campbell was Canadian. He had received an undergraduate and then a master's degree in computer science from the University of Alberta. His thesis advisor had been Tony Marsland, known for his chess program, Awit, and for his efforts to design a strong selective search program, meant to resemble the selective procedures thought to be used by the top chess players. Marsland had worked on Awit for some 15 years, continually refining it. While the program did reach the Expert level, Marsland was unable to strengthen it any further. Awit was, perhaps, the last strong selective search program.

Campbell's master's thesis involved parallel search and, more specifically, how to search a chess tree using a network of computers to obtain a significant increase in speed. He wrote his doctoral thesis at Carnegie Mellon University under the supervision of Hans Berliner. During this period, Campbell assisted in testing Berliner's Hitech and in developing the program's opening book. While continuing to work with his supervisor, Campbell joined with classmates CB Hsu and Thomas Anantharaman in the autumn of 1986 to work on their program Chiptest. Campbell walked a fine line to maintain good relations with Berliner while teaming up with rivals Hsu and Anantharaman. Berliner was frustrated at the success Hsu and Anantharaman were having with their program, especially because Hsu had decided to go off on his own. Hsu had felt that the special-purpose chess circuits in Hitech didn't have the potential for improvement as did those in Ken Thompson's Belle, and he based his own design on Thompson's circuits. The rivalry between Berliner and Hsu would continue for a decade.

When Randy Moulic left IBM Research, he was supervising several projects — the GF-11, the Vulcan, and the chess project. Tan was investigating applications that ran on the RP3 and was supervising research related to the design of a VLIW (very long instruction word) computer. The two had previously been managers of different aspects of building the RP3, and when that effort wound down, they continued on independent efforts related to parallel processing research. When Moulic left, research on parallel processing architecture at IBM Research was reorganized, leaving Tan in charge of the Vulcan project, the design of a VLIW computer, and the chess project.

Tan's first job was to reexamine the project, where it should fit in, or more crucially, whether it should fit in at all. He came to the conclusion that Hsu's dream machine would never fly. He reasoned that if it were ever assembled, all kinds of system software would have to be developed to support the hardware. In addition, Tan was concerned that the two cabinets, when loaded down with all the anticipated electronics, would generate too much heat — in spite of Jerry Brody's tests. Moreover, the system would be too specialized to be marketable as a commercial product, and with IBM in financial difficulties, the cost of developing an expensive, one-of-a-kind computer could not be justified. Tan understood that the old IBM philosophy of basic research for the sake of science was being replaced with a new philosophy: basic research tied to solutions for real customers. The chess project would have to be modified to fit in.

Tan, with Zeev Barzilai's strong support, convinced higher management that he had a singularly special group. Although many talented researchers were leaving IBM, including world class physicists, the young group and the chess project should be kept together. However, he realized he could no longer justify the project within IBM Research as just a "Grand Challenge" project. As a result of discussions with Barzilai, Tan decided to repackage the project as an application designed to run on the new RS/6000 SP2 architecture. If it could be the world's best chess player, it could also be the world's best weather forecaster or DNA decipherer. That argument might sell computers. In the late 1980s and early 1990s, IBM's largest computers were mainframe systems; these systems were losing ground badly to systems that networked many small computers and workstations. The SP-series computers were IBM's effort to recapture the market, which preferred the advantages of these more flexible networked systems. The chess program would showcase how the RS/6000 SP2 architecture could solve highly complex problems.

Tan discussed this approach with Hsu, Campbell, and Hoane. After weighing their options, they accepted the proposal; the RS/6000 SP2 would be the new home for the chess program. Besides deciding on the SP2, they agreed that Campbell and Hoane would concentrate on improving the software, while Hsu would concentrate on completing his new VLSI chess chip and accelerator card. Previously, the VLSI chess chip was said to be on a "board," but the term "accelerator card" was now introduced to reflect the fact that the VLSI chess chip and board accelerated the move generation process, just as some computers use a "floating-point accelerator card" to speed up the calculation of floating-point numbers. To measure progress, Tan planned several high-profile matches, hoping to culminate in a 1995 match with World Champion Garry Kasparov. Tan went back to his superiors to confirm the team's agreement with the modified plans, and he received their support.

Along with Tan's reorientation of the project, the PR office at IBM Research felt a more appropriate name than Deep Thought II was needed for the chess program, and so a small internal naming contest was held. Jerry Present invited researchers to make suggestions, and over the next few weeks, about a dozen names were proposed. The name Deep Blue was selected, and those developing it, the Deep Blue team. This combined "Big Blue" and "Deep Thought" in a way that preserved the original name of the chess program while closely identifying it with IBM.

Anticipating the arrival of Hsu's new VLSI chess chip and accelerator card and the birth of Deep Blue in late 1992, Tan organized several events for the following year. Each event was expected to suggest hardware and software improvements for future versions of the system. The first was scheduled for February 1993 in Copenhagen against the entire National Chess Team of Denmark; the team was headed by Denmark's top player, Grandmaster Bent Larsen. The second was a single game in April against Grandmaster Michael Rohde. It would take place at New York University in lower Manhattan. The third was a two-game match in August at the team's Hawthorn Annex against Hungarian Grandmaster Judit Polgar.

The team passed up defending its title as world champion at the seventh such competition held in Madrid in November of 1992. It felt that participating in the event would delay completing the new system and that there was no need for additional recognition. This left Cray Blitz as the only program to successfully defend its title over the course of the first seven world championships. In computer-chess circles, some felt that history was repeating itself. Like others that had been world champion and subsequently faded away, passing up this event could signify the beginning of the end for the IBM chess program. To stay at the forefront of this addicted passionate group of code producers and circuit designers, all hoping to produce the world's best chess program, meant never stopping for a breather, as the competition was likely to sail by if you did.

In addition to passing up the world championship, the team chose to skip the 23rd ACM International Computer Chess Championship held in Indianapolis in February of 1993, preferring to participate in a major event in Denmark against human competition. The team was focusing on an eventual showdown with the human world chess champion, and there was more to be learned in Denmark than in Indianapolis.

In Denmark two separate matches were scheduled to take place during February 24–28, 1993 [1]. The Copenhagen Chess Union, in cooperation with IBM Denmark, organized a four-game match against Larsen and the second four-game match against the National Chess Team of Denmark, which included Larsen as a member. One Larsen game, the fourth, counted as part of both matches, and thus only seven games were played.

Anticipating that Hsu's VLSI chess chip would finally be ready for Denmark, the Deep Blue team had advertised that the matches would be played with the new Deep Blue. However, while Hsu had been working like a tiger throughout 1992, the system was not ready, and the team had to revert to its Deep Thought II program, though this time, it consisted of 14 enhanced first-generation VLSI chess chips, two per card, housed in a box by themselves and connected to an RS/6000 workstation. New, improved software was used, and in an attempt to distinguish the new system from the old and from what was to come, the system was named Nordic Deep Blue. That is, Nordic Deep Blue was Deep Thought II with improved software.

The Deep Blue team travelled to Denmark, bringing with them 16 first-generation chess chips on eight cards to be tied into a locally-provided workstation. Unfortunately, the system overheated when they were setting up, frying one card, leaving seven for the match. Over time, the cards were slowly being degraded, going from 12 when Deep Thought II was born to seven for this match. In his report of the match, Hsu estimated the approximate cost of the chess-specific hardware at $24,000.

Larsen, it might be recalled, had been upset by Deep Thought 0.02 in the 1988 Software Toolbox Chess Championship, and he was eager to avenge the loss. The whole team, not only Larsen, prepared extensively for the match, with team coach Jens Nielsen putting together a book of Deep Thought games for his teammates to study. Nevertheless, Nordic Deep Blue performed admirably, winning 1.5 of the 4 points against Larsen and 3 of the 4 points against the National Chess Team of Denmark. Against Larsen, Nordic Deep Blue lost the first game and then drew the following three. Against the team, Nordic Deep Blue defeated Henrik Danielsen and Lars Bo Hansen while drawing against Larsen and Carsten Hoi. The games were played at a rate of the first 40 moves in 2 hours, and then the remaining moves in 30 minutes; a game could last at most 5 hours.

Given the level of the competition, Nordic Deep Blue could be credited with a performance rating of approximately 2575. Moreover, there were several drawn games in which the computer had the better position, and thus on Nordic Deep Blue's behalf, one might argue that the 2575 figure was conservative. But still, Kasparov's better-than-2800 rating loomed far above.

There were lessons to be learned from every match, and these two were no exceptions. In discussing the matches in the *ICCA Journal*, Hsu pointed out that in the first two games with Larsen, Nordic Deep Blue wound up with a bishop pair, which received a positive evaluation; it didn't understand that in this case it was best to trade off pawns to give the bishops greater range. Other adjustments to the search heuristics were made after the first round, improving the computer's play in later rounds.

On Friday, February 18, 1993, one week before the matches, the Deep Blue team met with Garry Kasparov over a dinner of reindeer meat, considered a delicacy in Denmark, and discussed chess. On the following day, Kasparov gave a talk attended by 500 devotees, and he used Nordic Deep Blue as his assistant when analyzing several famous positions. According to Campbell, a match with Deep Blue was one of many topics of discussion, with Kasparov saying that he wanted to play the computer before he was 30 (two months hence), while he still had energy.

After the Danish matches, on April 20, 1993, the IBM chess program — now called Deep Blue Prototype though still essentially Deep Thought II —

next took on Grandmaster Michael Rohde in a one-game match played at New York University [2]. Rohde had defeated Deep Thought in 1989 at the 1st Harvard Cup playing White; this time it would be Deep Blue Prototype's turn with White. Deep Blue Prototype, running out of the Hawthorn Annex, used 16 VLSI chess chips on eight accelerator cards compared to the 14 and seven used in Denmark, but otherwise it was essentially the same system. Vishwananthan Anand, the world's second-ranked chess player at that time, was visiting the Hawthorn Annex during the match, accompanied by Frederic Friedel, and he provided his observations to the researchers watching there. Anand had earlier played several scrimmage games with Deep Thought II, and according to Murray Campbell, Deep Thought II held its own.

The game with Michael Rohde turned out to be a tactical battle in which Deep Blue Prototype obtained two passed queenside pawns. Rohde soon found himself very short of time and then, worse, backed into a position in which the computer announced mate in eight! After being marched along the path toward oblivion for several moves, Rohde threw in the towel. He had defeated Deep Thought at the 1989 Harvard Cup. Now, four years later, the tables were reversed.

Deep Blue Prototype's next challenge came on August 20, 1993, when Judit Polgar, the 17-year-old Hungarian chess whizkid came to the IBM Hawthorn Annex to play Deep Blue Prototype in a two-game match [3]. Judit is the youngest of three exceptional sisters and is now the top-ranked woman in the world. Her older sister, Zsuzsa, is a grandmaster, while her younger sister, Zsofia, is a master. The three sisters were taught to play chess when they were very young by their parents, who were interested in shedding light on the question of whether geniuses are made or born [4].

Earlier, in March of 1993, Dan Edelman had proposed to IBM a much larger event with Polgar in which IBM would showcase the new Deep Blue. But when it became clear that the system wouldn't be ready and that Deep Blue Prototype was to be used, plans were scaled back a second time. Deep Blue Prototype was continuing to be improved through the usual evolutionary changes in its software and the filtering out of subtle bugs, but the new Deep Blue's maiden appearance would have to wait.

Judit Polgar, her mother Klara Polgar, and the Hungarian Consul-General and his wife arrived at the Hawthorn Annex in a Rolls Royce. A Hungarian television crew covered the match along with a number of other journalists, including Robert Byrne. The Professional Chess Association's Commissioner Bob Rice attended. The PCA was established that year by Kasparov and British Grandmaster Nigel Short and backed by Intel. Short had lost his challenge for the world championship against Kasparov the previous year. Tan invited me to attend in my capacity as head of the

ACM Computer Chess Committee. I sat in the audience with approximately 30 other invitees.

In his report on the match, Hsu said that Polgar had prepared for the match, and she was "probably better prepared against the machine than Karpov was, but not as well as the Danish players and certainly not as well as Kasparov, Mr. Prepared himself." Her 2630 FIDE rating at that time placed her about 170–190 points weaker than Kasparov. I was impressed by the combination of her mature composure and her youthful, easygoing, and outwardly relaxed nature.

The games were played at the fast rate of all moves in 30 minutes; a game would last no more than one hour. In the first game Deep Thought II, playing White, opened with the usual advance of its king's pawn. Polgar countered with a Sicilian defense and, while putting up a good fight, gradually succumbed to the computer, being tactically outplayed, and giving up on the 73rd move. After a 45-minute break, the second game began. Again, the machine obtained a very strong position, but Polgar recovered around the 50th move and was able to force a draw. Following the two games, she discharged the typical battle cry, "I need some practice, then I will kill it!"

CB Hsu at the terminal talking to Judit Polgar with
Zeev Barzilai and CJ Tan looking on.

Late in 1993, in an attempt to initiate negotiations for a match with Garry Kasparov, Tan contacted PCA Commissioner Bob Rice and made plans to meet in the latter's Wall Street office. Tan and Campbell went there together with a proposal for a major event with Kasparov, while Rice had in mind obtaining IBM corporate sponsorship for the PCA. At that time, the PCA was also negotiating to extend its existing contract with Intel, but there was concern over the slow progress. Rice suggested to IBM that it support a series of major PCA events including a Kasparov versus Deep Blue match. According to Tan, the proposal was given consideration back at IBM Research and at IBM Corporate Headquarters at Armonk. However, while there was support for a match between Kasparov and Deep Blue, more extensive support for the PCA was not forthcoming. In mid-1994 the talks ended with no agreement, putting the chess project in serious jeopardy.

In early 1994 Deep Blue and the Deep Blue team moved from the Hawthorn Annex to IBM's premier research quarters in Yorktown Heights. Yorktown Heights is an hour's drive north of Manhattan in Westchester County. Gentle rolling hills covered with tall graceful trees provide seclusion for large stately estates and environmentally clean corporations. The research center was built in 1961 and currently is home to approxi-

Judit Polgar and Murray Campbell observing Deep Thought II.

mately 1400 of IBM's top researchers. While IBM has other prominent research centers and laboratories — in Haifa, Beijing, Tokyo, Zurich, Delhi, and in San Jose, California, and Austin, Texas — the Yorktown facility is its largest and traditionally considered its finest.

From outside, the three-story building's black-tinted glass and enormous quarter-mile-wide semicircular shape make it an impressive structure. A long uphill driveway leads from the highway, New York Route 134, to the main entrance. Deer and Canadian geese — permanent New York State residents, in this case — wander nonchalantly around the grass-covered grounds at sunrise and dusk, disappearing into the shrubbery during midday, oblivious of the exciting work going on only yards away. Photographs and accomplishments of the "who's who" of the research center — and of the computer world — are proudly displayed in the entrance lobby. Early calculating devices exhibited in the lobby contrast sharply with the advanced technology that permeates the interior offices and laboratories.

The researchers have a large parking area at the back, hiding hundreds of cars from view, and giving visitors who arrive at the front of the building the feeling that there may be no one at home! But stashed away in about 120 rows of some 25 offices each are some of the world's most prominent researchers. The environment is relaxed and congenial, concealing the intensity of the work. A large, cheery cafeteria serves as one of many places where researchers can sit quietly and discuss ideas. A comfortable auditorium is the site of presentations by visitors from all corners of the world. On the top floor facing outward toward the deer and geese is a first-rate technical library. The researchers come and go at irregular hours and dress casually, like many of the world's top minds. Several tennis courts and a soccer field, also hidden behind the building, are available to exercise the bodies of the exceptional individuals who work inside.

The Deep Blue team was assigned to rows 26 and 27 on the third floor; Tan had the head office in row 26. The others had their own individual offices, while laboratories filled with experimental computing equipment and meeting rooms occupied the remaining space. On my visits there while preparing this book, I found blackboards covered with chalked technical ideas, plans, and schedules. Trophies previously won by the team are on display in a small meeting room next to the Deep Blue Grandmaster Laboratory. Enlarged photographs of the numerous successes cover the walls. A few chess sets could be found along with many books on chess and, in particular, books on chess openings.

So the "Hawthorn Years" came to an end, and so continued the countdown to catching Garry Kasparov with the team in its new Yorktown Heights quarters. The chess project had survived the corporate recession, had been assigned a new leader, and had discarded Hsu's special-purpose chess-playing system for the RS/6000 SP2 computer. Deep Thought II had had a good year, improving during the course of the Copenhagen event, and then defeating both Michael Rohde and Judit Polgar. Perhaps a rating of 2650 was in order, still 150 points shy of Kasparov. But Hsu's new chip was not yet ready, and that problem would continue for some time. To achieve its goal, the team had to improve its system by at least 150 points — and, when ready and not before, it had to find a way to bring Kasparov to the table.

References

[1] Feng-hsiung Hsu, "IBM Deep Blue in Copenhagen," *ICCA Journal*, 16(1), pp. 53–56, March 1993.

[2] Mark Ginsburg, "The Deep Blue Challenge," *ICCA Journal*, 16(2), pp. 111–113, June 1993.

[3] Feng-hsiung Hsu, "Deep Thought versus Judit Polgar," *ICCA Journal*, 16(3), pp. 150–151, September 1993.

[4] Christopher Chabris, "The girl who would be king," *Games*, pp. 12–14, 65–66, February 1994.

IBM's Thomas J. Watson Research Center, Yorktown Heights.

Summary of Matches during the Period
January 1, 1992 – December 31, 1993

Dates: February 24–28, 1993
Location: Copenhagen, Denmark
Event: There were two matches. Seven games were played, with Larsen's
      4th game counted in both matches.
(1) 4 Game Match — Nordic Deep Blue and Grandmaster Bent Larsen
(2) 4 Game Match — Nordic Deep Blue and Danish National Team
Time Control: Some games were played 40/2, 20/1, then sudden death in
      1. Others were played 40/2, All/1 or 40/2, 20/1, All/30.
Results: (1) Larsen 2.5 — Nordic Deep Blue 1.5
      (2) Nordic Deep Blue 3 — Danish National Team 1

Versus	Color	Result
Bent Larsen	Black	Nordic Deep Blue Lost
Bent Larsen	White	Draw
Bent Larsen	Black	Draw
Bent Larsen	White	Draw
Henrik Danielsen	Black	Nordic Deep Blue Won
Carsten Hoi	White	Draw
Lars Bo Hansen	Black	Draw

Date: April 20, 1993
Location: New York University, New York
Event: The Deep Blue Challenge
Time Control: 40/2, 20/1 thereafter
Results: Deep Blue Prototype 1 — Rohde 0

Versus	Color	Result
Michael Rohde	White	Deep Blue Prototype Won

Date: August 20, 1993
Location: IBM T. J. Watson Research Center, Hawthorne, New York
Event: Exhibition Match with Grandmaster Judit Polgar
Time Control: All/30 minutes
Results: Deep Blue Prototype 1.5 — Polgar .5

Versus	Color	Result
Judit Polgar	White	Deep Blue Prototype Won
Judit Polgar	Black	Draw

5 From Cape May to Beijing

"Remote resuscitation efforts were unable to revive the system," Cape May, June 1994.

"To lose a game on time was something that shouldn't happen to a computer," Barcelona, September 1994.

"The position became disastrous when the communication link with Yorktown Heights suddenly broke off," Hong Kong, May 1995.

"Several moves later, the computer crashed again," Beijing, September 1995.

In late June of 1994, after almost a year's hiatus from competition against the human race, and a two-and-a-half-year's abstinence from competition against its own kind, the Deep Blue team took its creation to Cape May, New Jersey, a charming summer seaside resort at the southern tip of the state. Entered under the name of Deep Thought II rather than Deep Blue Prototype, the IBM program had come to participate in the five-round 24th ACM International Computer Chess Championship along with nine other leading programs [1]. The championship was part of a large conference organized by the ACM and the IEEE, the Sixth Annual ACM/IEEE Symposium on Parallel Algorithms and Architectures. It attracted several hundred leading computer scientists and engineers. CJ Tan and CB Hsu came to watch over their entry; Murray Campbell and Joe Hoane were off on summer vacations.

The field at Cape May included *Socrates, Mchess, Wchess, Zarkov, and Cray Blitz, making the event a de facto world championship. These programs, especially *Socrates and Mchess, were nipping at the toes of grandmasters. A single-processor version of *Socrates had finished with an even score at the 1993 Harvard Cup, defeating Grandmasters Michael Rohde and Alexander Ivanov, and drawing with Grandmaster Boris Gulko, earning a performance rating of 2588. The games at the Harvard Cup were played at a rate of all in 30 minutes, far faster than standard top-level tournament play and giving the computers a small edge over slower play, but nevertheless, *Socrates' performance was most impressive. In the same 1993 Harvard Cup, Mchess defeated Grandmaster Patrick Wolff and drew with Gulko.

The single-processor version of *Socrates had also won the 23rd ACM International Computer Chess Championship in Indianapolis in 1993 running on a 50 mips PC. Here at Cape May, the fact that *Socrates was running on a powerful 512-processor Connection Machine, manufactured by the Massachusetts-based company Thinking Machines, suggested that it would play even more strongly than in Boston and Indianapolis. Mchess was running on a 60-mips PC, much faster than the 12-mips PC it had used at the Indianapolis tournament, suggesting additional trouble for Deep Thought II.

The first two rounds were played on Sunday, June 25. Deep Thought II defeated a strong Zarkov in a wild game in Round 1. Then, just before the 7:00 scheduled start of the second round, a strong summer thunderstorm hit the Yorktown Heights laboratory, causing a temporary power failure. When electricity was restored, remote resuscitation efforts were unable to revive the system. The storm hit when there was no one at Yorktown Heights who had the required expertise to help. Despite Hsu's fervent efforts over a telephone line, he was unable to get the computer back online. After waiting several hours, the rules of the competition forced Tournament Director Mike Valvo to award the game to Deep Thought II's opponent, Marty Hirsch's Mchess. Hirsch had been most gracious, not pressing at all for a decision to be made. He was probably as interested in taking his chances on a miracle happening in the game, thereby raising the stock of his commercially available program, as he was in being generous to his program's opponent. He had little to lose by a loss and much to gain by an upset. The forfeit, however, was an unfortunate blow to the Deep Blue team.

At the end of two rounds and with three to go, two entries, *Socrates and Mchess, stood a full point ahead of Deep Thought II. To win the tournament outright, Deep Thought II would have to win all three remaining games, with neither *Socrates nor Mchess scoring better than even in their last three rounds. This seemed to be a highly unlikely scenario, given that *Socrates and Mchess had both done so well in the first two rounds, and moreover, both *Socrates and Mchess were running on greatly improved computing systems.

But Deep Thought II managed to do what it had to do. It wore down David Kittinger's Wchess in the third round, played a brilliant game to defeat *Socrates in the fourth round, and smashed Mchess in the final fifth round. Moreover, both *Socrates and Mchess failed to score better than even in their final three rounds. From the low point of the forfeit, with Deep

Thought II's chances to win the tournament looking impossible, to the high point of capturing the title with three straight decisive victories, the Deep Blue team went through one of its many emotional rollercoaster rides. It was a brilliant performance, reassuring anyone with doubts that Deep Thought II was the class of its field.

Meanwhile outside the world of chess, computers were making giant strides in other games. In August 1994 at the Boston Computer Museum, a computing landmark was established by Jonathan Schaeffer's checker-playing program Chinook. It took on the human world champion, Marion Tinsley, in a match for the "man-machine world championship." Tinsley had dominated the game of checkers for 40 years. He had last lost a game in competition in 1985 (to Asa Long), the one before that occurred in 1975, and the one before that in 1958! Tinsley took ill after the sixth round in the match with Schaeffer's program and had to forfeit, unable to play further. The match was called with the score even at 3–3. Don Lafferty, the world's second-best player, stepped in to replace Tinsley, now playing as the challenger to the new champion. Lafferty and Chinook played to a draw, leaving Chinook at the top of the world of checkers. Chinook defeated Lafferty the following year to clearly establish its position as the best checker player on planet Earth. Sadly, Tinsley passed away from cancer in April of 1995; he was already quite ill when he played Chinook [2].

With the best checker player now a computer, the day when the best chess player would be a computer was put into sharper focus. In some ways, it seemed natural that a computer would be programmed to play checkers better than any human before the same happened in chess. Checkers seemed less complex than chess and an easier programming task. Moreover, the world's best human chess player stood at the top of a much higher pyramid of knowledge-rich rivals than apparently did his checker-playing counterpart. On the other hand, compared with the huge effort invested in chess programming over the years, little had been devoted to the game of checkers, and it made some sense to believe that chess might fall first. Schaeffer's accomplishment was a notable marker on the road to developing a chess program that was also best on Earth.

In 1997 the human world champion at the game of Othello, Takeshi Murakami, was defeated 6–0 by Michael Buro's program Logistello in a six-game match [3]. According to Buro, an Othello program can play perfectly for the last 20-some moves of the game, a feat that is virtually impossible for checkers. While endgame databases help checker programs, they are of no use by Othello programs because of the large number of endgame positions. According to Buro, the scoring function is of greater importance in Othello than in checkers, where, in his opinion, deep search is more necessary.

It was during the Cape May event that CJ Tan, CB Hsu, and I first discussed the possibility of the ACM organizing a match between Deep Blue and Garry Kasparov. The discussion was very preliminary, but we left Cape May feeling there were possibilities. In the following weeks and on behalf of the ICCA, I approached Tan to see whether IBM would participate in and provide support for the next world computer chess championship, scheduled for sometime in 1995. We also continued our discussion about the possibility of the ACM organizing a Deep Blue versus Garry Kasparov match. Given that negotiations with Bob Rice weren't leading to where Tan hoped they would, he was more than willing to explore other possibilities. The Deep Blue team's ultimate goal of playing Kasparov was kept alive.

Meanwhile, Hsu's new VLSI chess chip and accelerator card were expected to be finally ready in 1995. Tan was on the lookout for a major event to use as a stepping stone and testing point on the road to an eventual match with Kasparov, while the ICCA was looking for a sponsor and location for its 8th World Computer Chess Championship. On behalf of the ICCA, I discussed with Tan various venues for a world championship over the next several months. One of them was in Asia. During this time, IBM was expanding its presence in the rapidly developing market of China. Among other activities, it was planning to open a new research facility near Beijing in late 1995. It occurred to Tan that a championship in Hong Kong might draw worldwide attention to IBM's efforts in that region. He thus agreed to throw IBM's support behind the event — the 8th World Computer Chess Championship in Hong Kong with the new Deep Blue participating. The ICCA was ecstatic. ICCA President Tony Marsland just happened to be spending his sabbatical year at the University of Hong Kong and would be there to coordinate the arrangements. Tan and I approached Omar Wing, then dean of the Engineering Faculty of the Chinese University of Hong Kong (and former professor of electrical engineering at Columbia University when Tan and I were there), regarding hosting the event at his university. Wing responded positively and called on Hon Tsang of the Department of Electrical Engineering to handle the local arrangements. And so it was that the group of us — CJ Tan, Omar Wing, Hon Tsang, Tony Marsland, and me, with help from ICCA Vice President David Levy — organized the greatest-yet world championship for computers. Wing provided space on an upper floor of the Ho Sin Hang Building, with a magnificent view of the Tolo Harbour and the Ma On Mountains. Hong Kong's mix of mountains and sea ranks it, along with San Francisco, Rio de Janeiro, and Vancouver, as one of the world's most spectacular cities.

Twenty-four programs participated, including entries from the United States, Germany, Israel, the United Kingdom, the Netherlands, Denmark, Spain, Hungary, France, and Canada. The first world championship outside North America and Europe, the Hong Kong event reflected the degree to which the world was becoming electronically connected. Eight of the entries ran on computers linked to Hong Kong via long-distance telephone lines including *Socrates (USA), Hitech (USA), Zugzwang (Germany), Frenchess (France), Ferret (USA), Cray Blitz (USA), Phoenix (Canada), and Deep Thought II (USA). (IBM entered the program under the name of Deep Blue Prototype, but it was really still Deep Thought II.) The other 19 entries used PCs rated at 90 mips located at the site of the competition.

A five-round world championship was planned, as was customary for these competitions. As the event approached and with Hsu's chip not ready, the Deep Blue team did a quick analysis of the odds of Deep Thought II's finishing in first place. They concluded that the odds were somewhere between 50% and 60%. They judged 10 other entries as each having about a 4% chance of upsetting the field. Concerned that a championship of five rounds was a bit short, Tan approached the organizers and suggested the number of rounds be increased to six. The more rounds played, of course, the less the chance of an upset. The request came too late, however, and the championship was played as the originally planned five-round event. At every computer-chess tournament, the participants want more rounds than the budget permits, and though the budget was there this time, the request, coming only a few weeks before the championship, simply came too late.

In November of 1994, as planning for Hong Kong progressed, I approached Tan with a concrete proposal for a match with Garry Kasparov. As chairman of the ACM Computer Chess Committee, I would attempt to have my committee put together a match in Philadelphia at the ACM's main annual event — ACM Computing Week '96 — scheduled for February of 1996. As part of the conference, the ACM was planning to celebrate the 50th anniversary of the birth of the digital computer, the ENIAC, built at the University of Pennsylvania in 1946. The conference would attract many of the leading names in computer science, serving as an ideal showcase for the new Deep Blue. When Tan assured me of his backing, I called the conference organizer, Frank Friedman, and then Joe DeBlasi, Executive Director of the ACM. Friedman, a professor of computer science at Temple University, was a longtime supporter of computer chess within the ACM and a prominent voice on many matters within the organization. His response was enthusiastic, and he agreed to lend his support. DeBlasi also was enthusiastic, ready to help if needed. In mid-December I visited IBM to discuss my proposal with Tan and his team, and I was assured of their participation if the ACM could put together the event.

Since 1970, when the ACM hosted the first tournament strictly for computers, the world's largest society for computer professionals had played a major catalytic role in the development of chess programs. ACM conferences provided a forum for progress in the field; annual competitions, often coupled with technical paper sessions, had been held for 24 years (the last being the competition in Cape May). It was thus quite fitting that the ACM should be involved in this classic event.

And so contract negotiations began. Through ICCA Vice President David Levy, a friend of Garry Kasparov's London-based agent Andrew Page, we contacted Kasparov in early January of 1995. The ACM's proposal was a six-game match in Philadelphia, with games beginning at 1:00. The ICCA would serve as the sanctioning body. The proposed rate of play for each player would be 40 moves in the first 2 hours and all the remaining moves in 1 hour (so that a game would last at most 6 hours). The ACM would offer a prize fund of $500,000, with $300,000 to the winner and $200,000 to the loser. In the event of a tie, the prize would be divided equally. There was also a complex rule for reducing the prize money awarded in the event of a defaulted game. IBM wanted all games played even if it meant Deep Blue would wind up with a 0–6 score.

Kasparov responded several days later. His agent contacted Levy, who then contacted me, and then I Tan, with Kasparov agreeing to most terms. He requested a day off between the second and third games and another between the fourth and fifth; he wanted the games to be played a little more slowly. His request was for each player to have 2 hours for the first 40 moves, 1 hour for the next 20 moves, and 30 more minutes for all the remaining moves. A game would last at most seven hours. To suit his biological clock, he also requested that games begin, not at 1:00, but at 3:00. These changes were all accepted by the other parties. His request to play "winner takes all" — rather than splitting the prize money between winner and loser — required further negotiation. Kasparov must have felt that there was no chance in the world of losing and that the prize money was essentially a charitable donation — to Garry Kasparov. IBM preferred a split. After another go-around, it was agreed that $400,000 of the $500,000 prize money would go to the winner, and in the case of a tie, the purse would be split equally. In most major chess matches, the split is 5–3, so in this regard, IBM went a good way toward meeting Kasparov's wishes.

During this period Kasparov proceeded very slowly. On the one hand, he did not want to cut ties with Intel while opportunities still seemed possible. On the other hand, if the California chipmaker stopped supporting him — likely a growing concern as time passed — the ACM match was worth considering as an introduction to future cooperation with IBM.

Joe DeBlasi was called upon early in the negotiations to coordinate the sticky aspects of the eventual contract. Along with Frank Friedman, David Levy, and Andrew Page, Tan, DeBlasi, and I worked together from that point on coordinating the negotiations among the four parties — Kasparov, the ICCA, the ACM, and IBM — while keeping in mind the limitations of the conference facilities in Philadelphia. A former IBM executive, DeBlasi was respected by both Kasparov and IBM, and threw his full support behind bringing the parties together. When he was younger, he was a tough baseball player — a shortstop, a position associated with leadership, with keeping cool, with keeping a team together — and he still had the same talent. He assigned his right-hand woman Terrie Phoenix to work on the public relations aspects of the match. Phoenix has a flamboyant personality and interacted with the press with style and great enthusiasm. For its part in assisting in the negotiations, the ICCA would assume the role of the sanctioning body.

Contract negotiations continued for several months although both IBM and Kasparov were committed to an agreement. In February of 1995 and early in the negotiations, IBM — and even Kasparov — became concerned that Deep Blue might not in fact be ready in time for the match. Kasparov was worried that he might have booked two weeks of his busy schedule and then find himself with no match and insufficient time to make other plans. IBM was concerned that Kasparov might cancel the match because of complications with Intel. To appease both parties, a paragraph was added to the proposed contract stating that either party could unilaterally withdraw from the match without penalty before October 31, 1995. After that date the ACM would provide the remaining contestant the sum of $100,000. At Kasparov's request, a paragraph was also added that obliged IBM to give him all officially played Deep Blue games over the previous 12-month period and from the signing date until the match.

In May 1995 Kasparov finally signed four copies of the contract and sent them off to Hong Kong in the hands of David Levy. In Hong Kong at the 8th World Computer Chess Championship and after five months of negotiations, the contracts were countersigned by IBM, the ACM, and the ICCA. At last the match took on a sense of inevitability.

The Hong Kong championship, however, turned out to be a disastrous ordeal for the Deep Blue team [4]. Entering the five-round world championship as the heavy favorite, Deep Thought II smashed its first three opponents, *Socrates, Hitech, and Cheiron, and looked like a certain winner. A fourth-round draw with Wchess was seen as a minor setback. Other than the Cape May forfeit, Deep Thought or Deep Thought II had won every game it played against other computers, dating back to the 20th ACM North American Computer Chess Championship in Reno, Nevada, when it lost a game to Mephisto. (In 1990 the old version, Deep Thought/88, had lost to Hitech.)

With three wins and a draw entering the fifth and final round, the Deep Blue team expected its computer to coast to the championship with a straightforward victory. Its opponent, Fritz4, had lost its first-round game due to an opening book bug, and its victories in the following three rounds were not over any of the main contenders. The championship therefore seemed a certain thing. The game started off as a routine Sicilian Defense with Deep Thought II playing the Black side. Then on move 13, Deep Thought II surprisingly found itself outbooked and in a difficult position. The position became disastrous when the communication link with Yorktown Heights suddenly broke off. The computer at home had been working hard to find a viable move and had, in fact, succeeded, but the telephone line had gone dead before the move was transmitted to Hong Kong. Joe Hoane, observing the computer in Yorktown Heights, told me Deep Thought II played 13 g3, leading to a weak but defensible position, one that still could have eventually led to a win.

However, when the connection was reestablished and the computer brought back online, Deep Thought II replayed the move, this time castling its king into a hungry nest of vultures. Its fall into a trap led to a quick loss and a disappointing third-place overall finish. As soon as the tragic 13th move was made, a large crowd quietly rushed to surround the playing table, watching in disbelief. IBM's own filming team, sent to Hong Kong to record the victory, found itself recording a major upset. In a five-minute period, Deep Thought II had gone from coasting to the world championship to finishing as just another strong contender. Hsu and Campbell sat motionless at the board as Deep Thought II's game gradually deteriorated. Tan went numb, watching from a few feet away. Two tournaments in a row, Cape May and now Hong Kong, had taken the Deep Blue team on emotional rollercoaster rides. Both rides were thanks to Mother Nature; one ended happily, the other ended in a big emotional letdown.

The loss was quickly put behind the Deep Blue team when the official contract signing at last took place at the end of the championship. A press conference was held in the game hall at which the Philadelphia match —the ACM Chess Challenge — was announced to the world in a totally different, less jovial mood than had been anticipated. Terrie Phoenix had come to Hong Kong for the explicit purpose of making the announcement and to distribute a hard copy of the press release to those present. She modified it at the last minute to declare IBM's chess computer as the "top-rated chess program" rather than as "world champion." Robert Byrne, attending the conference as a guest of the ICCA, was one of the first in the media to hear the news. Byrne was particularly well liked by the computer-chess community for his outstanding coverage of the subject over the years. Here in Hong Kong, the championship organizers had enjoyed spending their free moments with him, roaming the hilly streets of Hong Kong in search of interesting restaurants and old antique shops.

Hours after the announcement, news of the match was flashed to the world on CNN, and articles appeared the next day in *USA Today* and the *London Times*.

Clearly, IBM's preferred game plan was to play Garry Kasparov as the world computer chess champion. Even though computer-chess experts knew Deep Thought II was the best program and expected a significantly stronger Deep Blue, the official title had just slipped away. Making matters even more unsettling, Kasparov had to defend his title as world champion in a match scheduled for September of 1995 with Vishwananthan Anand. Until that match was over and Kasparov was victorious, there were concerns, albeit very small, that he might fail to maintain his world champion title. The Philadelphia match would then lose much of its significance. The $500,000 Philadelphia purse would be hard to justify if neither IBM's chess program nor Garry Kasparov was recognized as world champion.

Following the signing in Hong Kong, the Deep Blue team returned to Yorktown Heights, where CJ Tan initiated organizational plans for the match. First, he put a lid on the team's commitments for exhibition matches in the interim to just two — Spain in July and China in September. He called on Gabby Silberman to coordinate the technical infrastructure of the match in Spain, and he worked with George Wang to set up the Beijing event. He then met with Jerry Present to discuss and coordinate the public relations

Terrie Phoenix, head of PR for the ACM.

effort, he asked Jennifer Hall to coordinate the conference site with the ACM organizers, and he called on Carol Moore to prepare the web broadcast.

The Deep Blue team met to clarify priorities for the work to be done, dividing efforts between developing the RS/6000 SP2 system and improving the playing strength of the chess program. December 15, 1995, was established as the crucial deadline for having the chess software up and running on the RS/6000 SP2. October 9, 1995, became the target date for having Hsu's new VLSI chip and accelerator card up and running on a single computer of the RS/6000 SP2. Hsu's chip and card would be back from fabrication in September. The work on the software was divided into improving the evaluation function, incorporating endgame databases into the program, expanding opening preparation, further developing and refining the search, and carrying out extensive testing.

As part of the ACM's International Conference on Supercomputing, the Deep Blue team went to Barcelona, Spain, in early July of 1995. Gabby Silberman, fluent in Spanish from his childhood in Chile, served as IBM's interface with the conference's organizers. The IBM chess program would play Spain's Grandmaster Miguel Illescas a two-game exhibition match. Illescas was Spain's top-ranked chess player with a rating of 2625. Again, Deep Thought II was used since Deep Blue was still not ready. The first game, with Deep Thought II playing White, ended in a draw. The computer

Miguel Illescas having a conversation with Gabby Silberman.

lost the second game when a bug surfaced in a new time-control algorithm developed to handle the "Fischer clock." This was the first game Deep Thought II had played using this new move-timing system. Budgeting time when playing a game of chess is a complex problem, poorly done by humans. Humans often lose games because they fume and fret over a position. The amount of time consumed often has little correlation to the difficulty of the position or how crucial the position is to the game. However, to lose a game on time was something that shouldn't happen to a computer. The Deep Blue team realized that if and when it played Garry Kasparov, it couldn't afford to lose any games in this unnecessary way.

The Barcelona match with Miguel Illescas was Deep Thought II's final curtain call, but it also marked the beginning of a relationship with the Spanish grandmaster that would continue for some time.

The second exhibition match scheduled for Beijing on September 25, 1995, was especially important for the Deep Blue team. It was to serve as Deep Blue's debut, and the team was racing with the clock to complete everything on time. If Deep Blue wasn't ready for Beijing, Tan might have decided to postpone the big match with Kasparov for a while, or even to cancel it altogether.

Xie Jun surrounded (left to right) by her coach, Donald Tang (Assistant Director of IBM China Research Laboratory), CB Hsu, and CJ Tan.

Postponing the match with the world champion was preferable to challenging him with Deep Thought II, which, to date, had shown no evidence that it was any stronger than about 2650. Deep Thought II might have been improved in the final months leading up to the Philadelphia match, but not enough to defeat Kasparov. The team was optimistic that the new Deep Blue would be significantly stronger and be a real challenge to the world champion, and thus worth waiting for.

However, if Deep Blue wasn't ready for Beijing, it might well not be ready for another year or two — maybe never! And struggling with Deep Thought II had gone on long enough. Hong Kong, with its disastrous ending, was hard to forget, and Barcelona, with one more game lost because of a bug in the time-control algorithm, was hard to remember! Moreover, as things were going, there was a good possibility that other chess programs would edge out the IBM effort to catch Kasparov, as they, too, were rapidly improving.

When the Beijing exhibition match was first scheduled, it was anticipated that the entire Deep Blue system containing 30 RS/6000 computers would be ready, but delays with the chip fabrication forced a scaling down of plans. As the date of the match approached and it became clear that the entire Deep Blue system was not going to be ready, the team decided to prepare a small one-computer version named once again Deep Blue Prototype — but this was a real prototype. The computer contained one chess accelerator card with two VLSI chess chips. If the single-computer version worked as intended in Beijing, the team would add the remaining computers upon its return, and then modify the overall search algorithm to carry out the monstrous and complex parallel search of the chess tree on all the computers of the system. For Beijing there was time for just one computer.

IBM was establishing a major new research center in the Chinese capital city. The exhibition chess match, consisting of two games, was planned as part of the facility's official opening-day ceremonies. Tan and Hsu travelled with James McGroddy, who as head of IBM Research was instrumental in setting up the center. McGroddy would preside over the festivities. The center was the first major research laboratory of an international computer corporation to open in China. George Wang, who had been at Yorktown Heights and friends with Tan, was the recently named director. He had received a Columbia University doctorate in physics in 1977 and later a master's degree in computer science. He had joined IBM's Thomas J. Watson Research Center in 1978 and remained there until accepting the Beijing post.

About 100 people were there to celebrate the occasion, including the new staff of some 30 researchers, academicians, government dignitaries, and members of the news media. The center, located in the Shang Di suburb

of Beijing, was an hour's drive from downtown though congested traffic —
bicycles, buses, and pedestrians coming from all directions.

Xie Jun, the reigning women's world champion at the time, was Deep
Blue Prototype's opponent. Murray Campbell had suggested her to Tan,
who then approached her, and she gladly accepted. Xie Jun had previously been the women's world champion at Chinese chess and was a
popular national and even international personality [5]. She was born
in Baoding, China, in 1970, a city of about a million people located 100 miles
north of the Chinese capital.

Chess, that is western chess, is not particularly popular in China, but
with a population of over one billion people, even a small percentage of the
people playing the game amounts to a significant number of participants.
Furthermore, Chinese chess — known as "elephant chess" in China — and
Western chess are similar, and Chinese chess happens to be the most
popular board game in this populous country. Whatever properties that a
mind possesses to make it skillful at Chinese chess probably carry over to
Western chess, and vise versa. The complexity of the two games is similar,
although a small edge must be given to Chinese chess. Some pieces in
Chinese chess are similar to those in Western chess, while others are very

IBM China Research Laboratory.

different. Both games have 16 pieces per side. Chinese chess is played on
a board, a rectangular grid, with 90 squares — or points — while Western
chess is played on 64 squares. The goal for both is to checkmate the
opponent's king. Unlike Western chess, the king in Chinese chess cannot
roam the entire board but must stay in his palace, a region of nine points.
Two counselors are also restricted to moving only within the king's palace
and are meant to defend the king. Rooks and knights are present (two of
each per side) and move in ways somewhat similar to Western chess. A
canon and minister (again, two of each per side) replace Western chess's
bishop and queen since there were no bishops in ancient China and queens
generally kept a low profile in matters of politics and religion. Pawns, five
per side, move forward until they cross a river in the middle of the board,
whereupon they gain the additional ability to move sideways. Former
McGill University graduate, Hang-Tong Lau, published a delightful book
about the Chinese version of the game of chess [6].

Several weeks before the match, Hsu's new VLSI chess chips and
accelerator cards were finally delivered to the Thomas J. Watson Research
Center. The new chips, manufactured by VLSI Technology, were designed
using .6-micron CMOS circuitry — five times smaller than the 3-micron
CMOS circuitry used in Hsu's first chips a decade earlier. Two were placed
on an accelerator card, manufactured by Compunetics Incorporated.

However, initial tests carried out by Joe Hoane and Hsu revealed two
major and several minor problems. En passant moves weren't handled
correctly, and there were problems with capacitance between long lines —

 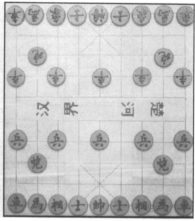

Initial configuration of pieces in
Western chess and in Chinese chess.

wires — on the cards that caused scores to be assigned to positions somewhat randomly. The bugs couldn't be fixed by modifying the circuitry on the chip; it was only possible to modify the programmable logic array on the accelerator card. Although Hoane and Hsu were able to correct the problems, the cures reduced the speed of the hardware by a factor of two. As soon as these problems were eliminated, others surfaced and remained uncorrected on the circuitry that went to Beijing.

Meanwhile Hoane worked night and day to eliminate the problems, finally managing to do so in the very hours leading up to the match. He electronically fired the new version of the software across the Pacific to IBM's downtown Beijing offices, where it was transferred to a diskette. The diskette was then driven — driven, because telephone lines from downtown to the center had too much noise running around on them to reliably transmit the software — through heavy traffic to the new center and installed on the RS/6000 there! Only the day before the new accelerator card had been installed on the RS/6000. Now with both the software and hardware apparently in order, the system was ready to go in the nick of time. A minimal one-computer, one-card, two-chip version of the much larger 30-computer system that would play Kasparov was at last up and running.

Hsu, who had been working at the Beijing research center the day before in his shorts and tee shirt, was cajoled into dressing up in a suit and tie for the big opening day. CJ Tan helped with the tie. James McGroddy looked impressed.

The two-game exhibition got underway at 1:00, with Deep Blue Prototype and Xie Jun in one room and the spectators in another nearby. Xie Jun's coach provided commentary on the chess; Tan provided commentary on the computer. The Deep Blue team hoped to come out of the match with an even score. Always somewhat concerned about the negative publicity that might result if an opponent was crushed, in this case the team would have been terribly disappointed if the computer, with its new VLSI chess chips and accelerator card, was defeated. Moreover, the match had parallels with the classic ping-pong match between a Chinese team and an American one in the 1970s. That match warmed political relations between the two countries; this one was expected to warm economic relations! Both sides wanted the other to be in good spirits at the end of the match. Given these sociopolitical-economic considerations and the precarious state of the new chess system, IBM's preferred to downplay the competitive side of the match. It was thus agreed that no record would be kept of the moves of the games. (For the curious chess player, the photo on page 83 suggests Deep Blue Prototype, playing Black, had chosen a Sicilian Defence.)

James McGroddy was keenly watching. His support of the Deep Blue team was crucial for the project's future and contingent on at least a respectable performance here. Midway through the first game, the worst fears of the Deep Blue team materialized: the computer crashed. Hsu restarted the program, then paced it through the game to the point of the crash. Several moves later, the computer crashed again. Hsu reluctantly resigned the game.

A victory in the second game took on added importance, since a loss or even a draw might result in major consequences for the Deep Blue project. If the same disastrous problem reappeared, and the odds were good, or maybe even a totally different one, two losses due to an unstable system would leave McGroddy concerned and Tan ready to give up. But Deep Blue Prototype came through with flying colors, forcing a resignation from Xie Jun. The match left everyone, let's say, tickled pink, from the Deep Blue team and Xie Jun to IBM China and, most importantly, to James McGroddy.

With the team having achieved its objective in the match with Xie Jun and with McGroddy providing support, IBM's management soon decided to continue with plans to hold the match with Kasparov. There were not quite six months remaining to prepare.

While the Deep Blue team was preoccupied with Beijing, Kasparov had been playing a 20-game title match against Vishwananthan Anand in New

Xie Jun and CB in a friendly match in Beijing.

York. The championship was played on the top floor of the 102-story World Trade Center from September 11 through October 10. The first eight games of the match were drawn. When Anand won the ninth, concerns surfaced that an upset was possible, but Kasparov came right back on the next game to even the score at the midpoint of the match. Kasparov then won three of the next four games to sew up the contest, coasting to victory over the following four games. The match was an outstanding success for Kasparov and Anand, with extensive media coverage. With the title secure, Kasparov was ready to set his sights on the next prize: Deep Blue in Philadelphia.

For its part, the Deep Blue team entered the final phase of preparations for Philadelphia upon its return from Beijing. There would be no more commitments for now. Only a few months remained to complete Deep Blue, to create a new system rated at Kasparov's world champion level. The days would pass very quickly.

Hsu made minor revisions to the VLSI design used in Beijing, sending the package back to VLSI Technology in early October for a second fabrication. Meanwhile, Tan managed to obtain the use of an SP2 at Yorktown Heights for the match. In December the new chips started coming back to IBM in small batches. They were twice as fast as those used in Beijing, and minus the problems that plagued them in Beijing. As the chips came back from VLSI Technology, Jerry Brody and Joe Hoane worked together to mount them on the accererator cards, six to eight chips per card, and then to install the cards in the SP2, one card per computer. At first they worked on the weekends and in the evenings when no one else was using the system, but as the match approached, they took full-time control of the system. The SP2 consisted of two cabinets containing 30 66-Mhz RS/6000 computers. When installed, the chips numbered somewhere between 220 and 250—nobody seems to know the exact number. The design plans called for 8 chips on each accelerator card and two accelerator cards per computer, but, as is usual in the world of VLSI design, many of the chips were found to have problems when tested prior to installation and not used. According to Joe Hoane, the system was in good shape and ready to go in late January of 1996.

In early December of 1995, CJ Tan hired Joel Benjamin as a consultant to provide a grandmaster's perspective to the team. Benjamin would help with the opening book and with the testing. Several weeks earlier the Deep Blue team had invited Benjamin, along with Grandmasters Patrick Wolff and Ilya Gurevich, to play two-game practice matches with Deep Blue Prototype at the same time limits as planned for Philadelphia. While there, the team had sized up each grandmaster as a potential addition to its ranks and had concluded that Benjamin was most appropriate, since, according to Campbell, Benjamin showed great enthusiasm for the project and was particularly interested in being involved. Benjamin's personality had the right ingredients to mesh with the Deep Blue team. He was particularly bright, rational, a fast learner, and outwardly, at least, calm. Benjamin's proximity — he lived in Manhattan — was also an asset. Benjamin's role with the team would turn out to be crucial.

Benjamin already had had a distinguished chess career. At the age of 13 he broke Bobby Fisher's record to become the youngest United States master ever. He became a grandmaster in 1986, one year after graduating from Yale University with a bachelor of arts degree in history. Benjamin maintained a strong academic record while pursuing his time-consuming passion. Among his many accomplishments as a chess player, Benjamin has to his credit the 1987 U.S. Championship. (Incidentally, he won it again in 1997 and finish second in 1998 — signs that his work with Deep Blue evidently didn't hurt his own chess career!)

Benjamin had faced Garry Kasparov at Horgen, Switzerland, in 1994 in a round-robin grandmaster tournament, playing the world champion to a draw. To his credit, he had been the only participant playing Black who hadn't lost to Kasparov. Benjamin discussed the event with me and spoke of the camaraderie that the organizers created among the players. The

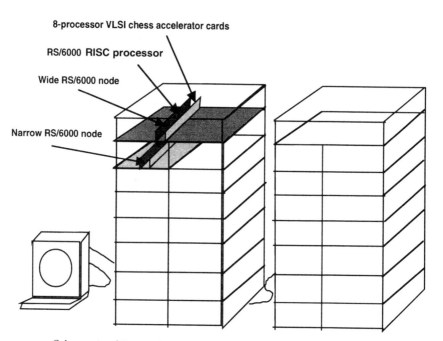

Schematic of Deep Blue: 30-processor RS\6000 SP with two chess accelerator cards per processor and 6-8 VLSI chess chips per card.

players, including Kasparov, usually had their meals together and "hung out" between rounds. Kasparov had come without his usual supporting team and, according to Benjamin, "was just another one of the guys."

With a rating of almost 2600, Benjamin had shown the Deep Blue team that he understood how to play computers by his three consecutive first-place finishes in the Harvard Cup that pitted a number of the leading chess programs against an approximately equal number of grandmasters. In the Sixth Harvard Cup in December of 1995, just prior to joining the Deep Blue team, Benjamin tied for first place with Michael Rohde, scoring 4.5 out of 6 points.

Benjamin made the daily trip from his Manhattan apartment to Yorktown Heights by train, arriving at about 11 a.m. and working in the Deep Blue Grandmaster Laboratory until time to go home. He would enter book lines and have Deep Blue check them out. He was particularly concerned that Deep Blue would be comfortable with the lines he entered. Because of Kasparov's preference for the Sicilian, that opening was booked far more extensively than any other.

In mid-December 1995 the Deep Blue project passed the usual year-end internal status review. James McGroddy, who would retire soon from IBM after a long and distinguished career, chaired the meeting; other research managers also attended. According to CJ Tan, McGroddy took the project under his wing when Zeev Barzilai left Yorktown Heights the year earlier.

Joel Benjamin.

A week before the review, Paul Horn was announced as McGroddy's successor. According to Tan, Horn came in near the end of the meeting and said that Deep Blue couldn't possibly beat Garry Kasparov. Tan defended the project, saying that the team was making fine progress, that it knew the computer's weaknesses and was working on them, and that it was now working with Grandmaster Joel Benjamin. Horn seemed reassured, adding that Benjamin was a good idea. According to Tan, Horn was a capable chess player, maybe an A-level player, good enough to understand that without top-level chess knowledge, Deep Blue couldn't defeat Garry Kasparov, but unaware of the specific work going on to strengthen Deep Blue. With his concerns relieved, the new head of IBM Research threw his weight behind the team.

One final shaky moment remained to be endured. Garry Kasparov was scheduled to play Fritz4 in a two-game match on December 13, 1995, in Germany. It marked the last Kasparov event that Intel would sponsor. Even though this match wasn't played under the standard time limits for world championship play, a defeat by Fritz4, who held the title of world computer-chess champion, would make the upcoming ACM Chess Challenge tragically anticlimactic. Kasparov, however, won the match, winning the first game and drawing the second. His victory in the first game was made easy by an error committed by Fritz4's human operator, who keyed in an incorrect move early in the game. When the error was discovered several moves later, nothing could be done. From that point on, the match was essentially a walkover.

References

[1] Monty Newborn, "The 24nd ACM International Computer-Chess Championship," *ICCA Journal*, 17(3), pp. 159–164, September 1994.

[2] Jonathan Schaeffer, *One Jump Ahead*, Springer-Verlag, New York, 1997.

[3] M. Buro, "The Othello match of the year: Takeshi Murakami vs. Logistello," *ICCA Journal*, 20(3), pp. 189–193, September 1997.

[4] H. K. Tsang and Don Beal, "The 8th World Computer-Chess Championship," *ICCA Journal*, 18(2), pp. 93–111, June 1995.

[5] Xie Jun, *Xie Jun — Chess Champion from China*, Gambit Publishers, 1998.

[6] H. T. Lau, *Chinese Chess*, Charles E. Tuttle Company, Inc, Rutland, VT, 1985.

Summary of Matches during the Period
January 1, 1994 – December 31, 1995

Dates: June 25–27, 1994
Location: Cape May, New Jersey
Event: 24th ACM ICCC
Time Control: 40/2, 20/1 thereafter
Results: Deep Thought II won 4 of 5 points, finishing in first place

Versus	Color	Result
Zarkov	White	Deep Thought II Won
Mchess	Black	Deep Thought II Lost (Forfeit)
Wchess	White	Deep Thought II Won
Star Socrates	Black	Deep Thought II Won
Mchess	White	Deep Thought II Won

Dates: May 25–30, 1995
Location: The Chinese University of Hong Kong, Hong Kong
Event: The 8th World Computer Chess Championship
Time Control: 40/2, 40/1 thereafter
Results: Deep Thought II won 3.5 of 5 points, finishing tied for third
          place in field of 24

Versus	Color	Result
Star Socrates	White	Deep Thought II Won
Hitech	Black	Deep Thought II Won
Cherion	White	Deep Thought II Won
Wchess	Black	Draw
Fritz3	White	Deep Thought II Lost

Dates: July 1995
Location: Barcelona, Spain
Event: Exhibition Match with Grandmaster Miguel Illescas
          Time Control: 40/2, Fischer clock
Results: Illescas 1.5, Deep Thought II .5

Versus	Color	Result
Miguel Illescas	White	Draw
Miguel Illescas	Black	Deep Thought II Lost (on time)

6 Philadelphia

"After all, we made the machine, didn't we?" Charles Krauthammer, *Time*, [47]. (Attributed by Krauthammer to his 10-year-old son.)

The Deep Blue team had spent six years preparing for this momentous occasion, the 1996 ACM Chess Challenge, the first time in history that a computer would go head to head against a human world champion in a match played at the slow, deliberate rate of a human world championship match. The team had gone from challenging World Champion Garry Kasparov in 1989 with a patched-together network of three SUN 4 workstations — each housing CB Hsu's graduate-student-designed VLSI chess chip — to challenging him in 1996 using IBM's premier supercomputing system — the new RS/6000 SP2 containing over 200 of Hsu's new second-generation VLSI chess chips. In 1989 two games were played, and rules limited the length of a game to three hours; the match was over in one day. This time, six games were scheduled over eight days — from February 10, 1996, through February 17, 1996 — and each game could last a grueling seven hours. Kasparov meanwhile had defeated Anatoly Karpov (1990), Nigel Short (1993), and Vishwananthan Anand (1995) in three world championship title defenses. He was now 32, and his career was rolling along in high gear.

The match took place in the massive Philadelphia Convention Center. Most of those involved stayed across the street in the Philadelphia Marriott Hotel, connected by an elevated pedestrian walkway to the convention center. In the cold February weather, the walkway was the preferred route to travel from one building to the other. At one time the building had been Philadelphia's main train station; in recent years it had been converted into a modern convention facility for large gatherings. The architects had maintained the structure's heritage, even preserving the railway tracks on the main hall's floor. The game room, the commentary room, the press-room, IBM's operations room, Kasparov's dressing room, and the VIP room were all on the ground floor in close proximity.

The 1000 ACM members attending their organization's Computing Week '96 Conference were given complementary tickets (a $20 value) as part of their registration package. The other ACM members who didn't attend — over 75,000, distinguished academicians and computing professionals — were able to see flashes of the organization's logo on the game table during CNN's hourly coverage. Many members followed the match on the Internet, either at IBM's website or at the ACM's website, which in turn was linked to the IBM website.

Kasparov entered the match as an overwhelming favorite, with leading grandmasters all predicting a lopsided result. Michael Antonoff's article in the March 1996 issue of *Popular Science* reported David Levy as saying he thought "Kasparov could win with a 6 to 0 score. ... I'd stake my life on it." In the same article Kasparov predicted a 4–2 score in his own favor. As he was writing the article, Antonoff told Levy of Kasparov's prediction, and Levy countered by saying,

> If he wants to, he can beat Deep Blue 6 to nil. But he may not want to. If he scores 3.5 points he gets $400,000. If he scores 6 points, he gets $400,000. He's not going to risk the money to try to make the score better. If he can make a perfect score without taking any risks, he'll do so.

CJ Tan was optimistic regarding Deep Blue's chances, telling Antonoff that "I'm very confident that we will win," and predicting a 4–2 score for Deep Blue [51].

On February 4, Kasparov arrived in Philadelphia with his then-fiancée Ioulia Vovk. I met them at the airport and escorted them to the Marriott. Kasparov had just finished playing a match against the Brazilian national team and was planning to rest for a few days before getting down to business. Vovk was a university student from Riga, Latvia, a charming young woman, a bit shy. She understood English quite well, but hesitated to speak it. The ACM's Terrie Phoenix also arrived on February 4 and took Vovk under her wing for the duration of the match, ensuring that she enjoyed every minute of her stay with shopping excursions, sightseeing, and visits to trendy restaurants. The ACM had arranged a large suite for Kasparov, Vovk, and Klara Kasparova. The latter two arrived on February 6 with Kasparov's coach Yuri Dokhoian, who had his own room across the hall from the Kasparov suite. Frederic Friedel also arrived before the match to make himself available to the world champion.

A proud mother who enjoyed accompanying her son on his fairytale travels, Klara Kasparova was there to serve as her son's manager. She supervised his daily schedule, making sure the game room met his requirements, making sure he ate properly, and always being nearby during the games to provide inspiration. Her English was excellent and she was quite articulate. She knew her son's needs and expressed them to the ACM organizers several days before the match. The lighting needed adjustment, noise from the air conditioning needed reducing, his nearby restroom needed security, and the seats in the game room had to be placed as far as possible from the game table.

Kasparov's coach, Yuri Dokhoian, was born in the Altai region of Russia in 1964 and began playing chess as a young boy, enrolling in a Moscow chess school at the age of 11. He reached the level of grandmaster at the age of 24. In 1993 he captured first place in three major tournaments — in Godesberg, Lublin, and Munster. He had a calm demeanor and was devoted to Kasparov. He seemed to be a good listener and handled himself in a professional way.

Frederic Friedel, with two decades of experience in the world of chess-playing computers, was there to serve as Kasparov's computer advisor. In addition to promoting computer-chess competitions in Europe, Friedel had founded the software company ChessBase in 1987. ChessBase has produced and marketed a database of hundreds of thousands of grandmaster games and also has developed the chess-playing program Fritz.

From the moment he arrived, Kasparov was under a steady deluge of media requests. Terrie Phoenix and IBM's Marcy Holle served as his interface with the media, arranging morning interviews with prominent writers including Peter Coy of *Businessweek*, Don Steinberg of *Gentlemen's Quarterly*, James Kim of *USA Today*, William Macklin of the *Philadelphia Inquirer*, and Bruce Weber of *The New York Times*. Holle had replaced Jerry Present in the summer of 1995 after Hong Kong. She hired the PR firm Technology Solutions Inc., headed by Kelly Fitzgerald, to help her during

Officials Mike Valvo and Ken Thompson, relaxing between games.

the match. Phoenix, Holle, and Fitzgerald were a dynamic PR three-some, catering to the needs of the media, Kasparov's team, and the Deep Blue team.

In the afternoons Kasparov found time for sightseeing at tourist favorites such as the Philadelphia Aquarium. In the evenings there was dinner out on the town until his mother arrived and final preparations for the match began. Kasparov liked sushi and took several of the group including me out to dinner one evening to one of Philadelphia's finest Japanese restaurants. Kasparov had earned a reputation for treating those around him generously.

When the world champion sits down to the board, he requires the equipment to be just right. The board and pieces must fulfill all his requirements. The board must be perfectly flat and produce no glare. Each square must measure 2.25 inches on a side and be colored brown and cream. The pieces must be wooden, seamless, glareless, well-weighted, and also colored brown and cream. The king must be 3.75 inches tall. Two sets must be brought to the game table in case one side promotes a pawn. His chair must be just right, not too hard and not too soft, with comfortable arms.

Flags, often present and on the table when major chess matches are played, were the subject of some discussion before the match. Since this was not meant to be a contest between individuals representing countries,

Commentator Maurice Ashley.

national flags were not necessarily appropriate. Nevertheless, when Kasparov requested a Russian flag, there was little choice for the Deep Blue team other than to request an American one.

On February 8 the Deep Blue team arrived along with Joe DeBlasi and David Levy. The next morning, with the whole cast now present, the play, a drama, began with an ACM-hosted press conference. As emcee, I first introduced the participants and then yielded the floor to them. Both Kasparov and Tan, who spoke on behalf of the Deep Blue team, expressed optimism over their chances. Next, David Levy supervised the selection of colors for the opening game, with Kasparov winning the choice and selecting to play with Black. Following about 30 minutes of questions, a buffet luncheon was served for the 100 or so in attendance.

That evening the ACM group gathered for dinner. Yasser Seirawan and Maurice Ashley were there, as were Ken Thompson and Mike Valvo. Yvette Nagel, who was soon to become Seirawan's wife, also joined us. Joe DeBlasi, David Levy, Pat DeBlasi (Joe's son), and I rounded out the group.

Seirawan and Ashley would serve as commentators for the match, and Valvo as the match arbiter. Thompson would serve as Valvo's assistant, responsible for monitoring both sides during the games. Kasparov, concerned that there might be inappropriate interaction with Deep Blue during the match, asked his computer advisor, Frederic Friedel, to request that the

Commentator Yasser Seirawan.

ACM have someone watch over the computer. Tan countered by raising the possibility that Kasparov might also receive inappropriate help, and after some negotiation, both sides agreed to have Thompson serve as an overseer. For Thompson, it was a great job. His inquisitive mind would know more about what Deep Blue was doing during the games than anyone except the Deep Blue team.

Seirawan and Ashley would provide outstanding commentary, making each slow-moving chess game sound more like a fast-moving tennis match. Seirawan, a grandmaster, had been ranked among the top players in the United States for many years. He was winner of the United States Championship three times. Ashley, a New Yorker, was on the verge of becoming a grandmaster, obtaining the title in March of 1999. They were a great team, with Ashley typically acting as the setup man, posing questions for Seirawan to answer. They had previously worked together at the 1995 Kasparov–Anand match, and their performance there led the ACM to seek them out for a repeat performance. Chess, incidently, is a great game for commentators. There are usually several minutes between each move, allowing lots of time for guessing and second-guessing. During the match Seirawan and Ashley called upon the audience for questions and ideas. At various times other leading players joined the two on stage to offer their expertise. Among them were Hans Berliner, Danny Kopec, David Levy,

Yuri Dokhoian, Garry Kasparov's coach.

and Dan Heisman. Members of the Deep Blue team also appeared. Fritz4, on stage with the commentators and supervised by Frederic Friedel, provided its own special analysis. Three large, 10-foot screens at the head of the commentary room displayed the board, the game room, and the   output of Fritz4. IBMer Matt Thoennes supervised the technical infrastructure surrounding the match, especially the game room and the commentary room.

On Saturday, February 10, 1997, at 3:00, the long-anticipated match finally got under way. Well, almost. After a decade of preparation for the big moment, CB Hsu was having last-minute problems getting Deep Blue started! This was Deep Blue's first serious game. Kasparov had arrived several minutes earlier, checked out everything, and sat down at the table to gather his thoughts. His mother, fiancée, and coach sat just offstage. Mike Valvo started Deep Blue's clock. Time was running but the computer wasn't! The main concern of the Deep Blue team and its supporters was the novelty of the system; it hadn't been checked out nearly enough, and there

CB Hsu and Murray Campbell making preparations before the match begins.

had to be many bugs just waiting to surface. Now, even before the first game started, problems appeared. Hsu, however, shortly solved the problem, and play began. Photographers initially crowded the game room, leaving under minor duress after the first several moves were played. Approximately 300 people gathered in the commentary room.

After the several-minute delay, Deep Blue opened with its usual first move, advancing its king's pawn two squares, and the greatest chess match in history thus far between man and machine was under way. Kasparov steered the game directly into his favorite Sicilian Defense. Deep Blue was well prepared, quickly playing the first nine moves from its opening book. Kasparov seemed to be testing Deep Blue but by the 17th move appeared unhappy and frustrated. PCA head Bob Rice was reported as saying that "now we know Kasparov does not deliberately pull those faces to disturb his opponents."

The position was considered equal by the 25th move, a far cry from the situation six years earlier when they first met. On the 26th move, Deep Blue's queen went on a dangerous fishing expedition, grabbing the weakest minnow on the board, Kasparov's pawn on b6. On the 29th move Deep Blue grabbed another pawn in a second more dubious gamble. But Deep Blue had meticulously calculated that there was time to grab this second pawn and then instigate an attack on its opponent's king. Kasparov, meanwhile, was setting up his own powerful attack on a completely abandoned Deep Blue king. The next 10 moves had the flavor of two sumo wrestlers battling one another at the edge of a high cliff. The slightest mistake by either side, and certain death would follow!

Deep Blue, with a tempo to spare, was the one still standing at the end. Kasparov resigned on the 37th move. His clock showed 5:42 minutes remaining to the 40-move time control, while Deep Blue had nearly an hour. Not only had Deep Blue won the game, it had done so making moves at approximately twice the speed of the human world champion. Kasparov faced a dilemma. He couldn't play any more slowly in the coming games. But playing faster would weaken his play. He walked a fine line in the coming games.

The outcome of the game stunned Kasparov and the chess world. History had been made. Deep Blue had became the first computer ever to force a world champion to resign in a regulation tournament game. Ed Gaulin began his report in the *Atlanta Journal and Constitution* by saying that "HAL would have been proud" [11]. Kasparov quickly got up from the table and left the scene.

The victory created an incredible high for the Deep Blue team. It was time to stop the experiment, go home, call the project a great success, and move on! But there were five more games to play. Could the good fortune continue for the Deep Blue team? Was the computer really better than Kasparov? With the next game coming the following day, there was little time for reflection, and the Deep Blue team adopted an attitude of "let's wait and see another round before drawing any conclusions, before becoming too optimistic." Kasparov was said to have had problems falling asleep that evening; Seirawan was sure he would awake "mean and hungry" for the second game.

And mean and hungry he was! In Game 2 Kasparov, playing White, turned the tables on Deep Blue, managing to avoid a tactical battle, wearing down the computer in what was the longest game played between the two contestants in this or any other match. Deep Blue started off badly. A human error was made loading the opening book into the computer, and as a result Deep Blue played without using this valuable resource. This had two negative consequences. First, the moves played in the resulting Catalan Opening by Deep Blue, while generally satisfactory, were not the sharpest possible. Second, valuable time was lost.

This second game turned out to be a 73-move 6-hour battle. While Kasparov was never in any serious danger of losing, the outcome looked drawish near the midpoint. However, some subtle long-term positional considerations related to the use of its king in the endgame turned out to be beyond the understanding of the computer and led to its eventual demise.

Delighted with his victory, Kasparov immediately went to the commentary room to meet the audience who, when he entered, stood and shouted, "Bravo, bravo." After observing how Kasparov turned the tables in this second game, some concluded that the first game was a fluke. But not Kasparov. During the discussion in the commentary room, he showed respect for his opponent. He said, "Now for the first time we are playing not with a computer, but with something that has its own intelligence." Kasparov said, "We are facing a new quality. We have all been playing with little computers. Like our laptops. ... like you are playing a five-year-old kid and suddenly big daddy comes."

The match was now even. Each side had been victorious when White while feeling the pangs of defeat when Black. We now understood that Deep Blue was only mortal.

With the score tied at one game apiece, the media attention picked up dramatically. On the 13th of February, the Deep Blue team and Kasparov were interviewed by ABC's "Good Morning America" host Joan Lunden and computer editor Gina Smith [54]. CNN's Natalie Allen, Bob Cain, and Brian Jenkens discussed the match with CJ Tan and Frederic Friedel on their "Early Prime" show [55].

For Game 3 Kasparov returned to the same Sicilian Defense played in the first game, determined this time to do better. He seemed unwilling to concede that he couldn't improve upon the first game using his favorite opening. Moves repeated until the 7th when Deep Blue, not Kasparov, veered off in a different direction. Joel Benjamin had modified Deep Blue's opening book before the round. Suspecting Kasparov would find a way to improve upon the line played in the first game, Benjamin directed Deep Blue to castle on the 7th move, thus avoiding the potential dangers that lurked ahead in some Kasparov innovation.

The game followed Deep Blue's opening book through the 12th move, up to another move Benjamin added just before the game was played. It wasn't thoroughly checked out by the Deep Blue team, and Kasparov came up with a refutation. A middlegame blood bath followed, leading to an early endgame. Kasparov had worn down Deep Blue in a difficult endgame in the previous round. Some speculated that he was counting on outmaneuvering and wearing down Deep Blue in a similar manner in the final phase of this game.

For a while Kasparov seemed to have the advantage, but Deep Blue played accurately and creatively and the human world champion found himself short on time and with insufficient material to win. With a king, rook, and four pawns per side, Kasparov offered a draw and the Deep Blue team accepted. According to Seirawan, late in the game Kasparov "was looking off into space with a kind of look as if to say 'what did I do wrong in this game?'" Ashley went on imagining Kasparov's words: "I feel I should have been able to milk more out of this position. And somewhere I let this thing off the hook."

The match remained tied now at 1.5 points each. Game 4 took place on February 14, Valentine's Day, and emotions, not particularly those of love, were high. Kasparov seemed to have the advantage in the early middlegame, but later found himself short of time. The game was drawn by agreement on move 50, with Deep Blue having a rook to bishop and pawn material advantage. Near the end of the game, Kasparov was so tired and stressed that his hand visibly shook when he made his moves. His position weakened to the point where, following the game, he said he was "quite happy that I escaped so narrowly at the end." He also said,

> I'm really tired. These games took a lot of energy. But if I play a normal human match, my opponent would also be exhausted. Here I have something that is not exhausted and just will play with the same strength. It is not stronger, but not weaker either. And the only thing I can do is just relax tomorrow and get some good rest and sleep . . . .

The media attention continued to pick up. CJ Tan and Yasser Seirawan were interviewed on PBS's "The News Hour with Jim Lehrer" [60].

Cartoonist Doug Marlette of Long Island's *Newsday* portrayed the battle as a real, live 20th-century version of the previous century's fabled showdown between John Henry and the automatic steel drill. Racing the drill while digging the Great Bend Railway Tunnel in West Virginia,

> John Henry, he drove fifteen feet
> The steam drill only made nine.
> ...
> But he worked so hard that it broke his poor heart
> And he laid down his hammer and he died.

The match was now deadlocked at two points apiece with two games remaining. The fifth game, played on Friday, February 16, attracted 700 chess devotees and ACM members, the largest crowd of the match thus far. This time Kasparov avoided his favorite Sicilian Defense. Twice unable to crack Deep Blue with it, he chose the Petroff, though soon found himself steered into a Four Knights Defense by his opponent. The dullest of all the games was unfolding until Kasparov electrified everyone when he

Cartoonist Doug Marlette captures the spirit in Philadelphia.
(*Newsday*, February 15, 1996; by permission of Tribune Media Services.)

offered a draw after making his 23rd move. Frederic Friedel told Bruce Weber that Kasparov must have thought, "Who knows if I can win it. Let's save some strength for tomorrow" [42].

CB Hsu, who was sitting across the board, relayed the offer to the IBM operations room. Joe Hoane, Joel Benjamin, Murray Campbell, and CJ Tan quickly gathered and, with time racing, weighed their options. Campbell told me they considered the fact that Kasparov was due to play White in the final round, and that the odds were bad Deep Blue would win the match by winning the last game. While Campbell had a bias toward accepting, Benjamin felt the game should continue, that it was still a bit early to take the draw. Deep Blue evaluated its own position as slightly behind. In retrospect, according to Benjamin, Deep Blue's scoring function should have evaluated the position even more negatively than it did. Kasparov's advanced kingside pawns weren't given enough credit, and the white knight in the middle of the board was given too much credit for its placement, given that it was pinned. In the end, after a hurried discussion, Tan accepted Benjamin's recommendation and made the decision not to accept the offer; the game continued. Kasparov quickly grabbed the lead and coasted to victory.

The IBM operations room with Joe Hoane, Ken Thompson,
and Jerry Brody watching Deep Blue.

Deep Blue could no longer win the match. Though the computer had played even with Kasparov for four rounds, its chances to draw the match looked very slim at this point. With White in the final game, Kasparov needed only a draw to walk away as victor. There remained, however, the question of whether he had learned how to play the computer. Could he take control of the game in their final battle? Would he show everyone why he was considered that greatest chess player in history?

On the following day the biggest crowd of all squeezed into the commentary room for the final game. Several hundred stood around the periphery of the room from beginning to end. For the third time, a Slav Defense ensued. Kasparov had a win and a draw playing it thus far. The moves followed those of Game 4 until Deep Blue veered off on the 5th move. Gradually, Deep Blue abandoned its king, and Kasparov confined the computer's pieces to the first two ranks. The computer resigned on the 43rd move without ever giving Kasparov a nervous moment.

The media immediately swarmed into the game room, clamoring for a few words from the victor, following him to the stage of the commentary room where he and the Deep Blue team met an enthusiastic audience. A long standing ovation greeted both sides, though it was directed mainly toward the winner. Seirawan and Ashley praised Kasparov for learning the computer's way and then putting the knowledge gathered into action in the final game.

That evening at an ACM conference dinner, the $500,000 in prize money was awarded. Kasparov was in great spirits, delighting the audience of several hundred computer specialists with his observations of the match. CJ Tan picked up IBM's share of the prize, turning it over to IBM Research, where it went toward supporting the team's future endeavors.

Campbell, when trying to explain to me what occurred in the final game, said,

> What he [Kasparov] happened to know happened to correspond well with what was required to make Deep Blue look bad in that game. I think he didn't have a very complete picture of Deep Blue's strengths and weaknesses, but how can you in only five games. But I think he had enough of an idea that he stumbled on something that he was able to exploit, and it worked very well.

Even at that, Campbell said that "the game looked very overwhelming to most observers, but that it wasn't quite that overwhelming and not quite as much at his control, not completely at his control as it may have seemed, but that he certainly demonstrated that he had some ideas about Deep Blue's weaknesses." Campbell said he didn't understand and appreciate

Kasparov's motives for many of his early effective moves. The game was being played at a level beyond his own expertise, but he watched as Deep Blue made a number of obvious weak replies. Campbell realized that the evaluation function had to be modified to discourage Deep Blue from getting its pieces forced off to the side of the board.

Kasparov was thus victorious in the end, though winning by a narrower margin than most experts had originally predicted, a score of 4–2. Actually, in retrospect, this was the score Kasparov had predicted. On Deep Blue's behalf, one might say that the match was closer than the final score reflected. Game 5 could have been drawn. The computer had the better chances late in Game 4, and it might have done better in Game 2 if it hadn't lost its opening book. On the other hand, Kasparov won the final two games in grand style and did have chances in both Games 3 and 4. Thus, while Kasparov won the match, the Deep Blue team also felt the match was a great success.

Kasparov went home from Philadelphia with the $400,000 winner's prize, not bad for a week's effort but, even more importantly, with expectations of participating in future events with IBM. After winning the final two games, he must have felt confident that he would have no serious troubles in winning a rematch, and maybe even a third match. His popularity reached unprecedented levels in his role of defending the human intellect, postponing the day when the inevitable would happen.

Several months prior to the match, David Levy asked a number of leading computer and chess experts including Kasparov when, if ever, a computer would usurp the top human player. According to David, Kasparov responded the year 2010 "or maybe never" [52]. Raymond Keene, Bryan Jacobs, and Tony Buzan concluded their book on the match, *Man v Machine, The ACM Chess Challenge Garry Kasparov v IBM's Deep Blue*, by saying,

> It would be interesting to pose the same question again now that Kasparov has actually played against Deep Blue at a classic time rate. Our own view is that Kasparov's second thought, 'maybe never', is closer to the truth. We have consistently explained throughout this book that the barrier of a draw is of immense aid to the human players and that human superiority in strategy will also be a giant hurdle for computers to surmount" [1].

The authors evidently were so impressed with Kasparov's performance that his prediction of "maybe never" looked like a better bet after the match than it did before the match. Seirawan felt that Kasparov had at least four more years, with the Deep Blue team having to improve its software [3]. Robert Byrne hedged his bets, asking "Is it really inevitable that computers will one day take over chess?" and answering, "The question still seems to be open" [10].

IBM, which had made its reputation selling computers that conduct business, found itself also king of the world of computers that play chess. The computer giant's image would never be the same. Under CEO Lou Gerstner, the company had made a remarkable financial recovery from its low point in the early 1990s. Deep Blue's success in Philadelphia was seen as a major step in helping to reshape the company's image as being at the cutting edge of technology and innovation, even in spite of the computer's loss to Kasparov. IBM was seen as playing a leading role in the most exciting scientific experiment to date with mankind's new tool, the tool that not only played great chess but was destined to evolve as our intellectual partner, the tool that some day will be at our sides in our travels through space. The Deep Blue story was more than just chess; it was a story that had major implications in the everyday lives of every one of us.

The Philadelphia match was also the largest Internet event to that time, a harbinger of the great potential of this new communications medium. It exceeded IBM's wildest expectations, overshadowing previous major Internet successes. In the year leading up to the match, IBM had developed websites for major tennis championships including the 1995 Wimbledon, the 1995 U.S. Open, and the 1996 Australian Open. It never imagined a chess

Bruce Weber, reporter for *The New York Times*.

match would attract a larger audience than these competitions. Perhaps Internet users, technology-oriented and typically younger than tennis fans, related to a contest between Deep Blue and Garry Kasparov with more personal interest than one featuring Pete Sampras, Andre Agassi, or their likes. It was a contest involving their beloved tool!

After the first game, it was clear that an expansion of the web server was necessary to meet the unprecedented demand coming in from all corners of the world. Carol Moore, responsible for the IBM website, obtained additional computing power on an RS/6000 SP2 located in IBM's White Plains office, the same kind of computer that was playing Kasparov. After the website was transferred to this new location, the response time dramatically improved. The original on-site staff of 10 people was expanded to 17 by the time the match was over. On the final day of the match, the IBM website received a record six million hits. According to Moore, this was the first big Internet event that attracted an audience of the size typically associated with broadcast TV.

The Internet was the ideal medium for communicating this event to the world. Thomas Mulligan, writing for the *Los Angeles Times* [30], said the match was "a perfect demonstration of how the global computer network can be more powerful even than television." He went on to say

Carol Moore, head of the IBM Internet team.

that, "The computer network's graphical, interactive and audience-targeting capabilities make it ideal for chess, which attracts a passionate—though limited—audience that wants not just to watch but to kibitz, even participate if possible."

For the Deep Blue team, the match, according to CJ Tan, completely satisfied its objectives. Though losing to Kasparov, Deep Blue demonstrated that it was playing near his level, and better than any computer ever played before. Deep Blue's first-round victory over Kasparov was the first time a computer ever defeated a human world champion in a regulation tournament-speed game and that victory, alone, made the match a success. In a post-match interview, Kasparov said,

> I would like, first, to congratulate the Deep Blue team for its outstanding achievement, because it is a worthy opponent. It is really a serious opponent. I won the match 4 to 2, but it was as tough as a world championship match and, believe me, I did not spare my strength playing it.

IBM's stock rose an impressive $6.62 dollars from its value of $113.50 at the close of trading on the day preceding the first round, that is Friday, February 9, 1996, to its value of $119.12 at the close of trading on Tuesday, February 20. (The final game was played on Saturday, February 17, and with Monday a holiday and the New York Stock Exchange closed, Tuesday, the 20, was the first day that the markets were open after the match ended.) With approximately 500,000,000 shares of common stock, this was equivalent to adding $3,310,000,000 to the value of the company in a little more than a week! Of course, how much of this can be attributed to the match is not clear, but estimating a figure of 10% implies the match was worth $331,000,000 to IBM. During the same period of time, the Dow Jones Industrial Average went the other way, dropping 97 points, from 5541 to 5458; if it were not for IBM's rise, the DJIA would have dropped more like 120 points. IBM's competitors Microsoft and Intel marked time during this same period; Microsoft slipped a quarter from $100.12 to $99.87 and Intel rose a modest $1.25 from $58 to $59.25.

In newspaper articles, magazine articles, TV stories, and editorials around the world, Deep Blue was the featured story. In the vernacular of the advertising world, Deep Blue received over one billion impressions in the days around the match. An impression is the equivalent of one person seeing or hearing about Deep Blue — that is, making an impression on that person. During the match, articles by Bruce Weber and Robert Byrne appeared regularly in *The New York Times* [4–10, 37–44]. James Kim reported on the match for *USA Today* with front-page coverage on three days [12–16], Jack Peters reported on the match for the *Los Angeles Times* [30–36], Joseph McLennen for the *Washington Post* [25–29], and William Macklin for the host-town *Philadelphia Inquirer* [17–23]. Stories appeared in *Sports Illustrated* [47], *Time* [49], *Newsweek* [50], *Businessweek* [46], and *U.S. News & World Report* [48]. Deep Blue lightened up David Letterman's "Late Show" on the 15th [56] and Jay Leno's "The Tonight Show" on the 14th and 15th [57,58]. Wide coverage of the match was given by news shows on CNN [55], ABC [53,54,61,62], CBS [59], and PBS [60].

The Philadelphia match was indeed a great success. But there was much more to come!

References

Books

[1] Raymond Keene and Byron Jacobs with Tony Buzan, *Man v Machine, The ACM Chess Challenge*, B. B. Enterprises, Brighton, Sussex, 1996.

[2] Monty Newborn, *Kasparov Versus Deep Blue: Computer Chess Comes of Age*, Springer-Verlag, 1997.

Grandmaster Chess Analysis

[3] Yasser Seirawan, "The Kasparov – Deep Blue Match," *ICCA Journal*, 19(1), pp. 41-57, March 1996.

Newspaper Articles

[4] Robert Byrne, "Cool under pressure, machine has moxie," *The New York Times*, February 11, 1996.

[5] Robert Byrne, "Cautiously and patiently, Kasparov outmaneuvers foe," *The New York Times*, February 12, 1996.

[6] Robert Byrne, "Kasparov and computer play to a draw," *The New York Times*, February 14, 1996.

[7] Robert Byrne, "Fourth chess game ends in a draw," *The New York Times*, February 15, 1996.

[8] Robert Byrne, "Chess computer refuses draw, falls to Kasparov," *The New York Times*, February 17, 1996.

[9] Robert Byrne, "Kasparov's winning strategy: slow strangulation," *The New York Times*, February 18, 1996.

[10] Robert Byrne, "Chess: A collision of brains and brawn," *The New York Times*, February 19, 1996.

[11] Ed Gaulin, "Computer 1, chess champion 0," *Atlanta Journal and Constitution*, February 11, 1996.

[12] James Kim, "Can this man save the human race?" *USA Today*, February 9, 1996.

[13] James Kim, "Kasparov wins, ties match with computer," *USA Today*, February 12, 1996.

[14] James Kim, "Man vs. machine," *USA Today*, February 13, 1996.

[15] James Kim, "Game 3 chess match a draw; IBM site up," *USA Today*, February 14, 1996.

[16] James Kim, "Human error helped Kasparov beat computer at chess," *USA Today*, February 19, 1996.

[17] William Macklin, "Man vs. computer, Game 1: The computer triumphs," *Philadelphia Inquirer*, February 11, 1996.

[18] William Macklin, "This time, Kasparov outfoxes computer," *Philadelphia Inquirer*, February 12, 1996.

[19] William Macklin, "Man and machine draw in chess match's Game 3," *Philadelphia Inquirer*, February 14, 1996.

[20] William Macklin, "Computer group glows in chess match's spotlight," *Philadelphia Inquirer*, February 15, 1996.

[21] William Macklin, "Quietly, Kasparov defeats computer," *Philadelphia Inquirer*, February 17, 1996.

[22] William Macklin, "Kasparov is the victor in man-vs.-machine," *Philadelphia Inquirer*, February 18, 1996.

[23] William Macklin, "Kasparov, computer tie again," *Philadelphia Inquirer*, February 15, 1996.

[24] Grant McCool, Reuters, "Brain beat chip — Kasparov wins," *USA Today*, February 19, 1996.

[25] Joseph McLellan, "The king vs. the thing," *The Washington Post*, February 13, 1996.

[26] Joseph McLellan, "Cyber-bout: Game 3 is a draw," *The Washington Post*, February 14, 1996.

[27] Joseph McLellan, "Kasparov wins Game 5," *The Washington Post*, February 17, 1996.

[28] Joseph McLellan, "Kasparov's tactics outfox, confuse computer's brute force," *The Washington Post*, February 18, 1996.

[29] Joseph McLellan, "Man, machine play to a draw," *The Washington Post*, February 15, 1996.

[30] Thomas Mulligan, "Match proves Internet can be king," *Los Angeles Times*, February 15, 1996.

[31] Jack Peters, "Computer beats world chess champion," *Los Angeles Times*, February 11, 1996.

[32] Jack Peters, "Kasparov bedevils Deep Blue with first win," *Los Angeles Times*, February 12, 1996.

[33] Jack Peters, "Computer beats world chess champion," *Los Angeles Times*, February 13, 1996.

[34] Jack Peters, "Man and machine agree to draw in chess match," *Los Angeles Times*, February 14, 1996.

[35] Jack Peters, "Kasparov, chess computer draw again," *Los Angeles Times*, February 15, 1996.

[36] Jack Peters, "Kasparov wins, clinches tie with computer," *Los Angeles Times*, February 17, 1996.

[37] Jack Peters, "Deep Blue is deep-sixed by Kasparov," *Los Angeles Times*, February 18, 1996.

[38] Bruce Weber, "Chess champ faces Deep Blue," *The New York Times*, February 9, 1996.

[39] Bruce Weber, "In upset, new chess computer beats Kasparov in first game," *The New York Times*, February 11, 1996.

[40] Bruce Weber, "In Kasparov vs computer, the chess scorecard is 1–1," *The New York Times*, February 12, 1996.

[41] Bruce Weber, "Representing people everywhere, Kasparov seems a lot more human," *The New York Times*, February 13, 1996.

[42] Bruce Weber, "Computer's ability against chess champion has surprised and intrigued," *The New York Times*, February 18, 1996.

[43] Bruce Weber, "It's man over machine as Kasparov beats computer in decisive game," *The New York Times*, February 18, 1996.

[44] Bruce Weber, "A mean chess-playing computer tears at the meaning of thought," *The New York Times*, February 19, 1996.

[45] Bruce Weber, "Deep Blue, deep thought," *The New York Times*, February 20, 1996.

Magazine Articles

[46] Peter Coy, "Your move, Deep Blue," *Businessweek*, February 19, 1996.

[47] Rick Reilly, "I was just a pawn," *Sports Illustrated*, February 23, 1996.

[48] Kenan Pollack, "Chess moves," *U.S. News and World Reports*, February 26, 1996.

[49] Charles Krauthammer, "Deep Blue funk," *Time*, February 26, 1996.

[50] Steven Levy, "Tangled up in Deep Blue," *Newsweek*, February 26, 1996.

[51] Michael Antonoff, "Curtains for Kasparov?" *Popular Science*, pp. 43–46, March 1996.

Miscellaneous Articles

[52] David Levy, "Extrapolation and speculation," *ICCA Journal*, 18(3), pp. 171–174, September 1995.

TV Coverage

[53] ABC World News Sunday, Aaron Brown, anchor, 6:30–7:00 p.m., February 10, 1996.

[54] ABC Good Morning America, Joan Lunden, Host with Gina Smith, 6:30–7:00a.m., February 13, 1996.

[55] CNN Early Prime, Natalie Allen and Bob Cain, Co-Anchors, 4:30–5:30 p.m., February 13, 1996.

[56] The Late Show, with David Letterman, CBS, 11:35 p.m., February 15, 1996.

[57] The Tonight Show, with Jay Leno, NBC, 11:35 p.m., February 14, 1996.

[58] The Tonight Show, with Jay Leno, NBC, 11:35 p.m., February 15, 1996.

[59] CBS Morning News, Troy Roberts, Anchor, 6:30–7:00a.m., February 15, 1996.

[60] The News Hour With Jim Lehrer, Jim Lehrer, Host, PBS Network, 7:00 p.m., February 15, 1996.

[61] ABC World News Sunday, Carole Simpson, Anchor, 6:30–7:00 p.m., February 18, 1996.

[62] ABC World News This Morning, Thalia Assuras, Anchor, 6:00–7:00 a.m., February 19, 1996.

7 Rematch Negotiations

> "A few years ago, it seemed like the gap between him and the other players was closing, but he's opened it up again," Joel Benjamin, April 1997.

Shortly after the Philadelphia match, Garry Kasparov, accompanied by Frederic Friedel and Owen Williams, triumphantly paid a visit to the Deep Blue team in Yorktown Heights. Negotiations for a rematch were launched. Both sides soon became committed to reaching an agreement, but the details of a contract would take months to work out.

The group arrived by limo from New York in the morning and stayed until late in the day. Kasparov was given a warm reception by the center's researchers, and in return he entertained them with a standing-room-only talk in their auditorium. His sharp wit was at its best as he interacted with an enthusiastic audience. Later after lunch, he discussed the match with the team and analyzed a few positions with Deep Blue's assistance. In the afternoon informal talks were initiated regarding a rematch, and the day concluded with a decision to hold more formal talks in April.

Following the Philadelphia match, Owen Williams was engaged by Andrew Page to handle Kasparov's chess-related activities. Williams, a tall, former world-class tennis player originally from South Africa and now living in Florida, had served as agent to some of the world's leading golfers. Kasparov was his first chess player, and he seemed out to impress his new client with his ability to negotiate a good deal. Page continued to manage Kasparov's other matters, particularly those in Moscow, ranging from real estate dealings to involvement in charitable organizations.

In April Kasparov and Williams returned to IBM, this time meeting the Deep Blue team at its corporate headquarters in Armonk. The day ended with both parties agreeing to the general framework of the rematch. CJ Tan and Marcy Holle were to negotiate the details of the contract with Kasparov and Williams.

If there were any doubts within IBM about holding a rematch, the great success of the first match and the optimism of the Deep Blue team on its chances in a rematch swung the balance in favor of another try. Further, when IBM took on the project in 1989, management intentions must certainly have included seeing this great scientific experiment through to completion, and now was not the time to stop. Moreover, though IBM was in the business of business machines, not chess-playing machines, the potential technical spinoffs from Deep Blue to other problems involving multiprocessing and special-purpose computing must have been alluring. And finally, it should be remembered that in 1958 an IBM 704 computer, programmed by IBMers Alex Bernstein, Michael de V. Roberts, Thomas Arbuckle, and Martin A. Belsky, was given widespread credit for playing the first full-scale game of chess [1]. A few years later, IBM's image had again been enhanced by Arthur Samuel's study of machine learning in the context of checkers [2,3].

In Philadelphia the match had been organized by the ACM and played under the auspices of the ICCA. This time IBM decided to organize the match themselves while offering the ACM the role of serving as the officials and commentators. The ACM gladly accepted this role, and Kasparov had no objections, but did want a voice in the people selected. Given the magnitude of the plans for the rematch and the resources at IBM's disposal, it made good sense for IBM to take control of what they envisioned as a Broadway-quality production.

In the summer of 1996 IBM began to organize the infrastructure surrounding the match under the assumption that the negotiations would eventually lead to an agreement. A communications team, headed by Marcy Holle, was formed to work with the Deep Blue team. TSI was rehired to assist Holle, while George Paul was called upon to assist Tan and Holle in the negotiations. Mark Bregman, general manager of the RS/6000 Division in Poughkipsee, would coordinate matters related to the SP2 supercomputer. Bregman's division had much to gain if Deep Blue was successful.

Holle's communications team met every other week at first, then every week as the match neared. They felt that Kasparov was keeping close tabs on everything that came out of IBM, and thus their message was meant for him as much as for the media. According to Tan, "The message was to tell Kasparov exactly what we were doing, and that we were extremely confident, which we were." He said that the message was that they were doing three things: (1) preparing a faster machine, (2) adding much better chess knowledge by working with Joel Benjamin, and (3) improving a number of tools to make the system more flexible. Tan felt that Kasparov didn't really believe what IBM was saying, that Kasparov felt Deep Blue couldn't be made that much smarter in one year, and that only the system would be faster. Tan felt this affected Kasparov's planning and eventually his play.

Kasparov, it turned out, had no objection to the officials selected by the ACM, although late in the planning, he expressed his concern over having Yasser Seirawan as a commentator. He saw Seirawan's large commercial website, insidechess.com, as a competitor to his own forthcoming major chess-based website. He eventually accepted Seirawan after the ACM pointed out that Seirawan was one of his staunchest supporters in Philadelphia, and that a commitment to Seirawan had already been made. Kasparov, at this time, seemed unconcerned that IBM was both organizer and competitor.

Kasparov and IBM were in negotiations for months, with Kasparov seeking IBM support for a range of chess activities, hoping IBM would take over the role that Intel had previously played. The agreed-upon 7–4 split of the $1,100,000 purse contrasted with the 4–1 split of $500,000 negotiated for the first match. The doubling of the purse was a sign of IBM's satisfaction with the results of the first match and its desire to hold a rematch. The 7–4 split was a sign of Kasparov's growing respect for Deep Blue. When negotiations for Philadelphia began in 1995, Kasparov had requested a winner-take-all split, feeling he had virtually no chance of losing; this time he was hedging his bets. If the rematch turned out to be closer than in Philadelphia where the score was 4–2, there was a chance that he would not come out on top.

A match of six games was agreed upon with conditions the same as in Philadelphia except that instead of one day off, there would be two days off between Games 4 and 5. This would give Kasparov an extra day to recover from playing the first four games in five days and an extra day to plot strategy for the final two games. This would also enable scheduling four of the six games on weekends when both the public and the media were more likely to show up. Since the final game, however, would take place on Sunday, Mother's Day, there was concern that attendance might be affected, although this didn't turn out to be the case.

Games were scheduled to start at 3:00 and were to be played at the same rate as in Philadelphia: each player would have to complete 40 moves in the first two hours, 20 moves in the next hour, and all remaining moves in an additional 30 minutes. A game could last up to seven hours. Draws offered by Kasparov could be accepted or rejected by the Deep Blue team, a rule left unchanged from the previous match — and the only way that human involvement was allowed in the Deep Blue decision-making process. Potentially the source of problems again, it turned out to be a non-issue this time.

Negotiations dragged on for some time, but finally contracts were signed near the end of February. The commercial issues surrounding the event and holding up a final agreement were at last worked out. On February 23, 1997, a joint press announcement was released and interviews were held in New York City with leading publications including *Time* and *Newsweek*. The IBM Kasparov Versus Deep Blue Rematch, or more briefly, the Rematch was on; the dates were May 3–11, 1997, and the place was New York City!

In the period between Philadelphia and the upcoming Rematch, Kasparov was clearly on a roll and possibly at the peak of his career. He led the Russian team to a first-place finish in the 1996 Chess Olympiad in Yerevan, Armenia, and won two major tournaments in Spain — Las Palmas in December 1996 and Linares in February 1997 — affirming his position at the top of the human race.

At the 1996 Chess Olympiad in Yerevan, Kasparov played top board for the Russian team, leading it to victory by scoring five wins and four draws. At Las Palmas, he finished a clear point ahead of Vishwananthan Anand, the only other player with a plus score, beating out an impressive list including Grandmasters Veselin Topalov, Vladimir Kramnik, Vassily Ivanchuk, and former World Champion Anatoly Karpov. At Linares, Kasparov finished first in the field of 12 grandmasters scoring 8.5 of 11 points, placing him one full point ahead of Kramnik. These three major events included 30 games, of which Kasparov won or drew all but one.

Kasparov was coming into the Rematch sporting a 2828 rating. This is the highest rating ever held by a human and 68 points higher than the 2760 rating of his main rival at that time, Vishwananthan Anand. Kasparov had now been world champion for a decade. He had successfully defended his title five times in matches against Karpov in 1986, 1987 and 1990, and against Nigel Short in 1993 and Anand in 1995.

Moreover, Kasparov's reign as world champion seemed likely to continue for some time. Unlike great athletes who seldom perform at world champion levels after about age 35, the strength of great chess players does not seem to diminish until much later in life. Wilhelm Steinitz, Emanuel Lasker, Alexander Alekhine, and Mikhail Botvinnik were all world champions after the age of 50! Steinitz, born in 1836, was still world champion in 1894 at the age of 58. Botvinnik, the most recent world champion of this group, was born in 1911 and gave up his world title for the third time in 1963 when he was 52. Just prior to the Rematch, Joel Benjamin told me, "A few years ago, it seemed like the gap between him [Kasparov] and the other players was closing, but he's opened it up again."

Of course, other forces were also at play. The number of players is much greater now, and the information available to them has increased. Players can now practice any time they wish with a chess program running on a PC that plays at near-grandmaster level. They can also find someone on the Internet 24 hours a day eager to serve as sparing partner. We have recently seen a 15-year-old grandmaster, Etienne Bacrot from France, who attained that rank at a younger age than anyone in history. Previously Judit Polgar held the record, and before her, Bobby Fischer.

Computers, however, were giving Kasparov increasing difficulties [4–7]. By the time of the Rematch, Kasparov had played almost 50 games against computers. In a simultaneous exhibition, his first encounter in 1985, he trounced 32 of them. Nine years later in 1994, playing against Fritz3 at accelerated time limits, he lost his first game to a computer. Losing at rapidly played games and then several years later losing at regulation rates has been a historical pattern followed by leading players. Would Kasparov be any different? In Philadelphia two years later, though he was still able to defeat Deep Blue, the 4 – 2 score of the match was far from one-sided, suggesting that any further improvement by the computer might mean serious problems for Kasparov.

In short, coming into the Rematch Kasparov had shown that he was clearly the best human chess player and was at the top of his game — a standout world champion. But it was also clear that computers were closing in.

References

[1] A. Bernstein, M. de V. Roberts, T. Arbuckle, and M. A. Belsky, "A chess playing program for the IBM 704, "*Proceedings of the Western Joint Computer Conference*, pp. 157–159, 1958.

[2] A. L. Samuel, "Some studies in machine learning using the game of checkers," *IBM Journal of Research and Development*, 3(3), pp. 211–229, 1959.

[3] A. L. Samuel, "Some studies in machine learning using the game of checkers, II," *IBM Journal of Research and Development*, 11(6), pp. 801–817, 1967.

[4] The Editors, "Chess grandmasters versus chess computers," *ICCA Journal*, 8, (1), pp. 51–53, March 1986.

[5] Christopher Chabris, "The Harvard Cup Man-Versus-Machine Chess Challenge," *ICCA Journal*, 16(1), pp. 57–61, March 1993.

[6] Frederic Friedel, "Pentium Genius beats Kasparov," *ICCA Journal*, 17(3), pp. 153–158, September 1994.

[7] Ossi Weiner, "A vengeful return," *ICCA Journal*, 18(2), pp. 125–126, June 1995.

1985, Hamburg. Simultaneous exhibition against 32 computers.
Results: Kasparov 32 – Computers 0.

October 23, 1989, New York. Kasparov Versus Deep Thought Exhibition.
All moves in 90 minutes.
Results: Kasparov 2 – Deep Thought 0.

October 28, 1989, Boston. Harvard Chess Festival, a simultaneous exhibition.
Results: Kasparov blanked eight opponents, seven humans, and Sargon IV.

May 1994, Munich. Intel World Chess Express Challenge.
All moves in five minutes.
Results: Fritz3 tied with Kasparov for first place in the 12-round event,
winning its round with Kasparov. Kasparov won playoff.

August 31, 1994, London. Intel Speed Chess Grand Prix.
All moves in 30 minutes.
Results: Pentium Chess Genius 1 – Kasparov 0.

May 1995, Cologne. Intel World Chess WDR.
All moves in 30 minutes.
Results: Kasparov 1.5 – Pentium Chess Genius .5.

December 14, 1995, London. Intel-Sponsored Match.
All moves in thirty minutes.
Results: Kasparov 1.5 – Fritz 0.5.

February 10–17, 1996, Philadelphia. ACM Computer Chess Challenge.
40 moves in 2 hours, then 20 in 1 hour, then all in 30 minutes.
Results: Kasparov 4 – Deep Blue 2.

Diary of Garry Kasparov's Computer Encounters

8 A Faster and Smarter Deep Blue

"Nobody would have guessed in the mid-1950s that it would take 100 million positions per second to play close to the level of the world champion," Murray Campbell, after the ACM Chess Challenge.

Following Philadelphia, the challenge for the Deep Blue team came down to improving Deep Blue by about 100 rating points to be on an even footing with Garry Kasparov. Of course, Deep Blue could win the Rematch even though it was the weaker player, and alternatively, it could lose the Rematch even though it was the better player. This often happens in competition. Moreover, Deep Blue could be strong in certain

Hsu's chip enlarged by approximatetly 40%.

aspects of the game and Kasparov in others, with the outcome decided by who dictated the terms of the games. Then again, that's part of the issue of who is better, since better players usually force their opponent to play the game on their terms. Following his 1989 victory over Deep Thought, Kasparov was quoted by Brad Leithauser in the *New York Times Magazine* [1] as saying, "The highest art of the chess player lies in not allowing your opponent to show you what he can do."

The 100-point estimate was made by Kasparov in Philadelphia, where after the third game, when asked what rating he would assign to Deep Blue, he said,

> I don't know. We have to play more games, the match is still in progress.
> . . . The machine's strength is varying from . . . an ELO rating of 3000 to
> maybe 2300. What is the average? I do not know. It depends very much
> on the number of positions that the computer can play well. I would say
> today it is in the 2700 range.

At a press conference following the final game, Kasparov reiterated his estimate of Deep Blue's rating, this time, in the range of 3000 to 2200. In theory, a 4–2 score against someone rated 2800, Kasparov's rating at the time of the match, merits a rating of 2700.

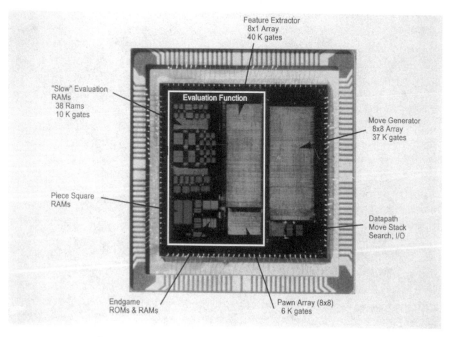

The functional features of Hsu's VLSI chess chip.

Thus, in April 1996, shortly after Kasparov's visit to the Yorktown Heights research center, the Deep Blue team members decided upon the improvements they wanted to carry out to raise Deep Blue's level of play. Work would focus on CB Hsu's VLSI chess processor and accelerator card, endgame databases, the opening book, tools for visualization and performance evaluation, the evaluation function, the memory tables, the search heuristics, and the time-control function. In addition, Joel Benjamin would be invited to return, and additional grandmaster support would be sought. Moreover, a new, faster SP2 was expected to be available for the match. In brief, Deep Blue would know more about chess and run on a faster computer.

Hsu redesigned his VLSI chip in the months after Philadelphia, coming up with what might be called Version 3. When CJ Tan and George Paul approached VLSI Technology in June 1996 to fabricate the chip, the chipmaker was not particularly interested since the chip was a small-quantity production effort at a time when the semiconductor industry was red-hot. Imagine, there was no time to fabricate Hsu's chip! Tan and Paul then visited VLSI to twist the arm of the company's VP marketing, and a commitment was finally made. The modified design went out to VLSI in August 1996, and the reworked chip came back to IBM Research in January 1997.

According to Hsu, the new chip ran at 24 Mhz — compared with 16–20 megahertz for the Philadelphia chip — and was three to five times stronger in terms of its overall contribution to the chess program strength. A die photo of the chess chip is shown on the previous page with functions indicated; a photo of the chip, is shown on the first page of this chapter. The chip, measuring 1.4 cm by 1.4 cm, contained approximately 1.5 million transistors, approximately one quarter the number of a Pentium 2 processor, the top microprocessor of the day. Hsu's description of the chip [2] outlined four components: a move generator, a smart move stack, an evaluation function, and a search controller.

The move generator offered a major advance over the move generator in the earlier Deep Thought chip (Version 1). In addition to generating captures at high speeds, the new version generated checking moves, check evasion moves, and attacking moves very quickly. The basic algorithm for move generation remained the same as used by the move generator in Ken Thompson's Belle [3,4].

The circuitry dealing with the evaluation function was sophisticated and advanced, allowing the chip to try first a fast evaluation and then, if necessary, a slow evaluation. The fast evaluation was mainly concerned with the value of material on the board. The slow evaluation, carried out on only about 15% of the positions, considered a slew of factors, including "square control, pins, x-rays, king safety, pawn structure, passed pawns, ray control, outposts, pawn majority, rook on the 7th, blockade, restraint, color complex, trapped pieces, development and so on." Proud of his accomplishment, Hsu says that the evaluation function was "perhaps more complicated than any chess evaluation function ever described in the literature."

Not present in the chip used in Philadelphia, the smart move stack helped the chip recognize draws through repetition of position. It also helped recognize when a move led to a repetition, showing that the side to move can at least claim a draw. It gave Deep Blue a far greater understanding of a draw; Campbell thought that this was significant in New York.

The search controller was in charge of the search of a position delivered from the host computer. It typically carried out a rapid four- or five-level search, returning information about the position to the host when done.

In the weeks leading up to the Rematch, Hsu tested a single-chip version of the system against some of the best commercial chess programs and reported that it won all but two points of the 40 games played. He also tested it against various grandmasters and reported it won 75% of the points. Hsu felt the single-chip system was playing at a level that would place it among the top 10 players in the world. The Deep Blue system that would play Garry Kasparov would have not one but hundreds of Hsu's VLSI chess chips!

In January of 1997 IBM announced a new processor, the Power Two Super Chip (P2SC) for the RS/6000. With a speed of 130 MHz, this RISC-based device made the computers of the SP2 twice as fast as those used by Deep Blue in Philadelphia. Each computer had one gigabyte of random-access memory. CJ Tan made plans to use the new processor against Kasparov, and spoke with Mark Bregman who, in turn, approached Eric Rosencrantz, director of marketing for the RS/6000 SP2. At the time, sales of SPs were on a roll, with new machines moving directly from test floor to customers. Rosencrantz was able to get his hands on one that was running benchmark programs for testing purposes.

The system contained 30 computers in two cabinets, the same size as the one used in Philadelphia. While being prepared, it remained in Poughkeepsie on the test floor, with Matt Thoennes traveling the 50 miles back and forth from Yorktown Heights, integrating the chess accelerator cards into the machine several at a time. With each card containing eight dedicated VLSI chess chips, and with two cards per computer, eventually the system would contain 480 chess chips on 60 accelerator cards housed in 30 RS/6000 computers. A communication line from Poughkeepsie to Yorktown Heights was used by the Deep Blue team to test the system during this development phase.

The match with Garry Kasparov was only a month away when, on April 1, 1997, the new SP2 was working with the new VLSI chess chips and accelerator cards. Two weeks later, on April 15, system testing was completed and the code, in theory, was frozen. On April 26 the two-cabinet system was loaded onto a truck and carefully driven the 100 miles from Poughkeepsie to the site of the match, the Equitable Center in midtown Manhattan. On Monday, April 28, it was up and running in its new temporary quarters.

Two backup systems were arranged, set up to follow the main SP2 from move to move and be ready to take over immediately if there was a problem. The system used in Philadelphia, the 30-computer RS/6000 SP2, now back at Yorktown Heights where it had been used to develop Deep Blue over the past year, was the first backup. A fast deskside RS/6000 workstation in the IBM operations room at the Equitable Center was the second backup. Tan said the team had learned from previous failures. In Philadelphia the team had used two backups, but the big difference this time was that the computer used for the match was on-site.

Thus by the time of the Rematch, Deep Blue was running on a system twice as fast as in Philadelphia, where it had searched 100,000,000 positions per second. In New York the new Deep Blue would search 200,000,000 positions per second. Searching one level deeper requires a computer to examine about six times as large a tree (approximately the square root of the average number of moves in a position), or where there are time constraints, to run about six times as fast. However, at search depth beyond about nine, information stored in large memory tables reduces this factor of six to somewhere between two and three. With Deep Blue sped up by a factor of two, it was now able to search almost one level deeper than in Philadelphia. During the Rematch, Deep Blue was typically searching all move sequences to a minimum depth of 10 to 12 levels in the middlegame and deeper in the endgame.

A natural question to ask at this point is, "How much stronger could one expect the new version of Deep Blue to be when running on the new faster system?" In particular, if nothing else was done to Deep Blue between matches except to increase the speed of the computer, how much improvement could one expect? Following the Philadelphia match, Robert Hyatt and I carried out an experiment aimed at answering this question. The reader with a mathematical bent is encouraged to follow the details of the experiment and analysis presented in Appendix H. A knowledge of high school algebra and an absolute minimal knowledge of probability theory are necessary to understand and appreciate the results — no more. We used Hyatt's program, Crafty, for the experiment, but the results extend to any chess program, including Deep Blue. The main conclusion from the experiment was that by doubling the speed of Deep Blue, its playing strength could be expected to increase by at least 100 rating points.

How much Deep Blue would improve as a result of software improvements was impossible to quantify, but the Deep Blue team believed it was a significant amount. In discussing the work done on the evaluation function, Campbell said,

> Not too long after the Philadelphia match, I recall a specific meeting, and we were talking about search extensions and improving the parallelism and all the issues of evaluation; all the issues were on the table about how we would improve for the next match and at some point, I said that we should devote all our efforts to the evaluation. The search, if not perfect, was reasonable; the parallel search, if not perfect, was reasonable, and that wasn't the reason we lost the games. And so we sort of agreed at that point that all our efforts would be devoted to evaluation. Now that included incorporating more knowledge into the evaluation function as it stood, and also for CB to incorporate more specific features into the chip, the next revision of the chip for the 1997 match. So CB spent a large part of his time in the redesign work, redesigning the logic for better understandability and especially efficiency, but a large part was adding new features to the evaluation function. A lot of work was done to better evaluate various pawn structures. Some of this was put into CB's chip, allowing for very rapid evaluation.

Campbell went on to say that

> rooks on open files — files where there were no pawns to hinder a rook's movement — were the object of one specific important modification. Joel Benjamin had noticed that Deep Blue would tend to prematurely open up files, put its rook on the files, and eventually the opponent, say, Kasparov, would be able to oppose rooks on the files and trade off all the rooks. Even though Deep Blue controlled the open file for a while, in the long run, it wasn't all that valuable. He observed that if you have the option of opening a file, that is, if the pawn structure is such that you are the one who can open the file whenever you want, then that's almost as good as having an open file. There is no need to actually open the file until the time is right. This helped in Game 2 in 1997 when Deep Blue played 23 Rec1 and certainly when it doubled rooks on the closed a-file. When it did open the file, it was at a particularly inconvenient time for Kasparov. Deep Blue didn't open the file prematurely, and it made threats on closed files. The same sort of thing was done for bishops. Closed diagonals for bishops were treated in a similar way.

Deep Blue's evaluation function was tuned with the help of Gerald Tesauro, who had previously developed a world-class backgammon program called TD-Gammon [3]. Tesauro used neural net methodologies to tune the function.

In addition to using a faster computer and improving the scoring function for New York, the team worked on the opening book intensively. It was a very tricky proposition. Should Kasparov's favorites be booked? Should one assume that he was going to play irregular openings? How much time should be devoted to his favorite, the Sicilian? The book was Joel Benjamin's primary responsibility, although in the last few weeks before the Rematch, The Deep Blue team brought in some heavy hitters for additional help. Miguel Illescas came to Yorktown Heights for a couple of weeks to add his expertise on the Sicilian. Two of Benjamin's grandmaster friends, John Fedorowicz and Nick DeFirmian, joined on in the weeks leading up the match, complementing Benjamin's opening expertise and playing scrimmage games as well. Three of the top 10 players in the United States plus the top player from Spain would thus work together to add the finishing touches to Deep Blue's book. DeFirmian was an "e4 expert"; Fedorowicz knew the Dragon variation of the Sicilian, one of Kasparov's favorites; Illescas had played a number of tournaments at the highest levels, including games with Kasparov, and had a large repertoire of openings. The grandmasters spent their time in the Deep Blue Grandmaster Laboratory, entering book lines, discussing them with Campbell, and playing games or segments of games against the computer, all the while searching for weaknesses. Every evening Deep Blue automatically checked every book move added and reported any problems back to the team in the morning. Scrimmage games with grandmasters and against old versions of Deep Blue were constantly going on. Benjamin, or one of the others, would play short game segments looking for weaknesses, then discuss the weaknesses with the team members and look for solutions. The burden of transforming Benjamin's ideas into working programming code fell on the shoulders of Campbell, Hoane, and Hsu.

Deep Blue often had had problems in the past with its time-control algorithm, and for New York nobody wanted any surprises. When I discussed this with Campbell, he said they

> . . . wanted a lot of time left at the end in case something happened at move 39. We didn't want to be frantically running around trying to get the system up. We did have a backup system, so it wouldn't have been that bad, of course, but we just wanted to have plenty of time, 20 or 30 minutes, so nobody was under any pressure to get a backup system up and running in three minutes. Also, we had found that the difference between computing for 1:40 and 2:20 was somewhat minimal; once in a while it would play a better move, but we figured that if we moved fairly quickly and kept

Kasparov under pressure in that sense, and didn't give him a lot of time to think on our time, that it would throw him a bit out of his rhythm. Most of his human opponents use a good majority of their time, except for maybe Vishwananthan Anand. Maybe around move 40 they only have a few minutes left, or a few seconds left. We just wanted to have a slightly different than usual rhythm, so we were moving at a minute and 30 seconds instead of every two minutes. Of course, it's unnatural already being so regular in the amount of time Deep Blue spends, except for when it goes into the panic mode. Then it spends a lot longer. It might use up a third to a half of the remaining time in a bad case. It could take up to 15 minutes on a critical position leading up to time control.

Several weeks before the Rematch was to take place, Grandmasters Larry Christiansen and Michael Rohde were invited to Yorktown Heights to take on the single-computer version of Deep Blue, previously called Deep Blue Prototype and named Deep Blue Junior after the Philadelphia match. Each grandmaster played two games against the computer under the same conditions that would be used for the Rematch. Deep Blue Junior searched identically to the full 30-computer system but ran on only one computer of the SP. These two tough players were offered an honorarium and expenses for their participation, as well as a financial incentive to win. Christiansen's rating at the time of the match was approximately 2630, and Rohde's was approximately 30 points less, thus placing them among the top 25 players in the United States. Deep Blue Junior played Black in two Reti Opening games, but the openings differed greatly from those in the rematch. Both Christiansen and Rohde drew their first games but lost the second. Their games appear in Appendix I.

Thus, with the improvements in hardware — a faster chip and a faster computer — and with improved chess knowledge, an improved opening book, and a year of extensive testing under the scrutiny of grandmaster-level talent, Deep Blue should have improved, in theory, by at least 100 rating points. If so, that would place it on a par with Garry Kasparov.

References

[1] Brad Leithauser, "Kasparov Beats Deep Thought," *The New York Times Magazine*, December 1989.

[2] Feng-hsiung Hsu, "The Chess Grandmaster Chips in the IBM Deep Blue Supercomputer," unpublished manuscript, 1999.

[3] Gerald Tesauro, "Temporal difference learning and TD-Gammon," *Communications of the ACM*, 3(3), pp. 58–68, March 1995.

9 Countdown to the Rematch

"At this point last year I didn't believe we could win. This year is different," Feng-hsiung Hsu, before the Rematch [15].

Garry Kasparov arrived in the Big Apple on April 23, settling in with his team at the Plaza Hotel at the corner of 5th Avenue and 59th Street, a convenient eight-block walk from the site of the match. Kasparov was accompanied by his coach, Yuri Dokhoian, his agent, Owen Williams, his computer advisor, Frederic Friedel, his mother, Klara Kasparova, and several computers equipped with Fritz4 and Hiarcs. Michael Khodarkovsky, a New Jersey-based chess master, was also part of the team. Born in 1958 in Odessa, Ukraine, Khodarkovsky made his career as a coach before emigrating to the United States in 1992. He took up

A 16-computer RS/6000 SP2. The Deep Blue
system consisted of two of these cabinets.

residence in New Jersey, where he continued coaching, serving as founder and executive director of the United States Branch of the Garry Kasparov International Chess School. Missing from the entourage was Julia Wolk; she and Kasparov had become proud parents during the interval between matches, and she chose to remain at home with her six-month-old son Vadim.

The Deep Blue team and most of the others involved in the Rematch stayed in the Michaelangelo Hotel located across the street from the Equitable. The Michaelangelo used to be the somewhat well-worn Taft Hotel in years gone by; it had been remodeled recently and turned into a small, for New York City, first-class hotel just off Times Square. IBM had initially attempted to hold the match in the Millennium Hotel, but the Millennium wanted IBM to agree to evacuate some of its space on the final day of the match for a wedding. No chance for that! IBM then opted for the Equitable Center, located at the corner of 51st and 7th Avenue, where the company had good relations with the management and where IBM corporate meetings had been held in the past.

I checked in on April 28, making myself available to the two teams. My Appeals Committee had scheduled a meeting with them on May 1 to resolve an issue concerning the clock.

The Deep Blue team began arriving on April 29. Herbert Liberman, who had retired from IBM, but was reactivated in May of 1996 to provide temporary assistance to CJ Tan, was there early to initiate IBM preparations. Liberman would serve as Tan's right-hand man, primarily keeping track of accounts, ensuring that bills were paid and records kept. In the months leading up to the match, he was responsible for keeping an eye on the timing of the project to make sure deadlines were met. Joel Benjamin, CB Hsu, Murray Campbell, Joe Hoane, and Jerry Brody also arrived on the 29th.

CJ Tan, Marcy Holle, and George Paul arrived on the 30th. They had been in Dallas that week for IBM's annual stockholders' meeting, where they proudly displayed the single-computer version of Deep Blue. Lou Gerstner had mentioned in his stockholders' address that the match was coming up soon and that Deep Blue was sitting in a nearby demonstration room. A number of upper-level executives visited the exhibit, including Gerstner.

Zeev Barzilai also checked in on the 30th. Barzilai was working at the time for IBM Israel in Tel Aviv and had come all the way to be on hand with his colleagues to celebrate in the event that Deep Blue won.

Matt Thoennes had been at the hotel from the day Deep Blue moved in. He was responsible for preparing the infrastructure at the Rematch, including the game room, the IBM operations room, Deep Blue's special place, the commentary auditorium, the press room, and the Internet room. The game room, actually a television studio, was on the Equitable's 35th floor.

Thoennes designed a stage set to give it the appearance of a professor's library, with partially filled bookshelves and paintings on the walls. The lighting was carefully arranged to give the game board the correct intensity for Kasparov. Several television cameras were mounted to cover the game room from various angles and provide close-ups of Kasparov, the Deep Blue team member running Deep Blue, the game board, and the clock. At the back were several seats for representatives of each side and a closed-off area for Kasparov to use when he wanted to get away from the board. Initially Kasparov had been given a dressing room located a short distance from the game room. When Klara Kasparova arrived to check out the facilities several days before the contest was to begin, she felt the room was too remote. She negotiated with the organizers to have part of the back of the game room set aside instead. During the match Kasparova ensured that Kasparov's staple refreshments were available. In much the same way as competing tennis players do, Kasparov had learned to refuel during a game with bananas for potassium, chocolate for sugar, and plenty of Evian bottled water.

Next to the game room were Deep Blue and the IBM operations room. Deep Blue was relegated to a dead-ended back hallway, where it was likely to remain relatively undisturbed. Its two six-foot cabinets sat quietly several feet apart. Occasionally someone would come to have a photo taken alongside. Jeanne Moos, of CNN's "Making the MOOSt of It," came to visit Deep Blue on the final day of the match, and with her usual wry sense of humor got a laugh by challenging it to a quick game of checkers.

The IBM Operations Room was bulging with computing equipment, including a monitor that observed Deep Blue's analytic process and a ready-to-go backup RS/6000 workstation for Deep Blue. The Equitable's television production control room was located between the game room and the IBM operations room. In the hallway, a large table filled with cold cuts and soft drinks was available for all involved.

Video cameras in the game room transmitted the games to the commentary auditorium and the press room. The press room was initially located on the 49th floor, but had to be moved up one floor to more spacious quarters following Game 2 when the number of media in attendance far exceeded expectations. The glorious New York skyline was a backdrop to the elegant press room.

A tiered commentary auditorium fitted with 500 soft and comfortable blue seats for the public was located one level below ground floor. Three large 10' x 10' video screens paneled the stage; an empty Deep Blue cabinet sat at the right side of the stage silently peering out at the audience. A laptop running Fritz4 occupied the commentators' table in the middle of the stage with its output connected to the middle video screen. During the games, a trained court stenographer typed in the commentary and shipped it off to the IBM Internet room, located adjacent to the rear of the stage and across a hallway. Never before had a chess match been held in such outstanding facilities.

Security was a concern for the organizers. Only two months earlier at an ACM conference in the San Jose Convention Center, a fake bomb scare preceding a demonstration given by the Deep Blue team emptied the hall. At the time, the "unabomber" had not yet been caught, and since it was known that he targeted high-tech individuals, the threat was taken seriously. Teddy Soohoo, normally responsible for maintaining security at the tranquil IBM Thomas J. Watson Research Center, found himself in charge of the dynamic and complex environment of the Equitable. Metal detectors were installed at the entrance to the commentary auditorium, and all traffic, especially that riding elevators to the upper floors, was carefully monitored. Fortunately, a crank e-mail was the most serious security issue Soohoo faced. Of course, some of the press felt they were entitled to be anywhere anytime, and Soohoo did his share of chasing an occasional overzealous member of the press from time to time.

Tickets sold for $25. For several games, there were more chess enthusiasts than seats available, and a small black market for tickets developed on the ground floor of the Equitable. And while the games lasted up to five hours, no one ever left early. With the exception of the final game, the spectators were always treated to a full day of chess with every game lasting more than 40 moves. Unlike many games between two grandmasters, no game was routinely drawn after 30 dull moves; with no adjournments, the audience never went home dissatisfied or frustrated by an uncompleted contest.

Ken Thompson, Mike Valvo, and I comprised the Appeals Committee, with Carol Jarecki under our direction and serving as Arbiter. Kasparov respected Jarecki, who had served as arbiter at the 1995 World Championship match between Kasparov and Vishwananthan Anand. If Jarecki could not solve a problem, it was put to the three of us. Jarecki, incidently, was a former nurse who had taken up a career as a professional arbiter several years earlier. With a flying license, she was known to hop around the United States from location to location, taking charge of major chess tournaments.

Ken Thompson again had the responsibility of observing the two sides to ensure that nothing irregular took place and that no one interacted with Deep Blue or Kasparov in an inappropriate manner. Thompson had had an easy job in Philadelphia, where there were no conflicts between the two contestants. This time, however, it wouldn't be quite so simple. Here, as in Philadelphia, he generally camped out in the IBM operations room.

Mike Valvo had served as arbiter in Philadelphia. This time IBM made a request, agreed to by the ACM and Kasparov, that he serve in a dual role of commentator and match official. Yasser Seirawan and Maurice Ashley repeated their Philadelphia performances as commentators, this time as part of a three-man team with Valvo. Valvo would balance the other two commentators' tendency to favor Kasparov. Ashley was the setup man, directing leading questions about the position to the other two.

Throughout the match, the three commentators invited questions and suggestions from the audience. They used Fritz4, with the help of Frederic Friedel, to run through variations from the current position. Among the leading players invited to the stage to comment on the games over the course of the match were Grandmasters Patrick Wolff, Zsuzsa Polgar, and Roman Dzindzichashvili. Members of the Deep Blue team were also invited to the stage to provide their perspectives of the match.

During the scheduled breaks, the three commentators took turns at leaving the stage and heading up to the press room to meet with the media, discuss the game with the grandmasters gathered there, and grab a bite to eat. Grandmasters and leading chess personalities were everywhere to be seen. There may have been more chess talent at the Equitable during the course of the match than at any other event in North America in the history of the game. Robert Byrne of *The New York Times* of course attended regularly, usually sitting at his unofficially reserved table in the press room. Shelby Lyman, syndicated chess columnist, attended. Grandmaster Ron Henley, who sometimes served as Anatoly Karpov's agent, attended. Grandmaster Lev Alburt attended. Grandmaster Ilya Gurevich attended. Grandmaster Lubomir Kavalek attended. Grandmaster Gabriel Schwartzman attended. British International Masters David Levy, Daniel King, and Malcolm Pein attended. United States women's champion Anjelina Belakovskaia attended. Bruce Pandolfini and Joshua Waitzkin, both characters portrayed in the movie *Searching for Bobby Fischer*, attended. International Master Danny Kopec attended.

A few months prior to the match, Audemars Piguet, a prominent Swiss watchmaker, had agreed to design a new chess clock for Kasparov with all the special features that a world champion could desire. Kasparov hoped the clock would become the standard timepiece for top-level chess events and planned to showcase the new instrument on the game table in New York. The clock had a special new feature that would give each player several seconds on each move to move his piece (or pieces) when there was only a little time left on the clock. This would help avoid situations where a game would be lost only because a player could not physically move the pieces at very fast speeds when under severe time pressure.

The inclusion of this new feature in the clock, however, created a problem for the Deep Blue team. The clock would function differently than the rules for time control agreed upon in the contract, and the Deep Blue team would have to modify the code for Deep Blue to take the difference into account. History had shown that modifications to the time-control code were dangerous and needed thorough testing. With only a few weeks left before the match, the Deep Blue team felt that spending unanticipated time on this complex issue was unreasonable.

When George Paul met with Audemars Piguet representatives Vincent Perriard and Henri Charton at IBM's Madison Avenue offices in New York on April 4, he found that the clock was not yet finished. Instead of observing the clock in operation, he was given a simulated demonstration on a PC. Moreover, Paul was concerned when he found that there was no way to set the time controls for the two players independently or to augment the time remaining for one of the players in case of a penalty. The Audemars Piguet representatives then gave Paul two diskettes containing copies of the program to take back to Yorktown Heights to explore further. When Paul attempted to examine the program on his laptop, he found the first diskette wouldn't load; the second loaded but failed to execute properly. Perriard sent Paul another diskette via overnight courier service with the problem found earlier corrected. Meanwhile, about now, Paul realized that programming modifications would have to be made to Deep Blue to use the

George Paul, IBM researcher in parallel computing,
provided assistance to the Deep Blue team.

clock if left as designed, but it was too late to perform the necessary complicated modifications. Moreover, further testing of the program revealed a number of other problems.

Paul was concerned and arranged a conference call with Kasparov in Moscow, Owen Williams in Florida, and Audemars Piguet representatives in Switzerland. Kasparov understood the problem. The feature adding time to the clock would have to be bypassed. Audemars Piguet representatives agreed to modify the clock's operation accordingly. Paul still had concerns about the clock's readiness for the match and requested my Appeals Committee examine it before the match and make a decision on its fitness. Kasparov agreed to accept the decision of the committee.

In addition to problems with the clock's functional operation, there was also concern that it didn't display the time on its two faces very well on the planned closed-circuit television setup. Unlike the clock used in Philadelphia, the faces of the clock were essentially perpendicular to the table and couldn't be seen by a ceiling-mounted television camera. The contract for the match, however, stipulated that Kasparov had the right to choose the clock, and the issue of its design was outside the jurisdiction of the Appeals Committee.

Garry Kasparov and CJ Tan with their New York Yankee baseball caps; Kasparov would play White in the first game.

Several days before the match began, at IBM's request the Appeals Committee met with the two parties to resolve this readiness issue. After a tense several-hour meeting during which the clock was tested by simulating typical game play, the Appeals Committee concluded it was operating adequately for the match.

The clock was quite complex and consisted of five components including the clock itself, a PC, two transformers, and a small switch box. Indeed, the committee was sufficiently concerned with the complicated nature of the operation of the clock that it required a representative of Audemars Piguet to be in the game room while the games were in progress. As a precautionary measure, on the morning of the first game, Arbiter Carol Jarecki was given a short 30-minute course to familiarize her with the device!

The Audemars Piguet clock was thus on the game table when the match began; an identical version sat under Carol Jarecki's table. After about an hour of play, it began to act strangely, flashing irregularly, evidently because of overheating. Jarecki briefly halted the game and had the backup clock placed on the game table, readying her own clock if the backup had problems. However, no additional problems occurred during the match.

Early in the planning for the stage set, IBM had asked Kasparov to leave the clock fixed on one side of the board throughout the match, and he agreed. It is customary for Black to decide on which side of the board to place the clock, but IBM preferred not to have the back of the clock showing on the television screen for half of the games.

Flags were agreed upon for the game table, a Russian one for Kasparov and an American one for Deep Blue. It had been a subject of some discussion before the first match, but this time it was a nonissue. The match was not meant to be viewed as competition between Russia and the United States in any sense, but flags are such a tradition in chess competition that omitting them is making more of a political statement than including them.

Colors for the opening game were decided at a press conference in the Equitable on May 1. Carol Jarecki and I stood side by side holding two identical boxes, each hiding a New York Yankee baseball cap, one white and one black. Kasparov was given the choice of boxes and drew the one with the white hat, leaving CJ Tan and Deep Blue with the one containing the black hat. Kasparov thus would play White in the opening round. This was a major stroke of luck for the Deep Blue team. It meant that Deep Blue would play White in Game 6, and that Kasparov could count slightly less on winning the match if it came down to the final game than if he had started with Black. In Philadelphia, when Kasparov offered a draw in the fifth game, he was counting on a victory in the sixth, but this time if the match turned out to be even after four rounds, Kasparov would be taking a greater risk offering a draw in the fifth game in expectation of winning the match in the sixth and final game as Black. It also meant that Deep Blue would be playing White in two of the three final games. It was anticipated that Kasparov might use the first few games to discover how Deep Blue played; having Black in two of the last three games would give him somewhat less flexibility in taking advantage of the knowledge gained. In Philadelphia Kasparov scored 2.5–0.5 in the final three games after playing even for the first three games. This led many to believe that he had learned from the first three games how to routinely defeat Deep Blue.

When Kasparov pulled the white Yankee cap, I asked him if he would like to put it on. I thought that it would make a great photo, likely to be used by the media, and endearing him to New Yorkers and to many other Americans living in the wild west across the Hudson River, especially those who didn't play chess (chess players already loved him). He wasn't interested, though, and declined my suggestion; he simply said it wouldn't fit. I had actually prepared for that reply by buying a cap with an adjustable head size, but there was no reason to get into that. Tan, with the black cap, similarly declined, respecting his opponent's decision.

Throughout the press conference, photographers flashed pictures of Kasparov from close up and from afar, probably several hundred flashes, and he was most obliging. I served as emcee, beginning by reading a proclamation from New York City Mayor Rudolph Giuliani that May 3–9 was New York City Chess Week. Tan then said a few words and introduced other members of his team. Kasparov followed, expressing his disappointment with not having any Deep Blue games to study. He also discussed the computers he would use to help him during the game. After the introductions and the selection of colors, Kasparov and the Deep Blue team answered a barrage of questions. A large buffet at the side of the room kept those in attendance well fed. Following the press conference, individual one-on-one interviews took place between members of the Deep Blue team, Kasparov and his team, and members of the media, lasting until late in the afternoon.

Predictions, predictions! Before the rematch began, predictions were everywhere. Phil Waga's article on August 21, 1996, in *The Reporter Dispatch* [3], quoted Shelby Lyman as saying that "I'd put my money on Kasparov," and Yasser Seirawan concurring, saying that "Kasparov will win, and win quicker and easier than he did the last time." Sean Hathorn, in a letter to the Editor in *USA Today* [18] on May 7 (perhaps already knowing the result of the first game since the first game was played on May 3) wrote "Deep Blue II will go down like the Titanic." Zsuzsa Polgar was quoted in *The New York Times* [14] several days before the match as saying, "The computer is better but Garry is better also."

Mark Saylor, writing in the *Los Angeles Times* [13] on May 1, 1997, thought Kasparov was about to milk the golden cow, writing,

> My prediction is that Kasparov will not only win, but win easily. This may not be evident either in the final score or in Kasparov's comments about how gruelling the match was. It is his intent to bring IBM back for another try next year with another lucrative prize fund.

Moreover, he went on to say,

> For a while IBM will keep coming back for the man versus machine PR. But if the company eventually concludes that Kasparov is pulling an elaborate con, it will probably throw in the towel and focus on selling more RS/6000s to grocery store chains so that computers can return to what they are supposed to do . . . .

And finally, he echoed the typical wishful thinking of all strong chess players: "The current programs will plateau about where they are because of limitations of computing power in exploring the game."

David Levy quantified his prediction to the half-point. "I predict he will win by at least 4.5 – 1.5. Kasparov will find it easier to put into practice what he learned last time than the Deep Blue team will" [12].

Kasparov, expressed self-confidence. James Kim's pre-match article in *USA Today* [16] on May 2, 1997, quoted Kasparov as saying, "I'm going to beat it absolutely," adding, "We will beat machines for some time to come."

About the only ones who felt Deep Blue had any chance were the members of the Deep Blue team. CB Hsu told Bruce Weber that "At this point last year I didn't believe we could win. This year is different" [15]. Murray Campbell was quoted in *Computing Canada* [7] in April 1997 as saying, "The match will be at a higher level than it was last year, and it will be very close." Joel Benjamin, when interviewed by Andy Soltis in an article that appeared in the *New York Post* [10] on April 28, 1997, said, "I think it's going to be a close match." CJ Tan was quite clear when talking to Steven Levy of *Newsweek*. He said, "I truly think we have a system which is far superior to what we had last year." He predicted that "we will win this match, overwhelmingly" [17].

References

[1] Bruce Weber, "The experts that built Deep Blue," *The New York Times*, July 6, 1996.

[2] Bruce Weber, "Rested, reprogrammed and ready," *The New York Times*, August 20, 1996.

[3] Phil Waga, "Kasparov, IBM plan man vs. machine rematch," *The Reporter Dispatch*, Gannett Suburban Newspapers, August 21, 1996.

[4] Michael Krantz, "Deeper in thought," *Time*, March 10, 1997.

[5] Randy Ray, "IBM's chess master is back for Round 2," *The Globe and Mail*, March 18, 1997.

[6] Brian Santo, "IBM tweaks Deep Blue for man–machine rematch," *EE Times*, March 24, 1997.

[7] Paula Anderton, "IBM takes on Kasparov in chess re-match," *Computing Canada*, April 1997.

[8] Robert Uhlig, "The king toppled?" *Daily Telegraph*, April 8, 1997.

[9] Andy Soltis, "Deep Blue set to re-boot for rematch," *New York Post*, April 13, 1997.

[10] Andy Soltis, "Chess king aims to send IBM foe back to cyberia," *New York Post*, April 28, 1997.

[11] Malcolm Pein, "Kasparov prepares for battle with Deep Blue," *Daily Telegraph*, April 29, 1997.

[12] Michael Antonoff, "Game, net & match," *Yahoo Internet Life*, May 1997.

[13] Mark Saylor, "Computers cast a long shadow on chessboard," *Los Angeles Times*, May 1, 1997.

[14] "Kasparov challenger receives an upgrade," *The New York Times*, May 1, 1997.

[15] Bruce Weber, "Man vs. machine: A rematch," *The New York Times*, May 1, 1997.

[16] James Kim, ""More than just chess. But not as simple as man vs. computer," *USA Today*, May 2, 1997.

[17] Steven Levy, "Man vs. machine," *Newsweek*, pp. 51–55, May 5, 1997.

[18] Sean Hathorn, "Mind will checkmate machine" (letter to the Editor), *USA Today*, May 7, 1997.

10   The Rematch – Game 1: Three Straight for Kasparov

> "It's already different from Philadelphia,"
> Garry Kasparov, after Game 1.

May 3, 1997, New York
Game 1, IBM Kasparov versus Deep Blue Rematch
White: Garry Kasparov   Black: Deep Blue
Reti Opening

On the morning of the first game of the IBM Kasparov versus Deep Blue Rematch, and on every subsequent morning throughout the match, the IBMers gathered around 8:30 over breakfast on the Michaelangelo Hotel's second-floor mezzanine to plan strategy for the day. The atmosphere was light. Discussions over breakfast revolved around the

Garry Kasparov and Feng-hsiung Hsu are all smiles as they shake hands before the beginning of the first game of the Rematch.

previous day's game and related newspaper articles. After breakfast, several organizational meetings were held, beginning with a general meeting to discuss such matters as media plans, the IBM website, and the games themselves. CJ Tan chaired the meeting, with Marcy Holle and George Paul helping out. The Deep Blue team then met to discuss strategy for the upcoming game, while Holle and the TSI group met to plan PR activities. Interviews with the media filled the rest of the morning. The lunch hour was unplanned, with most people grabbing a bite at nearby delis or sushi bars. Time flew by quickly in the hours leading up to the start of each game. In the evening after each game, members of the Deep Blue team remained working in the Equitable until they were shooed out. They then simply continued in their Michaelangelo rooms, looking over the logs of the previous games, and modifying Deep Blue's opening book for the upcoming game. Other members of the large IBM contingency were also occupied with preparations for the next game, but found time to enjoy dinner at the Michaelangelo and nearby restaurants.

Well in advance of the 3:00 start of the first game, the commentary auditorium was filling up. Chess and computer enthusiasts were sitting quietly, talking in low tones. Robert Morris (Tan's immediate boss), director of Personal Systems and Advanced Systems, opened the introductions, welcoming the several hundred attendees. Vice President Paul Horn followed, pointing out the importance of the event:

> IBM Research has pulled together what I believe is one of the strongest collections of technical talent ever assembled. You may know that that's the group that invented the disk drive, the DRAM, relational databases, RISC architecture — the list goes on and on. Five Nobel prize winners, numerous national medals for technology and science. And over the last eight years, some of the best of that technical talent has been focusing on a problem that's as old as computer science, the problem of computer chess. What we're talking about today and thinking about today goes far beyond the ability of a computer to supplement man's ability to play chess. It's one of the fundamental issues of the twenty-first century. IBM, just one company, has 170,000 home pages on the Internet. It would take a fast reader, operating seven days a week full time, five years to read it all. And that's just one company. We talk about the twenty-first century being the information age, but all that data is going to be useless unless it can be boiled down into something that is useful, transforming random pieces of information into useful information and ultimately into knowledge and potentially wisdom.

I followed Horn, reminding the audience of the results of last year's match, and adding that the Rematch ought to be even more exciting with both Deep Blue and Kasparov playing yet stronger chess. I then introduced the commentators, Maurice Ashley, Yasser Seirawan, and Mike Valvo, who proceeded to chat with the audience until the game started. Ashley asked Seirawan whether computers "had gotten good enough now to whip the best human being," to which Seirawan answered plainly and unequivocally "no," drawing relief and laughter from the audience. Valvo was less sure, venturing that "the computer definitely has a chance." Briefly discussing the future of the game of chess if Deep Blue should win, Seirawan observed, "I'll always want to beat my brother — or Maurice!" Of the three commentators, Seirawan was the tops on chess wizardry, Ashley in painting vivid and picturesque images of the battle, and Valvo in giving a balanced view of the games. Throughout the match, Seirawan and Ashley invariably saw Kasparov as having the better position while Valvo generally saw matters more evenhandedly.

Upstairs on the 35th floor, the game room was filling up. Marcy Holle was trying to maintain some semblance of order among the photographers as the two teams and officials took their places. Garry Kasparov arrived promptly five minutes before the 3:00 start looking "chipper" in Ashley's words, confident and relaxed, smartly dressed in a light-gray suit and vest. Feng-hsiung Hsu, who had been sitting at the board for some time making final preparations, rose to his feet to greet Kasparov, dressed his equal in a

Robert Morris.

dark-blue suit, looking no less confident though perhaps not quite as relaxed. He and Kasparov shook hands, both smiling ear to ear, while photographers captured the moment. There was great excitement in the air.

After the handshake, the players got down to business. They both sat down, while the photographers continued flashing away from all corners of the room. Kasparov's smiles of a few minutes earlier yielded to what Ashley referred to as his serious "game face," as the start of the match approached.

Methodically using his left hand, Kasparov first meticulously adjusted each of his pieces to the very center of its square, then readied his score sheet to the right of the board. Being left-handed, I always notice what other people use their left hand for. For Kasparov, it was limited to adjusting his pieces before each game, leaving the mechanics of moving pieces and punching the clock to his right.

Across the board, Hsu was calmly focused on a new futuristic flat-screen terminal that IBM had brought to the site. Deep Blue was all set to begin. Carol Jarecki sat quietly at her desk off to the front side of the room, preoccupied with concerns about the clock. Klara Kasparova and Kasparov's assistants were stationed at the back of the room. About 50 photographers squeezed their way into every available space in the minutes leading up to the start, shoving their cameras within inches of Kasparov's face trying for a close-up picture. There were, in fact, two shifts of photographers, each given about five minutes apiece to take pictures of the participants. They had to be virtually dragged out after overstaying their allotted time.

Kasparov had the first move. After a barely perceptible nod of his head in response to Jarecki's directive to begin, he brought out his knight to g3. The match was underway.*

In Philadelphia Kasparov opened all three games when playing White by bringing out his knight to f3, characterizing a Reti opening, and then advancing his queen's pawn to d4, winning two and a half of a possible three points. He returned to the same strategy here. However, instead of advancing his queen's pawn on the second move as he had done previously, he prepared to fianchetto his king's bishop — that is, placing it on the g2 square — by advancing his g-pawn one square. This alternate choice gave him the option of later transposing back into one of the lines played in Philadelphia, but this never happened. He was likely attempting to void work done by the Deep Blue team to thwart his strong, successful Reti opening. Further, he may have thought that this more passive line had better chances to elicit weak positional moves from his opponent. The Deep

---

* The moves from the games of this match appear, with the approximate time each player took, in Appendix J.

Blue team had invested considerable effort in the Reti, mostly in anticipation of Kasparov advancing his d-pawn, but Kasparov's choice of a move here also received some attention.

Deep Blue's second move, bishop to b4, played from its book, was an attempt to draw Kasparov into an early tactical skirmish. While probably not surprised by this popular move, Kasparov nevertheless, after playing his first two moves in a few seconds each, spent over three minutes on this one. This was an early indication by Kasparov that Deep Blue '97 might be more of a challenge than Deep Blue '96.

Kasparov's third move, advancing his b-pawn one square, took Deep Blue out of its opening book. According to Michael Khodarkovsky, Kasparov was more interested in learning about Deep Blue's evaluation function than fianchetting his king's bishop, and his third move gave Deep Blue the option of capturing the knight on f3 and doubling pawns in exchange for a bishop [3]. Kasparov observed that Deep Blue valued its bishop as worth more than its opponent's knight and doubled pawns, since it preferred to keep the bishop and to continue developing its pieces.

After his sixth move, Kasparov removed his watch, an Audemars Piguet Royal Oak, and placed it alongside his scorecard, a mechanical ritual in every one of his games, signaling the beginning of serious play. Over the next three moves, he continued his strategy of pursuing a quiet opening, intended to solicit an opening inaccuracy from his opponent. Kasparov's eighth move transposed the game back into Deep Blue's book, from which the computer selected its next two moves. On his ninth move, Kasparov again offered the exchange of his knight for a bishop, although this time without garnering himself with doubled pawns, and again Deep Blue backed off — this time though because the response, retreating the bishop to h5, was found in its opening book

After his 10th move, Kasparov got up from the table and took a short walk. After most of his moves and especially after the opening moves, he would leave the table for anywhere from a few seconds to several minutes. Sometimes he would get up immediately upon completing his move; at other times he would sit for a while before leaving. He would usually wait long enough to be sure Deep Blue wasn't ready to reply immediately to his move. He usually then went off to his small lounge area in the game room, although as the match progressed, he often simply paced behind the board. He usually returned when Deep Blue moved, but occasionally, when he had plenty of time on his clock, he returned as much as a minute later. When he left the table, he usually had a good idea how long it would be before Deep Blue would play. Deep Blue was fairly, but far from perfectly, predictable. In this first game, Kasparov left the table on all moves at one point or another except moves 1 through 9 of the opening phase, moves 26, 29, and 31 when the positions were filled with tactical complications, moves 37 through 40 when he wanted to be sure he would complete his first 40 moves in the allotted time, and moves 46 and 47, when he was waiting for Deep Blue to resign so he could go to dinner.

Deep Blue's 11th move took everyone by surprise — an unanticipated queen move to the far side of the board — and was just what Kasparov was waiting for. Kasparov made an assortment of faces. The queen had apparently taken a trip to Nowheresville! Daniel King called it a "truly ugly move" [2]. Since Deep Blue gives credit for queen mobility, with nothing in particular needing attention on the board, its move, in retrospect, was no major surprise. It is hard to train the queen not to wander off into open space. The audience in the commentary auditorium felt Deep Blue would soon be dead silicon if it played any more moves like this one. Could the computer get away with such an apparently miserable move?

With no targets to put pressure on, Deep Blue's 12th move, an unimpressive move by its bishop, again suggested that the computer was having difficulties in finding a purpose. Ashley conjectured that Kasparov was saying to himself, "How dare you play this move against me!" Seirawan took a poll of the audience and found 75% thought Kasparov was going to win the game. Imagine, after only 12 moves, 75% of the audience felt Deep Blue was finished! Deep Blue had now made two consecutive moves that the experts had panned.

Kasparov's 12th move, moving a knight to h4, was an invitation to Deep Blue to get itself into yet deeper trouble. Deep Blue obliged, advancing its g-pawn on its 13th move, dangerously weakening the defense of its king. Combined with the two previous weak moves, this move further convinced the audience that Kasparov was in for an easy ride. Kasparov himself must have concluded his opening strategy had been successful. Daniel King called Deep Blue's 13th move "quite daft" [2], while David Goodman and Raymond Keene described it as a "strategic blunder" [1]. Seirawan thought it was a "terrible positional concession" and considered "Black's position to be strategically lost" [15]. With Deep Blue's queen out of play and the defenses around its king softened, the experts felt that Kasparov was in good shape to coast to a routine victory.

Hsu, watching Deep Blue's calculations from his vantage point at the board, must have felt like an anxious father, hoping that his offspring would do as taught, suppressing his fears that it would do otherwise. For 12 years, Hsu had been training his electronic child; most of the time it listened to him but sometimes it didn't. He realized that the weak Deep Blue moves contradicted his training, and he was worried that others even more catastrophic might follow.

Beginning on the 15th move, Hsu could be seen unconsciously clinging to his Evian water bottle, like a small child holding on to his blanket. During the match, Hsu's anxieties were mostly internalized, but there were periods when he would cling to and fidget with whatever was near, usually his pen, water bottle, or tie. Kasparov is known for bringing out these sort of feelings in his human opponents, and Hsu, though not quite in that category, responded in kind.

Looking across the board at Hsu could not have been a positive experience for Kasparov either. His own at-the-board customary expressiveness would have no impact on his opponent. His deep stares at his opponent, his rising from the table when everything was in good shape on the board, his taking off and putting back on his watch — all were wasted moves if intended to affect an opponent. Every one of his movements did in fact receive attention in the commentary auditorium, but he was unaware of it.

Kasparov's circumstance cannot help but bring to mind Viktor Korchnoi's experience against Boris Spassky in a match for the world title in 1978. Spassky had been instructed by his handlers not to look at Korchnoi, to spend as much time as possible away from the game table, and to show up only to make his moves. Michael Stean, who covered the match for *Chess Life & Review*, wrote in the May 1978 issue that,

> I made a habit of turning up late for the start of a game (in fact, I'm always late for everything), but when I strolled in after some thirty or forty minutes of play in the 10th game, I sensed something was wrong. The crowd seemed restive, officials were running backwards and forwards with looks of blank bewilderment on their faces. I couldn't understand what the matter was until I glanced onto the stage. There was nobody there! Spassky's clock was running, his position was advertised on the two giant demonstration boards, but the two chairs at the chess table were empty. I asked what was happening and was informed that Spassky was spending his entire time away from the board and was only appearing on stage to make his move before retiring once more into oblivion. Very strange.

In a letter of complaint to the officials, Korchnoi claimed that,

> Spassky's behavior worries and distracts me. I am sitting at the board trying to concentrate and he will suddenly appear, make a move, then disappear. I do not know when he will come back, if he will come back. I do not have the sensation of playing a real game. It is like playing against a ghost.

Here in New York, Kasparov must have had some of the same feelings.

The decision to remove the game from an observing audience had been made at Kasparov's request. Somewhere along the line when the Philadelphia match was being organized, Kasparov had asked for a closed environment for the games, evidently concerned that an audience might distract him unfairly. But in fact, in the isolated environment in which the games were played, Kasparov missed out on feeling the strong support that his followers were indeed giving him in the commentary auditorium. Following the Rematch, Gabby Silberman suggested to me that in future matches with computers, Kasparov should again play in a room with an audience.

Great performers and athletes feed on the crowd, using the energy of the spectators to raise their level of play. Of course, this must be weighed against being distracted by the crowd, but great athletes have learned to cope. Pete Sampras has survived innumerable catcalls at inopportune times, and as in chess, concentration is an important factor in tennis. If Sampras can manage, so can Kasparov. In baseball the great hitters are constantly harassed by the catcher's banter as they try to hit a three-inch ball moving at 90 miles an hour, twisting and swerving on its path from the pitcher to home plate. Kasparov evidently thought the positive benefits of interactions with the crowd were outweighed by the distractions he might face while his opponent would be entirely unaffected.

Kasparov appeared hard at work for the first time on his 16th move, a move that continued the theme of giving Deep Blue nothing to shoot at. CJ Tan and Joe Hoane joined the commentators on stage at this point. Tan, with a big sheepish smile on his face, wanted to know what Fritz4 thought of the game! Hoane was questioned about Deep Blue's search techniques by the audience, to which he responded with great enthusiasm. Meanwhile, with little else happening on the board, Deep Blue set up an indirect attack on Kasparov's king on its 16th move. Kasparov was away from the board, as he had been for many moves, returning almost a minute after Deep Blue played, evidently reflecting satisfaction with his position.

Kasparov's 17th move, moving his queen to c1, was consistent with his waiting game. He was quietly building up an attack on the kingside. From her new c1 square, the queen became a distant attacker of Black's pawn on h6. Deep Blue's 18th move, advancing its pawn to a5, was another example of the goal of the computer's evaluation function to gain space.

Following Deep Blue's 18th move, CJ Tan thanked Mike Valvo and Yasser Seirawan for letting him know what Fritz4 thought of the situation, and then he and Hoane left the stage of the commentary auditorium, setting off for the IBM operations room.

After a pawn exchange initiated by Deep Blue on its 19th move, the computer then advanced a bishop to c5, threatening White's f-pawn. Despite increased mobility, Black's pawns were now awkwardly placed. The next few moves by both sides increased the tension on the board.

Then, when Deep Blue played its 22nd move, advancing a pawn to g4, Kasparov displayed a brief smirk on his face. Deep Blue seemed to be playing with fire here, putting its h-pawn in danger and potentially exposing its king to a devastating attack. Tactical complications on the board were increasing. Daniel King called this move "ugly" [2], while Yasser Seirawan [15] and King felt that 22 ... Bg6 was a better move in this position, defending the f5 square. On his 23rd move, Kasparov routinely captured Deep Blue's g-pawn with his h-pawn, and then Deep Blue recaptured with its knight.

Frederic Friedel joined the commentators on stage following the captures. He discussed Kasparov's use of computers and his preparation for the match, pointing out that Kasparov expends so much energy during a game that he loses two pounds. Meanwhile, in the game room, Kasparov was thinking long and hard before playing his 24th move, advancing a pawn to f3, a move that seemed to invite trouble for him by increasing tactical complications. Seirawan and King both suggested 24 Nxg4 Bxg4 25 Ne3 [15,2] as alternatives, and Benjamin concurred, adding one more move to the line, 25 ... Nf6 [65].

Knights were next exchanged on e3, and then Deep Blue retreated its bishop to e7, evidently planning to move it to g5. After the game, Kasparov said that he had overlooked this move. "Backward" moves by pieces seem to account for a disproportionate number of oversights by humans even at the highest levels of play. Computers search equally in all directions when calculating their moves.

Kasparov took eight minutes planning his 26th move. His legs shook under the table, releasing nervous energy. His head also shook back and forth, expressing his unhappiness with the position. Ashley, in the commentary auditorium, joked about how bad a poker player he would be. When Kasparov finally moved, he elected to move his king to the h1 square, temporarily relieving the pin on his knight on e3. For the first time since the opening stage of the game, he remained at the board thinking on Deep Blue's time.

Deep Blue followed through on its 26th move, placing a bishop on g5, once again pinning White's knight on e3, while simultaneously defending its own pawn on h6 [3]. Deep Blue was fighting back!

Kasparov, after playing 27 Re2 to beef up the defense of its pinned knight, had only 27 minutes remaining until the first time control, giving him an average of about two minutes per move.

The complications on the kingside of the board spread to the queenside when Deep Blue advanced its a-pawn one square on its 27th move. The move forced Kasparov to respond by advancing his b-pawn one square.

Deep Blue's 28th move, fearlessly advancing a pawn to f5, set the scene for a real blood bath. Ashley said the "board is in flames!" Deep Blue showed that its tactical play had improved over the past year. It calculated a material gain of a rook for a bishop and pawn, but underestimated the difficulties it would face from Kasparov's pawns and its own exposed king. When Kasparov captured on f5, Seirawan said that the "variations are very tricky and complex here. White has to work its way through a minefield of tactics . . . "[15]. For a rare second, Kasparov looked up at Hsu sitting across the table with his head lowered.

On the 29th move, Deep Blue advanced its e-pawn, continuing its fearless aggression. Kasparov countered by advancing his own f-pawn, accepting the exchange of a rook for his opponent's bishop and an earlier-sacrificed pawn. He was counting on his advanced kingside pawns and his opponent's exposed king to give him sufficient compensation.

After the exchange, Deep Blue advanced its knight to e5. It could not play 31 ... hxg5 because 32 Nc4 Bxc4 33 Qxg5+ is followed by mate. A smile broke across Hsu's face in a brief show of emotion.

From here until the end of the game, Kasparov held the upper hand. His 33rd move crushed any plans that Deep Blue might have had of moving its rook to the seventh rank. Though the rook controlled the d-file, there was no square to which it could move to improve its position.

Deep Blue's 33rd move, transferring its queen to b5, showed that it was willing to exchange queens, in part because its evaluation function was

Marcy Holle, Joe Hoane, CJ Tan, and Miguel Illescas talking
with members of the media halfway through Game 1.

happy to reduce material on the board when it possessed a material advantage. The move also slightly increased the mobility of its queen. In addition, Deep Blue must have noted Kasparov's queen taking dead aim on its defenseless pawn on h6. Deep Blue had little choice in this position where the momentum of the game was clearly with its opponent. In the commentary auditorium, Frederic Friedel wound up his observations on Kasparov and Fritz4, with Ashley thanking him for his visit to the stage.

Queens left the board after Kasparov, accepting Deep Blue's invitation to exchange them, played 34 Qf1. Kasparov's move was motivated in part by Deep Blue's threat to advance its queen to e2, potentially causing some havoc deep in Kasparov's territory. Kasparov's queen move foiled that plan.

Deep Blue may have had chances to draw the game as late as the 36th move. Although Kasparov had a clear advantage at this point, if Deep Blue had been able to exchange away sufficient material, Kasparov might have found himself unable to finish off his opponent. Instead of playing 36 ... Kf8, David Goodman and Raymond Keene [1] wrote that 36 ... Ng4 37 f6 Re6 38 Bh3 Rxf6 39 Bxg4 Rxg6 40 Bh3 Rxg3+ 41 Kh2 Rg5 42 Rf2 Rd6 leads to a "situation that is far from clear!" Hsu and Campbell, after testing the position on Deep Blue after the match, concluded that Deep Blue could have had "good drawing chances" if it had played 36 ... Ng4. This possibility was not considered at all in the commentary auditorium, where the game had been pretty well awarded to Kasparov. After 36 ... Kf8, Deep Blue's fate was clear: a loss in Game 1.

Occasionally sipping his bottled water, Hsu looked dejected as he watched Kasparov play 37 Bh3. Across the board, Kasparov exhibited the confidence of a tiger ready to pounce: highly excited, oozing energy, with his whole body in perpetual motion. His only challenge was a slight shortage of time on his clock, only 12 minutes to make four moves to time control. Though no serious problem, it did eliminate any long deliberation and contrasted sharply with Deep Blue's reservoir of 43 minutes.

After the 40th move, Campbell replaced Hsu at the board, internalizing many of the same anxieties as had Hsu. Kasparov completed his 40th move with about 4 minutes to spare, looking confident as the game wound down to his satisfaction. Deep Blue completed its 40th move with about 35 minutes to spare.

Deep Blue's position gradually deteriorated over the coming moves. On its 44th move, a devilish bug suddenly surfaced, causing a random, totally illogical move! Campbell later confided,

> The move was incredibly bad. Deep Blue's score dropped about 300 points, the equivalent of three pawns. The bug started showing up in 1996,

early 1997. It showed up in a game with Larry Christiansen, where Deep Blue gave away a pawn when it played 13 ... f5, though it was able to eventually draw the game. [See Game One between Deep Blue Junior and Larry Christiansen in Appendix I]. The bug was fixed then — almost. It turned out that the bug could arise in five ways, and only four of the five ways had been eliminated; the fifth was overlooked and sure enough, it came up here!

The logs confirmed the presence of the bug, and that evening Hoane worked to eliminate it.

According to Campbell, the move was of great consequence, because,

Kasparov saw this move and asked his own team why Deep Blue made it. They didn't know. They looked at alternatives, and found they lost also. So they conjectured that Deep Blue had looked 30–40 levels ahead at the alternatives — they were overestimating Deep Blue's talents here — and saw that all the moves lost, and that it didn't matter what was played, so it played a random move. Now, of course, this wasn't the case at all, but it perhaps gave Kasparov a false impression about what Deep Blue could do.

Campbell felt that this might have been a factor in the next game where, in the final position, Kasparov overestimated Deep Blue's strength.

On his 45th move, Kasparov advanced his g-pawn to the penultimate rank and then returned his watch to his wrist, signaling time for dinner. Ashley pointed out that "White is about to have a baby girl." In spite of the fact that Deep Blue hadn't reached the point where it would normally resign, Campbell tendered a resignation on the computer's behalf, extending his hand to Kasparov.

Kasparov and Campbell, who had sat across the table from one another in silence for some time, broke out into a friendly animated discussion about the game. Others on the Deep Blue team and on Kasparov's team quickly gathered alongside the game table for a minute of congratulations.

Kasparov and the Deep Blue team appeared on stage in the commentary auditorium several minutes later. The world champion arrived first, all smiles and savoring his victory in this tremendous struggle. He received a standing ovation, as did the Deep Blue team, which followed behind him. "It's already different from Philadelphia," Kasparov began, adding that he felt he had to survive the middlegame and then win the endgame. Once the queens were exchanged, he concluded he could no longer lose, and that after 37 Bh3 he was probably winning. Tan kidded Kasparov, pointing out that the match might repeat Philadelphia, where the winner of the first game was set on his/its ears in the second game. Campbell simply added, "We have some work to do tonight."

Based on this game, however, Kasparov's supporters questioned whether Deep Blue had improved since Philadelphia, contending that the computer's positional play showed no improvement. In his book, Daniel King says that there was "little evidence of any design or plan, ... little flow to its play," concluding that "perhaps one day we will have to accept that there are many ways to play chess successfully, but from the evidence of this game, it will be some time to come" [2].

It is interesting to observe that while Deep Blue lost Game 1, it was never behind in material, symptomatic of the tactical difficulties that Kasparov was about to face in the coming games. Of course, even though many chess games are won by the side down in material, there is often a correlation between having more material on the board and winning the game. In the Philadelphia match, for the record, Deep Blue was up two pawns at the end of its victorious first-round game, down two pawns at the end of its lost second-round game, equal in material in the drawn third-round game, and down a pawn in its lost fifth-round game. Though up a rook for a bishop and pawn in the fourth-round game, Deep Blue settled for a draw, and though up a pawn in the sixth-round game, it was outplayed otherwise and lost.

As a precursor of things to come, Deep Blue had diverted Kasparov away from his apparent game plan of avoiding a fierce tactical battle. Kasparov had smothered Deep Blue in Game 6 in Philadelphia, and many felt he could again impose his strategy at will. Although the first 20 moves of this first game of the Rematch went Kasparov's way, the very kind of fierce battle that he probably preferred to avoid did in fact take place over the next 10 moves or so.

Moreover, even late in the game, with Kasparov's pawns menacing, Deep Blue still might have been able to draw with 36 ... Ng4. This was amazing, given its moves that were so strongly criticized by the experts, including Daniel King's words, a "truly ugly" 11th move, a "horrible" 12th move, a "daft" 13th move, and an "ugly" 22nd move [2]! In his comments regarding the first 36 moves of the game, Yasser Seirawan placed a question mark — indicating a bad move — next to four of Deep Blue's moves (moves 11, 12, 13, and 22) and only one of Kasparov's moves (move 24), but placed an exclamation mark — indicating a good move —next to four of Deep Blue's moves (moves 25, 28, 31, and 35) and seven of Kasparov's moves (moves 15, 16, 18, 30, 32, 33, and 36) [15].

The fact that Deep Blue played its moves more quickly than Kasparov hinted at problems for Kasparov in the coming games. He couldn't afford to play more slowly than he had here, although Deep Blue could slow down a little. Deep Blue reached the 40-move time control with over 30 minutes to spare, while Kasparov reached the same point with only several minutes remaining. If Deep Blue seemed sufficiently reliable based on the experience of the first few rounds, its programmers could instruct it to play more slowly in later rounds, thus increasing its strength by some small but possibly significant factor.

Thus, while the Deep Blue team would have preferred to see its computer emerge victorious, the team members were focusing on the positive side of the defeat. It had tested the new version of Deep Blue against the old one and were confident the new version was much stronger. In head-to-head competition, the new version won about 80% of the points. In contrast, in Philadelphia Kasparov had won only 66% of the points (4–2), though six games is an insufficient number on which to base any strong conclusions. Moreover, the Deep Blue team observed that Deep Blue had held its own tactically in this game and that it hadn't allowed Kasparov to control the way the game was played. And finally, the team had learned long ago that one game was insufficient to establish a pattern.

With one round complete, Kasparov led Deep Blue with a 1–0 score.

11 The Rematch – Game 2:
Internet Finds Break for Deep Blue

"A computer program on the Internet Chess Club amusingly called Ferret had claimed the final position in Game 2 was a draw! Moreover, no GM could be found to refute this crazy notion," Malcolm Pein [16].

May 4, 1997, New York
Game 2, IBM Kasparov versus Deep Blue Rematch
White: Deep Blue   Black: Garry Kasparov
Ruy Lopez

Deep Blue had now lost three games in a row. Some argued that its chances looked bleak in the coming games. However, two of the three losses were last year, and the new Deep Blue had been worked on intensively since then. Moreover, even though Deep Blue lost the first game of this match, it put up a real fight. Nevertheless, for whatever reasons, it was now three straight losses.

As scheduled, Game 2 began at 3:00 sharp. Murray Campbell had arrived a few minutes earlier and readied the computer. Marcy Holle, George Paul, and TSI's Kelly Fitzgerald were trying to attend to the photographers. Downstairs in the commentary auditorium, the previous day's game was being reviewed by Yasser Seirawan, Maurice Ashley, and Mike Valvo. When Kasparov entered, Campbell rose, and the two shook hands briefly with warm smiles, but a lot less fanfare than the day before. Then it was down to business. Kasparov removed his watch, adjusted his pieces, and immediately went into his deep pre-game concentration.

Campbell provided me with the number of levels Deep Blue searched on each move of this second-round game. The first 17 moves played from its opening book involved no search by Deep Blue. After that, on each move,

Deep Blue examined a tree of moves to a depth of from 10 to 12 levels. The precise depth is included with the time consumed on each move in the game's presentation in Appendix J.

Deep Blue opened Game 2 with its usual advance of its e-pawn. Kasparov, playing Black, provided an immediate surprise by avoiding the Sicilian Defense, his favorite, and the Petroff, played in his Philadelphia Game 5 victory. Here he selected the Ruy Lopez, an opening he had played only a few times in his career. The Deep Blue team had given this classic Spanish opening little specific preparation. Joel Benjamin had played several Ruy Lopez games against the computer and found it handled them quite well. There seemed to be little reason to invest more effort in this particular opening when there were others that seemed more relevant. Almost all preparation had gone into the Sicilian Defense, a much more complex opening for the computer than the Ruy Lopez. It was far more likely to be played by Kasparov, according to Campbell, who claimed that,

> 90% of our opening book is dedicated to the Sicilian, maybe only 80%, because he doesn't play the Caro-Kann any more, not since he was a kid, and he doesn't play the Ruy Lopez (only four times in his career), and few Petroffs. We have book lines for these openings, but they are far from extensive, and we didn't spend a lot of time on them. Garry picked this Ruy Lopez to obtain a closed position, and that is what he got, but it was a bad

Garry takes his time before playing 9 ... h6,
while Murray Campbell looks on.

closed position. He had to suffer a long time. If he had wanted to draw, he would have had to suffer for many moves in a bad position, and it was too difficult.

With the exception of Kasparov's ninth move, each side played the first 17 moves in several seconds. On his ninth move, Kasparov didn't play immediately, but sat thinking for about seven minutes while the commentator tried to understand why. His move "was a bit of a surprise" according to Maurice Ashley, taking Deep Blue out of its book. Was Kasparov trying to determine the extent of the computer's opening book? Mike Valvo suggested that maybe Kasparov had reached a point where he was trying to decide between one of several moves, as there are a number of possibilities for Black in this position. Yasser Seirawan wasn't so sure. He felt that Kasparov was simply taking a breather, "kinda getting the Zen of the position. I don't think he thought he'd reach this position so quickly." The photographers were given walking orders while Kasparov was deciding on his move, so he might have taken some time to refocus his attention following the commotion they caused.

It was Deep Blue who unexpectedly forced a closed position by advancing its d-pawn on the 16th move. Experts argue that such positions are

Commentators Mike Valvo, Maurice Ashley, and Yasser Seirawan discussing Game 2 with the audience.

handled better by humans, not computers. However, guiding play here was not Deep Blue's search strategy, but rather its exploitation of the large database of grandmaster games stored in its extended opening book. Was this book leading the computer into a tricky positional opening that might be difficult to handle later? Would Deep Blue later have trouble finding good moves when depending on its own search of the chess tree? Time would tell.

On its 18th move and for the first time in the game, Deep Blue took more than several seconds to play its move, spending more than 4 minutes to carry out an 11-level search. Moves 10 though 17 were picked from the extended opening book, as were this 18th one and the next. However, unlike moves 10 through 17, the scores found in the extended opening book for moves 18 and 19 were not high enough to prevent Deep Blue from conducting a full search.

Playing the first 17 moves at a 5-second rate may have had an influence on Kasparov's choice of openings in later games. This Ruy Lopez was not an opening that he was expected to play. If Deep Blue was booked so extensively for this opening, Kasparov may have concluded that his favorite lines were booked even more extensively. The distinction between opening book moves and extended opening book moves was not obvious to him by the way the computer made its moves. That is, Kasparov couldn't have deduced that the first nine moves were selected from the opening book while the next series of moves were found in the extended opening book. He only would have noted that Deep Blue was taking five seconds to make each of its first 17 moves.

Kasparov's 19th move invited an exchange of knights. Deep Blue accepted. *Washington Post* chess correspondent Grandmaster Lubomir Kavalek was in the audience. When introduced and asked his opinion by Yasser Seirawan, Kavalek replied that he felt Kasparov's proposed exchange was a good idea and that, in general, Black best trade off some pieces to gain space. Perhaps Kasparov was hoping that Deep Blue would weaken the defense of its king by advancing its pawns, just as it had done in the first game. The knight exchange was necessary to permit the pawns to advance.

On the 21st move, Deep Blue positioned its queen to have influence on both the kingside and the queenside, forcing Kasparov to retreat his own queen for defensive purposes. For the first time, Kasparov seemed hard at work over the board.

After Kasparov retreated his queen on his 21st move, Deep Blue found itself in a good position to put pressure on Black. Kasparov had all his pieces restricted to the first two ranks, reminiscent of Deep Blue's misfortune in Game 6 of their Philadelphia match and almost a repeat of Kasparov's own state of affairs in Game 1 of this match.

When Deep Blue played its 22nd move, just three moves out of its extended book, Seirawan said, "I love White's position." Kasparov was not looking particularly happy at this point, looking intent on finding a way to proceed.

Maurice Ashley, among others, was very impressed with Deep Blue's 23rd rook move, "a deep positional move." It was a calculated investment on the part of Deep Blue, evidently encouraging Kasparov to advance his c-pawn on the next move. According to Murray Campbell, the rook move was a result of recent modifications to Deep Blue's evaluation function that gave credit for screened attacks. Kasparov pointed out after the game that 23 ... Qb7 was stronger than the move he had played — his pawn advance — which closed the queenside at a time when Black needed to do just the opposite. Joel Benjamin joined the commentators on stage at this point and proceeded to discuss his role in developing Deep Blue's opening book and Kasparov's concern over not having received any Deep Blue games played since the contract signing. The contract had a provision requiring the Deep Blue team to give Kasparov all officially-played games, but Benjamin said there just weren't any.

Over the next two moves, both sides jockeyed their pieces behind their respective pawn walls. Then, on its 26th move, Deep Blue advanced a pawn to f4, expanding its influence in the center and creating long-term opportunities for its rooks along that file. This created a second battlefront for Kasparov to be concerned about. Benjamin likened the move to "a basketball team spreading its players all over the court, forcing its opponent to do the same."

Following Kasparov's 26th move which centralized his knight, pawns were exchanged on e5. Then Deep Blue moved its queen to f1. It could have moved the queen to f2 at this point, instead of on its next move, but the move played kept this option open. In addition, moving the queen to f1 gave the queen a route to the queenside to add pressure on the a-file. Robert Byrne observed that "Deep Blue has the initiative here and superior mobility" [26]. Benjamin left the stage of the commentary auditorium at this juncture and returned upstairs to the IBM operations room.

When Kasparov makes a move, he usually makes it with a deliberate motion. His hand reaches out with confidence, and in a continuous motion, descends on the piece and transfers it to its new square. His 31st move was an exception everybody noticed. He extended his hand over the board, hesitated, and then several seconds later, moved his bishop to e7 and punched his clock. What raced through his mind in that brief period will remain a small mystery, but it was likely a reflection of his growing anxiety over his position.

Deep Blue's 31st and 32nd moves were thought out on Kasparov's time, giving him no chance to grab a breather. After Deep Blue's 32nd move, its clock showed 74 minutes to time control compared to Kasparov's 48 minutes.

Kasparov took approximately 18 minutes to make his 32nd move, retreating his bishop to f8. Instead of this move, Deep Blue was expecting Kasparov to recapture with his knight assigning a small advantage to itself. While Kasparov was deciding on his move, CB Hsu replaced Murray Campbell at the board, and Patrick Wolff, twice U.S. Champion, joined the commentators on stage. One of Patrick's first observations was that it looked "quite good for Deep Blue."

Deep Blue's 33rd move, posting its knight on f5, was "a dramatic decision," according to Maurice Ashley. Deep Blue was expecting 33 ... Nxf5 34 exf5 bxa4 with a small advantage for itself, but Kasparov chose to capture with the bishop. After Deep Blue recaptured with its e-pawn, Kasparov was left with few moves to improve his position. Hsu sat calmly holding a pen in his hand as he watched his protégé find one strong move after another.

Kasparov's 34th move, advancing his f-pawn one square, led to an even more closed position. This was a complete reversal of roles played in the sixth game in Philadelphia. Anatoly Karpov was quoted by Bruce Weber as

The audience in the commentary auditorium watching Kasparov as he waits for Deep Blue to play its 35th move.

saying "Black is dead" after this move [30]. Fritz4 was predicting 35 Bxd6 and crediting Deep Blue with a +96 score. A pawn is worth 100 points.

With over an hour remaining until time control and only having to play six moves, Deep Blue took an unusual 14 minutes to decide on capturing its opponent's bishop on its 35th move. When it completed a 10-level search, it felt the bishop capture on d6 was the best move with a score of +100. On the 11-level search, the capture was examined first and the score dropped to +78. Deep Blue then decided to continue the 11-level search, examining other moves and hoping to find one that didn't reduce the score as much, finally picking the capture.

Following Deep Blue's capture, Kasparov had little choice but to recapture. He remained at the board for a while after making his move, in deep concentration. Hsu, across the board, was glued to his computer's screen while his arm hung limply over the arm of the chair. When Deep Blue finally captured Black's pawn on b5 with its own a-pawn, it took its opponent by surprise. According to Michael Khodarkovsky, Kasparov was expecting 36 Qb6 and not 36 axb5, believing that Deep Blue would attempt to grab material [3]. His demeanor at the board suggested that he was preparing to accept the invasion of White's queen into his territory. When Deep Blue didn't invade, he looked relieved and surprised. Following the game, Kasparov reportedly returned to his hotel and examined the position on Fritz4 and Hiarcs and found what he thought: both programs, unlike Deep Blue, selected the queen move.

Bruce Weber interviewed the Deep Blue team after the match to find out why Deep Blue had played this move rather than invading Black's territory with 36 Qb6. He reported in The New York Times [38] on May 13, 1997, that Deep Blue's 36th move was made in a panic by Deep Blue. When Deep Blue played 35 Bxd6, it assumed that Kasparov would recapture with 35 ... Bxd6. Based on this assumption, it then began to calculate its 36th move. An eight-level search yielded a score of +87 points. The score dropped on the following nine-level search and still more on the 10-level search, during which time Kasparov played the move Deep Blue anticipated. Deep Blue continued its analysis of the ten-level search and then went on to an 11-level search. Midway through the 11-level search of 36 Qb6, Deep Blue became concerned that its evaluation of the position was dropping too much, by more than a quarter of a pawn, and so it added additional time — panic time — to consider its reply. After another 100 seconds, it completed the search of 36 Qb6, obtaining an evaluation of +48 points. It then considered the second move on its list, 36 axb5, assigning it a score of +63, enough of an improvement to end the search. Deep Blue rejected 36 Qb6 because it felt the 10-move continuation, 36 Qb6 Rxa2 37 Rxa2 Ra8 38 Rxa8 Qxa8 39 Qxd6 Qa1+ 40 Kh2 Qc1, was inferior to the selected line, which began with 36 axb5.

Deep Blue spent over 6 minutes on this 36th move. During the course of the match, there would be 11 other moves on which it spent more than 5 minutes. These were moves where, in general, Deep Blue became concerned as it searched deeper and deeper that its evaluation of the position was dropping. Appendix L presents the 12 troublesome positions in which moves by Deep Blue took more than 5 minutes to calculate.

In reply to Deep Blue's 36 axb5, Kasparov routinely recaptured and then he sat back in has chair to watch what his opponent would do.

Deep Blue's 37th move, playing its bishop to e4, was a monumental positional move, preventing Kasparov from creating havoc in White's territory by pushing his potentially troublesome e-pawn. It kept open the option of an invasion by its queen on the next move, generally sealing its opponent's fate. Kasparov had expected the queen invasion on this move, but Deep Blue was evidently more concerned with the trouble that Black's e-pawn might stir up if it had the opportunity to advance. Deep Blue judged that 37 Qb6 Rxa2 38 Rxa2 Ra8 39 Rxa8 Qxa8 40 Qxd6 Qa1+ 41 Kh2 Qc1 led to an equal game. If Kasparov's 33 Bc3 in Game 1 was effective in limiting Deep Blue's offensive possibilities, then this move was Deep Blue's unintended way of reciprocating.

Over the next several moves, Kasparov's expression grew less desperate, and there was increased talk in the commentary auditorium of a draw. Kasparov completed his first 40 moves with less than 2 minutes to spare on his clock, while Deep Blue had about 33 minutes.

However, Deep Blue continued to keep pressure on its opponent, checking the black king on the 41st move and then boldly prancing its queen behind Black's defenses on the next two moves. After the game, the commentators asked Joel Benjamin whether Deep Blue calculated that Kasparov had made any weak moves. Benjamin replied no, but that after Deep Blue played 41 Qa8+, the computer calculated that Kasparov should have responded with 41 ... Kh7. The commentators preferred Kasparov's move, 41 ... Kf7, feeling the king was needed to keep an eye on Deep Blue's advanced pawn on d5 and feeling that Kasparov risked getting mated in the corner.

Deep Blue offered an exchange of queens on its 43rd move, giving itself a passed pawn that would put even more pressure on Kasparov. The offer was declined.

Deep Blue eased pressure on Kasparov when it played 44 Kf1. This move kept alive Kasparov's chances for a draw by repetition. Had Deep Blue played 44 Kh1, the possibility would have been squelched. The analysis, however, was too deep for Deep Blue. After one more rook move by each side, Kasparov, evidently fed up with his position and tired of squirming for so long, abruptly resigned.

Kasparov left the game room and the Equitable Center immediately. When the world champion loses, he is generally not in a mood to meet with an audience. This game was no exception. The IBM team was left to appear alone on-stage in the commentary auditorium. After a long and loud welcoming applause, CJ Tan greeted the audience with, "I said in the very beginning this is going to be a long drawn out match, and we will see what happens in the next four games!" According to Benjamin, the machine always calculated it was ahead in the game, and that it had a large advantage at the end.

However, some were confused why Kasparov had resigned. There seemed to be enough life left in the position to make his resignation premature. Had he underestimated the worth of his position? There was some talk that he resigned to show himself to be a good sport, somewhat as the Deep Blue team had done in the first game, out of respect for his opponent's abilities. The first game might have continued on for some time, until all life was taken out of Deep Blue, and certainly until the computer, itself, was programmed to resign. In this second game, Kasparov had suffered for a number of moves and may have felt he didn't want to do so any longer.

While there was sentiment that Kasparov resigned early, no one in the audience — including the assembled 20 or so grandmasters — argued after the game that a draw was possible, according to Seirawan [15]. Even Robert Byrne wrote in *The New York Times* on the following day that a desperate attempt at a perpetual check with 45 ... Qe3 would fail after 46 Qxd6 Qc1+ 47 Ke2 Qb2+ 48 Kf3 Qxc3+ 49 Kg4 [22].

However, the Internet came alive in the hours following the game with an incredible, controversial finding: Kasparov may have mistakenly resigned! The word was circulating that he could have drawn by playing 45 ... Qe3. Malcolm Pein wrote, "About 1 1/2 hours after the close of play and on the screen I saw a message from GM Jon Tisdall of Norway, informing me that a computer program on the Internet Chess Club amusingly called Ferret, had claimed the final position in Game 2 was a draw! Moreover, no GM could be found to refute this crazy notion" [17]. B r u c e Weber's article in the May 12 issue of *The New York Times* gave Tim McGrew, a professor of philosophy at Western Michigan University, credit for finding 46 ... Re8 while he was discussing the position with colleagues at the Internet Chess Club (http://www.chessclub.com) [37]. Numerous grandmasters and chess-playing computers around the world were handed the position over the next several days and extensive analyses confirmed that Black could have drawn by playing 45 ... Qe3.

An in-depth examination of the final position appears in Appendix K. It is a composite of the analyses presented in references [1–3], [15], and [16] combined with some help from Fritz4. Suffice it to say here that if Kasparov had played 45 ... Qe3, then Deep Blue's 46 Qxd6 would have done no better than draw if Kasparov had then countered with 46 ... Re8!

At 2:00 in the morning Frederic Friedel read his e-mail; Game 2 was a draw, it said! The following morning, while Kasparov slept, he anxiously discussed the news with Yuri Dokhoian. Together they convinced themselves that the game was a draw. And so, on their walk down Fifth Avenue to an Italian restaurant for lunch, they broke the news to Kasparov. Friedel later said that it seemed preferable to tell Kasparov then than to have him hear it from his next taxi driver.

Michael Khodarkovsky, also there at the time, wrote that Kasparov initially said nothing, but soon began to wonder about the computer's inconsistent play [3]. How could the computer have been so clever as to play 37 Be4 and yet so dense as to let victory slip away with 45 Ra6? Playing 37 Be4 rather than 37 Qb6 didn't make sense when 37 Qb6 seemed to win material. How did Deep Blue pass up the opportunity? When Kasparov's computers were fed these positions, their performance evidently supported his contentions.

Kasparov asked Ken Thompson to examine Deep Blue's printout of the two moves in question. Thompson, in turn, approached the Deep Blue team for the information, but obtained it only prior to Game 5. An examination of the printout revealed nothing of concern. Thompson's observations were conveyed to Kasparov, but the long delay in obtaining the information troubled Kasparov to the point where he seemed to find it difficult to concentrate on the primary task at hand.

The entire team would have been put out to pasture immediately if the higher-ups at IBM ever got wind of any efforts to be anything more than 100% honest. Deep Blue had lost the previous match and, while feeling the computer's chances of winning this one were good, the team realized IBM could live with defeat. The first match had been such a good public relations event that win or lose the second, IBM could only come out looking like a champion.

The Deep Blue team preferred to give Kasparov as little information about Deep Blue as possible. The team was concerned with his ability to take advantage of anything he might obtain. It didn't want him to see any practice games, because if he had, it would have been necessary to rework parts of the opening book. Otherwise, Kasparov might have led Deep Blue down the same line to one of his own specially prepared concoctions. Deep Blue was not designed to be that flexible in opening play. If it played an opening against someone in the weeks leading up to the match, there was an excellent chance that it would play the same opening against

Kasparov. Kasparov knew that. In this regard, Kasparov had far greater flexibility.

The Deep Blue team also didn't want Kasparov to see any printout of Deep Blue's calculations. It was concerned that printouts would allow him to deduce exactly how deeply the program was searching. If he had all the printouts he wanted, he would have had a pretty good idea how the program's evaluation function weighted various features on the board.

Could it be that someone assisted Deep Blue's decision-making process, resulting in some of the moves that Kasparov questioned? Nothing has ever surfaced supporting this possibility. Moreover, if someone had helped Deep Blue, he or she must have skipped the first game in which so many of the computer's moves were criticized by the experts. The individual, almost necessarily a grandmaster, must have sat by squirming in agony while watching Deep Blue play moves called "truly ugly," "quite daft," and just plain "ugly" as Daniel King wrote. However, asking Deep Blue after the match to replay a move, for example, would prove nothing. The search carried out by Deep Blue cannot be duplicated. The process of arriving at a move by the RS/6000 SP2 involves sending thousands of messages from one computer to another, and the order in which these messages are sent and received affects the computation and is virtually impossible to repeat. In addition, information saved in various tables in memory depends on such things as the amount of time Deep Blue's opponent takes from move to move, and this too is impossible to duplicate because it depends on microsecond timing. As a consequence, the computer could not be tested at some later time to see if it would produce the same move that it did during the match.

Intrigue has been a part of other major chess events. One involved Kasparov, himself. During his 1986 defense of the world champion title in a match split between London and Leningrad, Kasparov came to the conclusion that one of his own coaches was passing along information on opening plans to his opponent, Anatoly Karpov. In Kasparov's autobiography with Donald Trelford, *Unlimited Challenge*, Kasparov said that after the fifth game he thought information was being leaked to Karpov, and after the 12th game he thought that it was being leaked by one of his own team. At first he thought it was Gennady Timoschenko, but when Timoschenko left the team after the 12th game and, in Kasparov's words, "the miracles continued," suspicions turned to another of his coaches, Yevgeny Vladimirov. Kasparov learned that Vladimirov was taking notes of the analyses made in their training sessions and concluded that these notes were being given to Karpov. After the 19th game and after three straight losses, Kasparov faced Vladimirov with the accusation; the latter denied it but nevertheless resigned from the team. Kasparov never knew for sure whether Vladimirov betrayed him. He said that he could not "say unequivocally that Vladimirov's notes were given to Karpov, but in my own mind three consecutive defeats can be explained more easily if they were" [11].

In a similar exhibit of intrigue, Anatoly Karpov had been suspicious of foul play by his opponent Viktor Korchnoi in their 1978 World Championship match. The match was held in the Philippines, far from Karpov's home in Moscow and Korchnoi's new home in Switzerland, where he had emigrated a year earlier from the USSR. Korchnoi came to the match upset with the Soviet government for denying his wife and son the right to join him in Switzerland; the Soviet government and Soviet chess officials came determined to teach Korchnoi a lesson for his effrontery in leaving his homeland. Raymond Keene, who was serving as a second to Korchnoi, wrote in the October 1978 issue of *Chess Life & Review* [59] that,

> Karpov accepted a chair from the organizers, but Korchnoi brought his own from Switzerland, an olive-green Stoll Giroflex costing $1300. Of course, Baturinsky [ed: a member of Karpov's entourage] insisted on X-raying the chair to see whether it contained any forbidden secret devices, so we had to trudge down to Baguio General Hospital and submit the chair to the X-ray theatre. All they found was foam rubber!

Keene retaliated, somewhat in jest, by submitting a protest letter to the organizers later after Karpov was given a yogurt during play, contending that the yogurt signalled some coded message. Keene wrote, "A yogurt after move 20 could signify: we instruct you to draw; or a sliced mango could mean: we order you to decline a draw; a dish of marinated quails eggs could mean: play Ng4 at once; and so on".

A similar display of suspicion hung over the 1972 World Championship match between Bobby Fischer and Boris Spassky. Fischer smashed Spassky, who was defending his title as world champion. Just before the match was to begin and on a day when haggling, rather than chess, was the only story coming out of Iceland — the match took place in Reykjavik — an article in *The New York Times* printed the following story of Soviet suspicions:

> The only levity of the day came with an announcement from Moscow that a group of Americans was using a computer in New York to help the 29-year-old United States star to win. These Americans would, by unexplained means, get the moves of each game in progress, feed them into a computer, and relay them back to Fischer during the game by equally unexplained means [58].

Imagine, in 1972, Fischer receiving help from a computer! In 1972 computers were playing at the level of good high school players, and to imagine Fischer placing his confidences in one is amusing. At that time there was only a handful of programs that Fischer could use, one being Ostrich, developed by George Arnold and myself. Shelby Lyman was giving commentary on the match on PBS and approached me at some point to see if I was willing to feed certain positions from the match into Ostrich to see how it would respond. I agreed, but he never called on me. I suspect he knew better than to expect anything of interest from a computer at that time, and he spared me potential embarrassment. Maybe this story, passed along a thousand times, was transformed into Ostrich helping Fischer! If there is another explanation, I'd love to hear it.

However, that someone in Moscow had given any credence to this possibility had to be based on the reputation that the Soviet chess program, Kaissa, was garnering [5]. In 1972 Kaissa had played a two-game match against the readers of *Komsomolskaia Pravda* with the newspaper serving as middleman. The readers submitted recommendations for moves, and the most popular one was fed to the computer and printed in the paper. The computer then searched for several hours, examining several million positions at about 12,000 positions per minute, and returned a reply. The games began in January 1972 and lasted throughout the year. Kaissa managed to draw one game and resigned on move 34 in the other. The previous year, Spassky had taken on the same readers in a similar two-game match; he won one game and drew the other. One might conclude that the level of play by both the readers and Kaissa couldn't have been too bad.

After two intensive days of chess over the weekend, both sides had Monday off. The Deep Blue team spent it trying to solve the problems that surfaced in Game 1: the wandering queen and the pawn moves that willingly weakened the defense of the king. The book needed last-minute preparations, and that was primarily Benjamin's responsibility.

With both Kasparov and Deep Blue having won their games with the white pieces, the Rematch stood tied at one point apiece after two games.

12 The Rematch – Games 3–5: Endgame Standoffs

> "Enter the endgame without fear even if you are not a Capablanca, Fischer, or Karpov.... In the endgame, your chances of outplaying the computer are probably greater than at any other stage of the game," Elliot Hearst, former captain of the U. S. Olympic Chess Team, 1983 [14].

May 6, 1997, New York
Game 3, IBM Kasparov versus Deep Blue Rematch
White: Garry Kasparov   Black: Deep Blue
English Opening

As 3:00 approached, the audience gathered in the commentary auditorium for the third game. The Tuesday afternoon crowd was smaller than the weekend throngs, but it still filled the majority of seats. Ambuj Goyal, vice president of IBM Research's Systems and Software and under whom the Deep Blue project was now situated, welcomed the crowd, expressing his pride in the computer's accomplishments thus far and pointing out how much they were learning about solving such complex problems. Upstairs in the game room, Joe Hoane was sitting at the board preparing Deep Blue. When Garry Kasparov arrived, he and Hoane shook hands briefly — no large smiles today — and then it was straight to business. For Kasparov, off with the watch and a quick adjustment of his pieces. Wearing a blue sport jacket and tan trousers, he was dressed more casually than for the first two games. More formally dressed in a dark blue suit with a Deep Blue pin on his lapel, Hoane also was wearing a very nervous smile.

Playing White for the second time, Kasparov was expected to fight hard for a win. But what opening would he choose? He might have concluded from the previous game that Deep Blue's book was greatly improved from the Philadelphia match. If he picked one of his favorites, he was sure his opponent would be well prepared.

"Oh, my God," said Mike Valvo, as he watched Kasparov play his first move. A first for the champion. Kasparov had decided to continue with his tactic of irregular openings by advancing his d-pawn one square. Deep Blue had a small book for this unusual opening and responded by advancing its own e-pawn two squares. Whenever an opponent fails to stake out a claim on the fourth rank, Deep Blue can be counted on to do so for itself.

Deep Blue developed its two knights to c6 and f6 on its second and third moves, while Kasparov moved a knight to f3 and advanced a pawn to c4.

On Kasparov's fourth move, he must have said to himself, "To heck with your big book!" as he advanced his a-pawn one square. Deep Blue, out of book, took four minutes to advance its d-pawn one square, to which Kasparov replied by developing his knight to c3.

Yasser Seirawan was unimpressed with Deep Blue's fifth move, pointing out Kasparov's early success here in setting up a position in which Deep Blue, when not finding a move in its opening book, seemed to play inaccurately. He pointed out that 5 ... g6 followed by the fianchetto of the black-squared bishop was the usual line of play, and that the bishop on e7 would inhibit the movement of other black pieces. Since Deep Blue generally prefers not to fianchetto its bishops, this move couldn't have been much of a surprise or concern to the Deep Blue team. According to Mike Valvo, Kasparov may have not been surprised either as he probably

Garry Kasparov paces behind the board after completing his fourth move, while Joe Hoane looks over the board.

experimented with this line on his PCs during his preparation and found that they, too, played this apparently weak move.

Both sides continued to develop their pieces over the next several moves. This included two kingside castling moves. The position was rather quiet after Deep Blue's eighth move.

Kasparov advanced his knight to g5 on his ninth move. The move defended against Black's attack on h3. It also tended to provoke Deep Blue into chasing the knight with its h-pawn, precipitating a weakening of the defenses around its king. Kasparov later reported on his website that he thought he would have won the game with 9 b4, but that 9 ... e4 bothered him. He pondered over this move for almost 28 minutes! According to Seirawan, it was an obvious move, and a mistake to fall behind on time so early in the game. Seirawan offered his own theory for why Kasparov thought so long: perhaps he was trying to see whether he could start a pawn avalanche on the kingside that would smash through to the Deep Blue king.

Murray Campbell reported that Deep Blue had gone down when calculating its ninth move, placing its bishop on f5, but was quickly

CJ Tan and Ambuj Goyal.

restarted. The unusual time consumed by this move, 3 minutes and 45 seconds, reflects about 45 seconds to get the system back on track. On his 10th move, Kasparov chased the black bishop from f5 to g4 when he advanced his e-pawn two squares.

On his eleventh move, Kasparov attacked the bishop a second time when he advanced his f-pawn one square. After playing his move, Kasparov got up to take one of his many breaks from the board, methodically pacing behind his chair exactly eight steps in each direction, looking over the board on each pass. Joining the commentators at this point, Campbell confirmed that Kasparov could have drawn the previous game. Campbell fed the final position into Deep Blue who saw the draw after playing through 45 ... Qe3 46 Qxd6 Re8.

Following Deep Blue's retreat of its bishop to h5 on its 11th move, Kasparov retreated his knight to h3. He hadn't succeeded in provoking Black to advancing its h-pawn. Seirawan's prediction of a pawn avalanche, which had been looking pretty good until this move by Kasparov, was put on hold, according to the discussion in the commentary auditorium.

When Deep Blue's knight jumped to d4, Kasparov looked frustrated for the first time. He moved his own knight to f2, watched as Deep Blue advanced its pawn to h6, then developed his bishop to e3.

View of Central Park from the press room.

Deep Blue advanced a pawn to c5 on its 14th move, a move that was crucial to the computer's survival. This move permanently iced Kasparov's plan to launch Seirawan's suggested pawn attack. Black's pawn on e4 would help to prevent an onslaught of white pawns.

On his 16th move, Kasparov placed a rook on the b-file, poised to eventually invade Black's territory. Meanwhile, on stage, Campbell had been talking with the commentators, discussing the chess lessons given to Deep Blue over the last year. He explained,

> It was an evolutionary process, with knowledge gradually added in an effort to teach the computer how to play a wide variety of positions. While the computer could follow the rules, there were always exceptions to the rules, and that was difficult for the computer. There were too many exceptions that the computer had to be told about. It also had to prepare for the real Garry and the anti-computer Garry.

His explanation finished, Campbell then hurriedly left the stage for the IBM operations room to see firsthand how things were going.

Kasparov had been playing much slower than Deep Blue. After initiating a pawn exchange on c5 on his 18th move, he found himself with only 41 minutes remaining to time control versus 1 hour and 19 minutes for his opponent. Grandmaster Roman Dzindzichashvili, reputed for having defeated more computers than any human alive, was invited to the stage of the commentary auditorium at this point. He was eager to present his own scenario as to how Deep Blue could have saved its victory in the previous game. He suggested that after 45 ... Qe3, Deep Blue should have played 46 Qxd6 Re8 47 Qc5 Qxe4 48 Kg1 Qxf5 49 Ra7+, contending that it was enough to win, evidently unaware that other experts had already called the game a draw.

After Kasparov played his 20th move, Hsu return to the helm of Deep Blue, relieving Hoane, while Kasparov was prowling about and pacing behind his chair.

Kasparov advanced his pawn to f4 on move 21. Pawns were then exchanged on that square, and his position as a whole looked solid. His rook on b2 was on a good file, and his bishops and knights were well placed. Deep Blue's strength rested on a well-placed knight on d4, although its bishops were immobilized. On its 22nd move, Deep Blue's queen set out on a fishing expedition, risking getting lost at sea. Kasparov responded by moving his bishop to d2. This encouraged Deep Blue's queen to continue on her voyage chasing after Kasparov's undefended a-pawn.

"Oh dear," observed Seirawan as Deep Blue did indeed grab the a-pawn on its 23rd move. Kasparov must have felt that having Black's queen somewhat out of play and having Black's bishops so ineffective — especially after the anticipated advance of his f-pawn — was adequate compensation. His reply, moving his rook to a2, was ready and waiting for Deep Blue, though it drew immediate criticism from the commentators and Dzindzichashvili, who was still on the stage. They felt that 24 Rb7 would have been a more forceful move, and they thought that that was Kasparov's intentions when gave up his a-pawn.

Kasparov next encouraged an exchange of queens over the coming moves, and Deep Blue gladly went along. The queens were exchanged on each side's 26th move. Deep Blue was happy to trade queens whenever it was ahead in material.

The next several moves were characterized by Kasparov's efforts to gain control of the center, gradually restricting Deep Blue's mobility. On its 27th move, Deep Blue backed up its bishop to h7, almost appearing to assist Kasparov's efforts to restrict its movement. While the alternate 26 ... Bh5 was playable, according to Benjamin who suggested 26 ... Bh5 27 Bxh5 Nxh5 28 Nd5 Bg5 29 Bxg5 hxg5 30 Rfa1, the computer seemed to fare no better [65]. Dzindzichashvili volunteered at this point that he found it "hard to decide which side has the advantage." This was in spite of the fact that White's bishops were free to roam while Black's were ineffective, and White's advanced f-pawn was an annoying thorn in Black's side.

The game lasted another 21 moves with neither side able to make further progress toward a victory. Deep Blue was forced to play defensively, but Kasparov, too, was forced to be cautious with little room for error. Kasparov gradually acquired control over more and more space, forcing Deep Blue to play from a severely cramped position. However, Deep Blue played strongly, defending its position with precision.

By the 33rd move, though up a pawn, Deep Blue's pieces had little mobility, and the computer was struggling to hold its position. Kasparov had 17 minutes to time control to complete his remaining seven moves. Following the 34th move, on which Deep Blue moved its king to g2, Fritz4 evaluated the game in Deep Blue's favor by 69 points, essentially giving Deep Blue a point for the extra pawn, but –31 points for its positional weaknesses.

At this point, the commentators introduced Grandmaster Zsuzsa Polgar, the world's leading woman player, who had been watching the proceedings from the rear of the commentary auditorium. Her younger sister Judit Polgar had played Deep Thought II in 1993. Looking quite elegant in a smart blue dress, Zsuzsa Polgar watched as Kasparov played his 36th move and immediately ventured that White had "no risk to lose," and that she still believed Kasparov would "win the match."

Frederic Friedel came on stage after Kasparov's 37th move, and was, of course, grilled on what had transpired in the Kasparov camp regarding Game 2. He remained on stage until near the end of the game, telling about the events from the perspective of the Kasparov team.

Deep Blue moved ahead by two pawns when it captured Kasparov's h-pawn on its 37th move. However, its own a-pawn and h-pawn would soon be dead ducks; Kasparov grabbed them back in the coming moves. The prospect of a draw loomed larger.

Deep Blue's 38th move signified it was ready to accept a draw by repetition of position, but Kasparov steered clear, wanting to continue on a bit longer, struggling in vain to find some way to make progress.

On its 40th move, Deep Blue evidently didn't see anything better than to propose a trade of its bishop and pawn for Kasparov's thorny all-purpose knight. Kasparov seemed delighted with the offer, displaying his biggest midgame smile of the match, nodding his head up and down. In retrospect, the move might have signaled, too, that Kasparov was prepared for a draw, giving away his well-placed knight for Deep Blue's relatively immobile bishop. Kasparov had used all but five minutes of his allotted time to complete his first 40 moves. Deep Blue had used all but 27 minutes, again moving considerably faster than its human opponent.

Deep Blue's material advantage disappeared on the 42nd move. From then point on, there was no way for either side to make progress. The two sides finally agreed to a draw after another hour's waltz around the board by their kings and rooks.

Umpire Carol Jarecki looking at one of the games.

Kasparov tried desperately to find a way to avoid a draw on his last two moves. He took almost 20 minutes to play his 47th move, searching for some way to make progress. His final, 48th move took over nine minutes. His hands were resting on his forehead, while Hsu sat across the table from him nervously and unconsciously doodling with the end of his tie. Kasparov finally played his 48th move, and then offered a draw to Hsu who, in turn, called the IBM operations room to discuss it with his team. Within all of about five seconds, a draw was agreed upon.

Following the game a 30–minute interview with Kasparov and the Deep Blue team took place in the commentary auditorium. Their arrival was met with enthusiastic applause. Maurice Ashley started the questioning and was eager to ask Kasparov about Game 2, beginning with, "What's your take now on this new Deeper Blue? Is it deeper?" Kasparov responded by saying that the machine had missed an elementary draw in the second game, and he had resigned in a position which was probably drawn. He said that against a human, he would have tried 45 ... Qe3, but he thought Deep Blue probably would have seen it. He went on to say that "anybody who plays chess and who knows a little bit about computers understands that Game 1 and Game 3 are very, very different from Game 2." He went on to say he couldn't understand Deep Blue's humanlike decision to play 37 Be4 while failing to realize that 44 Kh1 and not 44 Kf1 should have been played. Joel Benjamin responded by saying that Deep Blue had calculated 36 Qb6 would win two pawns but give up too much positionally in return, and that the following move, 37 Qb6, had the same difficulties. Benjamin went on to say that deeper search than done by Deep Blue was necessary to avoid 44 Kf1. Kasparov wasn't very satisfied, however, suggesting that some unseen forces were somehow helping Deep Blue. He recalled the goal scored by Argentina's Diego Maradona against England in the semifinals of the 1986 Soccer World Cup. The referees evidently missed noticing that the great soccer player had actually punched the ball into the goal. "It was the hand of God," Maradona said later. Kasparov wound up saying,

> I do not like to face things I do not understand, and I cannot get any viable explanation for my point of view. I know exactly what I'm dealing with. I know the power of Deep Blue. I know how strong it is, but Game 2 has definitely shaken my beliefs on what a machine can do (Game 3 has restored my confidence), and if miracles and surprises will not come again, I think I should win. I should win, but definitely Game 2 has shaken my confidences, especially because I've never resigned in a position which I could force a draw.

After three rounds, the score stood tied at 1.5 – 1.5.

May 7, 1997, New York
Game 4, IBM Kasparov versus Deep Blue Rematch
White: Deep Blue   Black: Garry Kasparov
Pribyl Defense

> "A chess match between the world's greatest chess player and Garry Kasparov," IBM CEO Lou Gerstner while visiting the Deep Blue team during this game.

On the morning of the fourth game, CJ Tan and Marcy Holle were alerted that Lou Gerstner might appear. The IBM CEO addressed a morning meeting of business people in Manhattan, and it was understood that he would drop in on the match if time permitted. He did find time, arriving during the middle of the game. He rode up to the Equitable's 35th floor and to the IBM operations room, keeping a low profile, not wanting to interfere with the game. He stayed for about a half-hour, giving the team a brief pep talk. "It's great what you've done," Gerstner told the team. "I think we should look at this as a chess match between the world's greatest chess player and Garry Kasparov." Bruce Weber and James Kim [31,48] happened to be present at the time and included the IBM chief's remarks in their reports on the match the following day. Deep Blue wasn't doing particularly well at that point, but evidently tuned in to the pep talk too, since soon after hearing Gerstner's words, it started to play better! The Deep Blue team was overjoyed with his visit, appreciating the recognition within IBM that the CEO's visit brought. Kasparov wouldn't forget Gerstner's remarks either.

   With the short six-game match tied at the midpoint, pressure was building on Kasparov. To win the match, he would need to secure two points from the remaining three games, two of which he would play with the black pieces. Deep Blue had played a strong Ruy Lopez in the second game, and Kasparov was expected to stay clear of this opening here — but what alternative would he choose?

   Deep Blue's initial move was no surprise, advancing its e-pawn two squares. Kasparov replied by advancing his c-pawn one square; a Sicilian was ruled out. Maybe a Caro-Kann? Deep Blue's second move was, again, no surprise, advancing its d-pawn two squares, but Kasparov surprised everyone when he replied by advancing his d-pawn just one square. This opening, the Pribyl Defense, named after the Czech Grandmaster Josef Pribyl, enabled Kasparov's pieces to stay completely out of Deep Blue's reach. Deep Blue expanded to fill the empty space with its standard pawn and knight moves, leading to good mobility for all its pieces.

Kasparov thought for over a half-hour on his 15th move, finally moving his knight to c7. Perhaps he was trying to find some way to refute Deep Blue's strange-looking previous rook move. Perhaps he was trying to find some way to launch an attack on the queenside. He was already beginning to show signs of fatigue even as early as this point in the game. Nevertheless, he paced behind the board on most moves when waiting for Deep Blue to play. In the first few rounds, he would go off to his small lounge in the corner of the room to relax, but here he was too intensely immersed in the action on the board to go even across the room. Klara Kasparova and Yuri Dokhoian remained in the game room at all times. His mother's attention was focused on him and the board, as if hoping to transmit her own invisible energy from herself to him.

Both sides were probably happy in their own ways when Deep Blue isolated Black's two g-file pawns on the 17th move — Kasparov, because he saw possibilities of using the f-file to invade his opponent's territory, and Deep Blue, because it counted doubled pawns as a negative feature for its opponent.

Kasparov, frustrated that he was making little progress, offered a pawn sacrifice on his 20th move in hopes of giving his pieces greater scope. Sacrifices are risky against Deep Blue; they are likely to lead to a permanent loss, although in this case the material was recouped 15 moves later!

Deep Blue's 22nd move hinted at eventually advancing its b-pawn and weakening its king's safety. Kasparov provided Deep Blue all the incentive necessary when, on his 23rd move, he placed a knight on c5. Deep Blue's 24th move, advancing its b-pawn to attack the knight, must have been expected by Kasparov.

Deep Blue took more time on its 30th move than on any other move of the match, a sign that things weren't going that well. Kasparov paced behind the game table a good part of the time. Eventually he stopped and leaned on his chair for a while, but then he returned to his pacing until Deep Blue finally moved.

Rather than capturing Deep Blue's queen on his 30th move, Kasparov said on his website that 30 ... Rf7 would have given him an extremely powerful position. However, he felt that exchanging queens was the correct way to play a computer. In every game, Kasparov consistently played more slowly than Deep Blue, and here he found himself having to make 10 moves in 14 minutes. Deep Blue had 35 minutes to do the same.

Deep Blue took several minutes to play the obvious recapture of Kasparov's queen, and the commentators panned the wasted time. In this particular case, no amount of searching would have found anything but the move Deep Blue selected, but it's not easy to spell out general rules for a chess program to avoid unnecessary search!

In spite of not playing 30 ... Rf7, Kasparov's position seemed to improve over the last several moves; his rooks were well placed and his king was one move better for the endgame.

Kasparov had his reply ready and waiting when Deep Blue played the obvious recapture of his queen. Yasser Seirawan got a chuckle from the audience when he noted that Kasparov had correctly anticipated Deep Blue's last move and responded immediately, just as his opponent often did.

On move 35, Kasparov finally drew even in material and seemed to have a clear advantage. But the road to victory was illusive. The four knights were removed from the board over the next several moves, leading to an endgame with two rooks and several pawns remaining on each side.

With evident relief on his face, Kasparov completed his 40th move. He had only about four minutes remaining on his clock. Deep Blue had a comfortable 25 minutes. The computer played strongly from here to the end of the game, surviving Kasparov's valiant attempts to hammer out a victory.

After Kasparov's 43rd move, CB Hsu replaced Murray Campbell at the board and immediately had to attend to correcting a second crash by Deep Blue. Kasparov delivered a scolding look as if to question Hsu's actions when he restarted the program. Deep Blue had only one legal move in the position, retreating its rook to b1, and thus the computer's problem had no effect on the move selected.

On his 44th move, Kasparov could have forced a draw, but he was still struggling to find a win. Deep Blue's moves showed it was content with a draw.

According to Campbell, Deep Blue was finding positions in its endgame database when it played its 45th move, just a small number of positions, but their discovery didn't play any role in the selection of moves. Hsu's chip had sufficient rook-and-pawn versus rook knowledge to correctly handle what transpired.

By move 50, the three commentators had gathered two unofficial assistants, Zsuzsa Polgar, who was invited on stage, and Ilya Gurevich, who joned in from the audience. The impromptu team of five tough competitors fiercely struggled in vain to find a winning line first for one side and then for the other.

After Deep Blue played its 56th move, Kasparov thought for seven minutes, desperately searching for a way to make some progress. Then, without making a move, he offered a draw to Hsu. Initially caught off guard by the offer, Hsu wasn't sure how to respond but, after a brief discussion, agreed to accept.

Garry Kasparov and the Deep Blue team headed down to meet the audience in the commentary auditorium and were given another standing ovation. Kasparov appeared tired and not particularly interested in discussing the game. He said he hadn't played well, but that he had been winning at some point. Campbell countered that Deep Blue never calculated the game was lost, although it barely hung on for several hours. Hoane made a point of acknowledging the use of Ken Thompson's endgame database during the game. Tan observed that the match was following the pattern from Philadelphia, implying an eventual Deep Blue victory. Finally, as soon as Maurice Ashley thanked both sides for coming on stage, everyone rushed out to dinner following the longest game of the match.

The IBM team headed for a Chinese restaurant on 49th Street. On the way there, it passed NBC's Electronic News Ticker Tape at Rockefeller Center. Among the other news headlines of the day, the tape was flashing the Rematch score of 2–2. Members of the Deep Blue team reacted to the moving stream of blinking lights like a bunch of high school kids on their prom evening, cheering and jumping up and down as they walked along. Over dinner, between gobbling down a variety of delicacies, they watched CNN spot stories on the match.

The next day was the first of a two-day intermission during which both sides prepared for the final two games. The score stood tied at two points apiece.

The Deep Blue team all smiles under
NBC's Electronic Ticker Tape at Rockefeller Center.

May 10, 1997, New York
Game 5, IBM Kasparov versus Deep Blue Rematch
White: Garry Kasparov   Black: Deep Blue
Reti Opening

> "If he loses or draws [today], the pressure will be on him in the last round, and he may have to attack when there just aren't any attacking chances," Ken Thompson [32].

Deep Blue was wakened early on this bright, sunny Saturday morning and taken for a stroll by its trainers down Sixth Avenue to Rockefeller Center. Matt Thoennes and his IBM colleagues wheeled the empty RS/6000 SP2 cabinet that sat on stage in the commentary auditorium out the door of the Equitable and on its half-mile round trip. Deep Blue had been invited for a brief appearance on NBC's News Today, where Janice Hutt asked a few questions regarding its success and the fact that the match was tied at 2–2 [67]. Then it was back to its place on stage. I imagine it was sort of like taking Big Bird for a walk.

As CJ Tan observed following Game 4, the match thus far had been the mirror image of Philadelphia. The first two games were won, but by the opposite player, and the next two games were drawn. How long would this pattern continue? Was Kasparov learning how to play against the computer, and thus could he be expected to play stronger in the final two games just as he had in the previous match, or was the match taking its toll on his energies? Or — was Deep Blue simply his equal?

Today was Kasparov's last easy chance to win the match. Bruce Weber quotes Ken Thompson as saying that "if he loses or draws [today], the pressure will be on him in the last round, and he may have to attack when there just aren't any attacking chances" [33].

The fifth game was played before a Saturday afternoon full house and began at the usual 3:00 starting time. A few tickets were sold by small-time scalpers for this game and the final one on Sunday. The commentators were warming up the audience while Campbell was warming up Deep Blue. When Kasparov arrived, the two shook hands briefly. Kasparov immediately sat down, removed his watch, adjusted his pieces and then went into his usual pregame concentration phase with his hands moving between his cheeks and temples.

The world champion returned to the Reti for his final effort with White. It was an opening with which he had had excellent success over the course of the two matches, including three victories and a draw. The game was a repeat of Game 1 for the first two moves. Kasparov could depend on Deep Blue for this. On his third move, Kasparov steered off in a different direction, although Deep Blue was left in book.

Kasparov's first four moves were all played in a matter of seconds. If he was planning to take Deep Blue down some precarious path in the opening, the speed at which he was making these moves suggested that all was going well so far. Kasparov must have expected that his quiet pawn advance on the fourth move would not be in Deep Blue's book and that the computer would need to search a large tree. He must have believed that Deep Blue's search and evaluation function would find it best to retreat the bishop.

But no, the bishop didn't retreat! The programmers had modified Deep Blue's evaluation function between rounds, reducing the value of a bishop relative to various developmental considerations in the early opening, and this time the computer decided to play the exchange. This must have surprised Kasparov. Murray Campbell said that he, himself, was surprised by the move. He said the Deep Blue team had modified its opening book to make sure the computer wouldn't be marched down one of the Reti lines previously played, but lines following Kasparov's 4 h3 hadn't been considered. Deep Blue's capture may have voided a number of hours of preparation by the world champion. He reflected his displeasure with the state of affairs by unbuttoning his shirt at the neck. No one will ever know how the game would have evolved if Deep Blue had played 4 ... Bh5 instead.

Deep Blue's seventh move was "a lemon," according to Maurice Ashley, although Yasser Seirawan liked it! It was nice to see that two players at such lofty levels could disagree so sharply.

On his ninth move, Kasparov faced an important early decision. Capturing Deep Blue's pawn on e4 with his own pawn would lead to an exchange of queens and an early endgame, something that the experts were arguing Kasparov seemed to have as a general goal in his games with Deep Blue. But he decided to avoid going into this phase of the game so early, perhaps feeling that there was more to reap from the opening. Deep Blue had played well in the last two games when the queens were off the board. In his analysis of the game in the *Informant* [65], Joel Benjamin pointed out that if Kasparov had played 9 dxe4, then Deep Blue's best line was not to capture the queen, but to play 9 ... Bb4+. If Kasparov then played 10 Nd2, Deep Blue should respond with 10 ... Qa5. If Deep Blue did capture the queen with 9 ... Qxd1, Benjamin indicated that 10 Kxd1 O–O–O 11 Ke2 gave White the better game.

Was there any possibility that Kasparov was pursuing lines leading to endgames by trading off queens as early as possible? The table on the next page presents data from three matches for consideration: the first, the world championship match with Vishwananthan Anand in 1995; the second, the ACM Chess Challenge; and the third, the first five games of this match. In the match with Anand, both queens stayed on the board until the end in eight of the 18 games. When they did come off the board, each player initiated the exchange an equal number of time. In Philadelphia queens stayed on the board in three of the six games. In New York one or both queens exited from the board in all but the second game. Furthermore, in Philadelphia, queens disappeared from the board in only one game before the 35th move, while in New York, one or both queens exited in five of the six games by the 35th move. In Philadelphia Kasparov had two wins and a draw with queens off the board when the games ended. In New York, however, he was unable to gain any advantage with this approach, winning 2.5/5 points in games with queens gone at the end. It's not clear to what extent Kasparov intentionally adapted this strategy or whether in the end it was simply the most appropriate strategy for the positions that arose.

Five of Kasparov's first 10 moves of this game were with his king's bishop. Somehow Deep Blue had forced him to violate one of the cardinal rules of opening theory, which says one shouldn't move the same piece more than once! Well, maybe sometimes twice and maybe even sometimes three times, but five times? Kasparov seemed frustrated that Deep Blue circumvented his opening preparation.

On its 11th move and with 48 legal moves in the position, Deep Blue picked a surprising, mystifying two-square advance of its h-pawn. Maurice Ashley observed that "Kasparov can't even write the move down. He's frozen! . . . We've seen some strange moves, and we've seen some strange moves, but that's a strange move!" Kasparov noted at his website that Deep Blue's move threw him off. He saw that it eventually led to a well-placed Black knight on f4, but he couldn't imagine that a computer could reason its way to this conclusion. Deep Blue was also threatening h4, leading to difficulties for White on the kingside. Initially panned by the experts, this move was later praised as an example of the excellent positional play that Deep Blue was capable of. The move suggested that Deep Blue was already planning to castle queenside, placing its queen's rook on an open file.

Kasparov took eight minutes to make a relatively obvious capture on his 17th move and drew the usual criticism from the commentators for taking so long. Kasparov also took extra time on his previous move, as well as on his coming 18th and 19th moves. These four moves consumed over 38 minutes. During the same period, Deep Blue spent about 10 minutes, playing at its typical 2.5-minute average.

Kasparov Versus Anand — 1995 World Championship

Game	Length of Game	How Queen Departed
1	27	Queens remained on board till end.
2	29	Kasparov initiated exchange on move 19.
3	36	Anand initiated exchange on move 34.
4	21	Queens remained on board till end.
5	27	Queens remained on board till end.
6	28	Anand initiated exchange on move 22.
7	25	Queens remained on board till end.
8	22	Kasparov initiated exchange on move 11.
9	35	Queens remained on board till end.
10	38	Anand initiated exchange on move 23.
11	31	Anand initiated exchange on move 21.
12	43	Kasparov initiated exchange on move 21.
13	25	Queens remained on board till end.
14	41	Anand initiated exchange on move 34.
15	16	Kasparov initiated exchange on move 34.
16	20	Queens remained on board till end.
17	63	Kasparov initiated exchange on move 19.
18	12	Queens remained on board till end.

1996 ACM Chess Challenge

Game	Length of Game	How Queen Departed
1	37	Queens remained on board till end.
2	73	Deep Blue initiated exchange on move 71.
3	34	Deep Blue initiated exchange on move 19.
4	50	Queens remained on board till end.
5	45	Deep Blue initiated exchange on move 35. (Kasparov queened a pawn on move 34.)
6	43	Queens remained on board till end.

The Rematch

Game	Length of Game	How Queen Departed
1	45	Deep Blue initiated exchange on move 34.
2	45	Queens remained on board till end.
3	48	Kasparov initiated exchange on move 25.
4	56	Kasparov initiated exchange on move 30.
5	49	Kasparov initiated exchange on move 30.

Queen departures in Kasparov games.

The table at the bottom of this page shows a breakdown of how the two sides spent their time during the rematch (including the yet-to-be-played sixth game). The number of moves that took less than 30 seconds, between 30 and 59 seconds, and so on is indicated for each side and for each game. The table shows, for example, that Deep Blue took more than 480 seconds (8 minutes) on two moves during the match; Kasparov took at least that much time on 22 moves, taking more than 16 minutes on six moves. Even though Deep Blue was thinking on Kasparov's time and sometimes moved immediately upon Kasparov's move, it was Kasparov that played more moves quickly — 97 moves versus 69 moves by Deep Blue in under 30 seconds. It is difficult to draw any conclusions from this information, however.

The only alternative to Kasparov's 17th move, taking with the pawn, would have resulted in an isolated White d-pawn and would have killed any idea of castling queenside. According to Joel Benjamin [65], Deep Blue preferred castling queenside on its 17th move. It felt castling kingside gave Kasparov an advantage with the game following along as: 18 O–O Bc5 19 Be3 Rhe8 20 Qf3 Ne5 21 Qf5+ Qd7 22 Bh3 Bd4 23 cxd4.

Although Kasparov had a pair of bishops, Deep Blue seems to have drawn even after playing 18 ... Ng4. Kasparov struggled hard over the coming moves to gain an advantage, while Deep Blue refused to give an inch.

Number of moves made by Garry Kasparov in range of seconds shown							
Game	1	2	3	4	5	6	All
Moves in <30 sec	12	23	15	18	18	11	97
Moves in 30–59 sec	7	2	5	11	7	1	33
Moves in 60–119 sec	6	3	11	5	5	2	32
Moves in 120–239 sec	10	5	9	10	8	1	43
Moves in 240–479 sec	7	7	3	8	7	3	35
Moves in 480–959 sec	3	3	3	3	3	1	16
Moves in ≥960 sec	0	2	2	1	1	0	6
Number of moves made by Deep Blue in range of seconds shown							
Game	1	2	3	4	5	6	All
Moves in <30 sec	9	20	10	10	9	11	69
Moves in 30–59 sec	3	1	0	4	1	0	9
Moves in 60–119 sec	3	2	4	12	3	2	25
Moves in 120–239 sec	28	12	31	25	31	5	133
Moves in 240–479 sec	2	10	3	3	5	1	24
Moves in 480–959 sec	0	0	0	2	0	0	2
Moves in ≥960 sec	0	0	0	0	0	0	0

Amount of time taken on moves by Garry Kasparov and Deep Blue.

While waiting for Kasparov to play his 24th move, Zsuzsa Polgar joined the commentators on stage and her book, *Queen of the King's Game* [6] was given a plug by Maurice Ashley. She said the game was close to even, although she preferred White but "not by much," mainly because of its good bishops. Kasparov took more time on this move —10 minutes — than on any other move of the game. Murray Campbell, across the table, watched the seconds tick by. When Kasparov finally moved, Deep Blue responded immediately, forcing the world champion to get right back down to the business of finding his next move.

Kasparov advanced his c-pawn on his 29th move, screwing it into the board when he did, a custom that all chess players use to indicate a move they are proud of. The practice can affect a human opponent but in this case, while the audience observed it, it sailed right by Deep Blue, who replied by inviting the exchange of queens. The exchange, however, would saddle the computer with doubled pawns. But with White's queen defending pawns on c4 and f2, the exchange would soon give Deep Blue a temporary one-pawn advantage. Kasparov had his choice of protecting one of his two en prise pawns and decided to keep the c-pawn. This had the effect of restricting the movement of Deep Blue's knight on b6.

Zsuzsa Polgar observed while waiting for Deep Blue to play its 31st move that "Black doesn't have much chance to win, White has some." Kasparov was now prowling behind his chair in his hungry lion mode. He had only 18 minutes to make his next nine moves, and he had to remain focused. There was pressure on him not to take too long on any single move during this critical stage of the game. Polgar left the stage several moves later and was given a big hand.

On move 33, the material was returned to a balance, but Kasparov seemed to have a definite positional advantage. He looked poised to gobble down Deep Blue's kingside pawns and then to advance his own g-pawn into the end zone.

After Kasparov played 35 Bd5, Deep Blue seemed to be in worse trouble, and Kasparov appeared optimistic. Patrick Wolff joined the commentators on stage and offered that the game was a seesaw battle but "now Garry has control of the position."

Over the next several moves, amazingly, Deep Blue improved its position while squirming like an eel. Its 36th move was a clever way to exchange its knight for Kasparov's bishop. By his 40th move, even Kasparov was evidently coming to the conclusion that he wasn't going to win this crucial game of the match, his last with the white pieces. His clock showed about 11 minutes remaining to time control. He paced back and forth behind the board for the entire time that Deep Blue was calculating its move. He had played each of his previous five moves in less than a minute, four of them in less than 15 seconds.

None of these moves by Kasparov was subsequently criticized in the literature, suggesting that even though he was playing quickly, he had nothing better to do. If that's the case, the game was effectively drawn as far back as move 35. Kasparov said after the game that he realized the game was drawn at move 40. But the remaining moves of the game were dramatic, nevertheless, with Deep Blue eventually mobilizing its king into an offensive role and threatening Kasparov with checkmate.

The audience and commentators were dumbfounded when Deep Blue captured Kasparov's a-pawn on its 42nd move. They felt Deep Blue couldn't afford to move its rook off to this relatively remote corner of the board when Kasparov's g-pawn was ready to roll, but Deep Blue knew better.

On move 45, Deep Blue's c-pawn came to life! "Kasparov looked perplexed, stunned, befuddled," Maurice said. Then, two moves later, from out of nowhere, Deep Blue's king also came to life! Deep Blue's c-pawn and king teamed up with its rook and knight, giving Kasparov no option but to settle for a draw. Kasparov sat looking over the board for several minutes after Deep Blue played its 49th move. Then suddenly, he extended his hand to Campbell. Game 5 was, indeed, a draw.

The game ended with Kasparov poised to promote the pawn but unable to prevent a draw by repetition through 50 b8Q Rd1+. Alternatively, it was suggested by Seirawan [14] that "50 Re2 Rd1+ 51 Kb2 c3+ 52 Kc2 Rc1+ 53 Kd3 Rd1+ 54 Ke4 Rd8 55 Nd5+ Kc4 56 Nf6 Nd4 57 Re1 b5!? is by no means clear." Daniel King wrote that [2] that "after 54 ... Rd8, Black can begin to advance its c-pawn, giving Garry enough concerns to offer the draw."

Kasparov was terribly upset at the conclusion of the game. He demanded a printout of Deep Blue's analysis of its play in this game be given to Carol Jarecki before he would leave the game room. His team huddled around him along with Ken Thompson and Carol Jarecki and CJ Tan. After some discussion, Tan agreed that printouts would be given to Jarecki as soon as they could be printed out; all 70 pages would be placed in a sealed envelope and given to her for safekeeping.

Shortly thereafter, Kasparov appeared in the commentary auditorium where he received a two-minute standing ovation, a loud and long outpouring of love by an appreciative audience. Everyone admired his great effort, and he slowly warmed to their support. When the cheering and applause finally stopped, he was a changed person, having recovered his usual poise and winning manner. After Kasparov had answered a number of questions, the Deep Blue team finally joined him on the stage and were met with a number of boos, not hostile boos, but more of an almost friendly, kidding booing. Everyone was in good spirits, much like at the end of a great theatrical production. The Deep Blue team had arrived on stage later than Kasparov because it was occupied in coordinating the printing of the game. The team was taken aback by the crowd's reaction, not realizing the nonhostile nature of the booing and the audience's efforts to raise Kasparov's spirits.

Maurice Ashley began with, "Garry, it's clear who the crowd is rooting for — who humanity is rooting for. What happened today?" Kasparov replied that this

> Was a very exciting and probably the cleanliest game in the match. I was very much amazed by h7–h5. Many, many discoveries in the match, and one of them that sometimes computer plays very human moves. h7–h5 is a good move. I have to praise the computer for understanding very, very deep positional factors. I think it is an outstanding scientific achievement. . . . the game was very tough, and at one point we reached a position that is very, very dangerous when you play the machine. I had not much time, and at one point I was very worried when the machine played 23...c5.... [I] managed to escape by a miracle.... [However] when I played 29 c4, I felt I was out of danger, and at that time it didn't play the same positional game as before, and suddenly White got a slight advantage in the endgame. And again it was very, very close, and I have to say it was a miracle that Black eventually was saved.

CJ Tan spoke briefly at that point, expressing satisfaction with Deep Blue's performance and congratulating both camps. "As the match progresses every game is better than the previous one, so I'm sure tomorrow the game will be probably the best game of all in the six-game series."

After Tan spoke, Ashley asked Kasparov about the next game: "Garry, you felt some piece of humanity was at stake in this match. How are your feelings now? You've been in many, many big games, more than we can even add up right now. Tomorrow's game? Same feelings?"

Kasparov replied,

> It's an important game for me, but it's probably more for the outside world than me. I'm playing a chess match, I feel really shaken after Game 2, and there are other factors than simply losing the game, and obviously the result of Game 2 had its impact on Game 3 and 4 — being completely disassembled after Game 2. I thought I would win one game, either 3 or 4, but it took time for me to recover and I managed to survive Game 4.... with virtually no preparation before the match, I have to be extremely cautious, and I think, with one exception, Game 2, I think I have managed quite well. And, in fact, if I hadn't resigned Game 2, that would have been a draw. The good thing up to now is that the computer hasn't won a game. I lost one.

For tomorrow, he concluded by saying that "I'll try to make the best moves."

With that, Kasparov and the Deep Blue team left the stage. As usual, everyone was hungry. The match stood at 2.5 – 2.5. One game remained.

13 The Rematch — Game 6: A Sacrifice and Surprising Patience

> "And instead of bringing out his bishop with bishop to e6, Kasparov has instead — whoa! Kasparov has played the move h7 to h6 and Deep Blue has instantly sacrificed with knight captures on e6, instantly, and Kasparov shook his head for a moment and played the move queen to e7, and Deep Blue has castled." Maurice Ashley, from the Commentary Auditorium, following the fast unfolding dramatic play of Game 6.

May 11, 1997, New York
Game 6, IBM Kasparov versus Deep Blue Rematch
White: Deep Blue   Black: Garry Kasparov

Caro–Kann Defense

The showdown between man and machine, between the world's greatest human chess player — possibly the greatest of all time — and the world's best chess-playing computer — definitely the greatest of all time — was set to begin at the customary three o'clock hour on this Mother's Day Sunday. Would this mark the day when man's very own creation, the computer, first defeated the world human chess champion in a legitimate match, symbolizing the beginning of a new era in the relationship between man and machine? Would IBM's Deep Blue team be able to accomplish the technological equivalent of landing a man on the moon? Or would the human race be given a reprieve with Kasparov postponing the inevitable? Would the landing have to wait for yet a greater effort? We would find out sooner than anyone ever could have imagined.

The score stood tied at two and a half points apiece after five rounds, and one final game remained to decide everything — all the drama and suspense of the seventh game of a World Series or a Stanley Cup Playoff. There would be no tomorrow.

With Deep Blue scheduled to play White in this crucial encounter, it was clear to all the pundits that Garry Kasparov was going to have a very difficult time winning the match, notwithstanding his capacity for lifting his game during just such moments. Kasparov had been there before and had come through. In 1985 he became world champion when he defeated Anatoly Karpov on the final 24th game of their match [11]. Kasparov went into that game up a point, needing only a draw to become world champion. But he did better than draw. Karpov opened by advancing his king's pawn, permitting his young challenger to counter with his favorite Sicilian Defense; Kasparov prevailed on that occasion with a 42-move victory. In his 1987 World Championship match with Karpov in Seville [12], Kasparov, now world champion, lost the 23rd game and found himself down one point and needing a victory in the final 24th game to even the score and retain his title. Again, here, he rose to the occasion, defeating Karpov in the greatest finale of any world championship match. Kasparov, playing White in that game, picked a quiet Reti opening. Karpov forced the exchange of valuable pieces in the middlegame, potentially leaving insufficient material for his opponent to win. However, Kasparov held fast while playing under severe time pressure, and despite several inaccuracies, managed to win an adjourned endgame on the following day.

Would Kasparov end this match with Deep Blue in a similar dramatic manner? Perhaps he had signaled his intentions a decade earlier in his autobiography when discussing preparations for the 24th game of his 1985 World Championship match with Karpov [11]. Kasparov said that, "Deciding my strategy for the final decisive battle was a serious problem. Playing with the sole aim of a draw is decidedly fraught with danger, and in any case goes completely against my view of chess." But he also realized that "In such extreme situations, when the opponents are playing at the limit of their nervous strength, much — if not all — is decided by how psychologically prepared you are, by your mental attitude. Victory goes to the player who proves to be cooler, more calculating, and more self-confident."

On the morning of the final game, Frederic Friedel was interviewed on ABC-TV's This Week, co-hosted by Sam Donaldson and Cokie Roberts [67]. When Roberts asked him what he thought was going to happen, Friedel said, "It's going to be difficult, and I'm very tense, of course, because it's our last chance, and with Black, and he should be a little bit daring, but that can go astray, you know." Friedel's words could have been echoed by any of the grandmasters who were following the match. While most felt that Kasparov should be more daring, they also concurred that that strategy had serious risks.

Now, though Friedel was a member of the Kasparov team, it is quite possible that he was unaware of Kasparov's planned opening moves. His answer to Roberts was his opinion of what he thought Kasparov should do. It was not based on his knowledge of what he knew Kasparov had planned. If Friedel had known Kasparov's plans, his loyalty would have probably prompted him to give a vague reply to the question. In fact, Friedel's answer might be construed as a confirmation that he did not know what Kasparov was going to do!

Meanwhile, according to Joel Benjamin, the Deep Blue team was not expecting a daring opening. The team felt Kasparov might play one final conservative game, hoping to win, but possibly quite satisfied with a draw after having had so much trouble in the match thus far. A draw would almost guarantee a third match with Deep Blue sometime in the following year or so with an even grander purse. Though the difference between winning and losing the game was worth $300,000 to Kasparov — not exactly pocket change for most of us — the purse was probably a secondary consideration at this point. His pride was at stake here. He had already received compensation from IBM for various promotional events in the months prior to the match. There was an IBM ad in *The New York Times* entitled "How do you make a computer blink" that featured him in a two-foot-high picture [66]. As a small but nifty part of his overall compensation, he had even received a new top-of-the-line Thinkpad from IBM that he had put to use against Deep Blue for analysis during the match! Moreover, IBM was talking about future cooperation on potentially lucrative Internet-related ventures.

The commentary auditorium quickly filled before the scheduled 3:00 start, and the commentators readied themselves. Maurice Ashley, Yasser Seirawan, and Mike Valvo were warming up the audience with their usual banter. In response to Ashley's "Yasser, what do you think his chances are today?" Seirawan answered,

> Before the match, I thought Garry was going to win very easily. I really thought that the computer hadn't made as much progress as it has and, I don't know, but I have a gut instinct that Garry is going to win. A real gut instinct, but he has put himself under a lot of pressure, playing the Black pieces in the final game, and when he was Black, he only managed to beat the computer once.

Joe Hoane was sitting at the game table preparing Deep Blue while his teammates were set to follow play from the IBM operations room. The Deep Blue team had methodically rotated CB Hsu, Murray Campbell, and Joe Hoane to the helm of Deep Blue, and this was Hoane's turn. An essentially shy guy and, of the group, the most intimidated by Kasparov's presence across the board, Hoane must have been hoping his shift would be during a relatively tranquil phase of the game. Little did he know.

Kasparov arrived several minutes late, his tardiness building up tensions already high with everyone but his opponent. In the seconds before his arrival, Carol Jarecki nervously went over to the board and aligned his knights to face dircectly across to the other side. When Kasparov arrived, Hoane stood up, and the two shook hands perfunctorily. Then they sat down for final preparations. As was his routine, Kasparov first removed his watch, placing it on the table to his right, and then using his left hand, quickly aligned his pieces to the very center of their squares. He immediately began to concentrate, gathering his thoughts, with his hands cupped over his forehead. Hoane calmly sat facing him with his hands folded in his lap.

The Internet was hopping, the photographers were furiously flashing close-ups of Kasparov, and the full house in the commentary auditorium was abuzz with anticipation.

While everyone was sure that Deep Blue would open with its usual advance of its king's pawn, the big question was what did Garry Kasparov have up his sleeve? What opening had he planned? Would he go to his strength with a Sicilian as he had done against Anatoly Karpov in 1985? Could he dare gamble on a victory with his favorite opening knowing that the Deep Blue team had invested extensive effort in countering it? He had seen how well Deep Blue was booked in Game 2 for his rarely played Ruy Lopez. He knew that every game he ever played with the Sicilian — as well as any other opening for that matter — was sitting in Deep Blue's opening book. Would he play another conservative, nonconfrontational, anticomputer opening as Joel Benjamin told me his team expected? Or would he try to improve on a line previously played in this match? Or would he select an opening that was totally different than any observed thus far, as he did with Karpov in 1987? The Deep Blue team believes Kasparov spent considerable time preparing something special for this monumental game, but what would it be?

Upon receiving the word from Carol Jarecki, Joe Hoane commanded Deep Blue to begin.

1 e4 [5s]

No surprise here. Deep Blue displayed 100% consistency in opening with this move, both in this match and in the Philadelphia match. Playing White, Deep Blue had had an even score with Kasparov in Philadelphia and had garnered a win and a draw thus far in New York. So there was no reason to try anything else. Kasparov most certainly anticipated this, nodding his head in concurrence when Hoane advanced the pawn. The first moment of decision had arrived!

1 ... c6 [15s]

Rule out the Sicilian! Kasparov had completely avoided his favorite opening in four consecutive games with Deep Blue, not playing it since the third game in Philadelphia when he and Deep Blue drew. To put his avoidance of the Sicilian in perspective, consider the following. When he played Vishwananthan Anand for the World Championship in 1995, he played the Sicilian in every one of his nine games with the Black pieces scoring two wins, six draws, and a loss. Further, at the three major events that Kasparov played during the period between Philadelphia and New York (The Olympiad, Las Palmas, and Linares), Kasparov played a Sicilian Defense every time his opponent opened with 1 e4. He won four games and drew two.

Given that Kasparov wasn't playing a Sicilian and that his first move was the same as that played in Game 4, the chances seemed good that he was planning to improve upon the line played in that game. He could be sure however that the Deep Blue team had spent considerable time booking for this possibility. He had developed a strong position in Game 4 by move 20, and perhaps he had found a way to do even better. In several of his games with Deep Blue, that is in fact what transpired — attempts were made to improve upon previously played lines. For example, the previous year in Philadelphia, Kasparov's moves in Game 3 followed those in Game 1 until Deep Blue, playing White, veered off by castling on the seventh move. Again in Philadelphia's Game 6, Kasparov's moves followed those of Game 4 until Deep Blue veered off with 5 ... c5. Kasparov showed in these two games that he was willing to go down previously played lines evidently expecting to do at least as well as he did the first time. It was only in Game 5 when he played a Petrov that a totally new direction was pursued.

Here in New York, Kasparov's moves in Game 5 followed those played in Game 1 until he veered off with 3 Bg2. However, except for this fifth-round game, Kasparov's openings were quite varied and hard to predict. This game would prove no exception.

2 d4 [10s]

This pawn advance was as likely to be played by Deep Blue as was its first move. So far, a repeat of Game 4.

2 ... d5 [10s]

A Caro–Kann! While generally thought to be a difficult opening for Black to win against an equal opponent, it was nevertheless "a real opening," according to Mike Valvo, who, like most strong chess players, felt Kasparov should stick to mainstream openings. It was now apparent that Kasparov hadn't found a way to improve upon the opening from Game 4. That possibility was put to rest by this move. But a Caro–Kann? Kasparov last played the black side of a Caro–Kann in 1982 against the Yugoslavian Grandmaster Dragoljub Velimirovic. Fifteen years had passed since then! Hundreds of games! Why now, and what could he be up to?

3 Nc3 [5s]

The most popular reply. Although the Caro–Kann cannot be blamed, Deep Blue's predecessor, Deep Thought, had lost to Anatoly Karpov playing this opening in a one-game exhibition match at Harvard University in 1990, playing 3 Nd2 instead of 3 Nc3 (see Appendix D). Of course, the Deep Blue book was very different from that of Deep Thought. For Kasparov, whether Deep Blue played 3 Nc3 or 3 Nd2 was all the same given that he was planning to capture the White e-pawn on the next move.

Garry Kasparov considering his fifth move, focusing his
attention around his king's squares.

3 ... dxe4 [1m25s]

Kasparov thought for about two minutes before playing this capture, seeming to gather his thoughts. After he took the pawn from the board, the first batch of 30 or so photographers was ushered from the room, and the second batch quickly filled the vacated space.

4 Nxe4 [10s]

Deep Blue had little choice here and played the necessary recapture. Kasparov must have believed that there was a good chance that the game would reach this particular position.

4 ... Nd7 [10s]

Kasparov played his fourth move in a matter of a few seconds, going into the Smyslov Variation of the Caro–Kann. This opening was studied by Aron Nimzowitsch, though named after Vasily Smyslov, the seventh in the line of world champions. In their 1989 coauthored book, *Batsford Chess Openings 2* [8], Kasparov and Raymond Keene investigated the main alternative 4 ... Bf5 extensively, but here, the world champion preferred to stay with the main line, the line of play currently in vogue by the top grandmasters. This kept his position a bit more closed than if he had played the alternate bishop move. A whole book is devoted to this 4 ... Nd7 line of the Caro–Kann [10].

5 Ng5 [15s]

Deep Blue's move was along the main line, and it's a good bet that Kasparov anticipated it. The move forced Kasparov to pay attention to an attack on the f7 square. Kasparov had played the white side of this variation of the Caro–Kann to this very position in two games of his 1987 world championship match with Anatoly Karpov in Seville. There he picked a less aggressive 5 Nf3 instead of Deep Blue's currently more popular confrontational and provocative 5 Ng5 move. Kasparov drew both games with Karpov, one in 20 moves and the other in 21 moves. In 1988 Kasparov played Deep Blue's 5 Ng5 when defeating Karpov in Amsterdam, and again in 1994 when defeating Gata Kamsky in Linares [10].

5 ... Ngf6 [4m50s]

Kasparov thought for about five minutes before routinely developing his kingside knight with 5 ... Ngf6. His eyes were focusing most of the time on the squares around his king. He seemed to be concentrating hard before making this move, with his hands in their customary places on his cheeks or folded on the table in front of the board, changing them from one position to the other from time to time. Was he considering alternatives to his knight move? There are 23 moves in this position but little choice other than 5 ... Ndf6, 5 ... Nb6 and 5 ... Ngf6, with 5 ... Ngf6 currently thought best by top players. Perhaps his mind was racing ahead to what was coming? The photographers were still present and flashing away, and maybe Kasparov was stalling, waiting for the mulling about by the media to run its course.

6 Bd3 [15s]

Deep Blue played another move from its opening book. The second batch of photographers was cleared out, and the atmosphere in the game room settled down completely. Arbiter Carol Jarecki watched nearby; Klara Kasparova and Yuri Dokhoian sat quietly at the back of the room; Gabby Silberman, CJ Tan, and Marcy Holle would occasionally look in from the back as well.

Michael Khodarkovsky, Owen Williams, and Maurice Ashley taking a coffee break.

6 ... e6 [50s]

Kasparov thought for about a minute before advancing his e-pawn one square, this time giving no indication, no clue, that other moves were under consideration. Nothing unusual so far. Sound moves along the main line of a popular opening.

7 N1f3 [5s]

The moves thus far have been played in thousands of games and, according to Benjamin, when Kasparov opened with the Caro–Kann, he must have believed that there was a strong possibility the game would reach this position. Unlike earlier games — except for Game 2 — where it seemed Kasparov was trying to steer Deep Blue into unfamiliar territory, thus far in this final game he seemed to be trying just the opposite. The real drama was now about to unfold. Events moved quickly, and just as no two witnesses to an auto accident have quite the same version of what happened, opinions here vary widely. The immediate question is whether Kasparov intended to play his next move or whether it was a mistake, a rare few seconds' lapse of concentration.

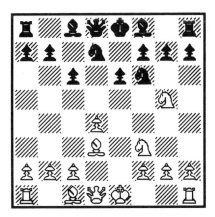

White: Deep Blue   Black: Garry Kasparov
Position after 7 Ng1f3; Kasparov played 7 ... h6.

7 ... h6 [45s]

A surprise of major proportions! Kasparov's move was a daring invitation to Deep Blue to sacrifice its knight on the next move in return for compensation in development. While grandmasters may be able to carry off the sacrifice, perhaps Kasparov thought the subtle positional aspects of how to proceed would be lost to Deep Blue, that if Deep Blue dared sacrifice its knight — the main-line move — its materialistic bent would eventually lead to its downfall. Rather than playing 7 ... h6, grandmasters usually play 7 ... Bd6 and then advance the h-pawn.

David Levy reported that he was watching Kasparov and believed that the world champion "had actually transposed moves in the opening [19]." Yasser Seirawan thought so too, as did Ilya Gurevich, who was quoted by AP writer Marcy Soltis as saying that "he mixed up his move order..." [60]. Daniel King said in his book that "Garry shook his head in disbelief. He had made a finger-slip allowing a known sacrifice, which, of course, was all in Deep Blue's database."

Robert Byrne wasn't quite so sure what happened. In his column that appeared in *The New York Times* on the following day, he said that "Kasparov either forgot the main line of the analysis or played the fatal 7 ... h6 to taunt the computer and lure it into sacrificing a knight with 8 Nxe6!?" [27].

The videotape of the game shows no indication of concern by Kasparov after this move. Further, what Murray Campbell, CB Hsu, and Joel Benjamin have conveyed to me in extensive talks and what information has appeared in print from the Kasparov team suggest that Kasparov intentionally steered off in this risky direction. Just before playing it, Campbell says one might have read into Kasparov's facial expression, "Well, here goes."

Supporting the belief that 7 ... h6 was planned was Bruce Weber's May 12th article in *The New York Times* in which he quoted comments made by Michael Khodarkovsky after the game:

> "It was a gamble," said Khodarkovsky, a close advisor to Mr. Kasparov, before the strategy collapsed. He said Mr. Kasparov was trying to capitalize on the computer's aversion to playing with a material disadvantage. "But the computer doesn't like to play in an unbalanced position," Mr. Khodarkovsky said. "He wants to win. He didn't come to play for a draw [37].

After the match, the Deep Blue team found that Fritz4 and Hiarcs avoided the sacrifice by simply retreating the knight to f3. However, Benjamin thinks that Kasparov believed Deep Blue would be booked to play the sacrifice. When the team forced these programs to play the sacrifice in reply to Black's 7 ... h6, they erroneously rushed to recapture the vulnerable pawn on e6 with their queens, opening up Black's position and allowing Black to eventually gain the upper hand. Benjamin thinks that Kasparov may have felt that whatever book lines Deep Blue had, they wouldn't go far enough to lead the computer through the minefield he planned.

Moreover, once out of book, Deep Blue's greedy nature wouldn't understand how to proceed.

Kasparov played the next three moves in approximately 10 seconds each. If he hadn't planned his seventh move, one suspects that he might have taken more time on these moves — especially on the next move where two possibilities had to be considered and the choice was crucial. Even though there was little choice on his ninth and tenth moves, he responded to Deep Blue's rapidly played moves just as rapidly.

In recent games, Anatoly Karpov and Gata Kamsky had both steered clear of playing 7 ... h6. However, neither could win with the alternate 7 ... Bd6. In 1996 Anatoly Karpov, playing Black, drew with Gata Kamsky at the 1996 FIDE World Championship in Elista, a city located in the southern Russian republic of Kalmukia and known for its interest in chess, in a game that went 7 ... Bd6 8 Qe2 h6 9 Ne4 Nxe4 10 Qxe4 Nf6 11 Qe2 Qc7 12 Bd2 b6 13 O-O-O Bb7 14 Rhe1 ending in a draw on move 54. Kasparov, in his Caro–Kann game against Kamsky at Linares in 1994, followed this current game until Kamsky played 7 ... Bd6 with the game continuing 8 Qe2 h6 9 Ne4 Nxe4 10 Qxe4 Qc7 11 Qg4, at which point Kamsky played 11 ... g5, eventually losing to Kasparov [10].

Kasparov's 7 ... h6 was played by Grandmaster Gennady Timoschenko just prior to the Rematch and reported in the March 1997 issue of the *ICCA Journal* [20], the last issue published before the rematch. Timoschenko, one of Kasparov's trainers during the middle 1980s, played an eight-game match against the team of Ingo Althofer and Fritz4 — a man versus man-and-machine match. In one of the games, Timoschenko as Black played the same Caro–Kann as played in this game including 7 ... h6. Timoshchenko's game and this sixth-round game continued identically for several more moves, diverging on Black's eleventh move. As will be seen, Kasparov played 11 ... b5 while Timoschenko played 11 ... Nd5. Timoschenko concluded that 11 ... Nd5 12 Bg3 Qb4 13 Qb1 Ne7 14 c3 Qa5 15 Bh4 Kc7 16 Bg3+ Kd8 17 Bh4 Kc7 forces White, now down a knight and with insufficient compensation to play for a win, to accept a draw by repetition with 18 Bg3.

Of course, Timoschenko's line gives Black only a draw. Had Kasparov, the particularly well-read opening expert, seen this article and found a line starting with 11 ... b5 that improved upon Timoschenko's insufficient drawing line? Benjamin thinks that Kasparov had examined 11 ... b5 in his preparation and concluded that he could, in fact, win with it against Deep Blue.

8 Nxe6 [10s]

It was not Kasparov's seventh move but this Deep Blue reply that really electrified the audience in the commentary auditorium; the sacrifice was played in a few seconds. Ashley, leading the discussion in the commentary auditorium, followed the fast unfolding dramatic play with the words,

> . . . and instead of bringing out his bishop with bishop to e6, Kasparov has instead — whoa! Kasparov has played the move h7 to h6 and Deep Blue has instantly sacrificed with knight captures on e6, instantly, and Kasparov shook his head for a moment and played the move queen to e7, and Deep Blue has castled.

Deep Blue knew what it was doing, still finding moves in its opening book. Benjamin had routinely checked this sacrifice out some time ago and found that Deep Blue could handle the tricky play that followed even though it would be down in material for some time to come. Kasparov shook his head and even seemed to smile at Deep Blue's chutzpah, implying that Deep Blue's move might have been a pleasant surprise for him. There was no sign of particular concern on his face at this point. Murray Campbell said it seemed to convey "I'm committed now."

8 ... Qe7 [15s]

With his right hand, Kasparov recorded Deep Blue's eighth move and then played his reply in one continuous motion. With two choices here, 8 ... Qe7 and 8 ... fxe6, Campbell felt that if Kasparov hadn't thought out his seventh move in advance, he probably would have taken more time to consider this move. Not only was Kasparov using none of his own time to deliberate over his moves, he was given no extra time by Deep Blue, which was rapidly selecting moves from its opening book.

Timoschenko says that while he played 8 ... Qe7 in his game against Althofer and Fritz4, Karpov recommends Black play 8 ... fxe6 9 Bg6+ Ke7 10 O–O Qc7 11 Re1 Kd8 12 c4 (not 12 Rxe6 Bd6 13 Re1 Nf8 14 Bd3 Bg4 which is better for Black) 12 ... Bb4 13 Re2 Nf8 14 Ne5 Nxg6 15 Nxg6 Re8 16 c5 Qf7! 17 Ne5 Qh5 18 Ne4 b5 with advantage for Black [20]. Neither 8 ... Qe7 or 8 ... fxe6 had been shown to lead to the victory Kasparov needed.

9 O–O [10s]

Deep Blue judiciously castled on this move. This was the first move selected from Campbell's extended book, which paid for the effort invested in it over the next several moves. With its own king safely behind cover, Deep Blue was ready to make life difficult for its opponent.

9 ... fxe6 [5s]

Kasparov had little choice here and played immediately. He could not take the knight with his queen because Deep Blue would have replied with

10 Re1 pinning the queen. Any other move would have left Deep Blue up a pawn and better positionally.

10 Bg6+ [20s]

Hoane, now a bundle of nerves as he watched Deep Blue trying to justify the sacrifice, picked up and started to move the wrong bishop, quickly correcting himself, but his error had little effect on Kasparov, who seemed to know what Deep Blue was going to play and that Hoane was making a mistake. White's 10 Bg6+ forced Black's king to a life on the lamb while tying down Black's rook on h8 to a life of inaction.

10 ... Kd8 [10s]

With two legal moves in this position, and with one giving up a queen for a bishop, Kasparov had little to consider and played 10 ... Kd8 in approximately 10 seconds. To this point, Deep Blue had consumed about 4 minutes of its allotted time, while Kasparov had consumed about 10 minutes. It was after this move and while waiting for Deep Blue to reply that Kasparov looked concerned with his position for the first time. He unbuttoned his shirt at the neck, loosened his tie, and closed his eyes for a few seconds. He remained in a state of intense concentration waiting for Deep Blue to play.

11 Bf4 [2m45s]

White: Deep Blue   Black: Garry Kasparov
Position after 11 Bf4; Kasparov played 11 ... b5.

Deep Blue's extended book regurgitated its final move. However, the score associated with the move wasn't sufficient to cause Deep Blue to terminate search quickly. The computer made its first 10 moves in only a few minutes. This 11th move, the first that took more than a few seconds, took two and a half minutes and may have given Kasparov the impression that the computer was now out of book. Mike Valvo, discussing the game in the commentary auditorium, said that this was "exactly the position he (Kasparov) didn't want the computer to have." In this position, Kasparov may have been hoping Deep Blue's greedy materialistic bent would lead it to incorrectly pursue his pawn on e6 with either 11 Qe2 or 11 Re1.

11 ... b5 [5m25s]

Kasparov thought for about five minutes before advancing his b-pawn, not a particularly long time, in Benjamin's opinion, given the importance of the move. For the first time in the game, Kasparov got up from the table and took a walk to his lounge area, returning only when Deep Blue played its 12th move. He walked away looking like a chef who had just put his special recipe into the oven. It was now out of his hands and he would take a little breather before returning to see how it was doing.

Was this the position that Kasparov was aiming for, and was he now setting up Deep Blue with this pawn advance? Benjamin felt that in the weeks leading up to the match Kasparov might have rehearsed this line through to this position and beyond, and that 11 ... b5 was an innovation that needed reconfirmation with several minutes of thought before proceeding. Benjamin thinks that he may have tested this on his computers.

In the commentary auditorium, the move was criticized for not relieving pressure on Black's cramped position. Some argued that 11 ... Qb4 or 11 ... Ne8 might have given Black better chances, although David Goodman and Raymond Keene point out that 11 ... Qb4 lost to 12 a3 Qxb2 13 Qe2 Nd5 14 Bd2 when Russian Grandmaster Efim Geller defeated Czech GM Eduard Meduna in the Black Sea resort of Sochi in 1986. Gennady Timoschenko's 11 ... Nd5 was considered in the discussion several paragraphs above following Kasparov's seventh move [1]. According to Deep Blue's log (in Appendix M), Deep Blue expected 11 ... Nd5 followed by 12 Bg3 b5 13 a4 a6 14 axb5 cxb5 15 Re1 Bb7 16 Qd2 Kc8, after which the computer felt it was ahead by 78/100 of a pawn. Perhaps Kasparov felt 11 ... b5 was first necessary to lay the groundwork for moving a knight to d5 on a subsequent move.

Michael Khodarkovsky says that Kasparov "came to Game 6 without any plan other than the Caro–Kann defense he considered playing three days [ed: it was actually four days] earlier [3]." This suggests that Kasparov studied this sacrificial line well in advance of the match. He started off in Game 4 as though he was going to play a Caro–Kann but switched on the second move to a less committing Pribyl. If he was planning to play the Caro–Kann in Game 4, then most logically he fell upon the plan before the match began. Otherwise, he would have had to do so between Games 2 and 3, a one-day interval during which he seemed occupied with issues related to Game 2.

12 a4 [3m20s]

Deep Blue, out of its extended book, had to rely on its monstrous search of a complex chess tree to decide upon this crucial 12th move. Deep Blue was relentless in keeping up pressure on its opponent, now threatening to increase its influence on the queenside. Again, here as on its previous move, Deep Blue could have played 12 Qe2, winning back Black's e-pawn in several moves. But this would have been a mistake, perhaps just what Kasparov was waiting for. Deep Blue's apparent lack of greed here was similar to that shown in Game 2, when on moves 36 and 37, it preferred to shore up its position rather than grab what seemed to be free material. On the other hand, Kasparov had witnessed Deep Blue's passion for grabbing anything available when it chased after his a-pawn in Game 3, capturing it on move 23 in what seemed to be a risky expedition. Moreover, in Game 1, even though Deep Blue won the exchange of a rook for bishop and pawn, it misunderstood how to handle the complex position that ensued.

12 ... Bb7 [25s]

Kasparov played this move after about 25 seconds of thought, giving the impression that he planned the move either when preparing for the game or when deciding on his previous move. He then stood up, looked over the board, and walked off toward his dressing room, returned and then walked off a second time, finally sitting back down when Deep Blue made its move. Meanwhile, it was reported in the commentary auditorium that Fritz4 felt Kasparov had a small quarter-of-a-pawn advantage.

13 Re1 [2m50s]

Hoane sat deep in his chair, trying to remain calm, showing no outward emotions, while he watched Deep Blue's score improving. Deep Blue continued to show surprising patience and restraint in not rushing to grab Black's e-pawn. Kasparov now went into a deep think, taking about 14 minutes for his next move. Two minutes into his thinking, he began looking exasperated, shaking his head in frustration. At this point, perhaps he realized that Deep Blue was better than he had previously given it credit for. The computer's 13 Re1 continued to strengthen White's position. Deep Blue's 12th and 13th moves essentially refuted Kasparov's gamble 11 ... b5, in turn, refuting 7 ... h6 as a way for Black to win.

The clock showed 1 hour 48 minutes remaining for White, 1 hour 37 minutes for Black; the game was only 35 minutes old. Fritz4 felt Kasparov had an advantage of almost half a pawn.

13 ... Nd5 [14m10s] 14 Bg3 [10s] Kc8 [10s]

Deep Blue had calculated its 14th move, 14 Bg3, essentially forced, while Kasparov was thinking about his 13th move. Kasparov, in turn, then played 14 ... Kc8 after only a few seconds of thought. If Kasparov had played 14 ... Qf6, White would have won Black's queen with 15 Bh4. Playing 14 ... N7f6 would have invited 15 Ne5, giving Black another major thorn in its side.

15 axb5 [8m20s]

Deep Blue's move showed that it wasn't interested in settling for a draw by playing 15 Bh4 Qd6 16 Bg3 Qe7. Deep Blue had no interest in settling for a half point, believing that it was ahead by about half a pawn. Deep Blue took over eight minutes to make this capturing move, with Kasparov at first

Ken Thompson relaxing for a few minutes.

concentrating hard on the board, then walking away. Hoane took advantage of Kasparov's absence to grab a quick drink of water. When his opponent sat across the table, Hoane would remain motionless except to type on his terminal or move the pieces on the board.

15 ... cxb5 [10s]

Kasparov immediately recaptured the pawn and walked away from the table.

16 Qd3 [1m55s]

White: Deep Blue   Black: Garry Kasparov
Position after 16 Qd3; Kasparov played 16 ... Bc6.

Every one of White's pieces were now on menacing squares. The queen was threatening to capture the pawn on b5, the rooks were on open files, the bishops were controlling vital squares in Black's territory, and the knight was posed and ready to charge to e5. Black's rooks were out of play and its queen, bishops, and knights were all ineffective.

16 ... Bc6 [2m50s]

Kasparov thought for about two minutes before making this move. He then continued to display great anguish, shaking his head sideways, then up and down, eyebrows raised. He walked away from the board one more time, returned and paced back and forth behind his chair, now with his hands clasped together behind his back. The clock showed 1 hour 37 minutes remaining for White, 1 hour 27 minutes for Black; the game was only 56 minutes old. In his write-up of the match in the *ICCA Journal*, Yasser Seirawan suggested [15] that Kasparov might have tried "16 ... Qb4 17 Rxe6 Be7 and hope," at least to avoid White's next powerful move.

In the IBM operations room, CJ Tan was hearing from the chess experts gathered there that Deep Blue was on the verge of wrapping up the game! He hurriedly called the PR team only to find it preoccupied with the usual matters at the beginning of games. They hadn't been following the progress of this game and now found themselves having to prepare for one of the most important press conferences in IBM's history in minutes, rather than the anticipated several hours!

17 Bf5 [3m10s]

Deep Blue offered Kasparov little choice but to exchange his bishop and rook for a Deep Blue queen and pawn, leaving Deep Blue with an overwhelming advantage. Deep Blue believed it was ahead now by almost a pawn and a half, seeing the game continuing: 17 ... exf5 18 Rxe7 Nxe7 19 Qc3 a5 20 Rxa5 Rxa5 21 Qxa5 Nd5 22 Qa6+ Bb7 23 Qe6 Kd8.

17 ... exf5 [3m10s]

After playing his move, Kasparov sat with his arms crossed on the table, shaking his head. He then put on his watch, looked toward his mother and coach and seemed to say a few words that conveyed his frustration. Maurice Ashley and Yasser Seirawan were slow in observing this, but when they did, they quickly pointed out to the audience Kasparov's symbolic gesture of putting his watch back on when he felt the game was coming to an end. Ashley interrupted Seirawan's analysis,

> I hate to interrupt but Kasparov is doing some very strange things right now. .... He's put the watch back on and that's as cryptic as ever in this position. Usually the watch comes on when he thinks the game is over for some reason, not usually for himself, but this is right in the middle of the game.

Even here, Ashley wasn't totally aware of the great difficulties Kasparov realized he faced.

18 Rxe7 [1m] Bxe7 [5s]

Kasparov played his 18th move in a few seconds, looking into space with what seemed to be glazed eyes, evidently resigned to losing. He slumped back in his chair and again looked toward his mother and coach, apparently saying something. In the commentary auditorium, Fritz4 was reported as finally seeing White well ahead, vividly showing the relative strength of Deep Blue over Fritz4.

Mike Valvo, who had been in the press room gathering information, returned to the stage at this point and said that he had discussed the game with Patrick Wolff. Patrick was sure Kasparov had planned the opening, that there was no erroneous permutation of moves, and that it was "very brave."

19 c4 [3m5s] Black resigns [5s]

Kasparov resigned immediately on Deep Blue's move. He quickly shook hands with Joe Hoane in a demonstration that the hand can be quicker than the eye, and then he walked away to talk with his mother and coach.

If Black had continued with 19 ... Nb4, then 20 Qxf5 Rf8 21 Qe6 would have sewn up Deep Blue's victory. The alternative 19 ... bxc4 is met with 20 Qxc4 resulting in overwhelming pressure on Black's King. Kasparov evidently had seen there was no way out of his predicament.

Thus Game 6 and the rematch went to Deep Blue. The final score of 3.5 – 2.5 was as close as a victory can be, but nevertheless, it was a gigantic victory. The member of the Deep Blue team must have felt they were on their way to seventh heaven as they rode the elevator up to the Equitable's 50th floor to meet the media.

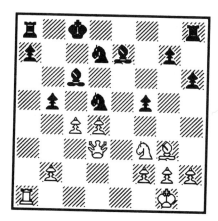

White: Deep Blue   Black: Garry Kasparov
Position after 19 c4 Black resigns.

References to Chapters 10 – 13

Books

[1] David Goodman and Raymond Keene, *Man Versus Machine, Kasparov Versus Deep Blue*, H3 Publications, Cambridge, MA, 1997.

[2] Daniel King, *Kasparov v Deeper Blue*, Batsford, London, 1997.

[3] Michael Khodarkovsky and Leonid Shamkovich, *A New Era: How Garry Kasparov Changed the World of Chess*, Ballentine Books, New York, 1997.

[4] Bruce Pandolfini, *Kasparov and Deep Blue*, Simon & Schuster, New York, 1997.

[5] Monty Newborn, *Kasparov Versus Deep Blue: Computer Chess Comes of Age*, Springer-Verlag, New York, 1997.

[6] Zsuzsa Polgar and Jacob Shutzman, *Queen of the King's Game*, Compchess Publishing, 1997.

[7] Anatoly Karpov and Ron Henley, *Elista Diaries*, Karpov-Kamsky 1996, Manasquan, NJ, 1996.

[8] Garry Kasparov and Raymond Keene, *Batsford Chess Openings 2*, B. T. Batsford, London, 1989.

[9] Anatoly Karpov and Alexander Beliavsky, *The Caro-Kann! In Black & White*, R & D (Chess) Publishing, Manasquan, NJ, 1994.

[10] Eduard Gufeld and Oleg Stetsko, *Caro-Kann: Smyslov System 4...Nd7*, Cadogan Chess Books, (Translated by Ken Neat), 1998.

[11] Garry Kasparov (with Donald Trelford), *Unlimited Challenge*, Grove Weidenfeld, New York, 1987. [An autobiography of Kasparov's life up to 1987, revised in 1990; originally published in Great Britain as *Child of Change* in 1987.]

[12] David Bronstein, *The World Chess Crown Challenge: Kasparov vs Karpov*, Seville 87, Raduga Publishers, Moscow, 1988.

[13] Jonathan Schaeffer, *One Jump Ahead*, Springer-Verlag, New York, 1997.

[14] Eliot Herst, "Man and machine: Chess achievements and chess thinking," in *Chess Skill in Man and Machine*, 2nd edition, P. Frey, ed., Springer-Verlag, pp. 166–200, 1983.

Grandmaster Chess Analysis Related to Games of the Match

[15] Yasser Seirawan, "The Kasparov – Deep Blue games," *International Computer Chess Association Journal*, 20(2), pp. 102–125, June 1997.

[16] Malcolm Pein with Garry Kasparov, "The king plays Deeper Blue," *Chess*, 62(3), June 1997, pp. 4–25.

[17] Malcolm Pein, "With Deep Blue in New York," *Chess*, 62(3), June 1997, pp. 26–32.

[18] Jonathan Schaeffer and A. Plaat, "Kasparov versus Deep Blue: The Rematch," *International Computer Chess Association Journal*, 20(2), pp. 95–101, June 1997.

[19] David Levy, "Crystal balls," *International Computer Chess Association Journal*, 20(2), pp. 71–78, June 1997.

[20] I. Althöfer, "A symbiosis of man and machine beats Grandmaster Timoshchenko," *International Computer Chess Association Journal*, 20(1), pp. 40–47, March 1997.

Newspaper Articles Covering the Games

[21] Robert Byrne, "In late flourish, a human outcalculates a calculator," *The New York Times*, May 4, 1997.

[22] Robert Byrne, "Deep Blue gently shows it has a nose for nuances," *The New York Times*, May 5, 1997.

[23] Robert Byrne, "After another stodgy start, a small gamble doesn't help," *The New York Times*, May 7, 1997.

[24] Robert Byrne, "Another 1-pawn gambit," *The New York Times*, May 8, 1997.

[25] Robert Byrne, "After another gamble, a fiery counterattack," *The New York Times*, May 9, 1997.

[26] Robert Byrne, "Kasparov loses after conservative variation," *The New York Times*, May 11, 1997.

[27] Robert Byrne, "How one champion is chewed up into small bits by another," *The New York Times*, May 12, 1997.

[28] Robert Byrne, "Why did Kasparov lose? Perhaps he tried too hard," *The New York Times*, p. B2, May 13, 1997.

[29] Bruce Weber, "Kasparov beats computer in first game of rematch," *The New York Times*, May 4, 1997.

[30] Bruce Weber, "Chess computer beats Kasparov, surprising experts with its skill," *The New York Times*, May 5, 1997.

[31] Bruce Weber, "Wary Kasparov and Deep Blue draw Game 3," *The New York Times*, May 7, 1997.

[32] Bruce Weber, "Kasparov and Deep Blue draw again in a tied match," *The New York Times*, May 8, 1997.

[33] Bruce Weber, "Saturday is D-day for Kasparov," *The New York Times*, May 10, 1997.

[34] Bruce Weber, "Fighting on down to the very last volt," *The New York Times*, May 11, 1997.

[35] Bruce Weber, "Deep Blue and Kasparov face final game," *The New York Times*, May 11, 1997.

[36] Bruce Weber, "Deep Blue escapes with draw to force decisive last game," *The New York Times*, May 11, 1997.

[37] Bruce Weber, "Swift and slashing, computer topples Kasparov," *The New York Times*, May 12, 1997.

[38] Bruce Weber, "Seconds of panic time aided nonhuman player," *The New York Times*, p. B2, May 13, 1997.

[39] Bruce Weber, "Kasparov, unbowed, looks to third bout with Deep Blue," *The New York Times*, May 13, 1997.

[40] Bruce Weber, "What Deep Blue learned in chess school," *The New York Times*, May 18, 1997.

[41] Jack Peters, "Kasparov defeats Deep Blue in 1st game," *Los Angeles Times*, May 4, 1997.

[42] Jack Peters, "Deep Blue turns tables on Kasparov, evens match," *Los Angeles Times*, May 5, 1997.

[43] Jack Peters, "Kasparov, Deep Blue draw in 3rd game," *Los Angeles Times*, May 7, 1997.

[44] Jack Peters, "Kasparov, Deep Blue remain tied at 2–2," *Los Angeles Times*, May 8, 1997.

[45] Jack Peters, "Kasparov, Deep Blue play to 3rd draw in a row," *Los Angeles Times*, May 11, 1997.

[46] Jack Peters, "After sudden defeat, it's Kasparov who's blue," *Los Angeles Times*, May 12, 1997.

[47] James Kim, "Chess score: Machine 1, man 1," *USA Today*, May 5, 1997.

[48] James Kim, "3rd Kasparov–computer match ends in a draw," *USA Today*, May 7, 1997.

[49] James Kim, "Kasparov, computer tied in chess match at 2 each," *USA Today*, May 8, 1997.

[50] James Kim, "Kasparov burns out in wild, wild, wild chess match," *USA Today*, May 12, 1997.

[51] Rajiv Chandrasekaren, "Aggressive playing style left little room for error," *The Washington Post*, May 4, 1997.

[52] Rajiv Chandrasekaren, "Across–the–board humanity lesson, Kasparov wins chess game with supercomputer," *The Washington Post*, May 4, 1997.

[53] Lubomir Kavalek and Joseph McLellan, "Deep Blue comes back for a draw," *The Washington Post*, May 7, 1997.

[54] Lubomir Kavalek and Joseph McLellan, "Almost a win for Kasparov," *The Washington Post*, May 8, 1997.

[55] Rajiv Chandrasekaren, "What the fans of Deep Blue see," *The Washington Post*, May 9, 1997.

[56] Lubomir Kavalek and Joseph McLellan, "Deep Blue, Kasparov draw again in Game 5," *The Washington Post*, May 11, 1997.

[57] Lubomir Kavalek and Joseph McLellan, "Blue Victory: Thanks to the Memory," *The Washington Post*, May 12, 1997.

Other Trade Articles

[58] Harold C. Schonberg, "Fischer apologizes to Spassky; plans for match still unsettled," *The New York Times*, July 6, 1972.

[59] Raymond Keene, "World chess championship," *Chess Life & Review*, pp. 538–541, October 1978.

[60] Marcy Soltis, "A 'TKO' Deep Blue defeats Kasparov," Associated Press Release, May 12, 1997.

[61] "The brain's last stand," *Newsweek*, May 5, 1997.

[62] Steven Levy, "Big Blue's hand of God," *Newsweek*, May 19, 1997.

[63] Steven Levy, "Garry sings the blues," *Newsweek*, May 26, 1997.

[64] "The rebirth of IBM," from *The Economist*, June 6, 1998.

[65] *Chess Informant 69*, Chess Informant, Belgrade, Yugoslavia, 1997.

[66] IBM Ad in *The New York Times*, "How do you make a computer blink?" May 1, 1997.

[67] This Week, Co-Hosts Sam Donaldson and Cokie Roberts, ABC, May 11, 1997, 10:30–11:30 a.m.

[68] News Today, with Janice Hutt, NBC, May 10, 1997.

[69] Raymond Keene and Michael Stean, "The candidates: Korchnoi–Spassky," *Chess Life & Review*, pp. 262–266, May 1978.

14 Deep Blue Is Triumphant

"We've got the wind in our sails," Lou Gerstner [1].

After only 19 moves and less than an hour of play, the final game was over, an abrupt and dramatic ending to a historic week of chess. The previous three games had been exciting, fierce battles; in each of these drawn games, the experts felt Garry Kasparov had the advantage at some point, but Deep Blue couldn't be toppled, baffling the world champion with its clever play. In the end, the computer prevailed.

Kasparov left the table at once and headed for the elevator. Accompanied by his assistants and his mother, he rode up to meet the media at a press conference and to participate in the presentation of awards. The Deep Blue team arrived several minutes later. Approximately 250 reporters gathered for the ceremony. Television production equipment and laptop computers were strewn about among dishes with half-eaten sandwiches. A video feed from the press room transmitted the proceedings to the spellbound audience in the commentary auditorium. Photographers were flashing away, mainly at Kasparov, at their usual voracious rate. The world champion sat there, stunned, visibly disappointed with the results.

On a small stage at the head of the room, Garry Kasparov and CJ Tan sat alongside ACM Executive Director Joe DeBlasi and me as I prepared for the honor of emceeing the proceedings. I began by introducing everyone — my team of officials, the Deep Blue team, Kasparov and his team, and DeBlasi. I then thanked Mike Valvo, Ken Thompson, and Carol Jarecki for the excellent job they had done. I went to great pains to explain to the press that the match had been played fairly — that my committee had observed nothing inappropriate in Deep Blue's play. I then introduced the Deep Blue team members, who were restraining their emotions in deference to Kasparov. Lastly I thanked a somber and disappointed human world champion for his participation in this exciting experiment with Deep Blue. As I began to introduce his supporting team — his mother, Klara Kasparova, Yuri Dokhoian, Frederic Friedel, and Michael Khodarkovsky — all sitting quietly side by side in the second row, Kasparov interrupted me, not letting me continue. I sensed that he wanted to accept full responsibility for the loss, saving his teammates the pain of being associated with what had happened.

I then turned the floor over to CJ Tan, who also thanked Kasparov for his participation and suggested that there was more to come. In particular, Tan brought attention to Web-based activities that were planned with Kasparov and expected to materialize shortly. Finally, he expressed his hopes for "continuing with Garry on a less competitive level." Before leaving the podium, he thanked the officials and congratulated his team.

Kasparov was next to the podium. The press gave him a long, standing ovation, echoed by those watching via the video feed in the commentary auditorium. He began by apologizing for his play in the final game. He had lost his will to win after the fifth game, he said. "For me, the match was over yesterday." His apology finished, he went on to say he felt that "the competition has just started." He expressed concern that Deep Blue had made moves beyond anybody's understanding, both human and computer, and that only the printout of several questionable moves might clarify what had happened. He indicated he felt he would have no problem defeating the computer in a rematch, saying, "It's time for Deep Blue to play real chess. I personally guarantee I will tear it to pieces." This marked the first time in Kasparov's career that he had lost a major match, and thus this ceremony must have been a particularly painful experience for him. He had established a pattern of not attending postgame press conferences whenever he lost a game, and had it not been in the contract that he attend this one, he likely would never have been present.

Joe DeBlasi talking with your author at the final press conference and just prior to awarding the prize money.

On behalf of the ACM, Joe DeBlasi then took the podium to award the trophies and prize money — $700,000 for the Deep Blue team and $400,000 for Kasparov. For the record, according to Robert Morris, the $700,000 went to support further research on parallel processing at IBM Research. DeBlasi congratulated the Deep Blue team and thanked Kasparov for his participation. He then underlined the great significance of the match. The ACM's involvement in this event was a fitting conclusion to the years of support the organization had given to computer chess. This was the culmination of more than a quarter century of playing a major role in the most exciting experiment in computer science and artificial intelligence.

Later that evening, IBM hosted a Mother's Day closing party in the Michaelangelo for everyone involved in the Rematch. The mood was ebullient, with toasts and short speeches intermixed with the dining. Two hundred attended the celebration, enjoying the sumptuous spread. The core of the Deep Blue team, that is, CB Hsu, Murray Campbell, and Joe Hoane, along with Jerry Brody, Joel Benjamin, and CJ Tan, was finally able to relax. Others who contributed were also there to celebrate: Gerald Tesauro, Miguel Illescas, Nick DeFirmian, and John Fedorowicz all helped raise Deep Blue's level of play; George Paul and Herbert Liberman had helped with the management; Marcy Holle and TSI's Debby Brown and Kelly Fitzgerald had led the PR efforts; Carol Moore had been responsible

The press questions the Deep Blue team and Garry Kasparov
at the final press conference.

for the outstanding IBM website; Matt Thoennes and Gabby Silberman were responsible for the complex infrastructure; Teddy Soohoo was in charge of security. Absent, but maybe there in spirit, were Thomas Anantharaman, who played a major role at the inception of the project, and the others at Carnegie Mellon who were involved during the pre-IBM days — in particular, Peter Jansen, Andreas Nowatzyk, and Mike Browne. And the many others who had worked on developing chess programs around the world for half a century? Their spirits must have been at the party too, floating around the room, celebrating as their ideas woven into Deep Blue passed the ultimate test.

Paul Horn, unable to attend, sent CJ Tan a note that was read to the team:

> Certain key events in history signal the start of a new era. Many people associate the legendary battle between John Henry and the Steam Drill with the start of the industrial age. I believe 100 years from now people will look back at the battles between Deep Blue and Garry Kasparov as the start of the information age. To the general public they mark the first time in history that a computer appeared to think, an event that will be commonplace 20 years from now.

Head of IBM Research Paul Horn.

Everyone I have talked to in IBM, including Mr. Gerstner, is incredibly proud of what you have accomplished. It is a great honor for me and for all of Research to be associated with the team that created Deep Blue. We shine bright in the brilliance reflected from your accomplishment.

Mark Bregman was proud of the Deep Blue team and particularly pleased that his RS/6000 SP played a significant role in the victory, showcasing the capabilities of the SP systems. In a letter addressed to IBM RS/6000 colleagues, he pointed out all the good publicity that the match generated for the RS/6000 SP, including broad coverage in the media and on the Internet. His division received a real shot in the arm from the match, increasing sales on a computer series that was already having great success.

The Deep Blue team members took Monday off, returning to their offices the following day. A large banner in the lobby welcomed them home and congratulated them for their triumph. The same banner was in the lobby of every IBM research center around the world and remained on display for months. The table on which the match took place, the pieces and board, and a mock-up of the clock were all prominently displayed in the Yorktown center's lobby. At 2:00, coffee, cookies and a specially baked white cake with blue icing were served in the company cafeteria, where several hundred of the team's colleagues gathered to give their heroes a rousing ovation. Robert Morris and Ambuj Goyal joined in the congratulations.

CEO Lou Gerstner sent a note to all IBM employees worldwide, expressing his congratulations to both Deep Blue and Garry Kasparov [2]. Written on Monday, May 12, 1997, it went as follows:

Dear Colleague:

I know I speak for IBM colleagues everywhere in congratulating the Deep Blue team on its outstanding performance. It was the culmination of years of research and exploration, and it will stand as a great example of IBM's technology leadership.

As much as I love to win (and I'm glad we did), I don't think the triumph of the match was that Deep Blue won and Garry Kasparov lost. The achievement was in demonstrating that powerful computers like Deep Blue can successfully tackle tough problems that require mind-bending high-speed analysis. Now we can apply what we have learned to help improve medical research, air traffic management, financial market analysis and many other fields our customers care about.

I also want to thank Garry Kasparov. There aren't many people in the world who would have been willing to match their intelligence and wits against an opponent like Deep Blue -- and under intense media scrutiny. Mr. Kasparov never considered this match a sideshow. He took it seriously, and his sincerity as our partner in this experiment made it the invaluable learning experience it was.

Lou

In the following months, accolades poured in one after the other. The Deep Blue team received the 1997 Innovation of the Year Award from *Popular Science,* essentially the same award from *Industry Week,* and they were an Innovation of the Year finalist in *Discover Magazine*'s 1997 competition. Further recognition of Deep Blue's achievement was *Businessweek*'s inclusion of the project in their special issue on "100 Years of Innovation," which appeared two years after the Rematch. Alongside the Internet, the assembly line, the Xerox machine, the triode, the transistor, and the supercomputer stood Deep Blue.

In July 1998 CB Hsu, Murray Campbell, and Joe Hoane received the Fredkin Prize of $100,000, the last jewel of the Triple Crown of the computer-chess world [3]. In 1980, MIT professor Ed Fredkin had established the prize for recognition of accomplishments in computer chess. Three prizes had been awarded over the years — the first to Belle (1983, $5000) for reaching the level of master, then Deep Thought (1988, $10,000) for reaching the level of grandmaster, and now Deep Blue for defeating the world champion (1997, $100,000). Chess programs had progressed from playing at the level of a master to defeating the world champion in 14 years. An interesting comparison shows that Garry Kasparov moved from master to world champion in approximately 10 years. (In 1975 he finished seventh in a field of more than 30 competitors in the USSR Junior Championship in Vilnius, a Master-level performance, and a decade later he won the world championship.)

IBM's Rematch website won the 1997 Cool Site of the Year Award in the Live Internet Event category [4]. InfiNet, sponsor of the competition, also recognized the Mars Pathfinder website, Webstock '96, The Gig, and the Tibetan Freedom Concert.

Marcy Holle and Ellen Beth van Buskirk, director of communications at IBM Research and to whom Holle reported, while working with Technology Solutions Inc.'s Debby Brown and Kelly Fitzgerald, won the CIPRA (Creativity in PR Awards) Gold for the best public relations campaign in 1997. They placed ahead of 500 entries representing companies of every industry and agencies of every size. The 1997 campaign made a whopping three billion plus impressions, a threefold increase over the staggering one billion impressions at the 1996 match in Philadelphia.

Even competing technology companies praised IBM. "It's an IBM team that did it. . . . My hat's off to them," was the reaction from Nathan Myhrvold, Microsoft's chief technologist, according to Laurence Zuckerman's article in *The New York Times* on May 12. Netscape cofounder Marc Andreessen offered, "It's a great way for them to show leadership in high-performance computing" [5].

Deep Blue had, indeed, become a real media personality. Three years after the match, a survey by Marketing Evaluations/TvQ rated Deep Blue's celebrity on a par with Batman, Austin Powers, rapper LL Cool J, radio talk show personality Howard Stern, and former "Baywatch" star Carmen Electra. The top-rated celebrities included Albert Einstein, Mickey Mouse, and Elvis Presley. Rated just behind Deep Blue were Larry King and Count Chocula.

Within IBM Research, there were many awards. Outstanding Contribution Awards were given to Marcy Holle for a PR success that had worldwide media impact and to Matt Thoennes for his efforts in coordinating the infrastructure at the match. Research Division Awards for the staging of the match were given to Jennifer Hall, Joefon Jann, Katherine Joyce, Dickson Lee, Geoffrey McNiven, George Paul, Gabby Silberman, Teddy Soohoo, Deborah Stanglin, and Charles Treppeda. More Research Division Awards for contributions to Deep Blue were given to V. Guruprasad, Herbert Liberman, Randy Moulic, and Gerald Tesauro. CB Hsu, Murray Campbell, Joe Hoane, Jerry Brody, and CJ Tan received special Corporate Awards directly from Lou Gerstner at an IBM technical awards program in June "for

Marcy Holle, Kathy Joyce, and Kelly Fitzgerald.

developing the IBM Deep Blue Chess Program." This gives an outsider some feel for the number of people who made significant contributions within IBM!

Having recovered his winning composure, Garry Kasparov appeared on CNN's "Larry King Live" on the May 15 [6]. When asked whether he was still angry, Kasparov responded,

> No, I'm not angry. If I'm angry, it's only with myself because, obviously, I made some bad mistakes, and — and lost the match.

Kasparov reiterated his interest in another match with Deep Blue. He told Larry King,

> I would like to play [Deep Blue] this fall, when I can be at my best form after a summer of vacation and preparation. And I'm ready to play for all or nothing, winner take all, just to show that it's not about money. Moreover, I think it would be advisable if IBM would step down as the organizer of the match. It should be organized independently.

At IBM there were mixed feelings on how to proceed. IBM certainly must have been unhappy with some of Kasparov's remarks during and after the match and concerned over the negative publicity that they could bring. On the other hand, IBM must have realized the great impact of the match in the computer world, where, along with the first match, the company's image as a dynamic, progressive organization was greatly enhanced. The project remained alive over the coming months, with the team exploring various possibilities. From time to time, CJ Tan called me to bounce around various ideas.

In the May 26, 1997, issue of *Time* [7], Kasparov outlined his challenge in detail: "a match of ten games, twenty days long, to play every second day." Given the fatigue factor, he might do well to consider even more than a day between games the next time. Great athletes of the world pace their performances carefully. The top football players can be called upon no more often than about once a week; marathon runners need weeks between performances. The best baseball pitchers need three or four days between starts. Two days would be too few while more than five would be considered too many, since pitchers lose their edge if they rest too long. They have a disciplined schedule between starts that usually involves light workouts after a day of rest. Based on these observations, Kasparov might best consider taking two days off between games: relaxing on the first day and then preparing for the next game on the following day. In a long match between two humans of similar strength, the minds of both combatants degenerate during the course of the battle at approximately the same rate, and while they might not be playing at their best at the end, their relative playing strength won't have changed that much. In a man versus machine battle, only one player is affected. By the sixth game of the Rematch, Kasparov's state of mind was likely similar to a truck driver who had driven from New York to San Francisco in a week, or to a student who had just finished a week of day-long college-board examinations.

Perhaps Kasparov would also improve his chances with different time controls. By the end of a typical game lasting four or five hours against a computer, not even considering the maximum of seven hours that a game could last, Kasparov would be mentally drained. This creates a dilemma for the future. When playing at high rates of speed — speed chess, for example, in which each side has five minutes on the clock — even the best humans lose some of their relative edge against computers because of careless errors. On the other hand, if the games take too long, the best players imperceptibly tire and are not playing their best by the end. Most sporting events never put an athlete through more than a several-hour test. Games of basketball, football, baseball, hockey, and tennis usually last no more than two or three hours, with time to rest in mid-contest. A seven-hour battle between man and machine is balanced to the machine's advantage. While hourly breaks of 10 or 20 minutes might help to equalize such a contest — for example, a tennis player can sit and rest during court changeovers — it is more difficult to escape the chessboard and to rest an overstimulated, adrenaline-saturated mind. In professional baseball, the pitcher is sent off to the showers at the slightest sign of tiring, and the bullpen is called upon. The team's pitching coach monitors the pitcher closely and uses a radar gun to measure the speed of every pitch. It's not so easy to put a radar gun on a chess player's mind! Nor do the rules of chess allow for a relief thinker!

In early June of 1997 Natan Scharansky, Israel's Minister of Industry and Trade, came to Yorktown Heights at the invitation of Zeev Barzilai to meet Deep Blue Junior and others at IBM. Sharansky had been imprisoned in the USSR on trumped-up charges of spying in the 1970s and spent a decade in captivity. Upon his release in 1986, he emigrated to Israel, where in recent years he has entered Israeli politics. Scharansky, born in 1948, had been a candidate for the Master's title when he was 15, and he was still an avid player. He had played to a draw with Garry Kasparov in a simultaneous exhibition given by the world champion in Israel in 1996. But here in Yorktown Heights and in head-to-head play, he was no match for Deep Blue Junior, losing several games before being reluctantly dragged away from the board to discuss other matters with his IBM hosts. He enjoyed his scrimmage with Deep Blue, observing, "I realize that against Deep Blue you do your best and just enjoy how it sees everything" [8].

There was contact between IBM and Kasparov through Owen Williams in the summer of 1997. According to CJ Tan, IBM told Kasparov in July that if he could obtain a sponsor and a suitable venue, another match would be given consideration. That never happened.

Meanwhile, Deep Blue Junior, accompanied by CB Hsu and CJ Tan, set off for Asia on a victory lap around the world. In September they held exhibitions and talks in Taiwan, Hong Kong, and Beijing. Everywhere Hsu and Tan went, they were given the welcome of conquering heroes. According to Tan, they received especially enthusiastic responses from the Asian media. Influential members of the government, industry, and academia hosted them wherever they traveled.

On September 23, 1997, Phil Waga reported in USA Today that "Deep Blue is checking out" [9]. Melinda McMullen, who had replaced Ellen Beth van Buskirk as director of communications at IBM Research, told the press that Deep Blue had been retired, that "we met the challenge, and our team is eager to use what they know and go on." The team members, with the exception of Hsu, were quite ready to move on. For Hsu, it was his special baby, while for the others, it was one exciting research problem in a world of exciting problems. Nevertheless, they would continue to schedule time for exhibitions. Kasparov was quoted by Reuter's Grant McCool as saying that he was "very disappointed," that it was not appropriate to quit at this point, and that there was still time to reconsider [10].

The Deep Blue team had achieved its goal of defeating World Champion Garry Kasparov. The Rematch had generated a tremendous amount of favorable publicity for IBM and its supercomputers. The Rematch was the world's largest Internet event up to that point in history, a giant feather in IBM's hat. However, an earlier informal survey of the media conducted by Marcy Holle revealed there might be less interest in a third match. IBM had concluded that enough was enough. In addition to these subjective arguments, the SP architecture was improving — both the individual RS/6000 processor and the interprocessor communication network — and the new version might well be too much for any human opponent, even for the world champion. A humiliating defeat might generate an unwanted backlash against Deep Blue and IBM. Some grandmasters were even complaining that Deep Blue was destroying chess, although this concern was not new. In fact, if anything, computers were popularizing chess as never before.

Outside IBM, many were eager to see a third match. Even if all the arguments against another match were valid, some members of the media saw fairness as the deciding factor. Even if the media ignored the match, even if the team lost interest and wanted to move on, even if the computer was expected to overwhelm Garry Kasparov, some members of the media felt that one more match was called for. James Coates of the *Chicago Tribune* put the case most succinctly in his October 12, 1997, article [11]:

> The geniuses who built a computer that whipped the world's best player fair and square in May need to learn here in October the first lesson that every back room poker player and pool shooter learns from the git go. I'm talking about the rules of threes. Say we're playing 9 ball or pingpong, and you wipe me out. I ask for a rematch and barely beat you. Then I say bye-bye, I'm the better player and now I'm going home? Legs have been broken for less.

Following its successful tour through Asia in September, Deep Blue Junior traveled to Europe with CJ Tan, George Paul, Murray Campbell, and Joe Hoane. Arriving in Milan on the 2nd of October, then on to Lisbon, Madrid, Paris (where Deep Blue Junior met Etienne Bacrot), Brussels, Stuttgart, Stockholm, Amsterdam, and London (where Deep Blue Junior met Malcolm Pein), Deep Blue Junior put on exhibitions while the team members gave talks and interviews and met with IBM sales staff and customers.

Since then, the team has gradually moved on. Murray Campbell has become interested in using supercomputers to attack problems in the world of electronic commerce. Joe Hoane took leave from IBM to pursue work with a new start-up company involved in digital signal processing. Jerry Brody retired after 15 years of service. Matt Thoennes took a leave from IBM to obtain a PhD. degree. Marcy Holle left IBM to join the high-tech world of Silicon Valley. Gabby Silberman was appointed director of the IBM Center for Advanced Studies. George Paul left Yorktown Heights and returned to his old specialty of scientific computing with IBM on the West Coast. Herbert Liberman returned to his retired life in Florida. CJ Tan became director of the E-Business Technology Institute, jointly associated with the University of Hong Kong and IBM China/Hong Kong. And as for CB Hsu? For him, it was more than a decade of passion and excitement. When I asked him what he planned next, he replied with a smile from ear to ear, "That's a secret!" I have heard recently that he has set out on his own, pursuing his dreams.

And where is Deep Blue now? And where will its eventual resting place be? Great racehorses are put out to pasture when their careers end. They spend their golden years courting the opposite gender while being pampered from their winning noses to their flying tails. But Deep Blue? The glorious years of its own special kind of mating are over. The two-cabinet supercomputer is stashed away in the Deep Blue Grandmaster Laboratory, quietly munching electrons fed to it through a long thick black cable attached to a power outlet on the wall, still calculating, standing there with the distinguished appearance of a champion. In an adjacent room, trophy clocks that Deep Blue won for its various accomplishments stand ticking on the shelves, reminding visitors of the glorious days gone by. There has been talk of eventually moving Deep Blue to Washington's Smithsonian Museum, where it would then assume its place among the many great creations of mankind.

References

[1] Michael Khodarkovsky and Leonid Shamkovich, *A New Era: How Garry Kasparov Changed the World of Chess*, Ballentine Books, New York, 1997

[2] Lou Gerstner, A letter addressed "Dear Colleague," *Think*, 63(2), 1997.

[3] Joann Loviglio, "Deep Blue team awarded $100,000 Fredkin prize," *The New York Times*, June 30, 1997.

[4] http://copli.infi.net/csoty97.html

[5] Laurence Zuckerman, "Grandmaster sat at the chessboard, but the real opponent was Gates," *The New York Times*, May 12, 1997.

[6] "Larry King Live," with Larry King, CNN, May 15, 1997, 9:00–10:00 p.m.

[7] Garry Kasparov, "IBM owes me a rematch," *Time*, pp. 38–39, May 26, 1997.

[8] Natan Sharansky, "Deep Blue dreams," http://www.forbes.com/asap/97/1201/060.htm

[9] Phil Waga, "IBM's Deep Blue checks out," *USA Today*, Sept. 23, 1997.

[10] Grant McCool, "IBM retires Deep Blue from chess matches," Reuters Information Service, September 24, 1997.

[11] James Coates, "PR gaffe gives Deep Blue a black eye," *Chicago Tribune*, October 12, 1997.

15 The Bottom Line

> "Yes, computers can think," Drew McDermott [4].
>
> "Those mindless machines," Martin Gardner [5].
>
> "It weighs 106 tons!" Lawrence Livermore National Laboratory about ASCI White.

The success of Deep Blue reverberated around the world following the match. The media and the general public tried to digest the outcome, focusing on the issue of artificial intelligence. The scientists who had been working on the project at IBM and elsewhere felt pride and joy at being part of this great, successful experiment. For IBM, the match had positive lasting effects, reflected in the sales of its computers and in the movement of its stock price.

When the Rematch ended, many felt compelled to draw some conclusions. While a computer had just shown that it can play chess as well as any human, some argued it certainly cannot do anything that we associate with our human intellectual uniqueness. In this regard, we are still safe and reign supreme on planet Earth [1–7].

Some said that chess is but a calculation, and computers are better at calculating than humans. OK! But, they cannot learn from experience, they have no intuition, and they cannot use what they have learned about chess to help solve other problems. But if chess is simply a calculation, then what isn't? Is it the ability to appreciate beauty, smell flowers or taste pickles, feel in love, sick, old, happy or sad, angry, take care of one's children? And if these intellectual processes are not calculations, then just what are they? Just where is the boundary between the calculating ability shown by Deep Blue when playing chess and the intellectual processes that say we are alive and well?

In a letter to the Editor in *The New York Times* [1], Yale University professor of molecular biophysics Mark Gerstein wanted to provide us some reassurance when he pointed out that Deep Blue couldn't even move its own pieces. In a letter following Gerstein's, Elliot Thomson went on to say that "Computers will never be 'handwringing' over their own meaning. They may crash, but they will never feel deep blue. And they may win

Employee of the Month awards, but they will never create such a program to lift the morale of their fellow computers" [2].

Possibly unnerving those who might have found any comfort in the previous paragraphs, Charles Krauthammer wrote in *The Weekly Standard* on May 26, 1997, that "if the speed and complexity of electrochemical events in the brain can produce thought and actual self-consciousness, why in principle could this not occur in sufficiently complex machines? If it can be done with carbon-based systems, why not with silicon (the stuff of computer chips)?" [3] Moreover, while Deep Blue was not moving its own pieces, a Novag chess computer that housed David Kittinger's Mchess program had done that more than a decade earlier.

The tangible lesson of Deep Blue's victory is that we have taken a major step forward in learning how to take advantage of the capabilities of our new electronic partner in solving difficult problems. A landmark has been established: in 50 years, computers have progressed on one important problem that we have argued demands great intelligence, progressed to the point where they can defeat the best human mind. These 50 years will seem like a drop in the bucket some day.

During these 50 years, progress in computer technology has been astonishing. The Deep Blue computing system performed about 50 billion calculations per second, compared to about 50,000 calculations per second on the vacuum tube IBM 704, the first computer to play chess in 1958. For round numbers, Deep Blue is one million times faster! To put this increase in a different context: in 1958 the fastest airplanes flew at approximately 1000 miles per hour. A trip to the moon would take about 10 days. If the speed of airplanes had increased as much as that of computers, airplanes would now be flying one billion miles per hour, exceeding even the speed of light — light travels at approximately 750 million miles per hour — and the 250,000-mile trip to the moon would take one second!

In the coming years, much faster computer can be expected. IBM has already produced supercomputers that dwarf Deep Blue. Working with the Department of Energy's Accelerated Strategic Computing Initiative (ASCI) program, IBM delivered ASCI Blue Pacific to the Lawrence Livermore National Laboratory in Livermore, California, in 1998. This $94-million RS/6000 SP supercomputer is capable of performing four trillion calculations per second, 80 times as many as Deep Blue. The system contains 5856 processors, with each processor being slightly more powerful than an Intel Pentium II chip. The system occupies about the same space as the infield at Yankee stadium, weighs as much as 700 people, and consumes the electricity of 300 hair dryers.

IBM delivered an even faster Deep Blue descendent, ASCI White, capable of 12 trillion calculations per second, more than 200 times as many as Deep Blue, to the Lawrence Livermore National Laboratory in August of 2001. This system has 8192 processors with 6 trillion bytes of memory and 160 terabytes of disk storage. It weighs 106 tons!

These powerful computers will be used to simulate nuclear explosions (possibly making it unnecessary ever again to detonate a nuclear device for experimental observation), study local weather patterns to improve forecasting accuracy, monitor global climate change, and improve techniques in medicine, manufacturing, and aviation.

IBM has plans for an even faster computer on the books. A 200-trillion-calculations-per-second computer, which, according to IBM, will have more computing power than the top 500 supercomputers in the world today, is due in 2005. In comparison, it will be 4000 times more powerful than Deep Blue. The computer, Blue Gene, will initially be used to model the folding of human proteins, hopefully giving medical researchers a better understanding of diseases and how to cure them. IBM Research recently set up the Deep Computing Institute and Computational Biology Group with

Novag robot moved the pieces for
David Kittinger's program Mchess.

approximately 50 researchers to work on Blue Gene and other problems that could use the power of the anticipated one million processor system.

For a long time, faster computers have been a consequence of smaller and smaller circuit components, and that trend should continue. According to Gordon Moore's Law, approximately every 18 months the density of computer circuits doubles, yielding a doubling in computing power. The Intel cofounder proposed this law in 1965, and it generally has held valid since then. With circuit components getting smaller and smaller, the laws of physics that set upper limits on just how small the components can be are being squeezed, and it's not clear for how many more years the decrease can continue. In 1997 Moore predicted that the pattern would continue until 2017.

Along with faster circuits, multiprocessing systems, such as ASCI White and Blue Gene, should permit computing power to increase for some time to come. In addition, the semiconductor industry has a third dimension to use for VLSI circuit design that should yield significant increases in computer power in the coming years. Computer chips are currently primarily two-dimensional. Hsu describes his chips as being 1.4 centimeters by 1.4 centimeters, omitting a value for the third dimension, the chip's thickness. In the future, this third dimension will be put to greater use.

As a small aside, it's no small miracle that silicon, and not gold, is the main constituent of integrated circuits; there is virtually an infinite supply of this element — for example, in the sand on the beaches — on Earth and it's cheap. Imagine if it weren't.

This dramatic increase in computer speed has been reflected in the size of the chess trees searched. In 1958 the Bernstein chess program, when running on an IBM 704, searched five chess positions per second; in 1997 Deep Blue searched 200 million chess positions per second, a 40 million-fold increase. Computers are now only one million times faster, but the search of chess trees is 40 million times faster. This difference, perhaps, can be accounted for by the use of better ways to store and process chess knowledge in the current programs, more than offsetting the increase in the amount of knowledge processed. The graph on page 32 shows the rapid increase.

Memory sizes have also been increasing at astounding rates. Deep Blue used one gigabyte of random access memory on each of its 30 computers, for a total of 30 gigabytes, or 240 billion bits. This high-speed memory compares with approximately 4000 36-bit words — 144,000 bits — on an IBM 704, an increase by a factor of approximately 17 million! The growth of memory sizes is more than keeping pace with increasing computing speeds.

An interesting comparison of the computing power of Deep Blue to that of the our brain can be drawn from Stuart Russell and Peter Norvig's book,

Artificial Intelligence, a Modern Approach [3]. According to their analysis, Deep Blue had approximately 1% of the processing capability of our brain! The gap between the processing power of the biggest computers and that of our brain is shrinking so quickly that the two will have comparable computing power soon. This assumes that information processing in the brain takes place at the level of neuronal message passing and neglects the processing of information at lower molecular levels. It's not clear how much of this takes place.

1958 was the time when a single computer might fill a room with its several thousand vacuum tubes burning out so frequently that a small maintenance staff with oscilloscopes in hand always had to be present to keep it running. Imagine, it was an era before the mouse and the video screen; large clunky teletypes and card-crumbling card readers were used to enter information. Decks of punched cards had to be dragged around by programmers. Now-extinct typewriters and typists then populated business offices. No floppy disks, no hard disks, no disks at all. Instead, information was stored in magnetic cores, on magnetic drums, and on long rolls of paper and magnetic tape. Time-shared computers didn't yet exist. E-mail and the Internet were nowhere to be seen.

The great progress made in the area of computer software is harder to quantify. Most programming tools used by the Deep Blue team, such as editors, debuggers, compilers, and assemblers, were in their infancy in 1958. The C programming language didn't exist. The edit-compile-assemble-debug-edit loop that now can be done in seconds then took hours. This loop is carried out by somebody who designs a chess program hundreds, if not thousands, of times. Developing a chess program used to be a very tedious process because of this.

When imagining what computers of the future will be like, we must remind ourselves that they are now in their infancy. During the coming century, they will be given the ability to see, hear, feel, and smell at levels far beyond their current ones. They will also be able to move with a flexibility and an agility that will exceed that of humans. They can already, to a limited degree, repair themselves.

But whether they will ever have any sense of self, be able to feel for the computers they create, or even for themselves, is far from clear. In the previous century we learned that the animals around us are much smarter than we imagined. The current century may well be remembered as the one in which intelligent life was found to exist or have existed beyond the confines of our Earth. It's a safe bet, however, that another century will pass before we create machines that truly become our intellectual equals.

On the road to designing a program to compete with Garry Kasparov, computer scientists have learned a great deal about how to program computers to carry out this important process of search. This research has been characterized by surprises and unanticipated results. And while the results have been discovered in the context of chess, they have important implications for other, similar artificial intelligence problems. What were some of these exciting results?

The effectiveness of brute-force search versus what is generally argued to be the more humanlike "selective" search is perhaps the biggest surprise. Early Carnegie Mellon researchers in Herbert Simon's group pioneered the selective search process they ascribed to good human players. But attempts to program computers to carry out this type of search have generally been unsuccessful. Too often, difficult chess positions contain exceptions to the heuristics — or rules of thumb, as the heuristics were sometimes called — used to eliminate moves.

Essentially, early chess programs used heuristics to weed out, or prune, moves at shallow levels in the search tree with the intention of saving time to examine other hopefully more relevant moves at deeper levels. When "shallow" and "deeper" are far apart, a program that carries out such a search is vulnerable to a sacrifice move. A sacrifice initially looks bad and is thus subject to elimination by shortsighted heuristics, but deeper analysis reveals a positive side. When searching to the depths carried out by Deep Blue, sacrifices abound! Some sacrifices are severe, involving the temporary loss of material, but many are small, subtle, positional sacrifices.

The attempt to design chess programs based on the selective search approach dominated the direction of chess program development until the middle 1970s. It was then that David Slate and Larry Atkin's Chess 4.0 totally eliminated pruning heuristics at shallow levels in the search tree. Their program was also the first to use iteratively deepening search, a technique suggested by Peter Frey, psychology professor at Northwestern University. Iteratively deepening search combined with brute-force search subsequently has been found effective in solving a wide variety of search problems, from speech recognition to automated theorem proving. Chess 4.0 carried out a sequence of deeper and deeper brute-force searches — iteratively deepening searches — for as long as time permitted. The fourth search, for example, examined all sequences of moves from a given position to a depth of four levels, two moves by each side. On each search, the program would look deeper yet along lines with unresolved tactical complications. At positions deep in the tree, it would then carry out a highly selective search. Each successive brute-force search yielded information that was used on the next, one-level-deeper brute-force search.

It took over a decade for brute-force iteratively deepening search to be picked up by other computer science researchers and used in other search problems, although it became a standard tool the following year or so in almost all chess programs. In 1976 the combination of brute-force search and iteratively deepening search, along with the use of Control Data Corporation's then-new Cyber 176 supercomputer, moved Slate and Atkin's program up to the Expert level, a rating of approximately 2100, a major surprise to all at the time.

Calling Deep Blue's search procedure a brute-force approach is somewhat misleading. The brute-force search procedure of Deep Blue actually has considerable flexibility. In particular, rather than pruning what seem to be bad moves, Deep Blue simply spends less time examining them. All moves at shallow levels in the tree get some attention, and they are searched and researched a number of times with improved information available each time. It is, in fact, the flexibility of brute-force search, coupled with the use of windowing techniques that narrow the search, and iteratively deepening search, all carried out on powerful computers, that has made the current chess programs so effective! Windowing techniques are used to focus the search to some range of values under the assumption that the value of a position doesn't change that much from one move to the next.

To date, the intellectual games of Othello, checkers, and chess have fallen to computers. Although it seems to go against current thinking, a world-class Go program may well need to use the same approach as Deep Blue — a brute-force, iteratively deepening search, and a powerful computer. Eliminating moves at shallow levels in the search tree will cause the same sort of errors that chess programs make when pruning moves at shallow levels. Good moves are too often not understood by nearsighted pruning heuristics.

A second major surprise occurred in the late 1970s when chess programs, starting to play at the expert and master levels, played much better against human opponents at speed chess than at slower speeds. Speed chess games are played with short time limits requiring all moves by one side to be played in five minutes. Chess 4.6 and Belle, the two best programs at that time, were able to do quite well in speed chess games against strong players, while performing not nearly as well when playing at slower speeds. This contradicted some popular thinking. Some people felt that human intuition played an important role in speed chess, and this was something that couldn't be programmed. But the reality was that humans made more mistakes than they realized. It was, in fact, when playing slowly that humans showed an edge over computers. Mike Valvo demonstrated this when he won both games of a two-game match against Deep Thought 0.02. The match was played over the Internet — way back in 1988–89 and took several months [9]. At the time, he was having difficulties defeating Deep Thought 0.02 at speed chess.

However, a pattern developed over the years where a strong player would lose to a computer at speed chess and then have difficulties winning at slower speeds several years later. Even Garry Kasparov's games against computers fit this pattern. Kasparov lost his first game to a computer at speed chess in 1994. Three years later in the Rematch, where moves were made more slowly, he was unable to win, finding himself under continual time pressure. In each of the six games, Kasparov played more slowly than his opponent, as summarized in table below. For each player and for each game, the table shows the total time taken, the average time per move, and the time remaining on the clock when the 40th move was made. In addition, the table shows the total number of moves and the elapsed time of each game. The bottom two rows summarize the data over all six games. As can be seen, Deep Blue averaged 2.3 minutes per move in contrast with Kasparov's 2.8 minutes per move. It was making the 40-minute time control, however, that showed the pressure on the world champion. In the five games that lasted at least 40 moves, Kasparov

Game	DB Time GK Time	DB Ave Time GK Ave Time	40–move Bal. 40–move Bal.	# Moves	Time of game
1	99 min 127 min	2.2 min 2.8 min	33 min 4 min	45	3h 46m
2	102 min 127 min	2.2 min 2.7 min	33 min 1 min	45	3h 49m
3	114 min 153 min	2.4 min 3.2 min	27 min 5 min	48	4h 27m
4	140 min 170 min	2.5 min 3.0 min	16 min 3 min	56	5h 10m
5	121 min 124 min	2.5 min 2.5 min	26 min 10 min	49	4h 05m
6	28 min 35 min	1.5 min 1.8 min	- - - - - - - -	19	1h 03m
All	604 min 736 min	2.3 min 2.8 min	- - - - - - - -	262	3h38m

Summary of time taken during games by
Garry Kasparov and Deep Blue.

consumed all but an average of about five minutes of his first two hours of allotted time. Time is a great equalizing factor in the game of chess, suggesting that faster computers will increase the difficulty of defeating them in coming years.

For computer scientists, that chess programs are now almost all written in the low-level programming language C is another major surprise. In the early years, there was talk of a need for a special-purpose chess language if a grandmaster-level program was to be created. The language should contain the words "fork," "pin," "check," "draw," and so on. But this language has yet to materialize. Instead, C gradually has taken over as the standard language for chess programs. C is portable. That is, a program written to run on one computer can also run on others, although minor modifications are sometimes necessary. C has excellent compilers, allowing programmers to efficiently manipulate information at the lowest levels. Deep Blue is written in a combination of C and microcode. Eventually, more sophisticated programming languages are likely to develop and maybe even one that can be tailored to chess, but their effectiveness will depend on having computers much faster than they are today. In essence, at this time in the evolution of computing technology, it is easier for us to talk to computers in their language than to teach them how to use ours.

There have been many surprises discovered by those who have built large opening databases and those who have built endgame databases. In both cases, mistakes permeate the literature generated by humans. Copying from books into a computer and using the information on the assumption that it contains no errors cannot be done safely. We saw that in 1991 Deep Thought lost two games (out of seven played) when it tried to use Maxim Dlugy's book, which was created in part just this way.

In the fourth game of the Rematch, Deep Blue managed to draw a complex endgame against Kasparov. Kasparov knew Deep Blue had a large endgame database and he preferred to stay clear of it. Positions from the database were found in the search, but turned out not to play a role in deciding which move to play. Deep Blue stored Ken Thompson's four-piece endgames in its random access memory. Five-piece endgames, as well as a few six-piece endgames from Larry Stiller's database, were available to Deep Blue but kept on slower disk memory. Eventually, maybe even in the next several years, all six-piece endgames will be available on a database. At the rate computer technology is progressing, a database of all seven-piece endgames may not be more than 20 years away.

Last but not least, the use of a large team of computers to search the chess tree in parallel is an incredibly exciting and challenging research problem. The surprise here is how difficult it is to develop an efficient procedure to carry out this process. While there are now computing systems with hundreds of processors, algorithms that carry out parallel search have had only moderate success in utilizing the available computing power. Ideally, using 100 computers to solve a problem should allow the problem to be solved 100 times faster than on one computer. But even using just a handful of computers, obtaining such a linear speedup by a chess program has not yet been accomplished. With each additional computer, the increased effectiveness becomes more marginal.

The problem is quite complex. Imagine a general who is assigned an army of soldiers with the mission of searching the desert for a lost comrade. Could you develop a strategy for effectively using the army? How would you spread the soldiers around? What would they say to one another and to the general? How often would they communicate and with whom? When they finished searching assigned areas, how would new assignments be determined?

If they all start at the same location, they would initially be falling over each others' feet, getting in each others' way as they spread out! How many soldiers would the general really need? Wouldn't the number depend on the size of the desert, and on the amount of time allotted? Given enough time, the missing soldier would be found by a one-soldier army. But time is always a factor, and the desert is large.

These were some of the issues faced by the Deep Blue team. Rather than searching the desert for a missing soldier using an army of soldiers, Deep Blue was searching a chess tree for the best sequence of chess moves using an army of VLSI processors. The search tree was huge, essentially a desert reaching almost to eternity, and time was constrained to an average of three minutes a move. Using a 30-computer IBM RS/6000 SP2 system with 16 Hsu-designed VLSI chess chips at each computer, Deep Blue effectively used approximately 480 VLSI chess chips during the Rematch. One RS/6000 SP node served as master or general, dishing out chess problems to the other 29 computers which, in turn dished them out to the 16 VLSI chess chips at that computer with each chess chip capable of examining several million chess positions per second.

The game of Go remains as the final frontier for researchers interested in developing game-playing programs that compete with the best human minds. Go has approximately 300 moves in a typical position, as contrasted with 30-40 in a typical chess position. Experience with parallel search in the context of chess suggests that the larger branching factor of the Go tree will make it easier to obtain significant increases in effective speed when carrying out parallel search. That is, while the Go tree has a branching factor about 10 times that of a chess tree, parallel search techniques will, in part, compensate for this more rapidly growing tree.

One of the quiet lessons of the match is how difficult it is to create a program without any bugs and how much testing and debugging are necessary to ensure that a complex program is relatively bugfree. Deep Blue had gone through months of testing and debugging, having played hundreds of games, and even with all this effort, small bugs surfaced in the very first few moves of the very first game. It was a testimony to the resilience of Deep Blue that it was able to perform as well as it did with the bugs present.

The match also vividly showed that computers don't tire on the job the way people do. In both matches Kasparov was not at his best by the end of the match. In Philadelphia he was sufficiently stronger than Deep Blue that it didn't matter. In New York fatigue was a factor. These considerations of reliability and endurance have enormous implications when using computers to perform difficult tasks in environments where errors cannot be tolerated.

Computers are now playing chess at a level that makes their moves often go beyond human understanding and explanation. When playing chess in the future, computers will make an increasing number of moves that defy explanation. The grandmasters following the Kasparov versus Deep Blue games were consistently critical of the computer's play because it wasn't making moves they expected; in retrospect, Deep Blue was doing fine. This phenomenon has been observed for many years in regard to certain endgames. Five-piece endgame databases play perfect chess in very complex positions, so complex that their moves are beyond reason, illogical. No practical amount of time would permit a strong player to understand why a move was selected. The same behavior is spreading to other stages of the game. The day is quickly approaching when computers will be making moves, each of which, to understand, might require careful reading of the equivalent of an encyclopedia.

For the United States, Deep Blue's triumph showed the great success of the nation's emigration policy, promoting a melting pot of ideas and creativity, benefiting from the great energies that individuals from other nations bring with them. CB Hsu came to the United States from his birthplace in Taiwan, Murray Campbell from Canada, and Thomas Anantharaman from India. Joe Hoane, Jerry Brody, and Joel Benjamin were all born in the United States. CJ Tan was born in China. The "International" in IBM was most befitting as the Deep Blue team was truly an international one.

And Deep Blue's triumph was a history lesson on modern politics! For over a week, a Russian world champion received standing ovations from a mainly American audience every time he stood before them. He was embraced by the American public as one of their own, a Russian American hero, maybe returning to his home in Moscow after the match, but in some sense a spiritual American forever. A far cry from the days of Bobby Fischer and Boris Spassky.

The success of Deep Blue was particularly important to IBM. The two matches showed the great potential of the Internet as a mass communication tool, and they showed IBM playing a leadership role in this regard. While the Philadelphia match was the largest Internet event to that point, the Rematch was larger yet. IBM's website received more than 74 million hits from over 4 million users during the six-game Rematch. One SP was defeating Kasparov, while others were busy winning the battle for the king of Internet broadcasting, supervising the distribution of the games to an audience from over 100 countries around the world.

Once upon a time, IBM ranked among the leaders in the world of supercomputers. In 1970, when the first major competition between computers that played chess was held, Hans Berliner pleaded with me as the organizer of the event to arrange for his chess program, Jbit, to run on Columbia University's IBM 360/91, one of the premier supercomputers of the day. He had designed it to run on a Digital Equipment Corporation PDP–10 computer at Carnegie Mellon, but he felt he could improve the program's chances by running it on the 360/91. Berliner came to New York in advance of the tournament to get his program up and running on the 360/91. His program did well in the event, though not well enough to win. For this 1970 tournament, half of the participating computers were large IBM

Columbia University's IBM 360/91 supercomputer, 1970,

systems, Columbia's 360/91 and two 360/65s (at Texas A&M and Bell Laboratories). Over the coming years, IBM supercomputers slowly lost ground to other systems. By the early 1990s, they were essentially nowhere to be seen.

Over the next several years, IBM went from near-zero visibility in the world of supercomputers to become the most prominent name in the field today [10]. The SP-series computers and their offspring now dominate the market of giant computers. The table below, in which the years 1993–2001 are summarized, dramatizes this striking growth by IBM supercomputers. The first column indicates the number of IBM supercomputers among the 10 largest in the world, the next column among the 25 largest, and the third column among the 100 largest computers in the world. The table shows that in 1993, there wasn't a single IBM computer among the 10, 25, and even 100 largest computers in the world. Eight years later, in 2001, there were 32 IBM computers among the 100 largest. As dramatic as that is, even more dramatic is that today half of the world's 10 largest computers and 12 of the world's 25 largest computers are IBM products.

How much of the success of IBM's supercomputer program can be attributed to the chess effort is hard to measure. However, at IBM they appreciate the value of the Deep Blue name. The world has turned to "Deep" and "Blue" for Big Blue: from ASCI Blue Pacific to Blue Gene to Deep Computing to even Deep Thunder (a project in the Deep Computing Institute for small-scale weather modeling such as thunder storms) and Blue Hammer (a software system intended to help e-commerce firms

	Number of IBM computers among largest		
Year	10	25	100
1993	0	0	0
1994	0	0	8
1995	3	3	9
1996	0	3	13
1997	0	1	13
1998	2	2	21
1999	2	4	25
2000	5	10	30
2001	5	12	32

Number of IBM computers among the
largest computers in the world for 1993–2001,

manage clusters of servers from a single point of control). Of course, even ASCI White conjures up visions of the color "blue" heating up to the point where it turns "white" hot!

IBM's stock soared during the course of the Rematch. The Philadelphia match saw an increase of 5.8% in its value. The Rematch saw a similar increase, from $162.12 at the close of trading on Friday, May 2 to $173.50 at the close of trading on May 12. This increase of $11.37 amounts to a 7% rise. IBM jumped $6.00 alone on the 12th. With approximately one billion shares of stock (IBM's stock had split between the two matches), the $11.37 represents an increase in the value of IBM of $11.4 billion in just over one week. As we argued earlier, if credit for 10% of the increase was due to the Rematch, the Rematch was worth $1.14 billion to IBM! Given that costs related to Deep Blue totalled in the neighborhood of an estimated $20 million over the lifetime of the project at IBM, that's not a bad return on investment: over a billion dollars for a $20 million investment for the two matches! This time, for what it is worth, the Dow Jones Industrial Average rose 3% during the same time (probably 1% due to the rise in IBM). Microsoft dropped $2.25 from $120.75 to $118.25, while Intel rose a modest $1.75, from $157.37 to $159.12. This $1.14 billion return is a conservative

CJ Tan demonstrating Deep Thunder to a group of Chinese visitors; next to IBM CEO Lou Gerstner on the extreme left is China's President Jaing Zemin.

estimate; the increase in IBM's stock price was probably more than 10% due to Deep Blue; most likely there was an increase in the value of IBM's stock due to Deep Blue that occurred outside the one-week timeframe of the two matches as well. This could increase the value of Deep Blue's contribution to IBM's stock value by two to three times the estimate. Let's leave it at $3 billion — hard to comprehend!

References

[1] Mark Gerstein, "How smart can it be?" *The New York Times*, Letters to the Editor, May 13, 1997.

[2] Elliot Thomson, "Computer morale," *The New York Times*, Letters to the Editor, May 13, 1997.

[3] George Johnson, "Conventional wisdom says machines cannot think," *The New York Times*, May 9, 1997.

[4] Drew McDermott, "Yes, computers can think," *The New York Times*, May 13, 1997.

IBM's ASCI White, the world's largest computer.

[5] Martin Gardner, "Those mindless machines," *The Washington Post*, May 25, 1997.

[6] David Gelernter, "How hard is chess?" *Time*, May 19, 1997.

[7] Charles Krauthammer, "Be afraid. The meaning of Deep Blue's victory," *The Weekly Standard*, pp. 19–23, May 26, 1997.

[8] Stuart Russell and Peter Norvig, *Artificial Intelligence, A Modern Approach*, Prentice-Hall, Englewood Cliffs, NJ, 1995.

[9] Mike Valvo, "The Valvo–Deep Thought UNIX mail match," *ICCA Journal*, 12(3), pp. 183–190, September 1989.

[10] www.top500.org.

16 The Light Side of Deep Blue

"It's demanding an agent . . . ," Duane
Powell, May 13, 1997.

Through cartoons, we often express our ideas more powerfully and with greater conciseness than we do through words. Inanimate objects come to life, see, hear, reason, and feel. In this regard, Deep Blue provided a field day for the masters of subtle — and sometimes not so subtle — wit, the cartoonists of the American press.

Dozens of cartoons appeared during and after the Philadelphia and New York matches. Those after New York were generally more favorable to the computer than those from the year-earlier Philadelphia match, after which little love was expressed between man and machine. Four cartoons, published after the Philadelphia match and appearing on the following pages, express this hostility. Another 11, published after New York and appearing next, show an entirely different attitude.

Jim Borgman shows that someday computers might take total control, with humans nowhere to be seen. His *Jacksonville Citizen Patriot* cartoon of February 23, 1996, is a spoof of the IBM – Apple battle of the mid-1990s when Apple looked like it was on its way out. IBM is shown crushing Apple, having captured all its pieces except the king, and telling it to find a move.

Cartoonist Jim Borgman, *Jacksonville Citizen Patriot*, February 23, 1996.
(By special permission of Jim Borgman and King Features Syndicate.)

Hostility came out in Mike Thompson's cartoon strip in the *Daily Hampshire Gazette* on February 24, 1996. It first shows the frustration of the human race with computers taking over jobs and making the average Joe feel inadequate; it then shows glee and relief that, at least at the game of chess, man has the upper hand. Thompson's computer can see and is able to read the newspaper article shoved in its screen — or face — about Garry Kasparov's 1996 victory over Deep Blue.

Mike Luckovich shows zero love between man and machine in his *Lawrence Daily Journal – World* cartoon of February 21, 1996, in which he pictures a computer jabbering while playing chess at a level that makes Kasparov sweat.

Finally, in the *Williamsport Sun-Gazette* on March 1, 1996, cartoonist Brian Duffy gives a computer other computers for friends and shows it understands natural language while being unpleasant, to say the least, when told the bad news about its friend, Deep Blue, losing to Kasparov.

These cartoons from the first match indicate no love lost between man and machine.

Cartoonist Mike Thompson, *Daily Hampshire Gazette*, February 24, 1996.
(By permission of Mike Thompson and Copley News Service.)

Cartoonist Mike Luckovich, *Lawrence Daily Journal –World*, February 21, 1996.
(By permission of Mike Luckovich and Creators Syndicate, Inc.)

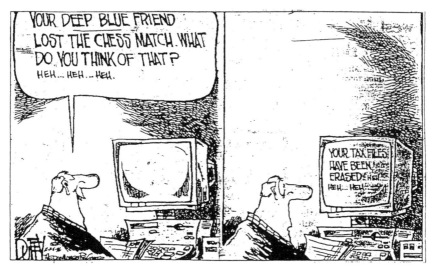

Cartoonist Brian Duffy, *Williamsport Sun-Gazette*, March 1, 1996.
(By permssion of Brian Duffy.)

During and following the rematch, a number of cartoons appeared with a markedly different flavor: the previous hostility between man and machine was gone. IBM's PR message that the RS/6000 SP is not only good at chess but can be used to solve other problems had succeeded. Deep Blue became another one of us.

In the *Arkansas Democrat-Gazette* on May 13, 1997, John Deering's cartoon features Deep Blue playing golf against Tiger Woods. The world's greatest golfer reacts with a touch of concern, saying "uh, oh," when realizing who his opponent is. Nobody intimidates Tiger very much.

In a cartoon drawn by Bill DeOre that appeared in *The Dallas Morning News* on May 13, 1997, Deep Blue is zipping along, looking for a partner with whom to enjoy a game of tennis.

Cartoonist Steve Breen shows Deep Blue ready to go head to head with Michael Jordan in a game of basketball (*Ashbury Park Press*, May 6, 1997).

These cartoons show Deep Blue as a capable and versatile athlete. Two show Deep Blue competing with the best athletes in their respective sport. In none are the hostile feelings that characterized the earlier cartoons present.

Cartoonist John Deering, *Arkansas Democrat-Gazette*, May 13, 1997.
(By permission of John Deering.)

DEORE'S WORLD

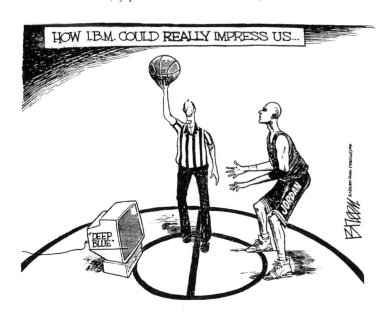

TENNIS, ANYONE?...

Bill DeOre/The Dallas Morning News

Cartoonist Bill DeOre, *The Dallas Morning News*, May 13, 1997.
(By permission of Bill DeOre.)

Cartoonist Steve Breen, *Ashbury Park Press*, May 6, 1997.
(By permission of Steve Breen and Copley News Service.)

Beyond playing basketball, Deep Blue is shown by Jeff Stahler in the *Cincinnati Post* on May 7, 1997, trying its hand at the headier occupation of coaching. Here, Coach Pitino is being replaced by a computer, but there is no hostility reflected by the tall team member who is about to meet his new coach — more a sense of bewilderment.

IBM must have been delighted when it saw then-President Clinton and Senate Majority Leader Lott calling upon Deep Blue to solve federal budget problems as depicted by Richard Crowson in the *Wichita Eagle* on May 13, 1997. Deep Blue has become an economic advisor to the highest levels of the U.S. government.

In the *Windsor Star* on May 13, 1997, cartoonist Mike Graston shows one typical Canadian youth aspiring to be Wayne Gretsky, Canada's greatest hockey player of all time, and a second aspiring to be Deep Blue, the greatest chess player of all time. No hostility here. Deep Blue's fame goes far beyond the borders of America, although, in this case, Windsor, Ontario, is no more than a bridge away from Detroit, Michigan.

Cartoonist Jeff Stahler, *Cincinnati Post*, May 7, 1997.
(stahler@United Feature Syndicate.)

CROWSON'S VIEW

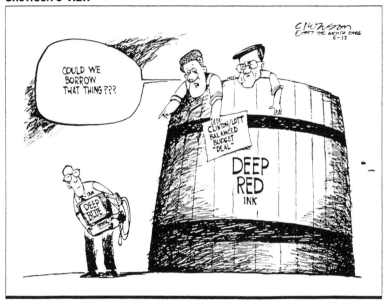

Cartoonist Richard Crowson, *Wichita Eagle*, May 13, 1997.
(By permission of Richard Crowson.)

Cartoonist Mike Graston, *Windsor Star*, May 13, 1997.
(By permission of Mike Graston.)

Deep Blue also became more human, learning to enjoy its newfound fame. Realizing its status, it demanded a few things every star is entitled to.

More money — as shown in a John Sherffius' cartoon in the *Ventura County Star* on May 9, 1997, even before polishing off Kasparov, threatening to jump ship and play for Apple if refused.

A Nike contract — requested only minutes after dispensing with Kasparov, to be negotiated by its agent, as Dwane Powell depicts in *The News & Observer* on May 13, 1997.

A life of leisure — relaxing poolside at a country club while its agent managed its commitments, as drawn by Richard Guindon of the *Detroit Free Press* on May 12, 1997.

Cartoonist John Sherffius, *Ventura County Star*, May 9, 1997.
(By permission of John Sherffius.)

Cartoonist Dwane Powell, *The News & Observer*, May 13, 1997.
(By permission of Dwane Powell and Creators Syndicate, Inc.)

Cartoonist Richard Guindon, *Detroit Free Press*, May 12, 1997.
(By permission of Richard Guindon and the *Detroit Free Press*.)

It takes a woman's psyche to imagine Deep Blue in love with a vacuum cleaner, as Etta Hulme portrays in the *Fort Worth Star-Telegram* on May 13, 1997. Hulme is the only woman of this somewhat randomly selected group of cartoonists. It's not clear how the vacuum cleaner feels!

Not everyone is ready to capitulate to Deep Blue's daunting capabilities, however. In a cartoon in *The St. Petersburg Times* on May 13, 1997, Don Addis depicts a young champion of Eleanor Abbott's game "Candy Land" coming to see Deep Blue. She has heard of Deep Blue's success and is there to teach it a lesson or two. "Deep Blue may be chess champ, but not Candy Land champ," she says to herself! It might be that she is coming to obtain advice from Deep Blue, rather than confronting it — one more person seeking help. Her facial expression conveys a combination of unhappiness, anxiety, and determination. The unhappiness and anxiety suggest she has come to learn, while the determination suggests battle. However, her strong knock on the door is the clincher, signaling it is battle she sought, as Don Addis, himself, confirmed to me in a brief appreciated note.

The last cartoon reflects a common theme: we can always pull the plug and end the pompous and annoying "checkmate" and "you got e-mail." In some cartoons, the plug is pulled quite by chance, as shown by Kirk Walters in his *Toledo Blade* cartoon on May 13, 1997; in others, it is pulled most deliberately, showing who does, in fact, have the final word. Whew!

Cartoonist Etta Hulme, *Fort Worth Star-Telegram*, May 13, 1997.
(By permission of Etta Hulme and the *Fort Worth Star-Telegram*.)

Cartoonist Don Addis, *The St. Petersburg Times*, May 13, 1997.
(By permission of Don Addis and *The St. Petersburg Times*.)

Cartoonist Kirk Walters, *Toledo Blade*, May 13, 1997.
(By permission of Kirk Walters and the *Toledo Blade*.)

Appendix A
Rules of Play for the Rematch

1. The rate of play shall be 40 moves per player in the first two hours of that player's time (the First Period), then 20 moves per player in the next one hour of that player's time (the Second Period), then all the remaining moves in an additional 30 minutes per player (the Final Period). Any time not consumed during the first period is carried forward to the second period and any time not consumed from the second period is carried forward to the final period.

2. Kasparov has the right of choice of the chess clock to be used during the Match. In the event of there being a faulty clock and if a replacement of the same type of clock is unavailable, the ACM has the right to substitute a chess clock of a different type.

3. During the opening ceremony, Kasparov will draw lots to determine his color in the first game of the Match and thereafter the colors will alternate, irrespective of game postponement or forfeiture.

4. Deep Blue shall be operated by an operator provided for this purpose by IBM. Provided that it is not Kasparov's turn to move, the operator may be replaced at any time or times during a game or the Match at IBM's discretion.

5. The operator, at his option, shall sit at the chess table facing Kasparov. Although the operator is free to move about in a nondistracting manner when it is Deep Blue's turn to move, the operator may not leave the table or move in a distracting manner when it is Kasparov's turn to move.

6. In the event of a technical fault or problem in any way relating to Deep Blue, the operator may, provided that it is not Kasparov's turn to move, communicate with any person he chooses in such a manner as to avoid any distraction which may reasonably be regarded as disturbing to Kasparov.

7. When it is Deep Blue's turn to move, Deep Blue's chess clock must remain running at all times even though there may be a technical fault (excluding

power failure or other conditions which make the game unplayable) which prevents Deep Blue's move from being made in the normal way.

8. When Kasparov has made his move, the IBM operator must promptly communicate this move to Deep Blue via equipment provided for this purpose, such equipment to operate in a manner which cannot reasonably be regarded as disturbing to Kasparov. In addition, the operator is required to promptly communicate to Deep Blue information about draw offers and draw refusals.

9. When Deep Blue has chosen its move and communicated its move to the operator, the operator shall make Deep Blue's move on the chess board and then press Deep Blue's side of the chess clock.

10. If the operator makes a mistake either in communicating Kasparov's move to Deep Blue or in making Deep Blue's move on the chess board, when the mistake is discovered, the Arbiter shall set up the pieces on the chess board to their positions immediately before the mistake, and adjust the players' clock times. If it is possible for the Arbiter to determine the times that should be showing on the players' clocks, then the Arbiter shall adjust the clocks accordingly. If this is not possible, then each player shall be allotted a time proportional to that indicated by his clock when the error was discovered such that the proportion is the same as the ratio of the number of moves made by that player up to the time the error was made divided by the number of moves made by that player up to the time the error was discovered. In addition, Kasparov will receive a recovery bonus of five minutes on his remaining clock time to compensate for the disturbance caused to his concentration.

11. At any time during the game when it is Deep Blue's turn to move, the operator may indicate to Deep Blue how much time remains on either or both sides of the chess clock.

12. If, during play, Deep Blue is unable to perform in the expected manner, for example being unable to accept a legal move, then the operator may set up in the computer the current board position and status along with the clock times of both players and any other information required by the program, but all such work is permitted only while it is not Kasparov's turn to move.

13. At any time during play, IBM may replace any or all of the computer hardware and/or software being used to play the games provided that any work carried out in the playing hall is only that which is absolutely

necessary and is carried out only when it is not Kasparov's turn to move. Any work which can be carried out via the mirror terminal in the Deep Blue control room shall be carried out there. In the case work is required to be performed in the playing hall, Kasparov will receive a recovery bonus of five minutes on his remaining clock time to compensate for the disturbance caused to his concentration by the onsite repairs.

14. The operator may offer a draw, accept a draw or resign on behalf of Deep Blue. This may be done with or without consulting Deep Blue.

15. Kasparov and the operator shall both keep a written record of the moves of the game at least up to move 60, after which it is optional for each of them to do as he wishes.

16. In the manner concerning the laws of chess and their interpretation, including those matters referred to in 1–15, the decision of the Arbiter shall be final.

17. The Arbiter shall be appointed by the ACM and shall be a person who is acceptable to the ACM, IBM and Kasparov. If the appointed Arbiter is unwell or unable to officiate for any reason, then the ACM may, at its sole discretion, appoint a replacement Arbiter but shall, if practical, consult with the players or their representatives over the choice of the replacement Arbiter.

18. The ACM shall be responsible for resolving chess rules during the Match and shall be responsible for the appointment of the arbiter and together with the arbiter will have the responsibility to oversee and to officiate the six games comprising the Match.

19. In the event Kasparov or IBM disagres with a decision of the Arbiter, the ACM Appeals Board will be called upon to make a final decision.

20. The ACM Appeals Board will monitor the playing hall and the accessory facilities used by both sides to ensure compliance with Match rules and to ensure that no inappropriate conduct by either side takes place. Any irregularities will be immediately acted upon and reported to IBM and Kasparov. The members of the Appeals Board will be agreeable to both sides.

Appendix B
Algebraic Chess Notation

The games in this book are described using what is called algebraic chess notation. The rows, columns, and squares of the chess board are assigned numbers and letters as shown here.

The six pieces, the king, queen, rook, bishop, knight and pawn, are abbreviated respectively as K, Q, R, B, N, and P. They are usually capitalized, though Deep Blue's printout in Appendix M shows white pieces in lowercase characters and black pieces in uppercase characters. A chess move can be characterized as being one of eight types.

> 1. **Transfer by a nonpawn from one square to another**. The moving piece is named, followed by the destination square. If two pieces can move to the same square, the original column of the moving piece is

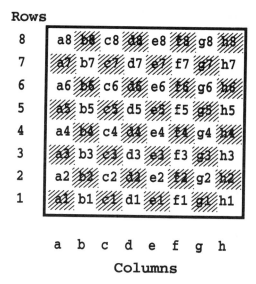

The assignment of letters and numbers to the rows,
columns, and squares of a chess board.

given before the destination square. If that leaves the move ambiguous, the row is given instead. In Deep Blue's printout of Game 6 of the Rematch, "full" algebraic notation is used where the moving piece is indicated first followed by the "from-square" and then the "to-square."

2. **Transfer by a pawn from one square to another**. The new square of the advancing pawn describes the move.

3. **Capture by a nonpawn**. The moving piece is named, followed by an "x" followed by the destination square. If two pieces can move to that square, the original column of the moving piece is given before the "x". If the move is still ambiguous, the row is given instead. Deep Blue adds the captured piece following the destination square.

4. **Capture by a pawn**. The original column of the capturing pawn is given, followed by an "x" followed by the destination square. This format is also adequate for en passant captures. Deep Blue adds the captured piece following the destination square.

5. **Castling move**. Kingside: O–O; queenside: O–O–O.

6. **Promotion**. The name of the new piece, a Q, R, B, or N, is added following the destination square.

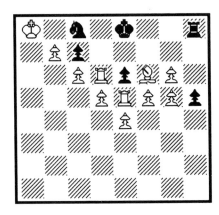

Chess position illustrating move notation.

7. **Checking move**. A "+" is appended to the end of the move description.

8. **Mating move**. A "#" is appended to the end of the description.

Consider the position shown at the bottom of the previous page. Assume Black last advanced its pawn from f7 to f5, or, in our notation, played f5. Then White's moves are Kb8, b8Q, b8R, b8B, b8N, bxc8Q, bxc8R, bxc8B, bxc8N+, Rdxe6+, Rd7+, Rd8, Rexe6+, Rxf5, dxe6, exf5, bxc6, g7, Bf8, Bg7.

Appendix C
Games from Chapter 2

Garry Kasparov versus Deep Thought Exhibition

October 23, 1989
New York
Time Control: All/90 minutes

Game 1
White: Deep Thought
Black: Garry Kasparov
Sicilian Defense

1	e4	c5	24	Ra2	Re6
2	c3	e6	25	Rae2	Rde8
3	d4	d5	26	Qd2	f6
4	exd5	exd5	27	Qc3	h5
5	Nf3	Bd6	28	b4	R8e7
6	Be3	c4	29	Kh1	g5
7	b3	cxb3	30	Kg1	g4
8	axb3	Ne7	31	h4	Re4
9	Na3	Nc6	32	Qb2	Na7
10	Nb5	Bb8	33	Qd2	R4e6
11	Bd3	Bf5	34	Qc1	Nb5
12	c4	O-O	35	Qd2	Na3
13	Ra4	Qd7	36	Qd1	Kf7
14	Nc3	Bc7	37	Qb3	Nc4
15	Bxf5	Qxf5	38	Kh2	Re4
16	Nh4	Qd7	39	g3	Qf3
17	O-O	Rad8	40	b5	a5
18	Re1	Rfe8	41	c6	f5
19	c5	Ba5	42	cxb7	Rxb7
20	Qd3	a6	43	Kg1	f4
21	h3	Bxc3	44	gxf4	g3
22	Qxc3	Nf5	45	Qd1	Rbe7
23	Nxf5	Qxf5	46	b6	gxf2+

47	Rxf2	Qxd1	51	Rxh5	a3
48	Rxd1	Rxe3	52	Rd2	Re2
49	Rg2	Nxb6		White resigns.	
50	Rg5	a4			

Game 2
White: Garry Kasparov
Black: Deep Thought
Queen's Gambit Accepted

1	d4	d5	20	Qxf3	Bb4+
2	c4	dxc4	21	Ke2	cxd5
3	e4	Nc6	22	Qg4	Be7
4	Nf3	Bg4	23	Rhc1	Kf8
5	d5	Ne5	24	Rc7	Bd6
6	Nc3	c6	25	Rb7	Nf6
7	Bf4	Ng6	26	Qa4	a5
8	Be3	cxd5	27	Rc1	h6
9	exd5	Ne5	28	Rc6	Ne8
10	Qd4	Nxf3+	29	b4	Bxh2
11	gxf3	Bxf3	30	bxa5	Kg8
12	Bxc4	Qd6	31	Qb4	Bd6
13	Nb5	Qf6	32	Rxd6	Nxd6
14	Qc5	Qb6	33	Rb8+	Rxb8
15	Qa3	e6	34	Qxb8+	Kh7
16	Nc7+	Qxc7	35	Qxd6	Rc8
17	Bb5+	Qc6	36	a4	Rc4
18	Bxc6+	bxc6	37	Qd7	Black
19	Bc5	Bxc5		resigns.	

Deep Thought at the First Harvard Cup

October 29, 1989
Boston, Massachusetts
Time Control: All/30 minutes

Round 1
White: Boris Gulko
Black: Deep Thought
Reti Opening

1 Nf3	d5	16 Bxe4	O-O
2 g3	Nf6	17 Qh5	g6
3 Bg2	c6	18 Qh4	Qb4
4 d3	Nbd7	19 Bh6	Rfb8
5 O-O	e5	20 Bxg6	fxg6
6 Nc3	d4	21 Qf6	Rf8
7 Nb1	Bd6	22 Bxf8	Rxf8
8 e4	Nc5	23 Qxe6+	Kg7
9 Nbd2	b5	24 Qe7+	Qxe7
10 Nxd4	exd4	25 Rxe7+	Rf7
11 e5	Bb7	26 Rae1	bxa4
12 exd6	Qxd6	27 R1e4	c5
13 Re1+	Ne6	28 R4e5	c4
14 a4	a6	29 dxc4	Black
15 Ne4	Nxe4	resigns.	

Round 2
White: Deep Thought
Black: Maxim Dlugy
Sicilian Defense

1 e4	c5	12 Bd3	dxe4
2 d4	cxd4	13 Bxe4	Qxd2
3 c3	dxc3	14 Bxd2	Bd7
4 Nxc3	d6	15 Rfe1	Rac8
5 Nf3	e6	16 Bf4	Bf6
6 Bc4	Be7	17 Rcd1	Rfd8
7 Bf4	Nc6	18 b3	Be8
8 Rc1	Nf6	19 a4	h6
9 O-O	O-O	20 h3	g5
10 Qd2	Nxe4	21 Be3	b6
11 Nxe4	d5	22 Rxd8	Bxd8

23 Rc1	f5	49 Rxd4+	Kc5
24 Bd3	f4	50 Rc4+	Kd6
25 Bd4	Bd7	51 Kg3	Rb1
26 Bb2	Na5	52 Rc3	Ke5
27 Rd1	Bc6	53 Re3+	Kd4
28 b4	Nb7	54 Kxf3	a6
29 Ba6	Be7	55 Bf7	b5
30 Rc1	Bxb4	56 Re6	bxa4
31 Ne5	Bc5	57 Rxa6	Rb4
32 Nxc6	Rxc6	58 Rxh6	Kc3
33 Bxb7	Rd6	59 Ke3	a3
34 Bc3	Kf7	60 Ra6	Kb2
35 Bf3	Kg6	61 Bd5	Rb5
36 Re1	Kf7	62 Bc4	Rb8
37 Bg4	Rc6	63 Ra5	Rc8
38 Bh5+	Ke7	64 Rb5+	Ka1
39 Bg7	Bb4	65 Kd3	Rf8
40 Re4	Rc1+	66 Rf5	Rh8
41 Kh2	Bd6	67 Re5	Rxh3+
42 Bg4	f3+	68 Kc2	Rh1
43 g3	Rf1	69 Ra5	Rh3
44 Bd4	Bc5	70 Bd5	Rd3
45 Bxe6	Kd6	71 Kxd3	Kb2
46 Bc4	Rc1	72 Rb5+	Ka1
47 Bb3	Rf1	73 Kc2	Black
48 g4	Bxd4	resigns.	

Round 3
White: Deep Thought
Black: Lev Alburt
Alekhine's Defense

1 e4	Nf6	13 gxf3	N8d7
2 e5	Nd5	14 f4	Nc5
3 d4	Nb6	15 Be3	Nxd3+
4 a4	a5	16 Qxd3	Nd5
5 Bb5	c6	17 Nxd5	Qxd5
6 Bd3	d6	18 Qxd5	cxd5
7 Qh5	g6	19 Rg1	f6
8 Qe2	Bg7	20 f5	fxe5
9 Nc3	O-O	21 fxg6	d4
10 Nf3	dxe5	22 Bd2	Rf3
11 dxe5	Bg4	23 Rg3	Rxg3
12 h3	Bxf3	24 gxh7+	Kxh7

25	fxg3	e4
26	Bg5	e5
27	Ra3	Kg6
28	Bh4	Rc8
29	c3	d3
30	Rb3	e3
31	Rxb7	Rf8
32	Rb6+	Kf5
33	Be7	Rf7

34	Bg5	Kxg5
35	h4+	Kg4
36	Rd6	e4
37	Re6	Kf3
38	Kf1	d2
39	Rd6	e2+
40	Kg1	White
	resigns.	

Deep Thought at the 20th ACM North American Computer Chess Championship

November 12–15, 1989
Reno, Nevada
Time Control: 40/2, 20/1 thereafter

Round 4
White: Michael Rohde
Black: Deep Thought
Reti Opening

1	Nf3	d5
2	c4	d4
3	g3	Nc6
4	Bg2	e5
5	O-O	e4
6	Ne1	Nf6
7	d3	exd3
8	Nxd3	Bd7
9	Bg5	h6
10	Bxf6	Qxf6
11	Nd2	Qf5
12	Ne4	O-O-O
13	b4	Bxb4
14	Rb1	a5
15	a3	Bxa3
16	Rb5	Qg6
17	Qa4	f5
18	Nec5	Bxc5
19	Nxc5	b6
20	Nxd7	Rxd7
21	c5	Na7
22	Rb2	d3

23	cxb6	cxb6
24	exd3	Qf6
25	Rfb1	Rd6
26	Qc4+	Kd7
27	Qa6	Rc8
28	Qxa7	Rc7
29	Qa6	Ke8
30	Rxb6	Rxb6
31	Rxb6	Qd4
32	Rb1	Kf7
33	Qxa5	Rc5
34	Qa8	Kg6
35	Qg8	Qd6
36	Re1	Re5
37	Rxe5	Qxe5
38	Qd5	Qe1+
39	Bf1	h5
40	h4	Kf6
41	d4	g6
42	Kg2	Black
	resigns.	

Round 1
White: Sun Phoenix
Black: Deep Thought
English Opening

1	c4	e5
2	Nc3	d6
3	Nf3	f5
4	d4	e4
5	Bg5	Be7
6	Bxe7	Nxe7
7	Nd2	c5
8	Nb3	Qb6
9	e3	Be6
10	Be2	Nd7
11	d5	Bf7
12	f3	exf3
13	gxf3	Nf6
14	O-O	a5
15	Qc2	Nd7
16	Bd3	Bg6
17	Nc1	Ra6
18	N1e2	Ne5
19	Nf4	Nxd3
20	Qa4+	Kf8
21	Nxd3	Be8
22	Qc2	Qd8
23	Nf4	Bd7
24	Kh1	Kg8
25	Rg1	g6
26	Nb5	Qf8
27	Nc7	Ra7
28	Nce6	Qf7
29	Qc3	Bxe6

30	Nxe6	b5
31	Rg2	bxc4
32	Qxc4	Ra8
33	Rag1	Qf6
34	Qd3	Kf7
35	e4	Rhb8
36	Qe3	Rb4
37	a3	Rb6
38	Qh6	Rh8
39	Re1	Kg8
40	Qd2	Rb5
41	Nc7	Rb7
42	Ne8	Qd4
43	Qxd4	cxd4
44	Nxd6	Rb3
45	exf5	Re3
46	Rxe3	dxe3
47	fxg6	hxg6
48	Nc4	Nxd5
49	Rxg6+	Kh7
50	Rg1	e2
51	Re1	Nf4
52	b3	Re8
53	Nb2	Rc8
54	Nc4	a4
55	h4	axb3
56	Nb2	Rc2
	White resigns.	

Round 2
White: Deep Thought
Black: BP
Petroff Defense

1	e4	e5	13	Rdg1	Re8
2	Nf3	Nf6	14	Bd4	Bf6
3	Nxe5	d6	15	Qf4	Re5
4	Nf3	Nxe4	16	Bxe5	dxe5
5	Nc3	Nxc3	17	Rxg7+	Bxg7
6	dxc3	Be7	18	Qxf7+	Kh8
7	Be3	Nd7	19	Qg6	Bh6+
8	Qd2	O-O	20	Rxh6	Qd7
9	O-O-O	Nc5	21	Bf7	Nb3+
10	h4	Bg4	22	cxb3	Qd2+
11	Bc4	Bxf3	23	Kxd2	Black
12	gxf3	Bxh4		resigns.	

Round 3
White: Hitech
Black: Deep Thought
Queen's Gambit Accepted

1	d4	d5	17	dxc6	Rxc6
2	c4	dxc4	18	Rxg5	fxg5
3	e4	Nc6	19	Qxh8	Nf6
4	Nf3	Bg4	20	Bf1	Qa5
5	d5	Ne5	21	Bd4	Qb4
6	Nc3	Nf6	22	Bxf6	Rxf6
7	Bf4	Nfd7	23	Rd1	Bxd1
8	Qa4	Nxf3+	24	a3	Qxb2
9	gxf3	Bxf3	25	Nxd1	Qxa3
10	Rg1	a6	26	Qxh7	Qa5+
11	Qxc4	Rc8	27	Ke2	Rd6
12	Rg3	Bh5	28	Qh5+	Kd8
13	Bh3	f6	29	Qxg5	Bh6
14	Qb4	g5	30	Qg8+	Kc7
15	Be3	b5		White resigns.	
16	Qd4	c5			

Round 4
White: Deep Thought
Black: Rebel
Caro-Kann

1	e4	c6	6	Ng3	e6
2	d4	d5	7	Bd3	Be7
3	Nd2	dxe4	8	O-O	O-O
4	Nxe4	Nd7	9	Qe2	c5
5	Nf3	Ngf6	10	Rd1	cxd4

11	Nxd4	Nc5	26	Nf3	Bc6
12	Bc4	Bd7	27	Rd6	Bxf3
13	Bg5	Qb6	28	gxf3	Rd8
14	b3	Rae8	29	Rb6	Rd7
15	c3	h6	30	Rab1	Rfd8
16	Bf4	Nd5	31	Kg2	Qc8
17	Bd2	Bd6	32	Qe4	e5
18	Qf3	Ne7	33	Qxe5	Rc7
19	Be3	Ng6	34	Bxh6	gxh6
20	b4	Ne5	35	Qg3+	Kf8
21	Qe2	Nxc4	36	Rxh6	Rxc5
22	Qxc4	Bxg3	37	Re1	Rh5
23	bxc5	Bxh2+	38	Rxh5	Black
24	Kxh2	Qc7+		resigns.	
25	Kg1	a6			

Round 5
White: Mephisto
Black: Deep Thought
Queen's Gambit Accepted

1	d4	d5	23	Rxh3	Rxh3
2	c4	dxc4	24	Ne4	Qc7
3	Nf3	Nf6	25	Kb1	g5
4	e3	Bg4	26	Rc1	Kb7
5	Bxc4	e6	27	Ba4	Nb8
6	h3	Bh5	28	Nd2	Qd7
7	Nc3	Nbd7	29	Bb3	Na6
8	g4	Bg6	30	Qe4	Nb4
9	Nh4	Be4	31	a3	Nd5
10	Nxe4	Nxe4	32	Qg2	Rh8
11	Nf3	Nd6	33	Ne4	f6
12	Bb3	Qe7	34	Qg3	Rg8
13	Bd2	h5	35	Rh1	f5
14	Rg1	hxg4	36	gxf5	exf5
15	hxg4	O-O-O	37	Qh3	Rf8
16	Ba5	b6	38	Nd2	Bf6
17	Bb4	a5	39	Qh7	Rf7
18	Bxd6	Qxd6	40	Qh6	Qe6
19	Qc2	Be7	41	Qg6	Rg7
20	O-O-O	Rh3	42	Rh7	Rxh7
21	Nd2	c6	43	Qxh7+	Be7
22	Rh1	Rdh8	44	Kc1	Kc7

45	Nf3	Kd8
46	Ne5	g4
47	Qh8+	Kc7
48	Kd2	Kb7
49	Nxc6	Qxc6
50	Qe5	Nc7
51	Qxe7	Qg2
52	Qh4	f4
53	exf4	Qe4
54	Qxg4	Qxd4+
55	Kc1	Qxf2

56	Qf5	Qf3
57	Kc2	Kc6
58	Qe5	Nd5
59	Qe6+	Kc5
60	Bxd5	Qxd5
61	Qxd5+	Kxd5
62	Kd3	a4
63	Kc3	Kc5
64	f5	Black
	resigns.	

David Levy versus Deep Thought

December 1989
London
Time Control: 40/2, 20/1 thereafter

Game 1
White: David Levy
Black: Deep Thought
Dutch Defense

1	d4	f5
2	Bg5	h6
3	Bh4	g5
4	e3	Nf6
5	Bg3	d6
6	c3	Bg7
7	Nd2	O-O
8	f3	Nc6
9	Bc4+	d5
10	Bd3	Nh5
11	Bf2	e5
12	Qb3	f4
13	e4	exd4
14	cxd4	Bxd4
15	exd5	Na5
16	Qc2	Bxf2+
17	Kxf2	Qxd5
18	Ne2	Bf5
19	Ne4	Qc6

20	N2c3	Qb6+
21	Kf1	Rad8
22	Rd1	Rfe8
23	Be2	Rxd1+
24	Qxd1	Bxe4
25	Nxe4	Nf6
26	Qa4	Re5
27	Qd1	Nd5
28	Qa4	Qxb2
29	Qd7	Qc1+
30	Kf2	Qxh1
31	Qd8+	Kg7
32	Qd7+	Ne7
33	Qxc7	Nac6
34	Nd6	Rxe2+
35	Kxe2	Qxg2+
36	Ke1	Qh1+
	White resigns.	

Game 2
White: Deep Thought
Black: David Levy
English Opening

1	c4	d6
2	Nc3	g6
3	d4	Bg7
4	e4	a6
5	Be3	Nf6
6	Be2	O-O
7	f4	c6

8	e5	Ne8
9	Nf3	d5
10	O-O	Nc7
11	Rc1	e6
12	Qe1	b5
13	cxd5	cxd5
14	Nd1	Ra7

15	Nf2	Nd7
16	Qa5	Na8
17	Qa3	Qb6
18	Bd2	a5
19	Qd6	b4
20	Rc6	Qd8
21	Rfc1	Bb7
22	R6c2	Ndb6
23	Qxd8	Rxd8
24	Be3	Rc8
25	Rc5	Bf8
26	Bd3	Rd8
27	R5c2	Rc8
28	Rxc8	Bxc8
29	Ng4	Be7

30	Nf6+	Bxf6
31	exf6	Rc7
32	Ne5	Rxc1+
33	Bxc1	Bb7
34	a3	Nc7
35	axb4	axb4
36	Bd2	Na4
37	Bxb4	Nxb2
38	Ng4	e5
39	Nh6+	Kh8
40	Nxf7+	Kg8
41	Nh6+	Kh8
42	f5	Black

resigns.

13	h3	Bd7
14	Nf3	Qa5
15	a3	Rad8
16	b4	Qc7
17	Rac1	b6
18	Bd3	Qb7
19	Qf2	Rb8
20	e5	Nh5
21	b5	axb5
22	cxb5	Nd8
23	g4	Bh8
24	gxh5	Bxh3

25	hxg6	hxg6
26	Rfd1	Qd7
27	Ng5	Bg4
28	Qh4	Bg7
29	Rd2	Bh5
30	Nd5	Qa7
31	Rc7	Rb7
32	exd6	exd6
33	Rc8	Qxa3
34	Ne4	Black

resigns.

Game 3
White: David Levy
Black: Deep Thought
Dutch Defense

1	d4	f5
2	Bg5	c6
3	c3	h6
4	Bf4	Nf6
5	Nd2	d6
6	e4	g5
7	e5	Nh7
8	Nc4	gxf4
9	Qh5+	Kd7
10	Qxf5+	Kc7
11	Qxf4	Be6
12	Nf3	Rg8

13	Ne3	Ng5
14	exd6	exd6
15	d5	Bxd5
16	Nxd5+	cxd5
17	Nd4	Qe7+
18	Be2	Nc6
19	Nb5+	Kb8
20	h4	Ne6
21	Qf3	Ne5
22	Qxd5	Nf4

White resigns.

Game 4
White: Deep Thought
Black: David Levy
English Opening

1	c4	d6
2	Nc3	Nd7
3	d4	g6
4	Nf3	Bg7
5	e4	c5
6	Be2	cxd4

7	Nxd4	Ngf6
8	Be3	O-O
9	O-O	a6
10	f3	Re8
11	Qd2	Ne5
12	f4	Nc6

Appendix D
Games from Chapter 3

Anatoly Karpov versus Deep Thought

February 2, 1990
Boston
Time Control: All/1

White: Anatoly Karpov
Black: Deep Thought
Caro-Kann Defense

1	e4	c6	26	Rxd1	exf3
2	d4	d5	27	gxf3	Ra7
3	Nd2	g6	28	Bd5	Rd8
4	c3	Bg7	29	Rb5	Ra6
5	e5	f6	30	Bc4	Ra7
6	f4	Nh6	31	Bd5	Ra6
7	Ngf3	O-O	32	Rc5	Rd7
8	Be2	fxe5	33	Kg2	Rb6
9	fxe5	c5	34	Bxc6	bxc6
10	Nb3	cxd4	35	Kf2	Rd5
11	cxd4	Nc6	36	Rxd5	cxd5
12	O-O	Qb6	37	Rc1	Rb4
13	Kh1	a5	38	Ke3	Rxa4
14	a4	Bf5	39	Rc5	e6
15	Bg5	Be4	40	Rc7+	Kg8
16	Nc5	Qxb2	41	Re7	Ra3+
17	Nxe4	dxe4	42	Kf4	Rd3
18	Rb1	Qa3	43	Rxe6	Rxd4+
19	Bc1	Qc3	44	Kg5	Kf7
20	Bd2	Qa3	45	Ra6	a4
21	Bc1	Qc3	46	f4	h6+
22	Rb3	Qa1	47	Kg4	Rc4
23	Bc4+	Kh8	48	h4	Rd4
24	Bxh6	Qxd1	49	Rf6+	Kg7
25	Bxg7+	Kxg7	50	Ra6	Kf7

51	h5	gxh5+	59	Rh7	h5
52	Kf5	Kg7	60	Ke5	h3
53	Ra7+	Kf8	61	f5	Kg8
54	e6	Re4	62	Rxh5	a3
55	Rd7	Rc4	63	Rxh3	a2
56	Rxd5	h4	64	Ra3	Rc5+
57	Rd3	Ke7	65	Kf6	Black
58	Rd7+	Kf8		resigns.	

Helmut Pfleger versus Deep Thought

February 1990
Time Control: 40/2, 20/1 thereafter

Game 1
White: Helmut Pfleger
Black: Deep Thought
English Opening

1	c4	e5	27	Nc3	exf4		
2	Nc3	d6	28	gxf4	Rc7		
3	g3	g6	29	Nd1	d5		
4	Bg2	Bg7	30	cxd5	cxd5		
5	Nf3	f5	31	Nb4	d4		
6	d3	Nf6	32	Kf2	Bf6		
7	0-0	0-0	33	Rc1	Rxc1		
8	Rb1	a5	34	Bxc1	Nb6		
9	a3	Nh5	35	Nb2	Bh4+		
10	Bg5	Nf6	36	Kf1	Kg7		
11	Qd2	Nc6	37	Bd2	Bf6		
12	b4	axb4	38	Na6	Ned5		
13	axb4	Be6	39	Nc5	Bf7		
14	b5	Ne7	40	Nca4	Nxa4		
15	Ra1	Qc8	41	Nxa4	Ne3+		
16	Rxa8	Qxa8	42	Bxe3	dxe3		
17	Ne1	c6	43	Nb6	Bd4		
18	Nc2	Qe8	44	Nc4	Bxc4		
19	Rb1	Qd7	45	dxc4	Bc5		
20	Na4	Qc7	46	Bd5	Bd6		
21	bxc6	bxc6	47	c5	Bxc5		
22	Qb4	h6	48	Kg2	g5		
23	Bd2	Nd7	49	fxg5	hxg5		
24	Qb7	Rc8	50	h3			
25	Qxc7	Rxc7	Drawn by				
26	f4	Ra7	agreement.				

7	0-0	d6
8	d3	Bd7
9	h3	Ne8
10	f4	f5
11	Rb1	Rb8
12	Be3	Nd4
13	b4	b6
14	bxc5	bxc5
15	Qd2	Nc7
16	exf5	gxf5
17	Rxb8	Qxb8
18	Rb1	Qc8
19	Kh2	e6
20	Qd1	Qa6
21	Bd2	Bc6
22	Bxc6	Qxc6
23	Nxd4	Bxd4
24	Qh1	d5
25	Ne2	Bg7
26	Be3	Rd8
27	a3	Qa6
28	Qc1	dxc4
29	dxc4	Bf8
30	Bg1	Qc6
31	Qe3	Ne8
32	Nc3	Nf6
33	Re1	Kf7
34	Bf2	a6
35	a4	h5
36	Qe2	Rb8
37	Rd1	Bg7
38	Kg1	Rb3

39	Be1	Kg6
40	Qg2	Qxg2+
41	Kxg2	Ne4
42	Nxe4	fxe4
43	Bf2	e3
44	Bg1	Bd4
45	Kf3	Kf6
46	a5	Ra3
47	g4	Rxa5
48	Rd3	Ra4
49	Bxe3	Rxc4
50	gxh5	a5
51	h6	Kg6
52	Bxd4	Rxd4
53	Rb3	Rd6
54	Rb7	Kxh6
55	Ra7	c4
56	Rxa5	Rc6
57	Ke2	c3
58	Kd1	Kg6
59	Kc2	Rc4
60	Re5	Kf6
61	Rh5	Rxf4
62	Kxc3	e5
63	h4	Rf3+
64	Kc4	Ke6
65	Rh8	Rh3
66	h5	Kf5
Drawn by		
agreement.		

Game 2
White: Deep Thought
Black: Helmut Pfleger
English Opening

1	c4	Nf6	4	Bg2	Bg7
2	Nc3	c5	5	e4	Nc6
3	g3	g6	6	Nge2	0-0

Deep Thought/88 at the 21st ACM North American Computer Chess Championship

November 11–14, 1990
New York
Time Control: All/2

Round 1
White: Deep Thought/88
Black: Bebe
Benoni Opening

1	d4	Nf6	23	a5	b5
2	c4	c5	24	Qe2	Rac8
3	d5	e6	25	Nxe8	Rxe8
4	Nc3	exd5	26	Kh1	Qh3
5	cxd5	d6	27	Rf2	f5
6	Nf3	g6	28	Qxb5	fxe4
7	Nd2	Bg7	29	fxe4	Rb8
8	e4	0-0	30	Qf1	Qxe3
9	Be2	Re8	31	Re1	Qg5
10	0-0	Na6	32	Rf7+	Kh8
11	f3	Nc7	33	Rxd7	Qd2
12	a4	b6	34	Re2	Qd3
13	Nc4	Ba6	35	Rxa7	Bxb2
14	Bg5	h6	36	Re1	Qd2
15	Be3	Bxc4	37	Rb1	Rg8
16	Bxc4	Nd7	38	Qg2	Bc3
17	Be2	Be5	39	Qxd2	Bxd2
18	Qd2	Qh4	40	a6	c4
19	g3	Bxg3	41	Rc7	Be3
20	Bb5	Nxb5	42	Rbb7	Black
21	Nxb5	Be5		resigns.	
22	Nc7	Kh7			

Round 2
White: Belle
Black: Deep Thought/88
Sicilian Defense

1	e4	c5	32	Ng5	fxg4
2	c3	d5	33	Nxe6	gxf3+
3	exd5	Qxd5	34	Kxf3	g6
4	Nf3	Nc6	35	Rg7+	Kh8
5	d4	Bg4	36	Re7	h5
6	Be2	cxd4	37	Nf4	Rg4
7	cxd4	e6	38	Rd7	Rg5
8	Nc3	Qa5	39	Nd5	Rf5+
9	0-0	Nf6	40	Ke4	Bg1
10	h3	Bh5	41	b4	h4
11	a3	Be7	42	Nf4	Rg5
12	Be3	Rd8	43	Rd6	Kh7
13	Bb5	0-0	44	Rd7+	Kh6
14	Bxc6	bxc6	45	Nh3	Rg4+
15	g4	Bg6	46	Ke5	Bh2+
16	Ne5	Qa6	47	Ke6	Rg3
17	f3	c5	48	Nf2	Bg1
18	Qe2	Bd3	49	Ne4	Re3
19	Qxd3	Qxd3	50	Ke5	h3
20	Nxd3	cxd4	51	Rd8	h2
21	Bxd4	Rxd4	52	Rh8+	Kg7
22	Rfd1	Rfd8	53	Rh4	Rf3
23	Nf2	Bc5	54	Nd6	g5
24	Kf1	Rd2	55	Rh5	Kg6
25	Rxd2	Rxd2	56	Rh8	Bf2
26	Nce4	Nxe4	57	Rxh2	Bg3+
27	Nxe4	Rh2	58	Ke4	Rf4+
28	Rd1	Bb6	59	Kd5	Bxh2
29	Rd2	Rxh3	60	Nc4	White
30	Kg2	Rh4		resigns.	
31	Rd7	f5			

Round 3
White: Deep Thought/88
Black: Mephisto

1	Nf3	d5	32	Nde5+ fxe5
2	e3	Nf6	33	Nxe5+ Kf6
3	c4	e6	34	Qxa5 Nxa5
4	Be2	Nc6	35	Rxb8 Rhxb8
5	d4	Bb4+	36	Rxb8 Rxb8
6	Bd2	O-O	37	Nd7+ Ke7
7	Bxb4	Nxb4	38	Nxb8 Nc4
8	a3	Nc6	39	Nxa6 Kd8
9	O-O	Na5	40	a4 Nb2
10	c5	b6	41	Kg1 Nxa4
11	b4	Nc6	42	Kf1 Kd7
12	Nc3	bxc5	43	f3 Nc3
13	bxc5	Qe7	44	Nb8+ Kc8
14	Rb1	Bd7	45	Nc6 Kd7
15	Bb5	Rfb8	46	Ne5+ Ke7
16	Qa4	Nd8	47	Ke1 g5
17	Bxd7	Nxd7	48	Kd2 Nb5
18	Qa5	Rc8	49	Kc2 Kf6
19	Nb5	a6	50	Kb3 Na7
20	Nc3	Qf6	51	Kb4 h5
21	Rb3	Qg6	52	Ka5 Nc8
22	Rfb1	f6	53	g4 hxg4
23	R1b2	h6	54	fxg4 Ne7
24	Kh1	Qd3	55	Ka6 Ng8
25	Ne2	Qd1+	56	Kb7 Ke7
26	Nfg1	Nc6	57	Kxc7 Nf6
27	Qa4	Ndb8	58	c6 Ne8+
28	Nf4	Kf7	59	Kc8 Kd6
29	Nd3	Rh8	60	Kb7 Black
30	Rb1	Qd2		resigns.
31	Nf3	Qa5		

Reti Opening
Round 4
White: Hitech
Black: Deep Thought/88
Sicilian Defense

1	e4	c5	6	Re1 O-O
2	Nf3	Nc6	7	d4 cxd4
3	Bb5	g6	8	cxd4 d5
4	O-O	Bg7	9	e5 Ne4
5	c3	Nf6	10	Nc3 Nxc3

11	bxc3	Bg4	32	Bd6 Bb5
12	h3	Bf5	33	Ne5 Bxe5
13	Bxc6	bxc6	34	Bxe5 Qxe5
14	Ba3	Rb8	35	Qxe5 Bxc6
15	Bc5	Qc7	36	Qe6 Rb1+
16	Qc1	Rb7	37	Rxb1 Rxb1+
17	Nh4	Be4	38	Kh2 Rb6
18	Qe3	Rfb8	39	g4 Bb7
19	f3	Bc2	40	Qg8+ Kc7
20	Rec1	Ba4	41	Qf7 Bc6
21	f4	Bb5	42	Qxe7+ Bd7
22	f5	Kh8	43	Qc5+ Rc6
23	e6	Bf6	44	Qxd5 Re6
24	exf7	Kg7	45	Kg3 Re1
25	Nf3	gxf5	46	c4 Re2
26	Re1	Kxf7	47	Qa5+ Kb7
27	Qh6	Qg3	48	Qb4+ Kc8
28	Qxh7+	Ke8	49	Qa3 Kb8
29	Qxf5	Qg7	50	d5 Re4
30	Re6	Bc4	51	c5 Bxg4
31	Rxc6	Kd8		Black resigns.

Round 5
White: Deep Thought/88
Black: Zarkov
Reti Opening

1	c4	c5	20	Rxa1 Na6
2	Nc3	Nc6	21	Rb1 Rb8
3	g3	g6	22	Nd4 e5
4	Bg2	Bg7	23	Nb5 Bxb5
5	e4	d6	24	Rxb5 Nc5
6	Nge2	Nf6	25	Nc3 Qc6
7	O-O	Bg4	26	Nd5 a4
8	f3	Bd7	27	d4 Nb3
9	d3	O-O	28	Qb4 exd4
10	Bg5	a6	29	Bf4 Nc5
11	Qd2	Re8	30	e5 Qc8
12	Rfd1	b6	31	Rxb6 Rxb6
13	a3	Ra7	32	Qxb6 Rb7
14	b4	cxb4	33	Nf6+ Kg7
15	axb4	Nxb4	34	Bxb7 Qxb7
16	Rdb1	Qc7	35	Qd8 Qb1+
17	Be3	a5	36	Kg2 Qb7+
18	Na2	Nxe4	37	Kh3 Qd7+
19	fxe4	Bxa1		Black resigns.

Deep Thought at Hanover Grandmaster Tournament

May 1991
Hanover, Germany
Time Control: 40/2, 20/1 thereafter

Round 1
White: H. Grunberg
Black: Deep Thought
Queen's Gambit Accepted

1	d4	d5
2	c4	dxc4
3	Nf3	a6
4	e4	b5
5	a4	Bb7
6	axb5	axb5
7	Rxa8	Bxa8
8	Nc3	c6
9	Be2	e6
10	O-O	Nd7
11	e5	Ne7
12	Bg5	Qb8
13	Ne4	Nd5
14	Qc2	h6
15	Bh4	c5
16	Ra1	cxd4
17	Nxd4	Nb4
18	Rxa8	Qxa8
19	Nxb5	Nxe5
20	Qd1	Nd5
21	Nec3	Kd7
22	Bg3	Nd3
23	b3	Nxc3
24	Nxc3	Qa5

25	Bxd3	cxd3
26	Qxd3+	Ke8
27	h3	Bb4
28	Nb5	Kf8
29	Kh2	Kg8
30	Nc7	h5
31	h4	Rh6
32	Qd8+	Kh7
33	Qd3+	Rg6
34	Nb5	Be7
35	f3	Bb4
36	Nd6	Be1
37	Bxe1	Qxe1
38	Ne4	Qxh4+
39	Kg1	Qe1+
40	Qf1	Qe3+
41	Qf2	Qxb3
42	Qh4	Qb6+
43	Nf2	Qb1+
44	Kh2	Qe1
45	g4	Qf1
46	Kg3	Qg1+
47	Kh3	f5

White resigns.

Round 2
White: Deep Thought
Black: K. Bischoff
Nimzo-Indian Defense

1	d4	Nf6
2	c4	e6

3	Nc3	Bb4
4	Qc2	d6

5	Bg5	Nbd7
6	e3	c5
7	Nf3	Qa5
8	Bd3	cxd4
9	exd4	Bxc3+
10	bxc3	Qc7
11	O-O	O-O
12	Rfe1	b6
13	Nd2	Bb7
14	f3	Rfe8
15	Bh4	h6
16	Re3	Rac8
17	Qb3	Nh5
18	Qa3	Ndf6
19	Bc2	Red8
20	Ne4	Bxe4
21	fxe4	e5
22	Bd3	Re8
23	Rae1	Nh7
24	Be2	Nf4
25	Bg4	Ra8
26	Qa4	Ng6
27	Bd7	Rf8
28	Bg3	Rfd8
29	Bg4	Nhf8
30	Rf1	Re8
31	Ref3	Re7
32	Bf5	Qb7

33	Qb4	Qc6
34	Qb5	Qxb5
35	cxb5	Rc7
36	Re3	Re8
37	Kh1	f6
38	Rd3	Kf7
39	Bg4	Ke7
40	Rfd1	Rb8
41	Bf5	Nh8
42	Be1	h5
43	Kg1	g6
44	Bh3	Nf7
45	Bd2	Rbb7
46	Rf1	Rc4
47	a3	Rbc7
48	g4	h4
49	Bg2	g5
50	Rb1	Ne6
51	d5	Nf4
52	Re3	Ra4
53	Rb3	Nd8
54	Bf1	Nb7
55	c4	Nc5
56	Rb2	a6
57	bxa6	Rxa6
58	Bb4	Ng6
59	Kh1	Drawn

by agreement.

Round 3
White: Eric Lobron
Black: Deep Thought
Reti Opening

1	Nf3	d5
2	g3	c6
3	Bg2	Bg4
4	c4	e6
5	b3	dxc4
6	bxc4	Nd7
7	Bb2	Qb6
8	Qc2	Ngf6
9	O-O	Bd6
10	d3	O-O
11	Nbd2	e5

12	Rab1	Qa6
13	h3	Be6
14	Ng5	Bf5
15	Bc3	Nc5
16	e4	Bg6
17	f4	exf4
18	gxf4	Na4
19	Ba1	Nd7
20	e5	Bc5+
21	Kh2	Be3
22	Nge4	Bxd2

23	Nxd2	Bf5
24	Be4	Bxe4
25	Nxe4	Nac5
26	Nd6	b6
27	Rg1	g6
28	f5	Nb7

29	Ne4	Qa3
30	Qd2	Nbc5
31	Qh6	Qxa2+
32	Rg2	Black
	resigns.	

Round 4
White: Deep Thought
Black: Uwe Bonsch
Queen's Gambit Declined

1	d4	Nf6
2	c4	e6
3	Nc3	d5
4	Bg5	Be7
5	Nf3	h6
6	Bxf6	Bxf6
7	e3	O-O
8	Qd2	a6
9	Be2	Nc6
10	O-O	dxc4
11	Bxc4	e5
12	d5	Ne7
13	Ne4	Nf5
14	Qc3	Re8
15	Bb3	Nd6
16	Nxf6+	Qxf6
17	Qxc7	Bg4
18	Nd2	Rac8
19	Qb6	e4
20	Rab1	Qg6
21	Kh1	Be2
22	Rfe1	Bd3
23	Rbd1	Re5
24	f4	Rh5
25	Kg1	Rh4
26	Nb1	Bxb1
27	Rxb1	Rg4
28	Re2	Qf6
29	Bd1	Rg6
30	Rc2	Rxc2
31	Bxc2	Qf5
32	Qd4	Qg4
33	g3	h5
34	Bxe4	f5

35	Bd3	h4
36	Kg2	Ne4
37	Qc4	Nxg3
38	h3	Qh5
39	Kf2	Kh7
40	Qb4	a5
41	Qe7	Qh6
42	Qxb7	Rd6
43	Qb5	Qg6
44	Qc5	Rb6
45	b3	Nh1+
46	Ke1	Rf6
47	Qxa5	Qg2
48	Qc5	Ng3
49	d6	Ne4
50	Bxe4	Qxe4
51	Rc1	Rg6
52	Kd2	Rg2+
53	Kc3	Re2
54	d7	Rxe3+
55	Kb2	Rd3
56	Qf2	Qe7
57	Rc7	Rxh3
58	Qd2	Qf6+
59	Kb1	Rh1+
60	Kc2	Qa1
61	d8Q	Qxa2+
62	Kc3	Qa5+
63	Kc4	Qa6+
64	Kc5	Qa3+
65	b4	Rc1+
66	Kb5	Black
	resigns.	

Round 5
White: W. Unzicker
Black: Deep Thought
Reti Opening

1	Nf3	d5
2	c4	dxc4
3	e3	c5
4	Bxc4	e6
5	O-O	a6
6	b3	b5
7	Be2	Bb7
8	Bb2	Nd7
9	a4	Qb6
10	axb5	axb5
11	Rxa8+	Bxa8
12	Na3	Bc6
13	d4	Ngf6
14	dxc5	Bxc5
15	Nd4	Bxd4
16	Qxd4	b4
17	Nc2	Qxd4
18	Bxd4	Nd5
19	f3	e5
20	Bb2	O-O
21	e4	Nf4
22	Bc4	Rb8
23	Rd1	Ng6
24	Rd6	Ne7
25	Bc1	Nf6
26	Bg5	Be8
27	Bxf6	gxf6
28	Rxf6	Kg7
29	Rd6	Nc6
30	Bd5	Ne7
31	Bc4	Nc6
32	Kf1	h5
33	h4	Ne7
34	Ke1	Nc6
35	Kd2	f6

36	Bd5	Ne7
37	Ne3	Bf7
38	Bxf7	Kxf7
39	Ra6	Rb7
40	Nc4	Nc8
41	Rc6	Na7
42	Nd6+	Ke6
43	Ra6	Rd7
44	Ke2	Rxd6
45	Rxa7	Rb6
46	Rc7	Rb8
47	Rc6+	Ke7
48	Rc4	Kf7
49	Kf2	Kg6
50	Kg3	Rb6
51	Kh3	Kg7
52	Rc5	Rd6
53	Rc4	Rb6
54	g4	Kh6
55	Kg3	Kg6
56	Rc5	hxg4
57	Kxg4	Kg7
58	Kf5	Rd6
59	Rc7+	Kh6
60	Rf7	Rd3
61	Rxf6+	Kh5
62	Kxe5	Kxh4
63	f4	Rxb3
64	Rb6	Rb1
65	f5	Kg5
66	Ke6	Rf1
67	Rxb4	Ra1
68	Rd4	Ra8
69	f6	Black
	resigns.	

Round 6
White: Deep Thought
Black: M. Wahls
King's Indian Defense

1	d4	d6	16	Qb4	a6
2	c4	g6	17	Rd1	Rfc8
3	Nc3	Bg7	18	Nd5	Bxd5
4	e4	Nf6	19	Rxd5	b5
5	f3	O-O	20	a4	bxa4
6	Be3	e5	21	Qxd6	Qb7
7	Nge2	c6	22	bxa4	Bf8
8	Qd2	Nbd7	23	Qxd7	Qb4+
9	d5	cxd5	24	Rd2	Rd8
10	Nxd5	Nxd5	25	Qxd8	Rxd8
11	Qxd5	Nb6	26	Be3	Bc5
12	Qb5	Bh6	27	Bg5	Rd6
13	Bf2	Be6	28	Ke2	Rxd2+
14	Nc3	Qc7		White resigns.	
15	b3	Nd7			

Round 7
White: R. Tuschbierek
Black: Deep Thought
Sicilian Defense

1	e4	c5	13	g3	Bg5
2	Nc3	Nc6	14	Rf2	Bxc1
3	Nge2	e5	15	Qxc1	Bc6
4	Nd5	d6	16	f6	gxf6
5	Nec3	Nge7	17	Qh6	Qb6
6	Bc4	Nxd5	18	Qxf6	Be8
7	Bxd5	Be7	19	Raf1	Qxb2
8	d3	Nd4	20	Qg5+	Kh8
9	O-O	Bh4	21	Nd1	Qb4
10	f4	O-O	22	c3	Qa3
11	f5	Rb8		Black resigns.	
12	a4	Bd7			

Darryl Johansen versus Deep Thought Exhibition Match

Sydney, Australia
August 28, 1991
Time Control: All/1

Game 1
White: Deep Thought
Black: Darryl Johanson
English Opening

1	d4	e6	24	Rh4	Ka7
2	Nf3	c5	25	Bg4	Qf7
3	e3	b6	26	Rdh1	d6
4	d5	exd5	27	Rh7	b5
5	Qxd5	Nc6	28	Kc1	b4
6	Bc4	Qe7	29	Nd5	Bxd5
7	Ne5	Qxe5	30	exd5	Rae8
8	Qxf7+	Kd8	31	Qd3	Qxd5
9	Qxf8+	Kc7	32	c3	bxc3
10	Nc3	Nce7	33	bxc3	Nb3+
11	Qf3	Kb8	34	Kc2	Qg2+
12	e4	Ng6	35	Kb1	Qe4
13	h4	h5	36	Rxg7+	Kb6
14	Bg5	N8e7	37	Rd1	Qxd3+
15	Rd1	a6	38	Rxd3	Re1+
16	Qe3	Rf8	39	Kc2	Na5
17	Be2	Nf4	40	Rxd6+	Kb5
18	Bf3	Nc6	41	a4+	Kxa4
19	g3	Ne6	42	Bd7+	Ka3
20	Bxh5	Ncd4	43	Rxa6	Re2+
21	Kd2	Nxg5	44	Kd3	Black
22	hxg5	Bb7		resigns.	
23	f4	Qe6			

Game 2
White: Darryl Johanson
Black: Deep Thought
English Opening

Deep Thought II at the 22nd ACM North American Computer Chess Championship

November 17-20, 1991
Albuquerque, New Mexico
Time Control: 40/2, 20/1 thereafter

1	e3	e5
2	c4	Nf6
3	Nc3	Bb4
4	Nge2	O-O
5	a3	Be7
6	d4	d6
7	d5	c6
8	Ng3	Bg4
9	f3	Bd7
10	Be2	cxd5
11	cxd5	Be8
12	O-O	Nbd7
13	Kh1	Rc8
14	e4	a6
15	Be3	Kh8
16	Rc1	h6
17	Nf5	Nc5
18	b4	Ncd7
19	a4	Ng8

20	a5	Ngf6
21	Qd2	Rg8
22	Na4	Bf8
23	Nb6	Nxb6
24	Bxb6	Qd7
25	Rxc8	Qxc8
26	Rc1	Qa8
27	Bc7	Nh5
28	Nxd6	Bxd6
29	Bxd6	f6
30	Qe3	Ba4
31	g3	Rc8
32	Bc7	Be8
33	Qb6	Bf7
34	b5	axb5
35	Bxb5	Be8
36	d6	Bxb5
37	Qxb5	Black
	resigns.	

Round 1
White: Deep Thought II
Black: Zarkov
Ruy Lopez

1	e4	e5
2	Nf3	Nc6
3	Bb5	a6
4	Ba4	Nf6
5	O-O	Be7
6	Re1	b5
7	Bb3	d6
8	c3	O-O
9	h3	Na5
10	Bc2	c5
11	d4	Qc7
12	Nbd2	cxd4
13	cxd4	Bd7
14	Nf1	Rac8
15	Re2	exd4
16	Nxd4	Nc6
17	Be3	h6
18	Ng3	Nxd4
19	Bxd4	Be6
20	Nf5	Bxf5
21	exf5	Rfd8
22	a4	b4
23	Bd3	a5
24	Ba6	Rb8
25	Rc1	Qd7
26	Bb5	Qb7
27	Bc6	Qc7
28	Qe1	Kf8
29	Rec2	Ng8
30	Be4	Qd7

31	Rc7	Qxa4
32	Ba7	d5
33	Bxd5	Rxd5
34	Bxb8	Qe8
35	Ba7	Rd7
36	Bb6	Rxc7
37	Rxc7	Nf6
38	Qc1	Bd8
39	Rc8	Bxb6
40	Rxe8+	Kxe8
41	Qc6+	Nd7
42	Qa8+	Ke7
43	Kf1	Nf6
44	Qb7+	Nd7
45	Qd5	Ke8
46	Qe4+	Kf8
47	h4	Nf6
48	Qa8+	Ke7
49	Qb7+	Nd7
50	Qe4+	Kf8
51	h5	Nf6
52	Qa8+	Ke7
53	Qb7+	Nd7
54	Qe4+	Kf8
55	Qd5	Ke7
56	Ke2	Ke8
57	Qe4+	Black
	resigns.	

Round 2
White: Mchess
Black: Deep Thought II
Catalan Opening

1	d4	Nf6
2	c4	e6
3	g3	d5
4	Bg2	Be7
5	Nf3	O-O
6	O-O	dxc4
7	Qc2	a6
8	Qxc4	b5
9	Qc2	Bb7
10	Bd2	Be4
11	Qc1	Bb7
12	Bf4	Nd5
13	Nc3	Nxf4
14	Qxf4	Qd6
15	Qe3	Nd7
16	Ne4	Bxe4
17	Qxe4	c5
18	Rac1	Rac8
19	dxc5	Rxc5
20	Rcd1	Qc7
21	Nd4	Ne5
22	b3	Bf6
23	e3	Rd8
24	f4	Ng6
25	Qb7	Qxb7
26	Bxb7	Rb8
27	Be4	Ne7
28	Rc1	Rbc8
29	Rxc5	Rxc5
30	Kf2	Nd5
31	Ra1	h5

32	a4	b4
33	Bxd5	exd5
34	Rd1	Rc3
35	h3	h4
36	g4	Bxd4
37	Rxd4	Rxb3
38	Rxd5	Rb2+
39	Kg1	Ra2
40	Rd8+	Kh7
41	Rb8	a5
42	Kf1	Rxa4
43	Ke2	Ra2+
44	Kd3	g6
45	Rb5	Ra3+
46	Ke4	b3
47	Kd4	a4
48	Rb7	Kg7
49	Kc3	Ra1
50	Rb4	Re1
51	e4	Re3+
52	Kb2	Rxh3
53	Rxa4	Rg3
54	g5	h3
55	Ra1	h2
56	Rh1	Rh3
57	Kc1	f6
58	Kb2	fxg5
59	fxg5	Kf7
60	Kb1	Ke6

White resigns.

Round 3
White: Deep Thought II
Black: Hitech
French Defense

1	e4	e6
2	d4	d5
3	Nd2	c5
4	exd5	exd5
5	Ngf3	Nf6
6	Bb5+	Bd7
7	Bxd7+	Nbxd7
8	O-O	Be7
9	dxc5	Nxc5
10	Nb3	O-O

11	Nxc5	Bxc5
12	Bg5	d4
13	Qd3	h6
14	Bh4	Rc8
15	Rfd1	Re8
16	Qf5	Qb6
17	Bxf6	Qxf6
18	Qxf6	gxf6
19	Kf1	f5
20	Rac1	Rcd8
21	Rd3	Rd6
22	a3	a5
23	Rb3	b6
24	Ne1	Rc6
25	Rb5	Kg7
26	Nf3	Rd8
27	Ne5	Rc7
28	Nd3	a4
29	Re1	Bf8
30	Re2	Bc5
31	g3	Rdc8
32	Re5	Kf6
33	Rd5	Re7

34	c3	Re4
35	cxd4	Rxd4
36	Rxd4	Bxd4
37	Rb4	Rd8
38	Rxa4	Ke6
39	Rb4	Kd5
40	a4	Ra8
41	b3	Ra5
42	Ke2	b5
43	Rxb5+	Rxb5
44	axb5	Bb6
45	h4	Bc7
46	h5	Ba5
47	f4	f6
48	Nb2	Bb4
49	Nc4	Bc5
50	Kf3	Bf8
51	Ne3+	Kc5
52	Nxf5	Kxb5
53	Ke4	Kc5
54	Ne3	Kb4
55	Kf5	Black

resigns.

Round 4
White: Cray Blitz
Black: Deep Thought II
Sicilian Defense

1	e4	c5
2	Nf3	d6
3	d4	cxd4
4	Nxd4	Nf6
5	Nc3	Nc6
6	f4	e5
7	Nxc6	bxc6
8	fxe5	Ng4
9	Be2	Nxe5
10	Be3	Be7
11	O-O	Be6
12	Qd4	O-O
13	Rad1	f6
14	b3	Qe8
15	Na4	Qg6
16	Bf4	Rf7
17	Qe3	Raf8

18	Qxa7	Qxe4
19	Bd3	Qb4
20	Qe3	Ra8
21	c3	Qb7
22	Rf2	Qa7
23	Qxa7	Rxa7
24	Be3	Ra5
25	Bb6	Ra8
26	Bc2	Bf8
27	Re1	c5
28	Be4	Ra6
29	Rb1	f5
30	Bc2	Rb7
31	Bd8	g6
32	Re1	c4
33	Rb1	Bd7
34	Nb2	Ra8

35	Bg5	Rxa2	50	gxf4	Rxf4	47 Kf3 Re6	57 Ra7 Kf6
36	b4	Bb5	51	Kg3	h5	48 Rc5 Rb6	58 Kg3 Rc6
37	Re2	Bg7	52	Nd2	h4+	49 Rc7 Rd6	59 Kh4 Ke6
38	Nd1	Ra6	53	Kg2	Bc6+	50 Ra7 Rc6	60 Kh5 Kd5
39	Bd2	Nd3	54	Kg1	Rg4+	51 Ke4 Rb6	61 f5 Ke5
40	Ne3	Ra2	55	Kf2	Rg2+	52 Ra8 Rb4+	62 Re7+ Kf4
41	Bxd3	cxd3	56	Ke3	Bb5	53 Kf3 Rb6	63 Re6 Rc3
42	Rf2	Rxd2	57	Ra2	Rxh2	54 Rh8 Kg7	64 f6 Black
43	Rxd2	Bxc3	58	Ra5	Re2+	55 Rd8 Kf6	resigns.
44	Nf1	Bxd2	59	Kd4	h3	56 Rd7 Ke6	
45	Nxd2	Re7	60	Rxb5	Rg2		
46	Nf3	h6	61	Rb8+	Kg7		
47	Rb2	Re4	62	Rb7+	Kg6		
48	Kf2	g5		Black resigns.			
49	g3	f4					

Round 5
White: Deep Thought II
Black: Chess Machine
Ruy Lopez

1	e4	e5	24	Qe2	Rad8
2	Nf3	Nc6	25	b3	Nxe5
3	Bb5	a6	26	Qxe4	Rf5
4	Ba4	Nf6	27	Rae1	Re8
5	O-O	Nxe4	28	Re3	Qf6
6	d4	b5	29	Bxe5	Rfxe5
7	Bb3	d5	30	Qxg4+	Kh8
8	dxe5	Be6	31	Rxe5	Qxe5
9	c3	Be7	32	c4	Rd8
10	Bc2	O-O	33	Qh3	Qg5
11	Nbd2	f5	34	Qe6	bxc4
12	Nb3	Qd7	35	Qxc4	Rg8
13	Nbd4	Na5	36	g3	Rg6
14	Nxe6	Qxe6	37	Re1	Qf5
15	Bf4	c5	38	Re7	Qb1+
16	Qc1	h6	39	Kg2	Qf5
17	h3	g5	40	Qc3+	Qf6
18	Bh2	g4	41	Qxc5	Qc6+
19	hxg4	fxg4	42	Qxc6	Rxc6
20	Bxe4	dxe4	43	Re5	Kg7
21	Nd2	Bg5	44	Ra5	Kf6
22	Qe1	Bxd2	45	f4	Ke7
23	Qxd2	Nc4	46	g4	Kf6

Appendix E
Games from Chapter 4

**Deep Thought II versus
Bent Larsen and versus
the Danish National Team**

February 24–28, 1993
Copenhagen, Denmark
Time Control: 40/2, 20/1 thereafter

Game 1, Larsen Match
White: Bent Larsen
Black: Deep Thought II
Four Knights Opening

1 e4	e5	23 g5	Bxb3
2 Nf3	Nc6	24 cxb3	Rxd3
3 Nc3	Nf6	25 Qe2	hxg5
4 Bb5	Bb4	26 hxg5	fxg5
5 O-O	O-O	27 Rd1	Re3
6 Bxc6	dxc6	28 Qb2	Qxb3
7 d3	Qe7	29 Qxb3+	Rxb3
8 Ne2	Bg4	30 Rd5	Ra3
9 Ng3	Nh5	31 Rxe5	g4
10 h3	Nxg3	32 Kxg4	c4
11 fxg3	Bc5+	33 Rd2	Rxa4
12 Kh2	Bc8	34 Rd7	Rc8
13 g4	Be6	35 Ng5	Ra2
14 Qe2	f6	36 Rxc7	Ra8
15 Be3	Bxe3	37 g3	Rf2
16 Qxe3	h6	38 Ree7	Kh8
17 a4	Qb4	39 Rxg7	Rh2
18 b3	b6	40 e5	Rd8
19 Rf2	c5	41 Rh7+	Rxh7
20 Kg3	Qa5	42 Nxh7	Rg8+
21 h4	Qc3	43 Ng5	Black
22 Raf1	Rad8	resigns.	

Game 1, Danish Team Match
White: Henrik Danielsen
Black: Deep Thought II
Reti Defense

1 Nf3	Nf6	20 g4	Bd7
2 b3	g6	21 Rfd1	h6
3 g3	Bg7	22 a4	Bc6
4 Bb2	O-O	23 Rd6	h5
5 Bg2	d6	24 g5	Ne8
6 d4	c5	25 Rdd1	f5
7 O-O	cxd4	26 b4	f4
8 Nxd4	d5	27 bxa5	fxe3
9 Na3	e5	28 fxe3	Be5
10 Nf3	e4	29 c5	Rf5
11 Nd4	Nc6	30 Rd8	Rxg5
12 c4	Nxd4	31 a6	bxa6
13 Qxd4	Bg4	32 h4	Rg4
14 Qe3	Qe7	33 Rc8	Bc7
15 Rab1	Bf5	34 Rb7	Bxb7
16 h3	d4	35 Rxe8+	Kf7
17 Bxd4	Qxa3	36 Rh8	Be5
18 Bc5	Qa5	White resigns.	
19 Bxf8	Rxf8		

Game 2, Larsen Match
White: Deep Thought II
Black: Bent Larsen
Sicilian Defense

1 e4	c5	9 O-O	Bd7
2 Nf3	g6	10 Qd2	Nxd4
3 c4	Bg7	11 Bxd4	Bc6
4 d4	cxd4	12 f3	a5
5 Nxd4	Nc6	13 b3	Nd7
6 Be3	Nf6	14 Be3	Nc5
7 Nc3	O-O	15 Rab1	Qb6
8 Be2	d6	16 Rfc1	Rfc8

17 Rc2	h5
18 Nd5	Bxd5
19 cxd5	Qb4
20 Qxb4	axb4
21 Bd2	Na6
22 Rbc1	Bd4+
23 Kf1	Rxc2
24 Rxc2	Bc5
25 Bd3	Kf8
26 Bb5	Nc7
27 Bh6+	Kg8
28 Bd3	Ne8
29 Bd2	Nf6
30 Ke2	Kg7
31 Bb5	h4
32 h3	Rd8
33 Bg5	Rh8
34 Kd3	Rh5
35 Bf4	e5
36 dxe6	fxe6
37 Ba4	b6
38 Bc6	Kf7
39 Bd2	d5
40 exd5	exd5
41 Bf4	Rf5
42 Bc7	Nh5
43 Re2	Nf4+
44 Bxf4	Rxf4
45 Bxd5+	Kg7
46 Be4	Rf7
47 Kc4	Rd7
48 Bd5	Re7
49 Rc2	Re1
50 Bb7	Kf6
51 Be4	Rd1
52 Kb5	g5
53 Re2	Ra1
54 Bd3	Rd1
55 Bh7	Ra1
56 Kc4	Rg1
57 Kd5	Rd1+
58 Kc6	Rf1
59 Bd3	Rf2

Drawn by agreement.

Game 2, Danish Team Match
White: Deep Thought II
Black: Carsten Hoi
Irregular Opening

1 e4	d6
2 d4	g6
3 Nc3	Bg7
4 f4	Nf6
5 Nf3	c5
6 Bb5+	Bd7
7 e5	Ng4
8 e6	Bxb5
9 exf7+	Kd7
10 Nxb5	Qa5+
11 Nc3	cxd4
12 Nxd4	Bxd4
13 Qxd4	Nc6
14 Qc4	Qb6
15 Qe2	h5
16 Bd2	Nd4
17 Qe4	Nf5
18 Qa4+	Qc6
19 Qxc6+	bxc6
20 h3	Nge3
21 Bxe3	Nxe3
22 Kd2	Nc4+
23 Ke2	Raf8
24 b3	Nb6
25 Rhf1	Rxf7
26 Rf3	h4
27 Rd1	Rhf8
28 Ke3	e6
29 a3	a5
30 Rdf1	c5
31 Ke2	Kc6
32 Kd1	Nd5
33 Nxd5	exd5
34 a4	d4
35 R1f2	d5
36 g4	hxg3
37 Rxg3	Rf6
38 Rfg2	Rxf4
39 Rxg6+	R8f6
40 R2g5	Rf1+
41 Ke2	Rf2+
42 Ke1	Rf1+
43 Ke2	Rf2+
44 Ke1	

Drawn by agreement.

Game 3, Larsen Match
White: Bent Larsen
Black: Deep Thought II
Center Counter Defense

1 e4	d5
2 exd5	Qxd5
3 Nc3	Qa5
4 Nf3	Nf6
5 d4	Bf5
6 Be2	e6
7 O-O	Nbd7
8 a3	O-O-O
9 Bf4	Qb6
10 Nb5	Nd5
11 Bg3	a6
12 c4	axb5
13 cxd5	Bd6
14 Qb3	Bxg3
15 hxg3	Nf8
16 a4	Rxd5
17 axb5	Kd7
18 Bc4	Rd6
19 d5	Ke7
20 Rfe1	Nd7
21 Qc3	Nf6
22 Nh4	Bg4
23 Re3	Rhd8
24 dxe6	fxe6
25 Rae1	Rd1
26 Qe5	Rxe1+
27 Rxe1	Rd2
28 Nf5+	Bxf5
29 Qxf5	Rd1
30 Qe5	Rxe1+
31 Qxe1	Qd6
32 Qe2	h6
33 b3	Qd7
34 Qf3	b6
35 Qe2	Kf7
36 g4	Qd6
37 g3	Nd5
38 Kg2	Kf6
39 Qf3+	Ke7
40 Qe4	Nf6
41 Qg6	Kf8
42 g5	hxg5
43 Qxg5	Qd4
44 Qc1	Ke7
45 Qg5	Kf7
46 Qc1	Qe5
47 Qd2	Ke7
48 Qb4+	Kd7
49 Qd2+	Nd5
50 Qd3	g5
51 Qf3	Ke7
52 Kg1	Qd4
53 Qh5	Qg7
54 Qg4	Kd6
55 Qe4	Qa1+
56 Kg2	Qf6
57 Qc2	Qe5
58 Qc1	Kd7
59 Kg1	Ke7
60 Kf1	Kf6
61 Qa3	Kf7
62 Qc1	Ke7

Drawn by agreement.

Game 3, Danish Team Match
White: Lars Bo Hansen
Black: Deep Thought II
English Opening

1 Nf3	Nf6	28 Nxc5	Bh5
2 c4	e6	29 e4	Nd6
3 Nc3	d5	30 Nxd6	Qxd6
4 d4	Be7	31 Bf2	Qd2
5 Bf4	O-O	32 Qb3+	Bf7
6 e3	c5	33 Qh3	Rfd8
7 dxc5	Bxc5	34 Be3	Bxe3+
8 Qc2	Nc6	35 Rxe3	Bc4
9 a3	Qa5	36 Rfe1	Rb8
10 Nd2	Be7	37 Qg3	a5
11 Bg3	Bd7	38 Rc3	Qd4+
12 Be2	Qb6	39 Qe3	axb4
13 O-O	d4	40 Qxd4	Rxd4
14 Na4	Qd8	41 axb4	Rxb4
15 b4	Rc8	42 Kf2	Rb5
16 Nb2	e5	43 Na4	Ra5
17 Nb3	dxe3	44 Nb6	Ba6
18 fxe3	Qe8	45 Nd5	Bb7
19 Rad1	Ng4	46 Ne7+	Kf8
20 Qc3	Bg5	47 Nf5	Ra2+
21 Bxg4	Bxg4	48 Kf3	Rdd2
22 Rde1	f6	49 Rc7	Rf2+
23 c5	Nd8	50 Kg4	Rxg2+
24 Nd2	Qc6	51 Ng3	Raf2
25 Qc2	b6	52 h4	g6
26 Ne4	Nf7	White resigns.	
27 Nc4	bxc5		

Game 4, Larsen Match and
Game 4, Danish Team Match
White: Deep Thought II
Black: Bent Larsen
Sicilian Defense

1 e4	c5	6 a4	g6
2 Nf3	d6	7 Be2	Bg7
3 d4	cxd4	8 O-O	O-O
4 Nxd4	Nf6	9 f4	Nc6
5 Nc3	a6	10 Be3	Bd7

11 Nb3	Be6	33 axb6	Be3+
12 Ra3	Rc8	34 Kh1	Bxb6
13 Kh1	Re8	35 Qe4	Qc5
14 f5	Bxb3	36 Qb1	a5
15 Rxb3	Qd7	37 Be4	g5
16 fxg6	hxg6	38 Bh7	Kf8
17 Nd5	Nxd5	39 Bf5	Qf2
18 exd5	Ne5	40 Bg6	Kg7
19 a5	Bf6	41 Bh7	Kh8
20 c3	Kg7	42 Bf5	Kg7
21 Rb4	Rh8	43 Bd3	Be3
22 Qb3	Rc7	44 Bh7	Kh8
23 Bb6	Rcc8	45 b3	Bd2
24 Kg1	Rh4	46 c4	Be3
25 Bd4	Rc7	47 Bg6	Bd4
26 Bxe5	dxe5	48 Bf5	Bc5
27 Rxh4	Bxh4	49 Be4	Be3
28 Rxf7+	Kxf7	50 Qd1	Kg7
29 d6+	Kg7	51 Qa1	Bd4
30 dxc7	Qxc7	52 Qc1	Drawn
31 Qb4	Bg5	by agreement.	
32 Bf3	b5		

Michael Rohde versus Deep Thought II

Judit Polgar versus Deep Thought II

April 20, 1993
New York
Time Control: 40/2, 20/1 thereafter

August 20, 1993
Hawthorn, New York
Time Control: All/30 minutes

White: Deep Thought II
Black: Michael Rohde
Sicilian Defense,
Taimanov Variation

Game 1
White: Deep Thought II
Black: Judit Polgar
Sicilian Defense

1	e4	c5	26	Qxd5	Rxc2
2	Nf3	Nc6	27	Rxf4	Qg6
3	d4	cxd4	28	Rd4	Rfc8
4	Nxd4	Qc7	29	a5	R8c5
5	Nc3	e6	30	Qd8+	Kg7
6	Be2	a6	31	b4	Rf5
7	O-O	Nf6	32	Rd2	Qc6
8	Be3	Bb4	33	Qd4+	Kg6
9	Na4	O-O	34	Rb1	f6
10	Nxc6	bxc6	35	Rxc2	Qxc2
11	Nb6	Rb8	36	Qb2	Qd3
12	Nxc8	Rfxc8	37	Ra1	Qe3+
13	Bxa6	Rf8	38	Kh1	Rf2
14	Bd3	Bd6	39	Qb1+	Kh6
15	f4	e5	40	Qg1	Qd2
16	b3	exf4	41	a6	Qb2
17	Bd4	Be5	42	a7	Rxg2
18	Bxe5	Qxe5	43	a8Q	Rxg1+
19	Qf3	d5	44	Rxg1	Qxb4
20	exd5	Nxd5	45	Rf1	Kg7
21	Qe4	Qh5	46	Qd5	h6
22	Rae1	g6	47	Qd7+	Kg8
23	Bc4	Rbc8	48	Qe6+	Kh7
24	a4	g5	49	Qf7+	Black
25	Bxd5	cxd5			resigns.

1	e4	c5	31	Kf1	Kf7
2	Nf3	e6	32	c4	Rc8
3	d4	cxd4	33	Ba5	dxc4
4	Nxd4	Nc6	34	Nb6	Rb8
5	Nc3	Qc7	35	Nd7	Rc8
6	Be2	a6	36	Bb4	cxb3
7	O-O	Bb4	37	Nxf8	Rxf8
8	Nxc6	bxc6	38	axb3	Rb8
9	Qd4	Bd6	39	Bxe7	Kxe7
10	Qxg7	Bxh2+	40	Rd4	a5
11	Kh1	Be5	41	Ra4	Bc6
12	Bf4	Bxg7	42	Rxa5	Rxb3
13	Bxc7	d5	43	Ra7+	Kf6
14	Rad1	Ne7	44	Rxh7	Nf4
15	Na4	Ra7	45	g3	Bb5+
16	Bb6	Ra8	46	Kg1	Nh3+
17	c3	Ng6	47	Kg2	Ng5
18	Bc7	Ra7	48	Rh6+	Ke7
19	Bb8	Rb7	49	Re5	Bc6+
20	Bg3	O-O	50	Kf1	Rb1+
21	exd5	cxd5	51	Re1	Rb2
22	Rfe1	f5	52	Be2	Ne4
23	Bd6	Rd8	53	Rd1	Bd5
24	Ba3	Rc7	54	Rc1	Nd2+
25	Bb4	Rc6	55	Ke1	Ne4
26	Ba5	Rf8	56	Ra1	Nc3
27	Bb6	Rf7	57	Bd3	Na2
28	Kg1	Bf8	58	Kf1	Nb4
29	b3	Bb7	59	Bxf5	Nc6
30	Bh5	Re7	60	Rd1	Bc4+

61	Bd3	Bb3	68	f4	Nf7
62	Rb1	Rxb1	69	g4	e5
63	Bxb1	Bd5	70	g5+	Kg7
64	Rh7+	Kf6	71	Rh7+	Kg8
65	Rh4	Ne5	72	g6	exf4+
66	Ke2	Bf3+	73	Kxf4	Black
67	Ke3	Bc6		resigns.	

Game 2
White: Judit Polgar
Black: Deep Thought II
Reti Opening

1	Nf3	Nf6	32	Rg1	Kf8
2	g3	d5	33	Qe1	Rd4
3	d3	Nbd7	34	Bg2	Qf4
4	Nbd2	e5	35	Ng4	Qxf5
5	Bg2	c6	36	Qh4	Qg6
6	O-O	Bd6	37	Qh8+	Ke7
7	Nh4	O-O	38	Qh4+	Kd6
8	e4	Nc5	39	Qf2	c5
9	Re1	Bg4	40	Ne3	Kc7
10	f3	Be6	41	f4	exf4
11	Nf1	Qb6	42	Nd5+	Kd8
12	Kh1	dxe4	43	Nc3	Qd3
13	dxe4	Rfd8	44	Qb2	Re3
14	Qe2	Na4	45	Nb5	Rb4
15	g4	Bc5	46	Qxg7	Qxb5
16	Ne3	Bd4	47	Qf6+	Kc7
17	c3	Nxc3	48	Qxf7+	Qd7
18	bxc3	Bxc3	49	Qf8	Ra4
19	Nc2	Qa5	50	Qa8	Rxa2
20	Bg5	h6	51	Qb7+	Kd8
21	Be3	b6	52	Qb8+	Ke7
22	Nf5	Qa4	53	Qxf4	Qd4
23	g5	hxg5	54	Qc7+	Kf6
24	Bxg5	Bxe1	55	Rf1+	Kg5
25	Rxe1	Bxf5	56	Qf7	Ra1
26	exf5	Rd6	57	Qf5+	Kh6
27	Ne3	Re8	58	Qf8+	Kh5
28	Rg1	Nh7	59	Qf5+	Kh4
29	Bf1	Nxg5	60	Qh7+	Kg5
30	Rxg5	Qf4	61	Qf5+	
31	Rg4	Qh6		Drawn.	

Appendix F
Games from Chapter 5

Deep Thought II at the 24th ACM International Computer Chess Championship

June 25–27, 1994
Cape May, New Jersey
Time Control: 40/2, 20/1 thereafter

Round 1
White: Deep Thought II
Black: Zarkov
King's Gambit Accepted

1 e4	e5	22 Qb5	Qe6+
2 f4	exf4	23 Qe2	Qd7
3 Nf3	g5	24 Rd1	Re8
4 h4	g4	25 Ne4	Qa4
5 Ne5	Nf6	26 Rxd5	Rxe4
6 d4	d6	27 Rd8+	Kh7
7 Nd3	Nxe4	28 Be3	Bh6
8 Bxf4	Bg7	29 b3	Qc6
9 c3	O-O	30 Bg2	Rxe3
10 Nd2	Re8	31 Bxc6	bxc6
11 Nxe4	Rxe4+	32 Rd7	c4
12 Be2	Qe8	33 b4	Kg7
13 Kd2	h5	34 Kf2	Rxe2+
14 Re1	c5	35 Kxe2	c5
15 dxc5	dxc5	36 b5	Nb4
16 g3	Na6	37 cxb4	cxb4
17 Bf1	Bf5	38 Rxa7	b3
18 Qb3	Qc6	39 axb3	cxb3
19 Rxe4	Bxe4	40 Ra3	Kg6
20 Nf2	Rd8+	41 b6	Black
21 Ke1	Bd5	resigns.	

Round 2
White: M-Chess-Pro
Black: Deep Thought II

Deep Thought II forfeited the game because of a storm at Yorktown Heights. White wins.

Round 3
White: Deep Thought II
Black: Wchess
Reti Opening

1 Nf3	Nf6	23 Nd7	Rfd8
2 e3	Nc6	24 Nxf6+	Kh8
3 d4	e6	25 Rc1	Rd6
4 c4	d5	26 Ne4	Rh6
5 Be2	Be7	27 Rc4	Rb8
6 Nc3	O-O	28 Rd1	Kg8
7 O-O	Bd7	29 Neg5	b3
8 Bd2	dxc4	30 a3	Rc8
9 Bxc4	Bd6	31 Rd7	Rd6
10 Rc1	e5	32 Rxd6	Bxd6
11 d5	Ne7	33 Ne4	Bxa3
12 e4	b5	34 bxa3	b2
13 Bd3	b4	35 Nfd2	Rd8
14 Na4	c6	36 g4	Rd4
15 dxc6	Bxc6	37 Rxc6	Rxe4
16 Bg5	Bxe4	38 Rc8+	Kg7
17 Bxf6	Bxd3	39 Rb8	Rxg4+
18 Qxd3	gxf6	40 Kf1	b1Q+
19 Rcd1	Bc7	41 Rxb1	Ra4
20 Qa6	Qe8	42 Rb3	Kf6
21 Nc5	Qc6	43 Rh3	Ke6
22 Qxc6	Nxc6	44 Rxh7	Rxa3

45	Rh6+	Ke7
46	Nc4	Ra1+
47	Kg2	f6
48	Ne3	Kf7
49	h4	Kg7
50	Nf5+	Kf7
51	h5	Ke6
52	Ng3	Ra4
53	Rh7	f5
54	Rh6+	Kf7
55	Nxf5	Rg4+
56	Kh3	Rf4
57	Nd6+	Ke7
58	Kg3	a5
59	Nc8+	Kf8
60	Ra6	Kg7
61	Rxa5	Rf5
62	Kg4	Rxf2
63	Rxe5	Rg2+
64	Kh3	Ra2
65	Nd6	Kf6
66	Rc5	Ra6
67	Rf5+	Ke6
68	Rg5	Ra3+
69	Rg3	Ra1
70	Rg6+	Ke7
71	h6	Rd1
72	Kg2	Rd5
73	h7	Rh5
74	Nf5+	Kf7
75	Nh6+	Kxg6
76	h8Q	Rxh6
77	Qf8	Kg5
78	Kg3	Rf6
79	Qd8	Kh5
80	Qd5+	Kg6
81	Kg4	Kg7
82	Qd7+	Rf7
83	Qd8	Rf1
84	Qd4+	Kh6
85	Qe3+	Kg7
86	Kg5	Rf7
87	Qc3+	Kf8
88	Kg6	Rd7
89	Qe5	Rd1
90	Kf6	Rf1+
91	Ke6	Kg8

Black resigns.

27	Rd6	Rb8+
28	Kc1	Ra3
29	Rxc6	Rxa2
30	g3	Ra1+
31	Kd2	a4
32	Bg2	Rd8+
33	Ke2	Rxh1
34	Bxh1	Ra8
35	Rb6	Nd5
36	Rd6	Nc3+
37	Kd3	a3
38	Kxc3	a2
39	Rd1	a1Q+
40	Rxa1	Rxa1
41	Bg2	Rg1
42	Bh3	Rh1
43	Bc8	Rxh2
44	g4	Rf2
45	Bb7	g6
46	Kd3	h5
47	gxh5	gxh5
48	Be4	h4
49	Ke3	Rg2
50	Bf5	Rg5
51	Bh3	Rg3
52	Bf1	h3
53	Kf2	h2
54	Bg2	Rg7
55	f4	f5
56	Kf3	Kf7
57	Kf2	Rg4
58	Kf3	Ke7
59	Kf2	Rg8
60	Kf1	Kd6
61	Kf2	White resigns.

Round 4
White: Star Socrates
Black: Deep Thought II
Sicilian Defense

1	e4	c5
2	Nc3	Nc6
3	Nge2	Nf6
4	d4	cxd4
5	Nxd4	d6
6	Bg5	e6
7	Qd2	a6
8	0-0-0	h6
9	Bf4	Bd7
10	Nxc6	Bxc6
11	f3	d5
12	Qe1	Bb4
13	a3	Ba5
14	Bd2	0-0
15	exd5	exd5
16	Bd3	Re8
17	Qh4	d4
18	Na2	Bxd2+
19	Rxd2	a5
20	Bc4	b5
21	Rxd4	Qe7
22	Bf1	Qe3+
23	Rd2	b4
24	Qd4	bxa3
25	Qxe3	axb2+
26	Kxb2	Rxe3

Round 5
White: MChess
Black: Deep Thought II
Sicilian Defense

1	e4	c5
2	Nf3	Nc6
3	d4	cxd4
4	Nxd4	e5
5	Nb5	d6
6	N1c3	a6
7	Na3	b5
8	Nd5	Nce7
9	c4	Nxd5
10	exd5	bxc4
11	Nxc4	Nf6
12	Be3	Rb8
13	a4	Be7
14	Be2	0-0
15	0-0	Bf5
16	f4	Be4
17	fxe5	Nxd5
18	Qd4	Nxe3
19	Nxe3	d5
20	Bxa6	Rb4
21	Qa7	Rxb2
22	Qd4	Qb8
23	Bb5	Rb4
24	Qd2	Qxe5
25	Ng4	Qh5
26	h3	Bc5+
27	Kh2	Bd6+
28	Kg1	Rb3
29	Be2	Bc5+
30	Kh2	Qh4
31	Rf3	Bxf3
32	Bxf3	h5
33	Qxd5	hxg4
34	Qxb3	Bd6+
35	Kg1	gxf3

White resigns.

Deep Thought II at the 8th ICCA World Computer Chess Championship

May 25–29, 1995
Hong Kong
Time Control: 40/2, 20/1 thereafter

Round 1
White: Deep Thought II
Black: Star Socrates
Queen's Pawn Opening

1 d4	Nf6	27 Qxc7	Qxa2
2 Nf3	d5	28 Qe5	Qa4
3 e3	e6	29 d6	Qc2+
4 Bd3	Nc6	30 Kg3	Qd1
5 Nbd2	Bd6	31 Kh4	Qd2
6 e4	e5	32 f5	Qf2+
7 0-0	0-0	33 Qg3	Qd4
8 exd5	Nxd4	34 Qe3	Qd5
9 c4	Bg4	35 Qd2	Qxd2
10 Re1	Nd7	36 Bxd2	Nb6
11 h3	Bh5	37 fxg6	hxg6
12 g4	Bg6	38 Kg5	Rd8
13 Bxg6	fxg6	39 Bc3	Rd7
14 Kg2	Kh8	40 Kxg6	Kf8
15 Nxd4	exd4	41 Bd4	Nd5
16 Ne4	Ne5	42 Kf5	b6
17 Bg5	Qd7	43 h4	Nb4
18 f4	Nxc4	44 h5	Nc6
19 Qxd4	Nb6	45 Be3	Nd8
20 Nxd6	Qxd6	46 h6	Rf7+
21 Re5	Rae8	47 Ke4	g5
22 Rae1	Rxe5	48 Rg6	Rh7
23 Rxe5	Nc8	49 Bxg5	Nb7
24 Re6	Qd7	50 Kd5	Kf7
25 Kh2	Kg8	51 Rf6+	Black
26 Qe5	Qa4	resigns.	

Round 2
White: Hitech
Black: Deep Thought II
Sicilian Defense

1 e4	c5	21 g4	Rf4
2 c3	Nf6	22 Rc2	Ra4
3 d3	Nc6	23 Qe3	Nd3
4 Nf3	d6	24 Rxc8	Qxc8
5 Nbd2	e5	25 b3	Rxg4+
6 Qa4	Be7	26 Kh1	Rf4
7 d4	cxd4	27 Kg2	Rxf3
8 cxd4	Bd7	28 Nxf3	Nf4+
9 Bb5	a6	29 Qxf4	exf4
10 Bxc6	Bxc6	30 Bb2	Bxb2
11 Qc2	0-0	31 Re1	Qf5
12 d5	Bd7	32 a4	Bd7
13 0-0	Rc8	33 Ng1	f3+
14 Qb3	Bb5	34 Kh2	Be5+
15 Re1	Nd7	35 Kh1	Qf4
16 Re3	Nc5	36 Rxe5	dxe5
17 Qa3	f5	37 b4	Bxh3
18 exf5	Rxf5	38 Nxh3	Qg4
19 h3	a5	39 Nf4	exf4
20 Rc3	Bf6	40 bxa5	Qg2#

Round 3
White: Deep Thought II
Black: Cheiron
Reti Defense

1 Nf3	Nf6	12 Qe2	Rb8
2 b3	Nc6	13 Rg1	Qc8
3 Bb2	d6	14 d5	Qb7
4 e3	e5	15 Qf2	Nh5
5 Bb5	Be7	16 Ne2	Bd7
6 d4	e4	17 Nf4	Bf6
7 Nfd2	Bg4	18 Bxf6	Nxf6
8 f3	exf3	19 Qh4	Kh8
9 gxf3	Bh3	20 Rxg7	Qb6
10 Nc3	0-0	Black resigns.	
11 Bxc6	bxc6		

Round 4
White: Wchess
Black: Deep Thought II
Sicilian Defense

Round 5
White: Deep Thought II
Black: Fritz 3
Sicilian Defense

1 e4	c5	32 Nf1	Nb4	
2 c3	d5	33 Nd2	Bd5	
3 exd5	Qxd5	34 Rb1	Be6	
4 d4	Nf6	35 Ra7	Nd3+	
5 Nf3	e6	36 Ke2	Nc5	
6 Be2	Nc6	37 Rb4	Bd5	
7 O-O	cxd4	38 g3	Ra8	
8 cxd4	Be7	39 Rxa8+	Bxa8	
9 Nc3	Qd6	40 Rd4	Kh7	
10 Nb5	Qd8	41 Rd8	Bb7	
11 Bf4	Nd5	42 Rb8	Bh1	
12 Bg3	a6	43 Rc8	Ne6	
13 Nc3	O-O	44 e4	Bg2	
14 Qb3	Nf6	45 Ke3	Bh3	
15 Rfd1	b5	46 Rc6	f5	
16 a3	Bb7	47 Rxa6	Nc5	
17 Qa2	Na5	48 Rd6	Nxe4	
18 b4	Rc8	49 Nxe4	fxe4	
19 Rac1	Nc6	50 Kf2	Bg4	
20 Bf4	Re8	51 Rb6	Bf3	
21 d5	exd5	52 Rxb5	g5	
22 Nxd5	Nxd5	53 Ke3	Kg7	
23 Qxd5	Qxd5	54 Rb7+	Kg6	
24 Rxd5	Bxb4	55 Rb6+	Kg7	
25 axb4	Rxe2	56 Re6	h5	
26 Be3	Re8	57 Rd6	h4	
27 Rd7	Ba8	58 g4	Bxg4	
28 Nd2	Nxb4	59 Kxe4	Bh3	
29 Kf1	R2xe3	60 Rd3	Bg4	
30 fxe3	Nd5	Drawn by		
31 Kf2	h6	agreement.		

1 e4	c5	21 cxb5	Bxd5
2 Nf3	Nc6	22 exd5	Nb4
3 d4	cxd4	23 Bf5	Rc5
4 Nxd4	Nf6	24 bxa6	Nxa6
5 Nc3	e5	25 Nc2	Qd2
6 Ndb5	d6	26 Ne1	Rxd5
7 Bg5	a6	27 Nxf3	Qxf2
8 Na3	b5	28 Be4	Ra5
9 Bxf6	gxf6	29 Rg2	Qe3
10 Nd5	f5	30 Re1	Qh6
11 Bd3	Be6	31 Bc6+	Kd8
12 Qh5	f4	32 a3	f5
13 O-O	Rg8	33 Rc2	Rc5
14 Kh1	Rg6	34 Rxc5	Nxc5
15 Qd1	Rc8	35 Rf1	Be7
16 c4	Qh4	36 a4	f4
17 g3	Qh3	37 gxf4	Qxf4
18 Qd2	f3	38 Rg1	Nxa4
19 Rg1	Rh6	39 b4	Qxb4
20 Qxh6	Qxh6	White resigns.	

Miguel Illescas versus Deep Thought II

July 1995
Barcelona, Spain
Time Control: 40/2, Fischer Clock

Game 1
White: Deep Thought II
Black: Miguel Illescas
Queen's Gambit Declined

1	d4	d5	25	Qg4	f5
2	c4	c6	26	Qg6	Qf7
3	Nc3	Nf6	27	Qxf7+	Kxf7
4	e3	e6	28	Bd3	Nd6
5	Qc2	Nbd7	29	Be5	Rxc1
6	Bd2	Be7	30	Rxc1	Rc8
7	Nf3	O-O	31	Rxc8	Nxc8
8	Bd3	dxc4	32	a4	Bc6
9	Bxc4	c5	33	b3	Ne7
10	dxc5	Bxc5	34	axb5	Bxb5
11	O-O	b6	35	Bb1	Nc6
12	Rfd1	Bb7	36	Bd6	g6
13	Be2	h6	37	Kf2	a5
14	Rac1	Qb8	38	Bc7	a4
15	Nb5	a6	39	bxa4	Bxa4
16	Nc3	Rc8	40	e4	Bb3
17	Qa4	b5	41	h3	h5
18	Qh4	Bd6	42	g3	Ne7
19	a3	Ne5	43	Bd3	Ba2
20	Nxe5	Bxe5	44	Be5	Bb3
21	f3	Bd5	45	Bd4	Ba2
22	f4	Bxc3		Drawn by
23	Bxc3	Ne4		agreement.
24	Bd4	Qb7			

Game 2
White: Miguel Illescas
Black: Deep Thought II
English Opening

1	c4	e5	15	Be2	Ne4
2	Nc3	Nc6	16	Ba5	Rc8
3	Nf3	Nf6	17	f3	Nf6
4	d3	g6	18	e4	Qe7
5	e3	Bb4	19	Bc3	c6
6	Bd2	d6	20	dxc6	bxc6
7	Be2	Be6	21	f4	Ned7
8	O-O	h6	22	Bf3	Rfe8
9	a3	Bxc3	23	Re1	d5
10	Bxc3	O-O	24	e5	Nh7
11	d4	e4	25	Bg4	Nhf8
12	d5	exf3	26	Qd4	Black
13	Bxf3	Bxd5		resigns.
14	cxd5	Ne5			

Appendix G
Games from the ACM
Chess Challenge

February 10–17, 1996
Philadelphia, Pennsylvania
Time Control: 40/2, 20/1,
                30/thereafter

Game 1
White: Deep Blue
Black: Garry Kasparov
Sicilian Opening

1	e4	c5	
2	c3	d5	
3	exd5	Qxd5	
4	d4	Nf6	
5	Nf3	Bg4	
6	Be2	e6	
7	h3	Bh5	
8	O-O	Nc6	
9	Be3	cxd4	
10	cxd4	Bb4	
11	a3	Ba5	
12	Nc3	Qd6	
13	Nb5	Qe7	
14	Ne5	Bxe2	
15	Qxe2	O-O	
16	Rac1	Rac8	
17	Bg5	Bb6	
18	Bxf6	gxf6	
19	Nc4	Rfd8	
20	Nxb6	axb6	
21	Rfd1	f5	
22	Qe3	Qf6	
23	d5	Rxd5	
24	Rxd5	exd5	
25	b3	Kh8	
26	Qxb6	Rg8	
27	Qc5	d4	
28	Nd6	f4	
29	Nxb7	Ne5	
30	Qd5	f3	
31	g3	Nd3	
32	Rc7	Re8	
33	Nd6	Re1+	
34	Kh2	Nxf2	
35	Nxf7+	Kg7	
36	Ng5+	Kh6	
37	Rxh7+	Black	
	resigns.		

Game 2
White: Garry Kasparov
Black: Deep Blue
Catalan Opening

1	Nf3	d5	
2	d4	e6	
3	g3	c5	
4	Bg2	Nc6	

5	O-O	Nf6	
6	c4	dxc4	
7	Ne5	Bd7	
8	Na3	cxd4	
9	Naxc4	Bc5	
10	Qb3	O-O	
11	Qxb7	Nxe5	
12	Nxe5	Rb8	
13	Qf3	Bd6	
14	Nc6	Bxc6	
15	Qxc6	e5	
16	Rb1	Rb6	
17	Qa4	Qb8	
18	Bg5	Be7	
19	b4	Bxb4	
20	Bxf6	gxf6	
21	Qd7	Qc8	
22	Qxa7	Rb8	
23	Qa4	Bc3	
24	Rxb8	Qxb8	
25	Be4	Qc7	
26	Qa6	Kg7	
27	Qd3	Rb8	
28	Bxh7	Rb2	
29	Be4	Rxa2	
30	h4	Qc8	
31	Qf3	Ra1	
32	Rxa1	Bxa1	
33	Qh5	Qh8	
34	Qg4+	Kf8	
35	Qc8+	Kg7	
36	Qg4+	Kf8	
37	Bd5	Ke7	
38	Bc6	Kf8	
39	Bd5	Ke7	
40	Qf3	Bc3	
41	Bc4	Qc8	
42	Qd5	Qe6	
43	Qb5	Qd7	
44	Qc5+	Qd6	
45	Qa7+	Qd7	
46	Qa8	Qc7	
47	Qa3+	Qd6	
48	Qa2	f5	
49	Bxf7	e4	
50	Bh5	Qf6	
51	Qa3+	Kd7	
52	Qa7+	Kd8	
53	Qb8+	Kd7	
54	Be8+	Xe7	
55	Bb5	Bd2	
56	Qc7+	Kf8	
57	Bc4	Bc3	
58	Kg2	Be1	
59	Kf1	Bc3	
60	f4	exf3	
61	exf3	Bd2	
62	f4	Ke8	
63	Qc8+	Ke7	
64	Qc5+	Kd8	
65	Bd3	Be3	
66	Qxf5	Qc6	
67	Qf8+	Kc7	
68	Qe7+	Kc8	
69	Bf5+	Kb8	
70	Qd8+	Kb7	
71	Qd7+	Qxd7	
72	Bxd7	Kc7	
73	Bb5	Black	
	resigns.		

Game 3
White: Deep Blue
Black: Garry Kasparov
Sicilian Opening

1 e4	c5	21 Bb8	Ra4
2 c3	d5	22 Rb4	Ra5
3 exd5	Qxd5	23 Rc4	O-O
4 d4	Nf6	24 Bd6	Ra8
5 Nf3	Bg4	25 Rc6	b5
6 Be2	e6	26 Kf1	Ra4
7 O-O	Nc6	27 Rb1	a6
8 Be3	cxd4	28 Ke2	h5
9 cxd4	Bb4	29 Kd3	Rd8
10 a3	Ba5	30 Be7	Rd7
11 Nc3	Qd6	31 Bxf6	gxf6
12 Ne5	Bxe2	32 Rb3	Kg7
13 Qxe2	Bxc3	33 Ke3	e5
14 bxc3	Nxe5	34 g3	exd4+
15 Bf4	Nf3+	35 cxd4	Re7+
16 Qxf3	Qd5	36 Kf3	Rd7
17 Qd3	Rc8	37 Rd3	Raxd4
18 Rfc1	Qc4	38 Rxd4	Rxd4
19 Qxc4	Rxc4	39 Rxa6	b4
20 Rcb1	b6	Drawn by	
		agreement.	

Game 4
White: Garry Kasparov
Black: Deep Blue
Slav Defense

1 Nf3	d5	13 Qxd4	Bc5
2 d4	c6	14 Qc3	a5
3 c4	e6	15 a3	Nf6
4 Nbd2	Nf6	16 Be3	Bxe3
5 e3	Nbd7	17 Rxe3	Bg4
6 Bd3	Bd6	18 Ne5	Re8
7 e4	dxe4	19 Rae1	Be6
8 Nxe4	Nxe4	20 f4	Qc8
9 Bxe4	O-O	21 h3	b5
10 O-O	h6	22 f5	Bxc4
11 Bc2	e5	23 Nxc4	bxc4
12 Re1	exd4	24 Rxe8+	Nxe8

25 Re4	Nf6	39 Rc7	Qf8
26 Rxc4	Nd5	40 Ra7	Ne5
27 Qe5	Qd7	41 Rxa5	Qf7
28 Rg4	f6	42 Rxe5	fxe5
29 Qd4	Kh7	43 Qxe5	Re8
30 Re4	Rd8	44 Qf4	Qf6
31 Kh1	Qc7	45 Bh5	Rf8
32 Qf2	Qb8	46 Bg6+	Kh8
33 Ba4	c5	47 Qc7	Qd4
34 Bc6	c4	48 Kh2	Ra8
35 Rxc4	Nb4	49 Bh5	Qf6
36 Bf3	Nd3	50 Bg6	Rg8
37 Qh4	Qxb2	Drawn by	
38 Qg3	Qxa3	agreement.	

Game 5
White: Deep Blue
Black: Garry Kasparov
Scottish Four Knights

1 e4	e5	26 Qe3	Bf7
2 Nf3	Nf6	27 Qc3	f4
3 Nc3	Nc6	28 Rd2	Qf6
4 d4	exd4	29 g3	Rd5
5 Nxd4	Bb4	30 a3	Kh7
6 Nxc6	bxc6	31 Kg2	Qe5
7 Bd3	d5	32 f3	e3
8 exd5	cxd5	33 Rd3	e2
9 O-O	O-O	34 gxf4	e1Q
10 Bg5	c6	35 fxe5	Qxc3
11 Qf3	Be7	36 Rxc3	Rxd4
12 Rae1	Re8	37 b4	Bc4
13 Ne2	h6	38 Kf2	g5
14 Bf4	Bd6	39 Re3	Be6
15 Nd4	Bg4	40 Rc3	Bc4
16 Qg3	Bxf4	41 Re3	Rd2+
17 Qxf4	Qb6	42 Ke1	Rd3
18 c4	Bd7	43 Kf2	Kg6
19 cxd5	cxd5	44 Rxd3	Bxd3
20 Rxe8+	Rxe8	45 Ke3	Bc2
21 Qd2	Ne4	46 Kd4	Kf5
22 Bxe4	dxe4	47 Kd5	h5
23 b3	Rd8	White resigns.	
24 Qc3	f5		
25 Rd1	Be6		

Game 6
White: Garry Kasparov
Black: Deep Blue
Slav Defense

1	Nf3	d5	23	Qd3	g6
2	d4	c6	24	Re2	Nf5
3	c4	e6	25	Bc3	h5
4	Nbd2	Nf6	26	b5	Nce7
5	e3	c5	27	Bd2	Kg7
6	b3	Nc6	28	a4	Ra8
7	Bb2	cxd4	29	a5	a6
8	exd4	Be7	30	b6	Bb8
9	Rc1	O-O	31	Bc2	Nc6
10	Bd3	Bd7	32	Ba4	Re7
11	O-O	Nh5	33	Bc3	Ne5
12	Re1	Nf4	34	dxe5	Qxa4
13	Bb1	Bd6	35	Nd4	Nxd4
14	g3	Ng6	36	Qxd4	Qd7
15	Ne5	Rc8	37	Bd2	Re8
16	Nxd7	Qxd7	38	Bg5	Rc8
17	Nf3	Bb4	39	Bf6+	Kh7
18	Re3	Rfd8	40	c6	bxc6
19	h4	Nge7	41	Qc5	Kh6
20	a3	Ba5	42	Rb2	Qb7
21	b4	Bc7	43	Rb4	Black
22	c5	Re8		resigns.	

Appendix H
Chess Program Strength, Search Depth, and Computer Speed

In 1996, following Deep Blue's loss to Kasparov in Philadelphia, Bob Hyatt and I carried out the experiment described in this appendix. Its objective was to estimate how much the playing strength of a chess program, such as Deep Blue, increases as a result of deeper search or, equivalently, as a result of playing on a faster computer [1]. At that time, Deep Blue was carrying out approximately 10-level to 12-level searches. It was expected that the Deep Blue that would participate in New York would be faster than the one in Philadelphia, possibly twice as fast, and thus able to search deeper. But how much stronger would it play? Our answer, based on the analysis that follows, is at least 100 rating points.

We fed several hundred positions into Crafty from games that appear in *Kasparov Versus Deep Blue: Computer Chess Comes of Age*. Positions were selected from the 55 games presented in Chapters 8 and 9. Positions on moves 7, 14, 21, ... with White to move were selected no matter how easy or difficult. Crafty searched each position to a depth of 14 levels. Some positions took hours of computing to complete the deep search. Hyatt recruited a number of people who had Crafty on their systems to help us.

Data was collected on how often Crafty selected a different move, that is, changed its mind, when going from one search depth to the next. Similar data had been obtained using Belle a decade earlier, but only to a depth of 11 levels. In 1998 Dark Thought provided data similar to Belle and Crafty [2–5]. Because of the increased computer speeds in recent years, the data collected in the 1996 and 1998 experiments went three levels deeper than the data collected in the earlier experiment with Belle.

Crafty was found to change its mind when going from one search depth to the next, with the percentages shown in the table on the following page. It can be seen that even at search depths greater than eight levels, the percentages fall off quite slowly with increasing search depth, all the way up to 14 levels. The rate of change decreases to zero as the search depth increases, but the decrease goes quite slowly. It strongly suggests that deeper searches — or, equivalently, faster computers — will continue to yield significant improvements in the level of play.

The table on the next page shows that in 15.3% of the positions, Crafty changed its mind when going from the 13th level to the final, 14th level. That is, on about one move in six, Crafty's 14-level search found a different move from its 13-level search. During the course of a 40-move game, Crafty's 14-level search would select six or seven moves that were different from its 13-level search. This 15.3% figure was not much less than the 17.3% figure, the frequency at which Crafty picked moves on a nine-level search different from the ones selected on an eight-level search.

Just because the computer picked a different move when searching deeper doesn't mean that the deeper choice was the better move. But statistically that seems to be the case: deeper search yields better moves. Further, the probability that the change in moves was better can be assumed to be independent of search depth.

The data allow us to estimate how much stronger a program would perform as search depth increases or, equivalently, as computer speeds increase. Let's see how. Suppose some chess program that searches to a depth of four levels has a rating of 1320 — this is approximately correct for Crafty. Suppose also that the same program, when searching to a depth of five levels, has a rating of, say, 1570 — also approximately correct for Crafty. Now suppose one observes that when making moves in a large number of random game positions, a program searching to a depth of five levels picks moves different from those picked by the same four-level program, say, 30% of the time. Further, suppose the same program, now searching to a depth of six levels, always selects exactly the same move as the program searching to a depth of five levels. From this information, it follows that the rating of the six-level program should be the same as the rating of five-level program. That is, the six-level program should also be rated at 1570. That's easy.

Now suppose, instead, that the six-level program picks moves different from those picked by the five-level program 30% of the time — the same percent that the five-level program picked moves different

Search depth d	Percent of time Crafty's d-level search picked a different move than its $(d-1)$-level search.
4	30.0
5	30.5
6	27.4
7	23.3
8	23.3
9	17.3
10	17.9
11	16.7
12	17.0
13	14.4
14	15.3

For 347 test positions, percent of time Crafty's d-level search picked a different move than its $(d-1)$-level search.

from the four-level program. In this case, it seems reasonable to conclude that the rating of the six-level program should exceed the rating of the five-level program by the same amount that the rating of the five-level program exceeded that of the four-level program. That is, the six-level program should have a rating 250 points higher than the five-level program, or the rating of the six-level program should be 1820.

The reasoning of the previous paragraph can be generalized. Consider three versions of some program. Suppose one searches to a depth of d levels, another to a depth of $d+1$ levels, and the third to a depth of $d+2$ levels. Suppose also that Q percent of the time the program searching $d+1$ levels picks moves different from the program searching d levels, and that R percent of the time the program searching $d+2$ levels picks moves different from the program searching $d+1$ levels. Then, given the ratings of the d-level program and the $(d+1)$-level program, it is reasonable to assign a rating to the $(d+2)$-level program using the following formula:

Rating of $(d+2)$-level program = Rating of $(d+1)$-level program

+ (Rating of $(d+1)$-level program – Rating of d-level program)(R/Q)

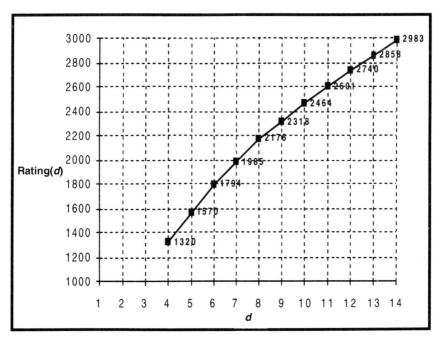

Rating of Crafty(d) for values of d studied in the 1997 experiment.

Using this formula, the percentages in the table on the previous page, the assumption of a rating of 1320 for Crafty when searching four levels, and the assumption of a rating of 1570 for Crafty when searching five levels, Crafty's ratings at search depths of from 6 to 14 levels were computed. The results are shown in the preceding graph. They show that an additional level of search always yields a rating improvement of more than 100 points over the search depths considered. For example, a 13-level search received a rating of 2858, an additional 118 rating points over a 12-level search, which received a rating of 2740. A 14-level search received a rating of 2983, an additional 125 rating points over a 13-level search.

Of course, one would expect the increase in strength when going from a 13-level search to a 14-level search to be less than the increase when going from a 12-level search to a 13-level search. The fact that the data show otherwise is probably due to an insufficiently extensive set of test positions. It may have also been due to the odd–even factor that crops up in many mathematical analyses of the search of chess trees. The graph does show an up–down behavior at search depths greater than eight.

Now, Deep Blue was carrying out 10-level to 12-level searches for which the graph indicates Crafty ratings in the range of 2464 to 2740. These ratings are likely approximately the same for Deep Blue; Deep Blue seemed to be playing approximately 2700-level chess in Philadelphia. An increase of one level of search by Crafty would yield ratings in the range of 2601 to 2858. A proportional increase — clearly more than 100 rating points — could be expected for Deep Blue. That is, because the SP to be used in New York would be twice as fast as the SP used in Philadelphia, Deep Blue could be expected to be at least 100 rating points stronger for the Rematch.

References

[1] Robert Hyatt and Monty Newborn, "Crafty goes deep," *ICCA Journal*, 20(2), pp. 79–86, June 1997.

[2] J. H. Condon and K. Thompson, "Belle chess hardware," in *Advances in Computer Chess 3*, M. R. B. Clarke, ed., Pergamon Press, Oxford, pp. 45–54, 1982.

[3] J. H. Condon and K. Thompson, "Belle," in *Chess Skill in Man and Machine*, 2nd ed., P. Frey, ed., Springer-Verlag, New York, pp. 201–210, 1983.

[4] M. Newborn, "A hypothesis concerning the strength of chess programs," *ICCA Journal*, 8(4), pp. 209–215, December 1985.

[5] Ernst A. Heinz, *Scalable Search in Computer Chess*, Vieweg Verlag, Wiesbaden, Germany, 2000.

Appendix I
Practice Games Played by
Deep Blue Junior in 1997

Deep Blue Junior played two practice matches leading up to the Rematch, one with Larry Christiansen, and the other with Michael Rhode. The games are presented here. A bug appeared in the first Christiansen game when Deep Blue Junior played 13 ... f5. In the second Christiansen game, Deep Blue Junior played 14 ... Qa5, a queen move to open space similar to 11 ... Qa5 in the first game of the Rematch! This second game saw Deep Blue Junior outmanoeuvre Christiansen in a subtle bishops and pawns endgame.

White: Deep Blue Junior
Black: Larry Christiansen
Position after Black played
12 ... Rc8; Deep Blue
Junior played 13 f5.

Location: IBM T. J. Watson Research Center, Yorktown Heights
Date: April 9, 1997
Game 1
White: Deep Blue Junior
Black: Larry Christiansen
French Defence

1	e4	e6
2	d4	d5
3	Nd2	Nf6
4	e5	Nfd7
5	c3	c5
6	Bd3	b6
7	Ne2	Ba6
8	Bxa6	Nxa6
9	0-0	b5
10	f4	g6
11	dxc5	Naxc5
12	Nb3	Rc8
13	f5	gxf5
14	Bf4	Ne4
15	Ng3	Nxg3
16	Bxg3	Bg7
17	Qd4	Qb6
18	Rae1	0-0
19	Qxb6	Nxb6
20	Nd4	a6
21	Bf4	Na4
22	Re2	h6
23	Rf3	Kh7
24	h3	Nc5
25	g4	fxg4
26	hxg4	Ne4
27	Rh2	Kg6
28	Nf5	exf5
29	gxf5+	Kh7
30	f6	Rg8
31	fxg7	Rxg7+
32	Kf1	Rc6
33	Rfh3	Rgg6
34	Ke2	Nc5
35	Ke3	a5
36	Rh5	Kg7
37	Rd2	b4
38	cxb4	axb4
39	Rxd5	Ne6
40	Rf5	b3
41	axb3	Rb6
42	b4	Rxb4
43	Rd7	Rb3+
44	Kf2	Rxb2+
45	Ke3	Rb3+
46	Kf2	Rb2+
	Drawn by	
	agreement.	

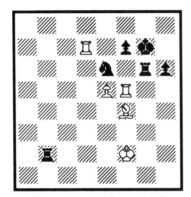

White: Deep Blue Junior
Black: Larry Christiansen
Position after 46 ... Rb2+
and drawn.

Location: IBM T. J. Watson
Research Center, Yorktown
Heights
Date: April 10, 1997
Game 2
White: Larry Christiansen
Black: Deep Blue Junior
Reti Opening

41	Be8	f6	48	d5	Bc4
42	Bf7+	Kc3	49	Bd4+	Kb3
43	Be8	Kb3	50	e4	a2
44	Bc5	a4	51	Ba1	Ba5
45	f3	exf3+	52	Bg8	Bc3
46	Kxf3	a3		White resigns.	
47	Bf7+	Kb2			

White: Larry Christiansen
Black: Deep Blue Junior
Position after 52 ... Bc3
and White resigns.

Location: IBM T. J. Watson
Research Center, Yorktown
Heights
Date: April 18, 1997
Game 1
White: Michael Rohde
Black: Deep Blue Junior
Reti Opening

1	Nf3	Nf6	21	Rd2	Reb8
2	c4	g6	22	h3	Rb1
3	g3	Bg7	23	Rxb1	Rxb1+
4	Bg2	O-O	24	Kh2	h5
5	O-O	c6	25	Rb2	Rxb2
6	d4	d5	26	Bxb2	Bb1
7	cxd5	cxd5	27	a3	e4
8	Ne5	Bf5	28	g4	h4
9	Nc3	Ne4	29	Bf1	Kf8
10	Qb3	Nc6	30	a4	Ke7
11	Be3	Nxc3	31	Kg1	Ke6
12	bxc3	e6	32	Ba3	a5
13	Nxc6	bxc6	33	c4	Bf6
14	Rac1	Qa5	34	Bc5	Bd8
15	Bf4	Rfe8	35	cxd5+	Kxd5
16	Bd6	Rad8	36	Ba6	Bc2
17	Qa3	Qxa3	37	Bc8	Bxa4
18	Bxa3	e5	38	Bd7	Bb5
19	e3	Rb8	39	Ba3	g5
20	Rfd1	Rb6	40	Kg2	Kc4

1	Nf3	d5	12	exd4	Nfxd4
2	c4	dxc4	13	Nxd4	exd4
3	Na3	c5	14	Re1	Kf7
4	Nxc4	Nc6	15	Bxc6	bxc6
5	g3	f6	16	Bxd4	Qd5
6	Bg2	e5	17	Ne3	Qb5
7	O-O	Be6	18	a4	Qa5
8	b3	Nh6	19	Qc2	c5
9	Bb2	Be7	20	Bc3	Qa6
10	e3	Nf5	21	Nf5	Rae8
11	d4	cxd4	22	Re3	Bd8

23	Rae1	Bd7
24	Rxe8	Rxe8
25	Rxe8	Bxe8
26	Qd1	Qe6
27	Nd6+	Ke7
28	Nxe8	Kxe8
29	Qh5+	Qf7
30	Qxc5	Qxb3
31	Qc6+	Kf7
32	a5	a6
33	Qd7+	Be7
34	Bd4	Qe6
35	Qa4	Qe1+
36	Kg2	Qe4+
37	Kg1	h5
38	h4	Kf8
39	Qd7	Qe1+
40	Kh2	Qxa5
41	Qc8+	Qd8
42	Qc4	Qd6
43	Be3	a5
44	Kg2	Qd7
45	Kh2	a4
46	Bc5	a3
47	Bxe7+	Qxe7
48	Qa6	g6
49	Qa5	Kf7
50	Kg1	f5
51	Kg2	Qd6
52	Kg1	Kf8

53	Kg2	Ke7
54	Kg1	Kf7
55	Kg2	Ke6
56	Kg1	Qe7
57	Kf1	Kf6
58	Kg1	Kg7
59	Kf1	Kh7
60	Kg1	Kh8
61	Kf1	Qd6
62	Kg2	Kg8
63	Kg1	Qe7
64	Kf1	Kg7
65	Kg1	Qd6
66	Kg2	Kf8
67	Kg1	Kg8
68	Kg2	Kg7
69	Kg1	Qf8
70	Qa7+	Kh6
71	Qa5	f4
72	gxf4	Qe7
73	Kf1	Qd6
74	Kg2	Kh7
75	Kg3	Qd3+
76	f3	Qd6
77	Qa4	Qe7
78	Qa5	Kg7
79	Qc3+	Kg8

Drawn by
agreement.

Location: IBM T. J. Watson
Research Center, Yorktown
Heights
Date: April 18, 1997
Game 2
White: Deep Blue Junior
Black: Michael Rohde
French Defence

1	e4	e6
2	d4	d5
3	Nd2	Be7
4	Ngf3	Nf6
5	e5	Nfd7
6	Bd3	c5
7	c3	Nc6
8	O-O	Qb6
9	dxc5	Nxc5
10	Bc2	Qc7
11	Re1	b6
12	Nb3	Bb7
13	Nfd4	a6
14	Nxc6	Bxc6
15	Qg4	O-O-O
16	Nd4	h5
17	Qf3	Be8

18	b4	Nd7
19	Qg3	g6
20	h4	Nb8
21	a4	Nc6
22	Bd3	Nxd4
23	cxd4	Bxb4
24	Bxa6+	Kb8
25	Re3	Ka7
26	Rb3	Ba5
27	Qd3	Bc6
28	Bg5	Rb8
29	Rb2	Qd7
30	Rc2	Rhc8
31	Bxc8	Rxc8
32	Bd2	Black
	resigns.	

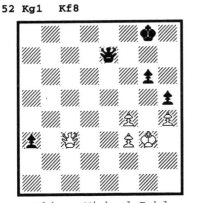

White: Michael Rohde
Black: Deep Blue Junior
Position after 79 ... Kg8
and drawn.

White: Deep Blue Junior
Black: Michael Rohde
Position after 32 Bd2 and
Black resigns.

Appendix J
Games from the Rematch

May 3–11, 1997
New York
Time Control: 40/2, 20/1,
          remaining moves/30 min

The time taken by each move is printed in square brackets following each move. The times were obtained by viewing videotapes of the games and rounded off the observed time to the nearest five seconds because of the difficulties in determining a more accurate figure. No move was recorded as taking less than five seconds even though there were moves made in the matter of a second or so.

Game 1
White: Kasparov
Black: Deep Blue
Reti Opening

1 Nf3 [5s]		d5 [10s]
2 g3 [10s]		Bg4 [5s]
3 b3 [3m25s]		Nd7 [3m15s]
4 Bb2 [1m]		e6 [2m20s]
5 Bg2 [2m5s]		Ngf6 [45s]
6 O-O [2m25s]		c6 [2m]
7 d3 [7m30s]		Bd6 [5s]
8 Nbd2 [5s]		O-O [10s]
9 h3 [5s]		Bh5 [5s]
10 e3 [55s]		h6 [3m]
11 Qe1 [2m45s]		Qa5 [3m10s]
12 a3 [45s]		Bc7 [2m45s]
13 Nh4 [5m10s]		g5 [3m]

W: GK B: DB after 13 ... g5;
    Kasparov played 14 Nhf3.

14 Nhf3 [20s]	e5 [3m20s]
15 e4 [5m25s]	Rfe8 [1m50s]
16 Nh2 [7m30s]	Qb6 [2m]
17 Qc1 [15m30s]	a5 [4m]
18 Re1 [30s]	Bd6 [2m50s]
19 Ndf1 [2m10s]	dxe4 [2m25s]
20 dxe4 [5m25s]	Bc5 [5s]
21 Ne3 [10s]	Rad8 [3m15s]
22 Nhf1 [3m10s]	g4 [5s]
23 hxg4 [35s]	Nxg4 [2m40s]

W: GK B: DB after 23...Nxg4;
    Kasparov played 24 f3.

24 f3 [13m35s]   Nxe3 [3m10s]
25 Nxe3 [10s]   Be7 [2m40s]
26 Kh1 [7m55s]   Bg5 [2m40s]
27 Re2 [15s]   a4 [1m35s]
28 b4 [2m30s]   f5 [5s]

W: GK   B: DB after 28 ... f5;
Kasparov played 29 exf5.

29 exf5 [50s]   e4 [1m45s]
30 f4 [10s]   Bxe2 [3m20s]
31 fxg5 [10s]   Ne5 [2m10s]
32 g6 [1m45s]   Bf3 [55s]
33 Bc3 [4m25s]   ...

W: GK   B: DB   after 33 Bc3;
Deep Blue played 33 ... Qb5.

33 ...   Qb5 [3m25s]
34 Qf1 [1m50s]   Qxf1 [3m]

35 Rxf1 [10s]   h5 [2m40s]
36 Kg1 [45s]   ...

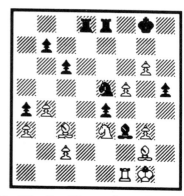

W: GK   B: DB   after 36 Kg1;
Deep Blue played 36 ... Kf8
Could Deep Blue draw
with 36 ...Ng4?

36 ...   Kf8 [2m45s]
37 Bh3 [2m30s]   b5 [3m40s]
38 Kf2 [1m55s]   Kg7 [1m55s]
39 g4 [50s]   Kh6 [3m15s]
40 Rg1 [7m55s]   hxg4 [3m10s]
41 Bxg4 [1m15s]   Bxg4 [2m5s]
42 Nxg4+ [3m35s] Nxg4+ [5s]
43 Rxg4 [5s]   Rd5 [7m50s]
44 f6 [1m]   Rd1 [2m30s]
45 g7 [4m55s]   Black resigns
[35s].

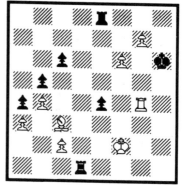

W: GK   B: DB   after 45 g7;
Kasparov resigns.

Game 2
White: Deep Blue
Black: Kasparov
Ruy Lopez

1 e4 [5s]	e5 [20s]
2 Nf3 [10s]	Nc6 [5s]
3 Bb5 [10s]	a6 [10s]
4 Ba4 [10s]	Nf6 [10s]
5 O-O [10s]	Be7 [20s]
6 Re1 [5s]	b5 [10s]
7 Bb3 [15s]	d6 [5s]
8 c3 [15s]	O-O [15s]
9 h3 [5s]	...

W: DB B: GK   after 9 h3;
Kasparov took about seven
minutes before
playing 9 ... h6

9 ...	h6 [7m]
10 d4 [15s]	Re8 [5s]
11 Nbd2 [10s]	Bf8 [10s]
12 Nf1 [10s]	Bd7 [15s]
13 Ng3 [10s]	Na5 [10s]
14 Bc2 [10s]	c5 [5s]
15 b3 [20s]	Nc6 [1m5s]
16 d5 [5s]	Ne7 [20s]
17 Be3 [10s]	Ng6 [10s]
18 Qd2 [4m10s,11]	Nh7 [1m30s]
19 a4 [2m30s,10]	Nh4 [2m55s]
20 Nxh4 [4m10s,11]	Qxh4 [20s]

21 Qe2 [4m15s,10]	Qd8 [20s]
22 b4 [3m45s,10]	Qc7 [9m20s]
23 Rec1 [3m50s,10]	c4 [6m55s]
24 Ra3 [10s,11]	Rec8 [2m20s]
25 Rca1 [1m30s,11]	Qd8 [10s]

W: DB B: GK after 25 ...Qd8;
Deep Blue played 26 f4

26 f4 [3m45s,11]	Nf6 [4m15s]
27 fxe5 [4m25s,10]	dxe5 [15s]
28 Qf1 [3m40s,10	Ne8 [16m40s]
29 Qf2 [4m,11]	Nd6 [2m]
30 Bb6 [1m55s,11]	Qe8 [3m45s]
31 R3a2 [30s,11]	Be7 [5m10s]
32 Bc5 [10s,10]	Bf8 [18m]

W: DB B: GK after 32...Bf8;
Deep Blue played 33 Nf5

33 Nf5 [5m20s,11] Bxf5 [9m10s]
34 exf5 [4m45s,11] f6 [25s]
35 Bxd6 [14m,11] Bxd6 [10s]

W: DB B: GK after 35 ...Bxd6;
Deep Blue played 36 axb5,
finding this move better
than 36 Qb6.

36 axb5 [6m40s,11] axb5 [40s]

W: DB B: GK after 36 ...axb5;
Deep Blue played 37 Be4,
passing over 37 Qb6.

37 Be4 [2m25s,12] Rxa2 [9m15s]
38 Qxa2 [3m35s,12] Qd7 [1m5s]
39 Qa7 [3m30s,11] Rc7 [7m55s]
40 Qb6 [10s,12] Rb7 [45s]

41 Ra8+ [2m25s,12] ...

W: DB B: GK after 41 Ra8+;
Kasparov played 41 ... Kf7.

41 ... Kf7 [10s]
42 Qa6 [4m20s,11] Qc7 [10s]
43 Qc6 [3m15s,11] Qb6+ [2m40s]
44 Kf1 [3m25s,11] Rb8 [5s]
45 Ra6 [3m20s,12] Black
resigns [4m30s].

W: DB B: GK after 45 Ra6;
Deep Blue resigns.

Game 3
White: Kasparov
Black: Deep Blue
English Opening

1	d3	[5s]	e5	[10s]
2	Nf3	[20s]	Nc6	[5s]
3	c4	[5s]	Nf6	[10s]
4	a3	[20s]	d6	[3m50s]
5	Nc3	[3m30s]	Be7	[2m55s]
6	g3	[40s]	O-O	[2m5s]
7	Bg2	[5s]	Be6	[2m45s]
8	O-O	[2m50s]	Qd7	[10s]

W: GK B: DB after 8 ... Qd7;
Kasparov played 9 Ng5 after
    thinking for 28 minutes!

9	Ng5	[27m45s]	Bf5	[3m45s]
10	e4	[1m10s]	Bg4	[3m]
11	f3	[10s]	Bh5	[2m55s]
12	Nh3	[55s]	Nd4	[4m]
13	Nf2	[45s]	h6	[2m10s]
14	Be3	[1m45s]	c5	[2m55s]
15	b4	[3m45s]	b6	[3m5s]
16	Rb1	[7m40s]	Kh8	[2m55s]
17	Rb2	[14m10s]	a6	[4m30s]
18	bxc5	[12m5s]	bxc5	[2m50s]
19	Bh3	[20s]	Qc7	[3m15s]
20	Bg4	[2m30s]	Bg6	[10s]
21	f4	[50s]	exf4	[2m40s]
22	gxf4	[60s]	Qa5	[3m30s]
23	Bd2	[25s]		

W: GK B: DB after 23 Bd2;
Deep Blue played 23... Qxa3.

23	...		Qxa3	[2m40s]
24	Ra2	[25s]	Qb3	[1m55s]
25	f5	[25s]	Qxd1	[2m5s]
26	Bxd1	[25s]	...	

W: GK B: DB after 26 Bxd1;
Deep Blue played 26 ... Bh7.

26	...		Bh7	[2m5s]
27	Nh3	[6m]	Rfb8	[2m50s]
28	Nf4	[1m55s]	Bd8	[30s]
29	Nfd5	[2m30s]	Nc6	[30s]
30	Bf4	[2m40s]	...	

W: GK B: DB after 30 Bf4;
Deep Blue played 30 ... Ne5
and a draw followed after
another 18 moves.

30 ...	Ne5 [10s]
31 Ba4 [1m30s]	Nxd5 [1m30s]
32 Nxd5 [20s]	a5 [3m10s]
33 Bb5 [1m45s]	Ra7 [1m30s]
34 Kg2 [2m55s]	g5 [3m10s]
35 Bxe5+ [1m5s]	dxe5 [3m5s]

W: GK B: DB after 35...dxe5;
Kasparov played 36 f6.

36 f6 [5s]	Bg6 [3m]
37 h4 [15s]	gxh4 [2m50s]
38 Kh3 [25s]	Kg8 [3m15s]
39 Kxh4 [1m45s]	Kh7 [1m40s]
40 Kg4 [5m45s]	...

W: GK B: DB after 40 Kg4;
Deep Blue responded
40 ... Bc7.

40 ...	Bc7 [3m30s]
41 Nxc7 [3m30s]	Rxc7 [5s]
42 Rxa5 [1m10s]	Rd8 [3m]
43 Rf3 [45s]	Kh8 [2m25s]
44 Kh4 [3m55s]	Kg8 [3m20s]
45 Ra3 [1m10s]	Kh8 [3m20s]
46 Ra6 [1m25s]	Kh7 [3m20s]
47 Ra3 [19m25s]	Kh8 [5m35s]
48 Ra6 [9m20s]	Drawn by
agreement [10s].	

W: GK B: DB after 48 Ra6;
drawn by agreement.

Game 4
White: Deep Blue
Black: Kasparov
Pribyl Defense

1 e4 [10s]	c6 [1m25s]
2 d4 [10s]	d6 [10s]
3 Nf3 [2m50s]	Nf6 [25s]
4 Nc3 [2m25s]	Bg4 [20s]
5 h3 [20s]	Bh5 [20s]
6 Bd3 [25s]	e6 [35s]
7 Qe2 [35s]	d5 [2m]
8 Bg5 [45s]	Be7 [4m20s]
9 e5 [3m10s]	Nfd7 [1m20s]
10 Bxe7 [1m45s]	Qxe7 [1m10s]
11 g4 [1m50s]	Bg6 [20s]
12 Bxg6 [2m45s]	hxg6 [3m40s]
13 h4 [3m15s]	Na6 [1m40s]
14 O-O-O [1m20s]	O-O-O [50s]
15 Rdg1 [2m15s]	Nc7 [32m]
16 Kb1 [5s]	...

W: DB B: GK after 16 Kb1;
Kasparov played 16 ... f6.

16 ...	f6 [8m]
17 exf6 [3m30s]	Qxf6 [40s]
18 Rg3 [6m55s]	Rde8 [35s]
19 Re1 [3m10s]	Rhf8 [5m5s]
20 Nd1 [3m10s]	

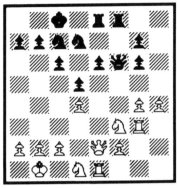

W: DB B: GK after 20 Nd1;
Kasparov played 20 ... e5.

20 ...	e5 [8m]
21 dxe5 [3m10s]	Qf4 [5s]
22 a3 [5m]	Ne6 [2m35s]
23 Nc3 [2m50s]	Ndc5 [2m40s]
24 b4 [9m10s]	Nd7 [15s]
25 Qd3 [2m30s]	Qf7 [6m5s]
26 b5 [10s]	Ndc5 [50s]
27 Qe3 [1m40s]	Qf4 [4m5s]
28 bxc6 [1m55s]	bxc6 [5s]
29 Rd1 [3m5s]	Kc7 [2m15s]
30 Ka1 [15m30s]	...

W: DB Black: GK after 30 Ka1;
Kasparov played 30 ... Qxe3.

30 ...	Qxe3 [5m15s]
31 fxe3 [1m45s]	Rf7 [5s]

32 Rh3 [2m55s]	Ref8 [3m50s]
33 Nd4 [10s]	Rf2 [40s]
34 Rb1 [2m]	Rg2 [2m15s]
35 Nce2 [1m40s]	Rxg4 [10s]

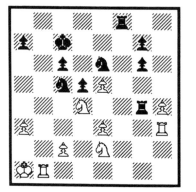

W: DB B: GK after 35... Rxg4;
Deep Blue played 36 Nxe6.

36 Nxe6 [1m55s]	Nxe6 [5s]
37 Nd4 [1m40s]	Nxd4 [1m25s]
38 exd4 [2m]	Rxd4 [5s]
39 Rg1 [2m]	Rc4 [15s]
40 Rxg6 [2m25s]	Rxc2 [50s]
41 Rxg7+ [1m55s]	Kb6 [15s]
42 Rb3+ [2m25s]	Kc5 [3m5s]
43 Rxa7 [20s]	Rf1+ [7m15s]
44 Rb1 [1m20s]	Rff2 [40s]

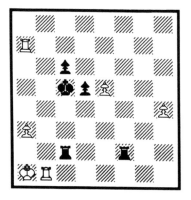

W: DB B: GK after 44... Rff2;
Deep Blue played 45 Rb4.

45 Rb4 [3m5s]	Rc1+ [14m40s]
46 Rb1 [15s]	Rcc2 [10s]
47 Rb4 [3m20s]	Rc1+ [7m15s]
48 Rb1 [10s]	Rxb1+ [55s]
49 Kxb1 [2m50s]	Re2 [5s]
50 Re7 [3m20s]	Rh2 [35s]
51 Rh7 [5m5s]	Kc4 [2m20s]
52 Rc7 [1m45s]	

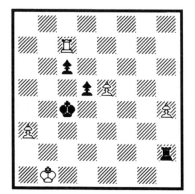

W: DB   B: GK   after 52 Rc7;
Kasparov played 52... c5.

52 ...	c5 [40s]
53 e6 [45s]	Rxh4 [10s]
54 e7 [3m10s]	Re4 [15s]
55 a4 [3m35s]	Kb3 [2m40s]
56 Kc1 [40s]	Drawn by
agreement [7m30s].	

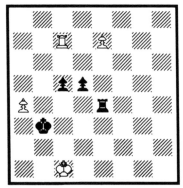

W: DB   B: GK   after 56 Kc1;
drawn by agreement.

Game 5
White: Kasparov
Black: Deep Blue
Reti Opening

1 Nf3 [10s]		d5 [10s]
2 g3 [10s]		Bg4 [10s]
3 Bg2 [10s]		Nd7 [10s]
4 h3 [10s]		...

W: GK B: DB   after 4 h3;
Deep Blue played 4 ... Bxf3.

4 ...		Bxf3 [4m]
5 Bxf3 [3m]		c6 [10s]
6 d3 [30s]		e6 [2m20s]
7 e4 [4m45s]		Ne5 [3m45s]
8 Bg2 [30s]		dxe4 [3m5s]
9 Bxe4 [1m50s]		Nf6 [1m10s]
10 Bg2 [20s]		Bb4+ [2m35s]
11 Nd2 [20s]		...

W: GK B: DB   after 11 Nd2;
Deep Blue played 11 ... h5.

11 ...		h5 [2m40s]
12 Qe2 [3m20s]		Qc7 [15s]
13 c3 [7m]		Be7 [10s]
14 d4 [20s]		Ng6 [3m10s]
15 h4 [2m]		e5 [1m]
16 Nf3 [7m30s]		exd4 [10s]

W: GK B: DB after 16...exd4;
Kasparov played 17 Nxd4.

17 Nxd4 [8m5s]		O-O-O [10s]
18 Bg5 [14m45s]		Ng4 [3m40s]
19 O-O-O [8m]		Rhe8 [6m]
20 Qc2 [45s]		Kb8 [3m35s]
21 Kb1 [5m]		Bxg5 [3m]
22 hxg5 [15s]		N6e5 [2m45s]
23 Rhe1[5m30s]		c5 [3m]
24 Nf3 [16m45s]		Rxd1+ [10s]
25 Rxd1 [45s]		...

W: GK B: DB   after 25 Rxd1;
Deep Blue played 25 ... Nc4.

25	...	Nc4 [2m10s]
26	Qa4 [4m40s]	Rd8 [3m15s]
27	Re1 [2m35s]	Nb6 [35s]
28	Qc2 [15s]	Qd6 [3m]
29	c4 [55s]	Qg6 [3m25s]
30	Qxg6 [1m15s]	fxg6 [2m]

W: GK B: DB after 30...fxg6;
Kasparov played 31 b3.

31	b3 [2m5s]	Nxf2[3m5s]
32	Re6 [25s]	Kc7 [3m30s]
33	Rxg6 [2m5s]	Rd7 [3m35s]
34	Nh4 [3m30s]	Nc8 [3m25s]
35	Bd5 [15s]	Nd6 [3m20s]
36	Re6 [15s]	Nb5 [4m10s]
37	cxb5 [15s]	Rxd5 [2m50s]
38	Rg6 [40s]	Rd7 [3m35s]
39	Nf5 [20s]	Ne4 [1m55s]
40	Nxg7 [1m30s]	...

W: GK B: DB after 40 Nxg7;
Deep Blue played 40 ... Rd1+.

40	...	Rd1+ [3m30s]
41	Kc2 [20s]	Rd2+ [2m40s]
42	Kc1 [6m30s]	Rxa2 [3m15s]
43	Nxh5 [45s]	Nd2 [2m20s]
44	Nf4 [4m30s]	Nxb3+ [6m30s]
45	Kb1 [1m]	Rd2 [1m55s]
46	Re6 [50s]	c4 [2m10s]
47	Re3 [1m45s]	...

W: GK B: DB after 47 Re3;
Deep Blue played 47 ... Kb6.

47	...	Kb6 [3m15s]
48	g6 [15s]	Kxb5 [2m45s]
49	g7 [10s]	Kb4 [2m50s]
Drawn by agreement [3m45s].		

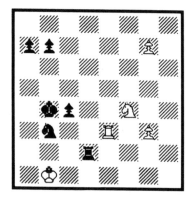

W: GK B: DB after Kb4;
drawn by agreement.

Game 6
White: Deep Blue
Black: Kasparov
Caro-Kann Defense

Note that the moves to this game as well as several positions from the game also appear in Chapter 13.

1 e4 [5s]	c6 [15s]
2 d4 [10s]	d5 [10s]
3 Nc3 [5s]	dxe4 [1m25s]
4 Nxe4 [10s]	Nd7 [10s]
5 Ng5 [15s]	Ngf6 [4m50s]
6 Bd3 [15s]	e6 [50s]
7 N1f3 [5s]	h6 [45s]
8 Nxe6 [10s]	Qe7 [15s]
9 O-O [10s]	fxe6 [5s]
10 Bg6+ [20s]	Kd8 [10s]
11 Bf4 [2m45s]	b5 [5m25s]
12 a4 [3m20s]	Bb7 [25s]
13 Re1 [2m50s]	Nd5 [14m10s]
14 Bg3 [10s]	Kc8 [10s]
15 axb5 [8m20s]	cxb5 [10s]
16 Qd3 [1m55s]	Bc6 [2m50s]
17 Bf5 [3m10s]	exf5 [3m10s]
18 Rxe7 [1m]	Bxe7 [5s]
19 c4 [3m5s]	Black resigns [5s].

Appendix K
Analysis of the Final Position
of Game 2

The analysis presented here of the final position from Game 2 is a composite of the analyses presented in references [1–5] combined with some help from Fritz4.

The conclusion of the analyses is that if Kasparov had played 45 ... Qe3, then 46 Qxd6 is only good enough to draw if 46 ... Re8! is played by Black. White's other alternative, 46 Qd7+, allows Black's king to escape: 46 ... Kg8 47 Qxd6 Rf8 48 Qe6+ Kh7, and then White will face the same perpetual check threats as it did after 46 Qxd6 Re8.

There was some speculation that Kasparov overlooked the strength of the crucial rook move 46 ... Re8 because he had convinced himself that Deep Blue, after having played so strongly in developing its crushing position, certainly wouldn't give him the opportunity to draw with such a simple and obvious ploy as 45 ... Qe3. Moreover, if 45 ... Qe3 didn't lead to a draw, then Kasparov must have believed that it was destined to lose. The rather quiet 47 h4 was recommended as White's best way to try to avoid a draw after 46 ... Re8, but this is countered by 47 ... h5, leaving White's king no way to escape perpetual checks. The alternative, 47 ... Qxe4, was also good enough to draw. Robert Byrne revised his earlier analysis and published the following drawing line after the match: 45 ... Qe3 46 Qxd6 Re8 47 h4 Qxe4 48 Ra7+ Kg8 49 Qd7 Qf4+ 50 Kg1 Qe3+ 51 Kh2 Qf4+ 52 Kh3 Re7 53 Qc8+ Kh7 54 Rxe7 h5 55 Rxg7 Kxg7 56 Qd7 Kh6 [6].

Deep Blue would have had to see lines of play to a depth of 20 to 25 levels to realize it was facing a draw when it played 45 Ra6. Specifically, it would have had to see that after 45 Ra6 Qe3 46 Qxd6 Re8 White has no move that does better than draw; that, in fact, as the analysis shows, the six moves 47 h4, 47 Qc5, 47 Qc6, 47 Qd7+, 47 Bf3 and 47 Qc7+ all lead at best to a drawn game. However, for Deep Blue to see that 47 Bf3, for example, was drawn would require the program to decide after exploring the first 16 moves 45 Ra6 Qe3 46 Qxd6 Re8 47 Bf3 Qc1+ 48 Kf2 Qd2+ 49 Be2 Qf4+ 50 Ke1 Qc1+ 51 Bd1 Qxc3+ 52 Kf1 Qc1, giving White a bishop for a pawn that it needed to look deeper at the quiet nonchecking, noncapturing move 52 ... Qc1. And if it did look deeper, it would have had to search even deeper along this line after exploring three more moves, 53 Ra7+ Kg8 54 Qd7, the last of which is

Final position in Game 2 Deep Blue had played 45 Ra6 and Kasparov reisgned.

White: Deep Blue Black: Garry Kasparov

Black to Move

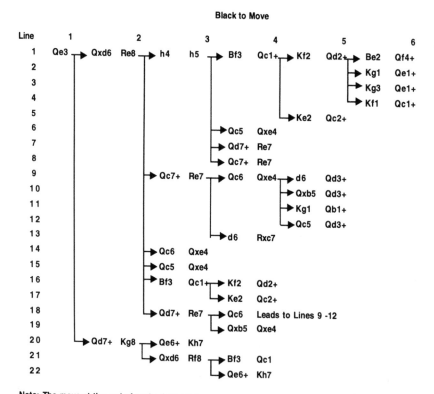

Note: The move at the end of each of the 22 lines was
scored a draw by Fritz4 after no more than 10 minutes.

again a nonchecking, noncapturing move that leaves White up a bishop for a pawn after 19 moves. In positions of this complexity, with 28 legal moves on the board for White and 31 for Black, Deep Blue was probably carrying out a 12-level brute force search followed by selective search at deeper levels. These quiet moves would have had to be picked up and searched in the selective search region of the tree that Deep Blue searched in order for the computer to see a draw. There is a good chance that they weren't.

References

[1] David Goodman and Raymond Keene, *Man Versus Machine, Kasparov Versus Deep Blue*, H3 Publications, Cambridge, MA, 1997.

[2] Daniel King. *Kasparov v Deeper Blue*, Batsford, London, 1997.

[3] Michael Khodarkovsky and Leonid Shamkovich, *A New Era: How Garry Kasparov Changed the World of Chess*, Ballentine Books, New York, 1997.

[4] Yasser Seirawan, "The Kasparov – Deep Blue games, *International Computer Chess Association Journal*," 20(2), pp. 102–125, June 1997.

[5] Malcolm Pein with Garry Kasparov, "The king plays Deeper Blue," *Chess*, 62(3), pp. 4–25, June 1997.

[6] Robert Byrne, "Why did Kasparov lose? Perhaps he tried too hard," *The New York Times*, p. B2, May 13, 1997.

Appendix L
Difficult Positions for Deep Blue from the Rematch

Twelve positions that Deep Blue found troublesome are presented in this appendix. Each took the computer more than five minutes to choose a move. In general, they can be characterized as positions in which the evaluation by Deep Blue dropped with increasing search depth. Game 4 had the most troublesome positions with four and Game 2 was next with three.

GAME 2

W: Deep Blue B: Kasparov
after 32 ... Bf8;
DB played 33 Nf5
(5m 20s)

GAME 1

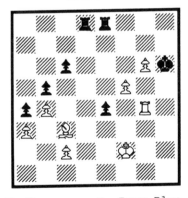

W: Kasparov B: Deep Blue
after 43 Rxg4
DB played 43 ... Rd5
(7m 50s)

W: Deep Blue B: Kasparov
after 34 ... f6;
DB played 35 Bxd6
(14m)

GAME 2
(cont.)

W: Deep Blue B: Kasparov
after 35 ... Bxd6;
DB played 36 axb5
(6m 40s)

GAME 4

W: Deep Blue B: Kasparov
after 17 ... Qxf6;
DB played 18 Rg3
(6m 55s)

GAME 3

W: Kasparov B: Deep Blue
after 47 Ra3;
DB played 47 ... Kh8
(5m 35s)

W: Deep Blue B: Kasparov
after 23 ... Ndc5;
DB played 24 b4
(9m 10s)

GAME 4
(cont.)

W: Deep Blue B: Kasparov
after 29 ... Kc7;
DB played 30 Ka1
(15m 30s)

GAME 5

W: Kasparov B: Deep Blue
after 19 O-O-O;
DB played 19 ... Rhe8
(6m)

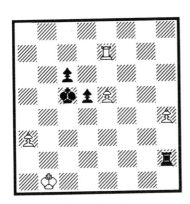

W: Deep Blue B: Kasparov
after 50 ... Rh2;
DB played 51 Rh7
(5m 5s)

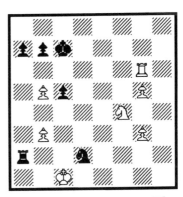

W: Kasparov B: Deep Blue
after 44 Nf4;
DB played 44 ... Nxb3
(7m)

GAME 6

W: Deep Blue   B: Kasparov
        after 14 ... Kc8;
        DB played 15 axb5
            (8m 20s)

Appendix M
Deep Blue's Printout
of Game 6 of the Rematch

Murray Campbell provided me with Deep Blue's printout of Game 6 of the rematch; it appears below. Deep Blue selected its first eleven moves from either its opening book or its extended opening book. The printout of this phase of the game has been condensed and cleaned up to show only moves by both sides and Deep Blue's guesses of its opponent's replies. The search of large trees was responsible for selecting the remaining eight moves. The material in bold lettering explains and elaborates on Deep Blue's somewhat cryptic printout.

```
1. e4  39/119:46     Guessing c5
```

[Deep Blue expected a Sicilian. 39 moves remain to be made to the first time control, and 119 minutes 46 seconds remain.]

```
1 ... Pc7c6  2. d4 38/119:41 (Guessing d5)  2 ... d5
3. Nc3 37/119:24  (Guessing dxe4)  3 ... dxe4
4. Nxe4 36/117:33 (Guessing Nd7)   4 ... Nd7
5. Ng5 35/117:12  (Guessing Ngf6)  5 ... Ngf6
6. Bd3 34/112:70  (Guessing e6)    6 ... e6
7. N1f3 33/111:60 (Guessing Bd6)   7 ... h6
8. Nxe6 32/111:10 (Guessing fxe6)  8 ... Qe7
9. o-o  31/110:56 (Guessing fxe6)  9 ... fxe6
10. Bg6+ 30/110:39  (Guessing Kd8)
```

[Deep Blue predicted 7 of the first 10 moves by Kasparov. It guessed Kasparov's previous move, 9 ... fxe6, and then, as the following printout shows, began a 5-level search for its own 11th move. When Deep Blue fails to guess correctly, it begins with a 3-level search. This time it is guessing Kasparov will play 10 ... Kd8.]

```
5 (4) [Re1] (-30) -30v  T=0   rf1e1 Kd8c7 bc1f4 Kc7b6 pc2c4
Pa7a6 ra1b1 Kb6a7 pb2b4
5 (5) [Re1] (-23) [Bf4] (30) 30^  T=0   bc1f4 Nf6d5 bf4g3
```

5 (5) [Bf4] (37) 37 T=0   bc1f4 Nf6d5 bf4g3

[The 5-level search concluded bc1f4 Nf6d5 bf4g3 was the best continuation. Deep Blue saw a score of +37 for itself; T=0 indicates the move consumed 0 seconds so far.]

6 (5) [Bf4] (46) 46 T=1   bc1f4 Nf6d5 bf4g3 Pb7b6

[The master computer carried out the search to this point by itself. The many processors of Deep Blue next divided up the deeper searches. A "#" was printed after each first-level move in the tree was searched.]

7 (5) #[Bf4] (41) ################################ 41
T=6   bc1f4 Pb7b6 rf1e1 Bc8b7 qd1e2 Kd8c8

[The 7-level search took 6 seconds and found the 6-move continuation bc1f4 Pb7b6 rf1e1 Bc8b7 qd1e2 Kd8c8 led to a score of +41.]

8 (6)<ch> 'kd8'

[cont] #[Bf4] (11) 11v T=37

[Kasparov made the guessed move after thinking for 37 seconds, and Deep Blue continued with its 8-level search. The score dropped to +11, so the 8-level search was repeated with a different window, leading the second time to a score of +32 after 50 seconds. The 9-level search was started, but even before search of the first move was completed, Deep Blue terminated search, selecting 11 Bf4 and assigning to it a score of +32.]

bc1f4 Nf6e8 qd1d3 Ne8d6 pc2c4 Nd6c4p qd3c4N Qe7f6 bg6b1
8 (6) #[Bf4] (32) ################################ 32
T=50   bc1f4 Nf6e8 qd1d3 Ne8d6 rf1e1 Kd8c7 pc2c4 Pb7b6
ra1c1 Pc6c5 pb2b4 Bc8b7 bg6f5 Pc5b4p
9 (6) [TIMEOUT] 32 T=190   bc1f4 Nf6e8 bf4g3 Ne8d6 rf1e1
Pa7a5 re1e3 Kd8c7 qd1e1 Qe7d8 pc2c4 Pc6c5 re3e6P Ra8a6

```
-------------------------------
-->  11.  Bf4 <-- 29/107:55     Guessing Nd5
-------------------------------
```

3 (4) 30^ T=0   bf4g3 Qe7b4 qd1c1 Qb4c4 rf1e1 Kd8e7
3 (5) 61^ T=0   bf4g3 Qe7b4 qd1c1 Qb4c4 rf1e1 Kd8e7
3 (5) 69   T=1   bf4g3 Qe7b4 qd1c1 Qb4c4 rf1e1 Kd8e7
4 (5) 49   T=1   bf4g3 Qe7b4 qd1c1 Qb4c4 rf1e1 Kd8e7
5 (5) [Bg3] (67) 67 T=2 bf4g3 Qe7b4 qd1c1 Qb4c4 rf1e1 Kd8e7

```
6 (5) [Bg3] (73) 73  T=3    bf4g3 Qe7b4 qd1c1 Qb4c4 pc2c3
7 (5) #[Bg3] (73) ####################################
#### 73  T=3    bf4g3 Qe7b4 qd1c1 Qb4c4 pc2c3
8 (6) #[Bg3] (54) ####################################
## 54  T=19    bf4g3 Pb7b5 pa2a4 Pb5b4 qd1d3 Ph6h5 pc2c4
Pb4c3p/E
9 (6) #[Bg3](84)^  T=124    bf4g3 Pb7b5 pa2a4 Pb5b4 bg3h4 Nd7f6
nf3e5 Kd8c7 ne5f7 Qe7f7n bg6f7Q Nd5e3 bh4f6N
9 (6) #[Bg3] (78) ####################################
#### 78  T=331    bf4g3 Pb7b5 pa2a4 Pa7a6 pa4b5P Pc6b5p
rf1e1 Bc8b7 qd1d2 Kd8c8 qd2h6P Pg7h6q
10 (6)<ch> 'b5'
```

**[Deep Blue's guess of 11 ... Nd5 was wrong. It aborted the search based on
guessing this move and started the search of its 12th move from scratch. The
printout shows that Deep Blue had calculated for 331 seconds and had
calculated a 10-move sequence in reply to the guessed move. It alotted 191
seconds to finding a reply to Kasparov's 11 ... Nd5.]**

```
going to search for 191 seconds

[AB Pb7b5]

--------------------------------
--> Pb7b5 <--
--------------------------------


78  T=334    bf4g3 Pb7b5 pa2a4 Pa7a6 pa4b5P Pc6b5p rf1e1
Bc8b7 qd1d2 Kd8c8 bg6f5 Pe6f5b re1e7Q Bf8e7r

going to search for 191 seconds
3 (4) 60^  T=0    pa2a4 Nd7c5
3 (5) 13  T=1    pa2a4 Nf6d5 bf4g3 Pa7a6 pa4b5P Pc6b5p rf1e1
Bc8b7 qd1d2 Kd8c8 bg6f5 Pe6f5b re1e7Q Bf8e7r
4 (5) 60^  T=1    pa2a4 Nf6d5 bf4g3 Pa7a6 pa4b5P Pc6b5p
rf1e1 Bc8b7 qd1d2 Kd8c8 bg6f5 Pe6f5b re1e7Q Bf8e7r
4 (5) 13  T=1    pa2a4 Nf6d5 bf4g3 Pa7a6 pa4b5P Pc6b5p rf1e1
Bc8b7 qd1d2 Kd8c8 bg6f5 Pe6f5b re1e7Q Bf8e7r
5 (5) [a4] (60) 60^  T=1    pa2a4 Nf6d5 bf4g3 Pa7a6 pa4b5P
Pc6b5p rf1e1 Bc8b7 qd1d2 Kd8c8 bg6f5 Pe6f5b re1e7Q Bf8e7r
5 (5) [a4] (20) 20  T=1    pa2a4 Bc8a6 bg6d3
6 (5) [a4] (60) 60^  T=1    pa2a4 Bc8a6 bg6d3
6 (5) [a4] (44) 44  T=1    pa2a4 Pb5a4p ra1a4P Nf6d5
7 (5) #[a4] (14) 14v  T=2    pa2a4 Pb5a4p rf1e1 Nf6d5 bf4g3
Bc8a6 ra1a4P Ba6b5
7 (6) # [a4] (15) ####################################
##### 15  T=4    pa2a4 Pb5a4p rf1e1 Bc8a6 nf3e5 Nd7e5n bf4e5N
```

```
8 (6) #[a4] (22) ####################################
### 22  T=13   pa2a4 Pb5a4p rf1e1 Bc8a6 ra1a4P Ba6b5 ra4a5
Nf6d5 bf4g3 Kd8c8 bg3h4
9 (6) #[a4] (14) ####################################
## 14  T=159   pa2a4 Bc8b7 pa4b5P Pc6b5p qd1e2 Pa7a6 bf4g3
Qe7b4 pc2c3
10 (6) #[a4] (18) [TIMEOUT]  18  T=191
```

[Time is up.]

```
pa2a4 Bc8b7 pa4b5P Pc6b5p qd1e2 Pa7a6 rf1e1 Nf6d5 bf4g3
Ra8c8 pc2c3 Nd5f6 nf3e5
```

```
-------------------------------------------------
--> 12.   a4 <-- 28/104:39  Guessing Bb7
-------------------------------------------------
```

```
7 (4) #[axb5] (18) ####################################
###### 18  T=1   pa4b5P Pc6b5p qd1e2 Pa7a6 rf1e1 Nf6d5
bf4g3 Ra8c8 pc2c3 Nd5f6 nf3e5
8 (6) #[axb5] (20) ####################################
##### 20  T=5   pa4b5P Pc6b5p qd1e2 Pa7a6 rf1e1 Nf6d5 bf4g3
Ra8c8 pc2c3 Nd5f6 nf3e5
9 (6) #[axb5] (3)<ch> 'Bb7'
```

[Deep Blue guessed Kasparov's 12th move correctly.]

```
[cont] #[Re1] (9)
######################################### 9  T=100
rf1e1 Nf6d5 bf4g3 Pa7a6 pc2c3 Ph6h5 bg3h4 Nd7f6 bh4g3 Kd8c8
10 (6) #[Re1] (19) [TIMEOUT] 19  T=191   rf1e1 Nf6d5 bf4g3
Pa7a6 pc2c3 Kd8c8 bg6f5 Nd5c7 pb2b4 Pa6a5 bg3c7N
```

```
-------------------------------------------------
--> 13.   Re1 <-- 27/101:55 Guessing Nd5
-------------------------------------------------
```

```
7 (4) #[Bg3] (12) ####################################
######### 12  T=1   bf4g3 Pa7a6 pc2c3 Kd8c8 bg6f5 Nd5c7
pb2b4 Pa6a5 bg3c7N
8 (6) #[Bg3] (15) ####################################
######### 15  T=13   Pa7a6 nf3h4 Qe7f6 bg6h5 Kd8c8 qd1g4
Nd5c7
9 (6) #[Bg3] (27) ####################################
######### 27  T=71   bf4g3 Pa7a6 nf3h4 Qe7f6 bg6h5 Pg7g5
qd1g4 Nd5c7 nh4g6 Rh8g8
```

```
10 (6) #[Bg3] (31) ###################################
########## 31  T=351    bf4g3 Pa7a6 qd1d3 Qe7b4 re1e6P
Bf8e7 pb2b3 Nd7f8 re6e1 Qb4c3 qd3c3 Nd5c3q bg6f5 Pg7g6
11 (6)<ch> 'nd5'
```

[Deep Blue guessed correctly.]

```
bf4g3*
```

```
-------------------------------------------------------
--> 14.  Bg3 <-- 26/101:50 Guessing a6
-------------------------------------------------------
```

```
7 (4) #[Qd3] (23) ################################
####### 23   T=2    qd1d3 Nd5c7 bg3h4 Nd7f6 nf3e5 Kd8c8 bh4g3
Ph6h5 ne5f7 Rh8g8 nf7g5 Ph5h4 bg3h4P Rg8h8 bh4g3
8 (6) #[Qd3] (39) ##############<ch> 'kc8'
```

[Deep Blue guessed incorrectly. It must start the search over.]

```
going to search for 192 seconds
[AB Kd8c8]
```

```
-------------------------------------------------------
--> Kd8c8 <--
-------------------------------------------------------
```

```
39  T=11
qd1d3 Nd5c7 bg3h4 Nd7f6 nf3e5 Kd8c8 bh4g3 Ph6h5 ne5f7 Rh8g8
nf7g5 Ph5h4 bg3h4P Rg8h8 bh4g3
```

```
going to search for 192 seconds
3 (4) 30^  T=1    pa4b5P Pc6b5p bg6f5 Pe6f5b
3 (5) 61^  T=1    pa4b5P Pc6b5p bg6f5 Pe6f5b
3 (5) 68  T=1    pa4b5P Pc6b5p bg6f5 Pe6f5b
4 (5) 68  T=1    pa4b5P Pc6b5p bg6f5 Pe6f5b
5 (5) [axb5] (77) 77  T=1    pa4b5P Pc6b5p bg6f5 Pe6f5b
6 (5) [axb5] (86) 86  T=2    pa4b5P Pc6b5p bg6f5 Pe6f5b
7 (5) #[axb5] (56) 56v T=2    pa4b5P Pc6b5p bg6f5 Nd5c7 qd1d2
7 (6) #[axb5] (63) ################################
###### 63   T=5    pa4b5P Pc6b5p qd1c1 Nd5b6 bg6d3 Bb7f3n
8 (6) #[axb5] (63) ################################
##### 63   T=10    pa4b5P Pc6b5p qd1c1 Nd5b6 bg6d3 Bb7f3n
9 (6) #[axb5] (47) ############[FH qd1d3]][FH qd1d3]][FH
qd1d3]][FH qd1d3]]#[FH qd1d3]] ###[TIMEOUT] [et3 1698 sec]
######################## 47   T=433
```

[Deep Blue took 433 seconds to move. The 6-level evaluation was +86, but it dropped on the following iteration to +63, the same on the 8th iteration, but dropping to +47 on the 9th iteration. The 8th iteration was completed after 10 seconds, but the 9th took much longer. There were 42 moves in this position.]

```
pa4b5 Pc6b5p qd1c1 Nd7b6 bg6d3 Nd5c7 nf3e5 Qe7g5 qc1d1
[9999999 sec (sr.c:630)]
[record_time] 12. a4 Bb7   13. Re1 Nd5   14. Bg3 Kc8 15. axb5
```

```
------------------------------------------------------------
--> 15.   axb5 <-- 25/94:31 Guessing cxb5
------------------------------------------------------------
```

```
6 (4) [Qc1] (30) 30^ T=1    qd1c1 Nd7b6 bg6d3 Nd5c7 nf3e5
Qe7g5 qc1d1
6 (5) [Qc1] (26) [Qd3] (61) 61^ T=3    qd1d3 Nd5c7 qd3c3
Qe7d8 bg3c7N Qd8c7b qc3c7Q Kc8c7q ra1a7P Ra8a7r re1e6P
6 (5) [Qd3] (41) 41   T=6    qd1d3 Nd5c7 pc2c3 Qe7d8 bg6e4
7 (5) #[Qd3] (69) ###################################
## 69 T=11 qd1d3 Bb7c6 pc2c4 Nd5b4 qd3c3 Pb5c4p qc3c4P
Nd7b6
8 (6)<ch> 'cb5'
```

[Deep Blue guessed correctly.]

```
[cont] #[Qd3] (39) 37v  T=31    qd1d3 Nd5c7 pc2c4 Qe7b4
re1c1 Bf8d6 bg3d6B Qb4d6b ra1a7P Ra8a7r
8 (6) #[Qd3] (53) ###################################
53   T=52    qd1d3 Nd5c7 re1c1 Qe7b4 nf3d2 Pa7a6 pc2c3 Qb4e7
9 (6) #[Qd3] (41) ##[TIMEOUT] 41   T=183Kb7c7 qd3b5P Pa7a6
qb5a5 Qf6f5
```

```
------------------------------------------------------------
--> 16. Qd3 <-- 24/91:38    Guessing Nc7
------------------------------------------------------------
```

```
6 (4) [b3] (29) [Qc3] (30) 30^ T=1    qd3c3 Qe7d8 bg6f7
Pa7a5 bg3c7N Qd8c7b qc3c7Q Kc8c7q bf7e6P Bb7f3n
6 (5) [Qc3] (61) 61^  T=1    qd3c3 Qe7d8 bg6f7 Pa7a5 bg3c7N
Qd8c7b qc3c7Q Kc8c7q bf7e6P Bb7f3n
6 (5) [Qc3] (16) [c3] (32) [c4] (46) 46  T=5    pc2c4 Qe7b4
pb2b3 Bf8d6 bg3d6B Qb4d6b ra1a7P
7 (5) #[c4] (23) ###################################
#############[Ra3] (41)# 41   T=10    ra1a3 Bb7d5 bg3c7N
Kc8c7b qd3b5P Nd7b6 re1a1 Qe7b4
```

```
8 (6) #[Ra3] (11) 11v  T=14    ra1a3 Bb7d5 bg3c7N Kc8c7b
qd3b5P Nd7b6 re1a1 Pa7a5 qb5d5B Pe6d5q
8 (6) #[Ra3] (26) ####################################
############# 26  T=58    ra1a3 Bb7d5 re1a1 Bd5c4 qd3d2
Kc8b7 bg3c7N Kb7c7b ra3a7P
9 (6) #[Ra3] (35)#<ch> 'Bc6'
```

[Deep Blue guessed incorrectly.]

```
going to search for 184 seconds
[AB Bb7c6]

----------------------------------------------------
--> Bb7c6 <--
----------------------------------------------------

35  T=172
ra1a3 Bb7d5 bg3c7N Kc8c7b qd3b5P Nd7b6 re1a1 Pa7a5 ra3a5P
Ra8a5r ra1a5R Qe7b4

going to search for 184 seconds
3 (4) 30^  T=0    bg6f5 Qe7b4
3 (5) 48  T=0    bg6f5 Qe7b4
4 (5) 48  T=0    bg6f5 Qe7b4
5 (5) [Bf5] (18) 18v  T=0   bg6f5 Qe7b4 re1e6P
5 (5) [Bf5] (54) [c4] (78) 78^  T=0   pc2c4 Nn5b4
5 (5) [c4] (97) 97  T=1   pc2c4 Nd5b4
6 (5) [c4] (87) 87  T=2   pc2c4 Nd5b4 qd3c3
7 (5) #[c4] (87) ####################################
########### 87  T=3   pc2c4 Nd5b4 qd3e2 Pb5c4p qe2c4P Nd7b6
8 (6) #[c4] (57) 57v  T=8   pc2c4 Nd5b4 qd3e2 Pb5c4p qe2c4P
Nd7b6 qc4c6B Nb4c6q ra1a7P Nc6a7r
8 (6) #[c4] (56)#[Bf5] (117) 117^  T=16   bg6f5 Kc8b7
re1e6P Qe7b4 re6c6B Kb7c6r bf5d7N Kc6d7b nf3e5 Kd7e6 ne5g6
Qb4b2p qd3e4
8 (6) #[Bf5] (148) 148^  T=18   bg6f5 Kc8b7 re1e6P Qe7b4
re6c6B Kb7c6r bf5d7N Kc6d7b qd3f5 Kd7c6 qf5e6 Kc6b7 qe6d5N
8 (6) #[Bf5] (137) ####################################
############# 137  T=37   bg6f5 Pe6f5b re1e7Q Bf8e7r pc2c4
Pb5c4p qd3c4P Nd5b4 ra1a4 Kc8b7
9 (6) #[Bf5] (137) #[TIMEOUT] 137  T=184   bg6f5 Pe6f5b
Re1e7Q Nd5e7r qdc3 Pa7a5 ra1a5P Ra8a5r qc3a5R Ne7d5 qa5a6
Bc6b7 qa6e6 Kc8d8 qe6f5P


----------------------------------------------------
--> 17. Bf5 <-- 23/88:25   Guessing exf5
----------------------------------------------------
```

```
(30) 30^  T=0    re1e7Q Nd5e7r qd3c3 Pa7a5 ra1a5P Ra8a5r
qc3a5R Ne7d5 qa5a6 Bc6b7 qa6e6 Kc8d8 qe6f5P
6(5) [Rxe7] (61) 61^  T=0    re1e7Q Nd5e7r qd3c3 Pa7a5
ra1a5P Ra8a5r qc3a5R Ne7d5 qa5a6 Bc6b7 qa6e6 Kc8d8 qe6f5P
6 (5) [Rxe7] (106) 106  T=2    re1e7Q Nd5e7r qd3c3 Pa7a5
ra1a5P Ra8a5r qc3a5R Ne7d5 qa5a6 Bc6b7 qa6e6 Kc8d8 qe6f5P
7 (5) #[Rxe7] (126) ###############################
############# 126  T=3    re1e7Q Nd5e7r qd3c3 Pa7a5 ra1a5P
Ra8a5r qc3a5R Ne7d5 qa5a6 Bc6b7 qa6e6 Kc8d8 qe6f5P
8 (6) #[Rxe7] (126) ###############################
############# 126  T=5    re1e7Q Nd5e7r qd3c3 Pa7a5 ra1a5P
Ra8a5r qc3a5R Ne7d5 qa5a6 Bc6b7 qa6e6 Kc8d8 qe6f5P
9 (6) #[Rxe7] (153) ############################
############### 153  T=36    re1e7Q Nd5e7r qd3c3 Pa7a5
ra1a5P Ra8a5r qc3a5R Ne7d5 qa5a6 Bc6b7 qa6e6 Kc8d8 qe6f5P
Bf8e7
10 (6) #[Rxe7] (159) ################################
<ch> 'ef'
```

[Deep Blue guessed correctly. The search continues.]

```
[cont] ############# 159  T=135
re1e7Q Nd5e7r qd3c3 Kc8d8 bg3d6 Bc6e4 qc3a5 Kd8e8 qa5b5P
Pa7a6 ra1a6P Ra8a6r qb5a6R
11 (6) [TIMEOUT] 159  T=184   re1e7Q*
```

```
-------------------------------------------------------
--> 18. Rxe7 <-- 22/87:30  Guessing Nxe7
-------------------------------------------------------
```

```
7 (4) #[Qc3] (159) 159^ T=0
qd3c3 Kc8d8 bg3d6 Bc6e4 qc3a5 Kd8e8 qa5b5P Pa7a6 ra1a6P
Ra8a6r qb5a6R Ke8f7 qa6a4 Ne7c6
7 (6) #[Qc3] (123) #############################
########## 123  T=2    qd3c3 Kc8d8 bg3d6 Bc6e4 qc3a5 Kd8e8
qa5b5P Pa7a6 ra1a6P Ra8a6r qb5a6R Ke8f7 qa6a4 Ne7c6
8 (6) #[Qc3] (123) #############################
####### 123  T=7    qd3c3 Kc8d8 bg3d6 Bc6e4 qc3a5 Kd8e8
qa5b5P Pa7a6 ra1a6P Ra8a6r qb5a6R Ke8f7 qa6a4 Ne7c6
9 (6)<ch> 'Be7'
```

[Deep Blue guessed incorrectly.]

```
going to search for 182 secoends
[AB Bf8e7r]
```

```
------------------------------------------------------------
--> Bf8e7r
------------------------------------------------------------

123 T=7
qd3c3*

going to search for 181 seconds
3 (4) 95^  T=1
pc2c4 Pb5c4p qd3c4P Nd5b4 ra1e1 Kc8d8 re1e7B Kd8e7r
3 (5) 103  T=1
qd3f5P Kc8b7 qf5d7N
4 (5) 103  T=1    qd3f5P Kc8b7 qf5d7N
5 (5) [Qxf5] (97) [c4] (133) 133^  T=1    pc2c4 Pb5c4p
qd3c4P Nd5b4 ra1e1 Kc8d8 ra1e7B Kd8e7r
5 (5) [c4] (159) 159 T=1   pc2c4 Nd5f6 pd4d5 Pb5c4p qd3c4P
Nf6d5p
6 (5) [c4] (138) 138  T=1    pc2c4 Pb5c4p qd3c4P Nd5b4 ra1e1
Kc8d8 re1e7B Kd8e7r
7 (5) #[c4] (168) 168^  T=2    pc2c4 Pb5c4p qd3c4P Nd5b4
ra1e1 Kc8d8 re1e7B Kd8e7r
7 (6) #[c4] (169) ###############################
######## 169  T=2  pc2c4 Nd5b6 qd3f5P Nb6c4p qf5e6 Bc6f3n
8 (6) #[c4] (182) ###############################
######## 182  T=5  pc2c4 Pb5c4p qd3c4P Nd5b4 ra1e1 Rh8e8
re1e7B Re8e7r qc4b4N
9 (6) #[c4] (189) ###############################
########## 189  T=18    pc2c4 Pb5c4p qd3c4P Nd5b4 ra1e1
Rh8e8 nf3h4 Pf5f4 nh4f5 Nd7b6 qc4f7 Nb4d5
10 (6) #[c4] (219) 219^  T=21    pc2c4 Pb5c4p qd3c4P Nd5b4
ra1e1 Rh8e8 nf3h4 Pf5f4 nh4f5 Nd7b6 qc4f7 Pf4g3b nf5e7B
Re8e7n re1e7R
10 (6) #[c4] (220) ###################################
###### 189  T=43    pc2c4 Pb5c4p qd3c4P Nd5b4 ra1e1 Rh8e8
nf3h4 Pf5f4 nh4f5 Nd7b6 qc4f7 Re8f8 qf7e6 Bc6d7 nf5e7B
11 (6) #[c4] (250) 250^  T=56    pc2c4 Pb5c4p qd3c4P Nd5b4
ra1e1 Rh8e8 nf3h4 Pf5f4 nh4f5 Nd7b6 qc4f7 Re8f8 qf7e6 Bc6d7
nf5e7B Kc8c7 bg3f4P
11 (6) #[c4] (267) ##################[TIMEOUT] 267  T=181
pc2c4 Pb5c4p qd3c4P Nd5b4 ra1e1 Rh8e8 nf3h4 Nd7b6 qc4f7
Nb4d5 nh4f5P Kc8d8 nf5g7P Re8h8
```

**[Deep Blue had actually calculated a much longer continuation, but it only
printed the first 14 moves. According to Murray, it based this continuation on
a search of at least another six levels, calculating that it was ahead by a score
of 267 points.]**

```
----------------------------------------------------
--> 19. c4 <-- 21/84:24     Guessing bxc4
----------------------------------------------------

8 (4) #[Qxc4] (267) 267^  T=0    qd3c4P Nd5b4 ra1e1 Rh8e8
nf3h4 Nd7b6 qc4f7 Nb4d5 nh4f5P Kc8d8 nf5g7P Re8h8
8 (6) #[Qxc4] (213) ##############################
######## 213   T=4    qd3c4P Nd5b4 ra1e1 Rh8e8 nf3h4 Nd7b6
qc4f7 Nb4d5 nh4f5P Kc8d8 nf5g7P Re8h8
9 (6) #[Qxc4] (243) 243^  T=5    qd3c4P Nd5b4 ra1e1 Rh8e8
nf3h4 Nd7b6 qc4f7 Nb4d5 nh4f5P Kc8d8 nf5g7P Re8h8
9 (6) #[Qxc4] (247) ##################################
##### 247  T=10   qd3c4P Nd5b4 ra1e1 Rh8e8 nf3h4 Nd7b6
qc4f7 Nb4d5 nh4f5P Kc8d8 nf5g7P Re8h8
10 (6) #[Qxc4] (235)<ch> 'score game6'
```

Index

D

M

N